Behavior Change Contr

MW01671535

Choose a health behavior that you would like to change, stai
at the bottom to affirm your commitment to making a healthy change and ask a friend to witness

My behavior change will be:

___

My long-term goal for this behavior change is:

___

Barriers that I must overcome to make this behavior change are (things that I am currently doing or situations that contribute to this behavior or make it harder to change):

1. ___
2. ___
3. ___

The strategies I will use to overcome these barriers are:

1. ___
2. ___
3. ___

Resources I will use to help me change this behavior include:

a friend/partner/relative: ___
a school-based resource: ___
a community-based resource: ___
a book or reputable website: ___

In order to make my goal more attainable, I have devised these short-term goals

short-term goal	target date	reward
short-term goal	target date	reward
short-term goal	target date	reward

When I make the long-term behavior change described above, my reward will be:

___ target date: ___

I intend to make the behavior change described above. I will use the strategies and rewards to achieve the goals that will contribute to a healthy behavior change.

Signed: ___ Witness: ___

Behavior Change Contract

Choose a health behavior that you would like to change, starting this quarter or semester. Sign the contract at the bottom to affirm your commitment to making a healthy change and ask a friend to witness it.

My behavior change will be:

____

My long-term goal for this behavior change is:

____

Barriers that I must overcome to make this behavior change are (things that I am currently doing or situations that contribute to this behavior or make it harder to change):

1. ______________________________
2. ______________________________
3. ______________________________

The strategies I will use to overcome these barriers are:

1. ______________________________
2. ______________________________
3. ______________________________

Resources I will use to help me change this behavior include:

a friend/partner/relative: ______________________________

a school-based resource: ______________________________

a community-based resource: ______________________________

a book or reputable website: ______________________________

In order to make my goal more attainable, I have devised these short-term goals

short-term goal	target date	reward
short-term goal	target date	reward
short-term goal	target date	reward

When I make the long-term behavior change described above, my reward will be:

______________________________ target date: __________

I intend to make the behavior change described above. I will use the strategies and rewards to achieve the goals that will contribute to a healthy behavior change.

Signed: ______________________ Witness: ______________________

CUSTOM EDITION FOR
MONROE COMMUNITY COLLEGE

TOTAL FITNESS & WELLNESS

Scott K. Powers • Stephen L. Dodd

Taken from:

Total Fitness & Wellness, Fifth Edition
by Scott K. Powers and Stephen L. Dodd

Custom Publishing

New York Boston San Francisco
London Toronto Sydney Tokyo Singapore Madrid
Mexico City Munich Paris Cape Town Hong Kong Montreal

Cover image: courtesy of Corbis.

Taken from:

Total Fitness & Wellness, Fifth Edition
by Scott K. Powers and Stephen L. Dodd

Published by Benjamin Cummings
San Francisco, California 94111

Grateful acknowledgment is made to the following source for permission to reprint material copyrighted or controlled by them:

"Lab A3-1: The 12-Minute Run Test for Assessing Cardiorespiratory Endurance," reprinted from *Physical Fitness Assessments and Norms for Adults and Law Enforcement* (2002), by permission of The Cooper Institute, Dallas, Texas. www.cooperinstitute.org.

Printed in the United States of America

10 9 8 7 6 5 4 3 2 1

2008420054

KS/RH

Pearson Custom Publishing is a division of

PEARSON

www.pearsonhighered.com

ISBN 10: 0-555-02404-0
ISBN 13: 978-0-555-02404-1

Brief Contents

1 Understanding Fitness and Wellness 1

2 General Principles of Exercise for Health and Fitness 31

3 Cardiorespiratory Endurance: Assessment and Prescription 51

4 Improving Muscular Strength and Endurance 95

5 Improving Flexibility 139

6 Body Composition 169

7 Nutrition, Health, and Fitness 195

8 Exercise, Diet, and Weight Control 239

Answers to Study Questions A-1

Nutritive Value of Selected Foods and Fast Foods B-1

Photo Credits CR-1

Index I-1

Contents

1 Understanding Fitness and Wellness 1

What Is Wellness? 2

Six Components of Wellness 2
Interaction of Wellness Components 4

Make sure you know 5

Wellness Goals for the Nation 5

Make sure you know 5

What Is Exercise, and Why Should I Do It? 5

APPRECIATING DIVERSITY WELLNESS ISSUES ACROSS THE POPULATION 5

A CLOSER LOOK HEALTHY PEOPLE 2010 6

Exercise Is One Type of Physical Activity 6
There Are Numerous Health Benefits of Physical Activity 6

Make sure you know 9

Exercise and Activity for Health-Related Fitness 9

Cardiorespiratory Endurance 9
Muscular Strength 10
Muscular Endurance 10
Flexibility 10
Body Composition 10

Make sure you know 11

How Can You Make Healthier Behavior Choices? 11

The Stages of Change Model 11
Behavior Modification 12
Assessing Your Habits 12

STEPS FOR BEHAVIOR CHANGE
Do you have trouble making healthy behavior changes? 13

Identifying Behavior Change Barriers 13

CONSUMER CORNER FINDING CREDIBLE HEALTH INFORMATION 14

Changing Unhealthy Behaviors 14

Make sure you know 14

Specific Application of Behavior Modification 15

Smoking Cessation 15
Weight Loss 15

Make sure you know 16

Summary 16

Study Questions 16
Suggested Reading 17
References 18

Laboratory 1.1: Lifestyle Assessment Inventory 21

Laboratory 1.2: Changing Your Behavior 25

Laboratory 1.3: Medical History Check 27

Laboratory 1.4: PAR-Q and You 29

2 General Principles of Exercise for Health and Fitness 31

Principles of Exercise Training to Improve Physical Fitness 32

Overload Principle 32
Principle of Progression 32
Specificity of Exercise 33

CONSUMER CORNER BUYING THE BEST RUNNING SHOE FOR YOU 34

Principle of Recuperation 34
Reversibility of Training Effects 35

Make sure you know 36

A CLOSER LOOK TOO MUCH EXERCISE INCREASES YOUR RISK OF ILLNESS 36

Designing Your Exercise Program 36

Setting Goals 37
Selecting Activities 38
The Importance of a Warm-Up 38

The Workout 39

The Importance of the Cool-Down 39
Personalizing Your Workout 39

Make sure you know 40

Health Benefits of Exercise: How Much Is Enough? 40

STEPS FOR BEHAVIOR CHANGE
Are you a couch potato? 41

Make sure you know 42

Summary 42
Study Questions 42
Suggested Reading 43
References 43

Laboratory 2.1: Warming Up 45

Laboratory 2.2: Which Physical Activities Work Best for You? 47

Laboratory 2.3: Using a Pedometer to Count Your Steps 49

3 Cardiorespiratory Endurance: Assessment and Prescription 51

The Need for Cardiorespiratory Endurance in Daily Living 52

What Are Cardiorespiratory Endurance and the Cardiovascular System? 52

The Cardiovascular System 53
The Respiratory System 53

Make sure you know 53

How Do We Get Energy for Exercise? 55

Anaerobic Energy Production 55
Aerobic Energy Production 55
The Energy Continuum 56

Make sure you know 56

What Happens to the Cardiorespiratory System with Exercise and Training? 56

Responses to Exercise 56
Adaptations to Exercise 57
Body Composition 58

Make sure you know 58

What Are the Health Benefits of Cardiorespiratory Endurance? 59

Make sure you know 59

Evaluation of Cardiorespiratory Endurance 59

Make sure you know 60

Designing Your Aerobic Exercise Program 60

The Warm-Up 61
The Workout 61

A CLOSER LOOK AEROBIC WORKOUTS—FAQS 63

CONSUMER CORNER HOW GOOD ARE EXERCISE GADGETS? 64

The Cool-Down 64

Make sure you know 64

Developing an Individualized Exercise Prescription 64

Initial Conditioning Phase 64
Improvement Phase 65
Maintenance Phase 65
Sample Exercise Prescriptions 65

Make sure you know 65

Training Techniques 66

Cross Training 66
Interval Training 67

Make sure you know 68

How Can You Get Motivated to Be Active? 68

APPRECIATING DIVERSITY DON'T LET A DISABILITY STOP YOU! 69

A CLOSER LOOK SPINNING—REV IT UP? 69

STEPS FOR BEHAVIOR CHANGE

How good is your level of cardiorespiratory fitness? 70

Make sure you know 70

Summary 71

Study Questions 71

Suggested Reading 72

References 73

Laboratory 3.1A: Measuring Cardiorespiratory Fitness: The 1.5-Mile Run Test 75

Laboratory 3.1B: Measuring Cardiorespiratory Fitness: The 1-Mile Walk Test 77

Laboratory 3.1C: Measuring Cardiorespiratory Fitness: Submaximal Cycle Test 79

Lab A3-1: The 12-Minute Run Test for Assessing Cardiorespiratory Endurance

Laboratory 3.1D: Measuring Cardiorespiratory Fitness: Step Test 83

Laboratory 3.2: Assessing Cardiorespiratory Fitness for Individuals with Disabilities 87

Laboratory 3.3: Determining Target Heart Rate 89

Laboratory 3.4: Developing Your Personal Exercise Prescription 91

Laboratory 3.5: Determining Rate of Perceived Exertion 93

4 Improving Muscular Strength and Endurance 95

The Need for Muscular Strength and Endurance in Daily Living 96

Make sure you know 97

How Muscles Work: Structure and Function 97

Muscle Structure 97

Muscle Function 98

Muscle Exercise and Muscle Actions 99

Types of Muscle Fibers 100

Individual Variations in Fiber Type 100

Recruitment of Muscle Fibers during Exercise 101

Muscular Strength 102

A CLOSER LOOK ANABOLIC STEROID USE INCREASES MUSCLE SIZE BUT HAS SERIOUS SIDE EFFECTS 102

Make sure you know 103

Chapter 4 (continued)

Evaluation of Muscular Strength and Endurance 103

Make sure you know 103

Principles for Designing a Strength and Endurance Program 103

Progressive Resistance Exercise 104

Specificity of Training 104

Make sure you know 104

Strength Training: How the Body Adapts 104

Physiological Changes Due to Weight Training 104

Rate of Strength Improvement with Weight Training 104

Gender Differences in Response to Weight Training 105

Make sure you know 105

Designing a Training Program for Increasing Muscle Strength 105

Safety Concerns 105

Types of Weight-Training Programs 105

STEPS FOR BEHAVIOR CHANGE

Are you reluctant to strength train? 106

Make sure you know 107

Exercise Prescription for Weight Training 107

Make sure you know 108

Starting and Maintaining a Weight-Training Program 108

A CLOSER LOOK DO WEIGHT LIFTERS NEED LARGE AMOUNTS OF PROTEIN IN THEIR DIETS? 108

Developing an Individualized Exercise Prescription 109

Sample Exercise Prescription for Weight Training 109

Make sure you know 110

Motivation to Maintain Strength Fitness 110

Some Isotonic Exercises for Increasing Muscular Strength 111

APPRECIATING DIVERSITY STRENGTH TRAINING FOR OLDER ADULTS 118

Summary 118

Study Questions 119

Suggested Reading 120

References 120

Laboratory 4.1: Evaluating Muscular Strength: The 1 RM Test 123

Laboratory 4.2: Evaluating Muscular Strength: The Estimated 1 RM Test 127

Laboratory 4.3: Tracking Your Progress 129

Laboratory 4.4: Measuring Muscular Endurance: The Push-Up, Sit-Up, and Curl-Up Tests 131
Laboratory 4.5: Measuring Core Strength and Stability 137

5 Improving Flexibility 139

The Need for Flexibility in Daily Living 140
Make sure you know 140
How Flexibility Works: Muscles, Joints and Stretching 140
Structural Limitations to Movement 141
Stretching and the Stretch Reflex 141
Make sure you know 142
Benefits of Flexibility 142
Keeping Joints Healthy 142
Preventing Lower Back Pain 143
Make sure you know 143
Evaluating Flexibility 143
Make sure you know 144
Designing a Flexibility Training Program 144
Static Stretching 144
STEPS FOR BEHAVIOR CHANGE
Are you too stiff? 145
Proprioceptive Neuromuscular Facilitation 145
Passive and Active Stretching 146
Applying the FIT Principle 146
Make sure you know 147
A CLOSER LOOK PILATES—MORE THAN STRETCHING? 148
A CLOSER LOOK WHEN MUSCLES CRAMP 149
Motivation to Maintain Flexibility 149
Sample Flexibility Exercises 150
Alternatives for Unsafe Exercises 157
Summary 160
Study Questions 160
Suggested Reading 161
References 161
Laboratory 5.1: Assessing Flexibility: Trunk Flexion (Sit-and-Reach) Test and the Shoulder Flexibility Test 163
Laboratory 5.2: Flexibility Progression Log 165
Laboratory 5.3: Stretching to Prevent or Reduce Lower Back Pain 167

6 Body Composition 169

What Is Body Composition and What Does It Tell Us? 170

Make sure you know 170

How Is Body Composition Related to Health? 171

We Need Some Fat 171

APPRECIATING DIVERSITY THE SEARCH FOR OBESITY-RELATED GENES 173

Mental and Physical Health Benefits of a Healthy Weight 173
Overweight and Obesity in the United States 173
Chronic Conditions Associated with Overweight and Obesity 175
Health Effects of Underweight 176

Make sure you know 177

STEPS FOR BEHAVIOR CHANGE
Are you at risk for developing diabetes? 177

A CLOSER LOOK CAN YOU BE FIT AND FAT? 178

Assessing Body Composition 178

Field Methods 178
Laboratory Measures 180

Make sure you know 182

CONSUMER CORNER USE-AT-HOME MEASUREMENT DEVICES—ARE THEY WORTH THE MONEY? 182

Using Body Composition to Determine Your Ideal Body Weight 182

Make sure you know 183

Behavior Change: Set Goals and Get Regular Assessments 183

Make sure you know 183

Summary 183
Study Questions 184
Suggested Reading 184
References 185

Laboratory 6.1: Assessing Body Composition 187

Laboratory 6.2: Determining a Healthy Body Weight 193

7 Nutrition, Health, and Fitness 195

What Is Nutrition and Why Is It Important? 196

What Are Nutrients? 196

Macronutrients 197

APPRECIATING DIVERSITY SHOULD PREGNANT WOMEN EAT FISH? 200

Micronutrients 203

Water 205

Make sure you know 205

What Are the Guidelines for a Healthy Diet? 205

Eat More Fruits, Vegetables, and Whole Grains 206

Watch Your Intake of Calories, Sugar, Alcohol, Fat, and Sodium 206

Use the Recommended Dietary Allowances, MyPyramid, and Food Labels to Plan Healthy Meals 208

Watch for Special Dietary Considerations 209

STEPS FOR BEHAVIOR CHANGE
Do you consume too much sugar? 212

A CLOSER LOOK DIETARY REFERENCE INTAKES 213

A CLOSER LOOK WHAT IS THE GLYCEMIC INDEX AND WHEN IS IT HELPFUL? 215

Make sure you know 215

STEPS FOR BEHAVIOR CHANGE
Are you a fast food junkie? 216

How Does Nutrition Affect Physical Fitness? 216

Carbohydrates Are Used for Energy during Exercise 217

Protein Needs Can Be Met with a Healthy Diet 217

High Vitamin Intake Does Not Improve Performance 217

Antioxidants Help Prevent Oxidative Damage 218

Make sure you know 218

Do Supplements Provide an Edge for Health and Performance? 218

The Role of Supplements in a Healthy Diet 218

A CLOSER LOOK DO PHYTOCHEMICALS PROTECT AGAINST DISEASE? 219

Regulation of Supplements 219

CONSUMER CORNER DETECTING SUPPLEMENT FRAUD 221

Make sure you know 221

Topics in Food Safety and Technology 222

Foodborne Illness 222

Food Additives 222

A CLOSER LOOK KEEP HOT FOODS HOT AND COLD FOODS COLD TO AVOID FOODBORNE ILLNESS 223

Antibiotics, Hormones, and Organically Grown Foods 223

Irradiated and Bioengineered Foods 223

Make sure you know 224

Summary 224

Study Questions 225

Suggested Reading 226
References 227
Laboratory 7.1: Analyzing Your Diet 229
Laboratory 7.2: Setting Goals for a Healthy Diet 233
Laboratory 7.3: Planning a New Diet 235
Laboratory 7.4: Assessing Nutritional Habits 237

8 Exercise, Diet, and Weight Control 239

What Is Your Optimal Body Weight? 240
Make sure you know 241
What Factors Can Affect Weight Management? 241
Genetic Factors and Hormones 241
Environmental Factors 241
STEPS FOR BEHAVIOR CHANGE
What triggers your eating? 242
The Concept of Energy Balance 243
Make sure you know 244
Designing a Successful Weight-Loss Program 245
Set a Realistic Goal for Weight Loss 245
Assess and Modify Your Diet 246
A CLOSER LOOK FACTS AND MYTHS ABOUT LOW-FAT AND LOW-CARB DIETS 247
A CLOSER LOOK FREQUENTLY ASKED QUESTIONS ABOUT WEIGHT-LOSS DIETS 248
Plan Your Physical Activity 249
A CLOSER LOOK WHAT INTENSITY OF AEROBIC EXERCISE IS BEST FOR BURNING FAT? 250
APPRECIATING DIVERSITY EXERCISE PRESCRIPTIONS FOR OBESE INDIVIDUALS 250
Focus on Behavior Modification 251
Make sure you know 252
Exercise and Diet Programs to Gain Weight 252
Make sure you know 252
Lifetime Weight Management 252
Extreme Measures for Weight Loss 253
Surgery 253
Prescription Medications 253
What Is Disordered Eating? 254

Anorexia Nervosa 254
Bulimia Nervosa 255
Binge Eating Disorder 255
Make sure you know *256*
Summary *256*
Study Questions *256*
Suggested Reading *257*
References *257*
Laboratory 8.1: Determining Ideal Body Weight Using Percent Body Fat and the Body Mass Index 259
Laboratory 8.2: Estimating Daily Caloric Expenditure and the Caloric Deficit Required to Lose 1 Pound of Fat per Week 261
Laboratory 8.3: Weight-Loss Goals and Progress Report 263
Laboratory 8.4: Assessing Body Image 265
Laboratory 8.5: What Triggers Your Eating? 267

Answers to Study Questions A-1
Nutritive Value of Selected Foods and Fast Foods B-1
Photo Credits CR-1
Index I-1

Preface

Good health is our most precious possession. Although we tend to appreciate it only in times of illness or injury, more and more of us are realizing that good health is not simply the absence of disease. Indeed, there are degrees of health, or wellness, and lifestyle can have a major impact on many of its components.

Intended for an introductory college course, *Total Fitness and Wellness* focuses on helping students effect positive changes in their lifestyles, most notably in exercise and diet. The interaction of exercise and diet and the essential role of regular exercise and good nutrition in achieving total fitness and wellness are major themes of the text.

Total Fitness and Wellness, Fifth Edition, was built on a strong foundation of both exercise physiology and nutrition. The text provides clear, objective, research-based information to college students during their first course in physical fitness and wellness. By offering a research-based text, we hope to dispel many myths associated with exercise, nutrition, weight loss, and wellness. In particular, we show students how to evaluate their own wellness level with respect to the various wellness components, such as fitness level and nutritional status. Indeed, the title of the book reflects our goals.

Numerous physical fitness and wellness texts are available today. Our motivation in writing *Total Fitness and Wellness*, Fifth Edition, was to create a unique, well-balanced physical fitness text, one that not only covers primary concepts of physical fitness and wellness but also addresses important issues such as behavior change, exercise-related injuries, exercise and the environment, and prevention of cardiovascular disease.

Foundation in Exercise Physiology

We believe it is imperative that students develop an understanding of the basic physiological adaptations that occur in response to both acute exercise and regular exercise training. Without this understanding, it is impossible to plan, modify, and properly execute a lifetime exercise program.

Strong Emphasis on Behavior Change

We recognize that one of the most important aspects of teaching students about personal fitness is presenting them with ways to alter their own behaviors and make fitness and health a part of their own lives. In this fifth edition of *Total Fitness and Wellness*, we have expanded our coverage of behavior change and relocated it to the first chapter. Presenting the concepts of behavior change at the outset encourages students to think about strategies for incorporating fitness and wellness principles into their own lives as they progress through the chapters and the course.

Steps for Behavior Change boxes throughout the text present students with quick evaluations of their current health behaviors and offer simple and practical ways to modify those behaviors and work toward lasting change. Laboratories at the end of each chapter are exercises and activities that encourage the immediate development of healthy lifestyle choices and a core fitness plan. The Behavior Change Log Book with Wellness Journal, packaged with each new copy of the text, further motivates behavior change by providing students with hands-on material to track daily exercise and food intake and to create personal, long-term fitness and nutrition programs. New journaling activities and an updated table listing nutritional content of common foods have also been added.

Coverage of the Latest Scientific Research on Physical Fitness, Nutrition, and Wellness

We firmly believe that college physical fitness and wellness texts should contain the latest scientific information and include references for scientific studies to support key information about physical fitness, nutrition, and wellness. Accordingly, we offer the most current research in the arena of fitness and wellness in *Total Fitness and Wellness*, Fifth Edition. For example, it is now clear that exercise plays a role in reducing the risk of some cancers and can contribute to a longer life. Although it has long been speculated that exercise brings about significant health benefits, evidence has only recently become available. In the area of nutrition, scientific data now suggest that vitamins may play a new role in preventing certain diseases and combating the aging process. In addition, whereas it has been well accepted that fat in the diet increases our risk of heart disease, it has just lately been shown that dietary fat plays a greater role than other nutrients in weight gain. Source information documenting the validity of the content presented, along with suggestions for further reading, appear at the end of each chapter.

With any attempt to present the most current information, there is always the danger of presenting ideas that are not fully substantiated by good research. We have made a concerted effort to avoid such a risk by using information from the most highly respected scientific journals and by consulting with experts in the field.

New to the Fifth Edition

Each chapter of the Fifth Edition has been significantly revised to include the newest research developments in exercise, wellness, and health-related nutrition. In addition we have greatly revised the art and design to increase the book's visual appeal, added several new features, and undertaken a significant reorganization of content. These changes and improvements include the following:

- **Two new contributing authors,** Erica Jackson and Marilyn Miller, bring to the text their own expertise in fitness and first-hand knowledge of the current challenges fitness and wellness instructors face in the classroom.
- **A new chapter, Body Composition** (Chapter 6), has been added to emphasize the importance of body composition as one of the five major components of physical fitness.
- **Behavior change material** has been expanded and moved up from Chapter 10 to Chapter 1, to reflect the standard organization of the course.
- **Steps for Behavior Change** boxes focus students on evaluating their own behaviors (e.g., Are you a fast food junkie? Are you reluctant to strength train? Do you protect your skin from UV light?) and present them with practical steps they can take to make meaningful behavior change.
- **True or False? chapter-opening quizzes** addressing common fitness myths and misperceptions combine with a fresh new design throughout to make the text more accessible, engaging, and visually appealing than ever before.
- **Consider This!** features grab students' attention with surprising statistics, prompting them to pause and consider the long-term consequences of specific health behaviors.
- **Integration of fitness assessment material** throughout the book aligns the assessments with the topics to which they are relevant.
- **Updated exercise photos** serve as a valuable reference for students, who often take their book with them to the fitness center and use it when completing a Laboratory.
- **New and improved art and photos** have been added throughout the text.
- **New and updated references** appear in every chapter.

Continuing Features

Although many options have to be considered when developing a text, the best way to determine what content to include and in what order is to ask instructors. Therefore, with input from instructors across the country, we have retained and revised the following coverage, layout, and features:

- **Unique topics.** Several chapters in the Fifth Edition address topics not contained in other introductory fitness and wellness texts. For example, this book includes chapters on exercise and the environment and on preventing and rehabilitating exercise-related injuries. Further, in several chapters we have incorporated an elementary discussion of the physiology of exercise to improve students' knowledge of how the body operates and responds to regular exercise.
- **Updated coverage.** Citing references to new research, we have expanded our coverage of current topics of student interest, such as eating disorders, stress management strategies, Pilates, diabetes and prediabetes, ergogenic dietary supplements, at-home fitness equipment, antioxidants, and emotional health.
- **Informational boxes.** Each chapter features a variety of informational boxes. **A Closer Look** boxes give the reader insight into special topics, such as the effects of caffeine, the search for a cure for AIDS, road rage, muscle cramps, and anabolic steroids. **Appreciating Diversity** boxes present current health research, covering issues such as how the risk of cancer varies across the United States and how the incidence of drug abuse varies across populations. **Consumer Corner** boxes teach students to be smart and discerning health

and fitness consumers, guiding them to make the best fitness and wellness decisions in a market full of fads, gimmicks, and gadgets.

- **Laboratories.** Each chapter contains easy-to-follow, application-based lab exercises that allow students to apply textual information to practical issues, encouraging the immediate development of healthy lifestyle choices and a core fitness plan. New and revised labs reflect current trends in fitness and incorporate activities that students can do at home or outdoors and with less costly equipment. New topics include assessing tobacco use, selecting a health insurance plan, and measuring core strength and stability.
- **Pedagogical aids.** Throughout the text, **Make Sure You Know** features summarize key points, prompting students to recall and process main concepts covered. To emphasize and support understanding of material, important terms are boldfaced in the text and defined in a **running glossary** at the bottom of text pages. Also, several features appearing at the end of each chapter reinforce learning. For students' review, the **Chapter Summary** sections succinctly restate the most significant ideas presented in the chapter. **Study Questions** encourage analysis of chapter discussions and prepare students for tests. **Suggested Readings, Web links,** and **References** offer quality information sources for further study of fitness and wellness.
- **Food appendix.** To help students track and modify their food intake, we present caloric and nutrient content of common foods and fast foods in the Appendix.

Supplemental Materials

A complete resource package accompanies *Total Fitness and Wellness* to assist the instructor with classroom preparation and presentation.

Instructor Supplements

Teaching Tool Box

Developed to support adjunct and part-time faculty teaching the fitness and wellness course, and also to be invaluable to veteran instructors, this kit offers all the tools instructors need to guide students through the course. The box includes the Course-at-a-Glance Quick Reference Guide, Fitness Support Manual (with First-Time Teaching Tips), Instructor Resource Manual and Printed Test Bank, Media Manager with *ABC News* Lecture Launcher videos and TestGen, MyHealthLab Instructor Access Kit, *Great Ideas: Active Ways to Teach Health and Wellness,* and transparency acetates. The Tool Box also includes the supplemental materials for students, such as the Behavior Change Logbook and Wellness Journal, Take Charge of Your Health! Worksheets, *Eat Right!,* and *Live Right!*

- **Course-at-a-Glance Quick Reference Guide.** This valuable supplement acts as your roadmap to the Teaching Tool Box. The available resources are broken down by chapter, and further by page number, so you can easily see what resources are available for each chapter in the book. One side lists resources for instructors to use when preparing for a lecture or while in class. The other side outlines where to find the resources that students can use in their homework or in-class activities.
- **Fitness Support Manual: First Time Teaching Tips and Visual Lecture Outlines.** Organized chapter by chapter, this key manual provides a step-by-step guide to all the resources available to instructors. It provides information on available PowerPoint lectures with the accompanying figures and art; integrated *ABC News* Lecture Launcher videos; suggested classroom discussion questions; in-class activities, tips, and strategies for large classrooms; and the best strategies to promote active learning.
- **Instructor Resource Manual and Test Bank.** The Instructor Resource Manual and Test Bank includes suggestions for class discussion, student activities, readings, lecture outlines, learning objectives, chapter summaries, Web references, and media resources. The Test Bank includes over 1,000 multiple-choice, true-or-false, short-answer, and matching questions to use for student review or testing.
- **Media Manager.** This cross-platform CD-ROM includes all the PowerPoint lecture outlines with embedded links to *ABC News* Lecture Launcher video clips and new exercise videos that can be customized for any lecture presentation. In addition, game show quiz and classroom-response "clicker" questions are included, as well as all figures and tables from the book, Microsoft Word files of the Instructor Resource Manual and Test Bank, and the TestGen computerized test bank, which enables instructors to create lists, edit questions, and add their own material to existing exams.
- **Transparency Acetates.** Over 180 full-color transparency acetates include all figures and tables from the main text. The transparencies are excellent for presenting information in a clear manner consistent with the text.
- ***Great Ideas: Active Ways to Teach Health and Wellness.*** This booklet is loaded with teaching

tips from instructors on how to make class come alive, including collaborative and active learning techniques and effective use of technology in the classroom.

MyHealthLab

(www.aw-bc.com/myhealthlab) This online resource provides everything instructors need to teach fitness and wellness in one convenient location. MyHealthLab's course management system is loaded with valuable free teaching resources that make giving assignments and tracking student progress easy. Powered by CourseCompass™, the preloaded content in MyHealthLab includes interactive labs from the book, *ABC News* Lecture Launcher video clips, PowerPoint slides, Test Bank questions, Instructor Resource Manual material, and more. In addition, we have added new exercise videos showing proper techniques for both muscular strength and flexibility exercises.

Benjamin Cummings Health Video Series

In addition to the *ABC News* Lecture Launcher series, health and fitness videos are available to qualified adopters on a variety of topics.

Student Supplements

Behavior Change Log Book and Wellness Journal

This assessment tool helps students track their daily exercise and nutritional intake and create a long-term nutritional and fitness prescription plan. Packaged with each new copy of the text, it also includes a Behavior Change Contract and topics for journal-based activities.

Live Right! Beating Stress in College and Beyond

Live Right! gives students useful tips for coping with stressful life challenges both during college and for the rest of their lives. Topics include sleep, managing finances, time management, coping with academic pressure, and relationships. This book also presents an objective overview of some of the gimmicky health-oriented products now being advertised.

Eat Right! Healthy Eating in College and Beyond

Eat Right!, a handy, full-color 80-page booklet, provides students with practical guidelines, tips, shopper's guides and recipes that turn healthy eating principles into blueprints for action. Topics include healthy eating in the cafeteria, dorm room, and fast-food restaurants; planning meals on a budget; weight management; vegetarian alternatives; and the effects of alcohol on health.

MyHealthLab

(www.aw-bc.com/myhealthlab) MyHealthLab features online access to a selection of the print and media supplements for students and makes studying convenient and fun. The preloaded content on this website includes interactive labs from the book, which students can fill out and easily e-mail to instructors, an interactive e-book, self-assessment worksheets, Behavior Change Log Book and Wellness Journal, links to e-themes from the *New York Times*, Research Navigator, and the *ABC News* Lecture Launcher video clips. There are also new exercise videos demonstrating proper techniques for a variety of muscular strength and flexibility exercises.

Companion Website

(www.aw-bc.com/powers) The Total Fitness and Wellness Website offers students approximately 500 practice quiz questions, interactive activities, Web links to sites for further information, and e-themes from the *New York Times* containing articles reporting on the latest in health and wellness news and research. For the instructor, the site includes PowerPoint presentations and lecture outlines.

Take Charge of Your Health! Worksheets

A total of 50 self-assessment exercise worksheets give more opportunities for assessment.

MyDietAnalysis

Powered by ESHA Research, Inc., MyDietAnalysis features a database of nearly 20,000 foods and multiple reports. This easy-to-use program allows students to track their diet and activity for up to three profiles and to generate and submit reports electronically.

Tutor Center

Students can visit www.aw-bc.com/tutorcenter for round-the-clock support from tutors that can help clarify some of the more difficult concepts encountered in the fitness and wellness course.

Acknowledgments

First and foremost, this edition of *Total Fitness and Wellness* reflects the valuable feedback provided by many people throughout the country. Most notably, our contributing authors, Erica Jackson and Marilyn Miller, deserve great accolades. Their insights and skills have made major contributions to the content, as well as making the text very user-friendly.

As always, this edition could not have been completed without the work of an enormous number of people at Benjamin Cummings. From the campus sales representatives to the president of the company, they are truly first rate, and our interaction with them is always delightful.

There were several key people in the process. Our Acquisitions Editor, Sandra Lindelof, has been the primary force behind assembling the team and directing the process, and her input has been invaluable. Several new additions to the team have been important in both the revisions of the text and the production process. Claire Alexander has been a guiding presence over several editions, and her involvement is always appreciated. Specifically for this edition, Cheryl Cechvala has been a major force in the development of the text. She has directly supervised the revision, and has made contributions to the writing. Her input has been most valuable, and it has been a pleasure to work with her. Kari Hopperstead and Susan Scharf have also been major contributors to the editorial process and the development of ancillary materials. Their efforts have been most appreciated. Sharon Montooth has again served as Production Supervisor and has expertly guided the manuscript through each stage of production. Linda Jupiter again has coordinated the artwork for this edition, and, as before, her efforts have enhanced the look of the book and helped convey a message. Other specific duties were expertly handled by the following list of professionals. We offer them our utmost appreciation for their efforts: Erik P. Fortier, Media Producer; Jacob Evans, Editorial Assistant; Wendy Earl, Managing Editor; Renn Sminkey of Creative Digital Visions, Photographer; Kristin Piljay, Photo Researcher; Precision Graphics, Illustrator; tani hasegawa, Cover and Text Designer; Sally Peyrefitte, Copyeditor; Martha Ghent, Proofreader; Progressive Information Technologies, Compositor; Kathy Pitcoff, Indexer; Dorothy Cox, Manufacturing Supervisor; Caroline Gloodt, Permissions Editor.

Quinlyn Soltow at the University of Florida has made major contributions to the ancillaries. Her technical and editing work, informed by her expert knowledge of fitness and wellness, was exceptional.

Finally, there is a long list of professionals whose reviews of the text's content and style or participation in a fitness and wellness forum have helped to shape this book. We owe these individuals a tremendous debt of gratitude:

George Abboud,	*Salem State College*
Roxanne Allen,	*McNeese State University*
Arturo Arce,	*Louisiana State University*
Kym Atwood,	*University of West Florida*
J. Sunshine Cowan,	*University of Central Oklahoma*
Mandi Dupain,	*Millersville University*
Michael Dupper,	*University of Mississippi*
Ken Grace,	*Chabot College*
Peg Hamlett,	*University of Idaho*
Todd Hammonds,	*Lansing Community College*
Jerry Hawkins,	*Lander University*
Mary Kemp,	*Carroll Community College*
Gary Ladd,	*Southwestern Illinois College*
Rosemary Lindle,	*University of Maryland*
Amanda Nelson,	*University of Illinois*
Karen Poole,	*University of North Carolina-Greensboro*
Christopher Rasmussen,	*Baylor University*
Tammy Sabourin,	*Valencia Community College East*
Andrea Willis,	*Abraham Baldwin Agricultural College*

Many thanks to all!

Scott K. Powers
University of Florida

Stephen L. Dodd
University of Florida

1 Understanding Fitness and Wellness

true or false?

1. Your physical activity as a college student has no effect on your health later in life.
2. You definitely have a high level of wellness if you exercise and eat a healthy diet.
3. As little as 30 minutes of brisk walking most days of the week can improve your health.
4. Most people do not need help to make a health behavior change.
5. Smoking is the leading cause of preventable death in the United States.

Answers appear on the next page.

Maria is a college freshman who is away from home for the first time and starting to gain a little weight. In high school, Maria had been active with after-school sports, and her mother kept healthy food around the house and cooked meals for the family. After soccer or softball practice, Maria would go home, have dinner with her family, and study. Since coming to college, Maria has not been involved in sports and rarely finds time to go to the gym. Her eating habits are erratic, and she's spending more time partying with her friends, forgoing much study and sleep time in the process. Like many college students, Maria is excited to be away from home and "on her own," but she is a little overwhelmed by all of the choices she now has to make about what to eat and how to spend her time.

Do you relate to Maria? Are you less physically active now than when you were in high school? Has your diet changed for the worse since you've assumed control of what you eat? Do you think your level of wellness is better or worse than when you left home?

In this book, you will learn about behaviors that can put you on the path to optimal wellness. In this first chapter, we present the concept of wellness, discuss the health benefits of exercise, and outline the major components of physical fitness. Understanding the role that exercise plays in your own health and wellness can help motivate you to sustain a lifetime of physical fitness.

What Is Wellness?

Not so long ago, *good health* was defined as the absence of disease. But then, in the 1970s and 1980s, many exercise scientists and health educators became dissatisfied with this limited definition. These visionary health professionals believed that health includes physical fitness and emotional and spiritual health as well. Their revised concept of good health is called **wellness** (1). You can achieve a state of wellness by practicing a healthy lifestyle that includes regular physical activity, proper nutrition, eliminating unhealthy behaviors (that is, avoiding high-risk activities such as reckless driving, smoking, and drug use), and maintaining good emotional and spiritual health (1). Let's discuss the components of wellness, and what it means to enjoy a healthy lifestyle, in more depth now.

Six Components of Wellness

To enjoy an optimal state of wellness, you need to achieve physical, emotional, intellectual, spiritual, social, and environmental health. Do you get regular physical and dental exams? Do you stay close to and communicate with friends and family? Do you recycle? These choices and habits can all contribute to a healthy lifestyle, and they all fall under the components of wellness.

Wellness is also a dynamic concept in that the choices you make each day move you along a continuum. At one end is optimal well-being associated with a high level of functioning. At the other end is a low level of wellness that likely includes poor physical and mental health (Figure 1.1). You can move toward optimal well-being by eliminating unhealthy behaviors and adopting healthy ones.

Physical Health Physical health refers to all the behaviors that keep your body healthy. One of the key aspects for maintaining a healthy body is physical fitness. Physical fitness can have a positive effect on your

Answers

1. **FALSE** What you do as a college student will affect your health as you get older. Students who are active in college have lower risk for heart disease later in life.
2. **FALSE** Although exercising and eating a healthy diet are very positive wellness habits, they don't cover everything. There are six components that determine overall wellness, which you will learn about as you read this chapter.
3. **TRUE** Regular moderate exercise can produce a lot of health benefits. However, for certain goals, such as improving fitness, you will have to do more than 30 minutes of moderate activity.
4. **FALSE** To adopt and maintain a healthy behavior, you will need information, as well as support from friends, family, and possibly support groups.
5. **TRUE** Approximately 430,000 deaths per year are attributed to smoking. Most people are aware of the relationship between smoking and lung cancer. Moreover, smoking is also a major risk factor for heart disease.

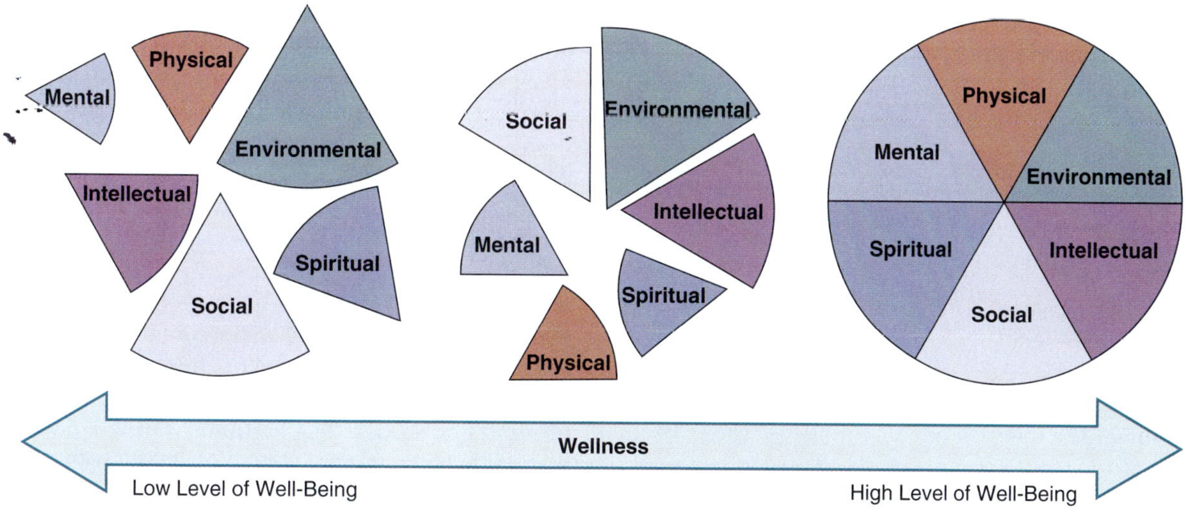

FIGURE 1.1
When the wellness components are well integrated and working together, you can enjoy the benefit of optimal well-being.

health by reducing your risk of disease and improving your quality of life. Proper nutrition, performing self-exams, and practicing personal safety are other important physical health behaviors.

Emotional Health Emotions play an important role in how you feel about yourself and others. Emotional health (also called mental health) includes your social skills and interpersonal relationships. Your levels of self-esteem and your ability to cope with the routine stress of daily living also are aspects of emotional health.

The cornerstone of emotional health is emotional stability, which describes how well you deal with the day-to-day stresses of personal interactions and the physical environment. Most people are well equipped to handle life's ups and downs, but the inability to handle everyday situations can lead to poor emotional health or mental health disorders, such as depression and anxiety disorders, in many people. In fact, mental disorders are the leading cause of disability for people aged 15–44 years (2). Emotional wellness means being able to respond to life situations in an appropriate manner and not remaining in extreme high or low emotional states.

CONSIDER THIS!

Approximately one in four adults between the ages of 18 and 44 has a diagnosable mental disorder in a given year.

Intellectual Health You can maintain intellectual health by keeping your mind active through lifelong learning. College is the ideal place to develop this wellness component, partly because it exposes you to new ideas and ways of thinking about life. Attending lectures, engaging in thoughtful discussions with friends or teachers, and reading are excellent ways to promote intellectual health. Maintaining good intellectual health can also increase your ability to define and solve problems, and continuous learning and thinking can provide you with a sense of fulfillment. Take advantage of opportunities to broaden your mind. Listen to audio books in the car, keep up with current events by reading the newspaper, and do not shy away from friendly debate.

Spiritual Health The term *spiritual* means different things to different people. Most definitions of *spiritual health* include having a sense of meaning and purpose. Many people define spiritual health according to their religious beliefs, but it is not limited to religion. People

wellness The state of healthy living achieved by the practice of a healthy lifestyle, which includes regular physical activity, proper nutrition, eliminating unhealthy behaviors, and maintaining good emotional and spiritual health.

Meditating or spending time outdoors can help you improve spiritual health.

may also find meaning in helping others and being altruistic, through prayer, or enjoying the beauty of nature. Whether you define spiritual health as religious beliefs or the establishment of personal values, it is an important aspect of wellness, is closely linked to emotional health, and also influences physical health (3).

Optimal spiritual health includes the ability to understand your basic purpose in life; to experience love, joy, pain, peace, and sorrow; and to care for and respect all living things. Anyone who has experienced a beautiful sunset or smelled the first scents of spring can appreciate the pleasure of maintaining optimal spiritual health.

Social Health Social health is the development and maintenance of meaningful interpersonal relationships. The result is the creation of a support network of friends and family. Good social health helps you feel confident in social interactions and provides you with emotional security. It is not necessarily the number of people in your support network that matters, but the quality of those relationships that is important. Developing strong communication skills is one behavior that is crucial for maintaining a strong social network.

Environmental Health Environmental health includes the influence of the environment on your health, as well as your behaviors that affect the condition of the environment. Our environment can have a positive or negative impact on our total wellness. For example, air pollution and water contamination are two important environmental factors that can harm physical health. Breathing polluted air can lead to a variety of respiratory disorders (e.g., asthma). Drinking water that has been contaminated with harmful bacteria can lead to infection, and drinking water that contains carcinogens (cancer-producing agents) increases the risk of certain types of cancers.

Your environment can also have a positive influence on wellness. For example, a safe environment invokes feelings of comfort and security, which impact your emotional health. Moreover, if your environment is safe, you are more likely to spend time outside being active and improving your physical health.

Our relationship with our environment is a two-way street. Just as our environment can have a positive or negative impact on us, we can have a positive or negative impact on it. Think about how your behavior affects the environment. Do you recycle regularly, or does much of your trash end up in a landfill? Do you carpool or take public transportation when you can, or are you leaving a large carbon footprint? Achieving total wellness requires learning about the environment and protecting yourself against environmental hazards that threaten your health and well-being, as well as being aware of your impact on the environment.

Interaction of Wellness Components

None of the components of wellness works in isolation; in fact, all six work closely together. For example, people with an anxiety or depressive disorder who also have a chronic physical illness report more physical symptoms than those who do not have a mental health disorder (4). Also, strong spirituality is associated with lower rates of mental disorders, better immune function, and greater participation in health-promoting behaviors (3, 5). Although the wellness components are interrelated, practicing healthy behaviors related to one aspect of wellness is not a guarantee of a high level of total wellness. Rather, total wellness is achieved through a balance of physical, intellectual, social, emotional, spiritual, and environmental health.

Make sure you know...

> *Wellness* is defined as a state of optimal health achieved by living a healthy lifestyle.

> There are six interacting components of wellness: physical health, emotional health, intellectual health, spiritual health, social health, and environmental health.

Wellness Goals for the Nation

All countries, including the United States, have a vested interest in having a healthy population. A nation of unhealthy people drains national resources by reducing worker productivity and increasing the amount of money the governments have to spend on health care. To improve the overall well-being of Americans, the U.S. government has established a set of wellness goals known as Healthy People.

The Healthy People initiative seeks to prevent unnecessary disease and improve the quality of life for all Americans. The wellness goals were first presented in *Healthy People* reports published in 1980 and have since been revised every 10 years based on the progress toward meeting the objectives. Each report includes a broad range of health and wellness objectives based on 10-year agendas. The current objectives, set forth in *Healthy People 2010*, are intended to help achieve two overarching goals: to increase the quantity and quality of healthy years of all Americans and to reduce health disparities across segments of the population in our society (see the Appreciating Diversity box below). For more details on the goals and objectives of *Healthy People 2010*, see the Closer Look box on the next page, or visit the Healthy People Web site at www.healthypeople.gov.

Make sure you know...

> *Healthy People 2010* is a set of wellness goals set by the U.S. government for the American people.

> The main goals of *Healthy People 2010* are to increase life spans and improve the quality of life and to eliminate health disparities.

What Is Exercise, and Why Should I Do It?

When you hear the word *exercise*, do you picture someone in a gym running on a treadmill? Or, do you imagine hiking up a scenic mountain with a group of friends? Actually, both activities can be exercise, and both are good for your health. In fact, there are numerous fun and interesting ways to exercise. So if going to the gym is not your thing, there are many other ways you can be active and improve your health. One part of designing your personal fitness program is to find out what works best for *you*.

APPRECIATING DIVERSITY WELLNESS ISSUES ACROSS THE POPULATION

Your behaviors have a significant impact on your level of health and wellness. However, there are factors beyond your control that contribute to your wellness and your risk for certain chronic diseases and conditions. Ethnicity, sex, age, family history, and socioeconomic status affect the risk of developing diabetes, cancer, cardiovascular disease (CVD), obesity, and other conditions.

For example, black Americans have a higher risk of developing hypertension (high blood pressure) compared to the U.S. population as a whole. Similarly, diabetes is more common in Native Americans and Latinos than people from other ethnic backgrounds. Further, men and women differ in their risk for heart disease, osteoporosis, and certain types of cancer.

Aging also can affect the ability to achieve wellness. For instance, the risk of chronic diseases (e.g., heart disease and cancer) increases with age. Finally, people with low socioeconomic status often have less access to quality health care and experience higher rates of obesity, heart disease, and drug abuse. The goal for everyone is to achieve optimal wellness, but individual and demographic differences can present special challenges in achieving wellness. This important issue will be discussed throughout this book.

A CLOSER LOOK

HEALTHY PEOPLE 2010

Selected *Healthy People 2010* objectives include the following:

- Increase the proportion of people who engage in daily physical activity.
- Reduce activity limitation due to chronic back conditions.
- Reduce the prevalence of cigarette smoking.
- Increase the consumption of fruits and vegetables.
- Reduce the lung cancer death rate.
- Reduce the prostate cancer death rate.
- Reduce the melanoma death rate.
- Reduce the number of college students engaging in heavy drinking of alcoholic beverages.
- Reduce the proportion of people who experience adverse health effects from stress each year.
- Reduce the prevalence of overweight people (aged 20 and older).

Improving the number and quality of healthy years and eliminating health disparities are lofty goals. To meet these goals outlined in *Healthy People 2010,* the government, health agencies, and individuals must work together to address a broad range of health behaviors across numerous populations.

Source: U.S. Department of Health and Human Services, Office of Disease Prevention and Health Promotion, www.healthypeople.gov.

Exercise Is One Type of Physical Activity

Although the terms *physical activity* and *exercise* are often used interchangeably, they do not mean the same thing. **Physical activity** includes all physical movement, regardless of the level of energy expenditure or the reason you do it (6). Physical activity can be occupational, lifestyle, or leisure time. Occupational activity is the activity that you carry out in the course of your job as, for example, a restaurant server or construction worker. Lifestyle activity includes housework, walking to class, or climbing the stairs to get to your apartment or dorm room. Leisure-time physical activity is any activity you choose to do in your free time.

Exercise is a type of leisure-time physical activity (6). Virtually all conditioning activities and sports are considered exercise because they are planned and help maintain or improve physical fitness. The main thing that distinguishes exercise from other types of physical activity is that exercise is done specifically for health and fitness.

When we use the term *physical activity,* it encompasses exercise, but exercise does not include all types of physical activity. For example, riding your bike to work for transportation is lifestyle physical activity, and lifting heavy boxes at work is occupational physical activity. Both of these activities will improve health and are examples of how an active lifestyle or job can affect health even when a person does not participate in a regular structured exercise program. Typically, exercise produces the greatest health benefits (you'll learn more about this in Chapter 2), but you still can receive a lot of health benefits with regular physical activity.

There Are Numerous Health Benefits of Physical Activity

If you ask people whether they exercise regularly, the answer often is no. People have many reasons for not exercising. However, most of us are aware there are many health benefits of regular physical activity and exercise. In addition to making us look better by improving muscle tone and levels of body fat, regular exercise helps improve our energy levels and our ability to perform everyday tasks. Perhaps even more important, it can help you achieve total wellness (2, 7–15).

The importance of regular physical activity in promoting good health and wellness is emphasized in the 1996 Surgeon General's report on physical activity and health (16). This report concludes that lack of physical activity is a major public health problem in the United States and that all Americans can improve their health by engaging in as little as 30 minutes of light-to-moderate-intensity physical activity most days of the week. The Surgeon General's report recognizes numerous health benefits of physical activity and exercise (Figure 1.2), which we will discuss next. Keep in mind that different levels of physical activity or exercise are needed for different health benefits. You will learn more about the recommended amounts of activity needed for health and fitness throughout the book.

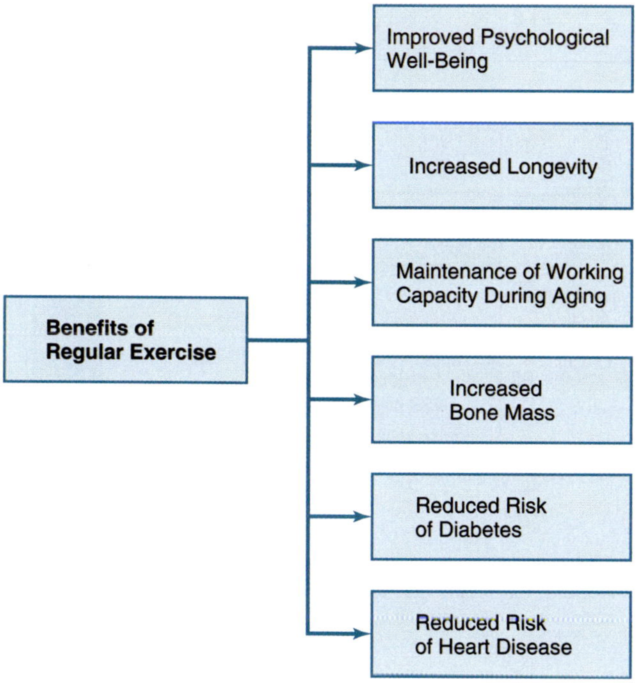

FIGURE 1.2
Regular exercise can yield several long-term benefits for your health.

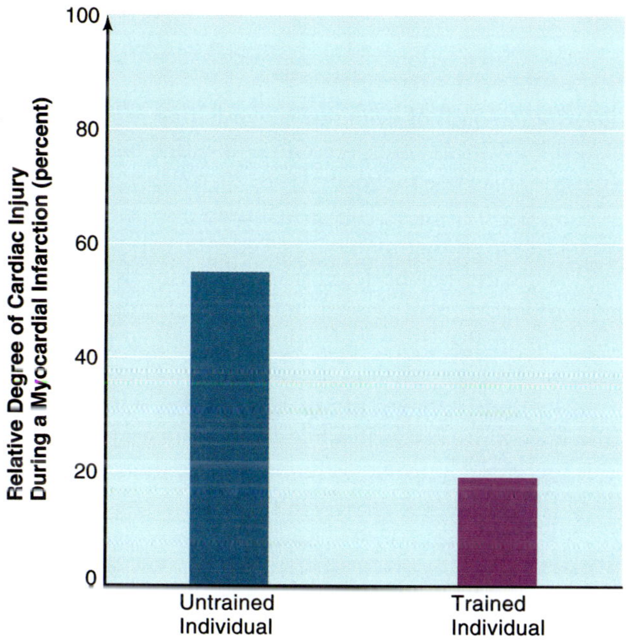

FIGURE 1.3
Regular endurance exercise protects the heart against injury during heart attack. This figure illustrates that during a myocardial infarction (a heart attack), exercise-trained individuals suffer less cardiac injury compared to untrained individuals.

Source: Data from Yamashita, N. et al. Exercise provides direct biphasic cardioprotection via manganese superoxide dismutase activation. *Journal of Experimental Medicine* 189:1699–1706, 1999.

Reduced Risk of Heart Disease **Cardiovascular disease (CVD)** (i.e., any ailment of the heart and blood vessels) is a major cause of death in the United States. In fact, one of every two Americans dies of CVD (17). Regular physical activity and exercise can significantly reduce your risk of developing CVD (1, 7, 8, 10, 11, 17–21). Further, strong evidence suggests that regular physical activity reduces the risk of dying during a heart attack (Figure 1.3) (22–25). Note from Figure 1.3 that exercise training can reduce the magnitude of cardiac injury during a heart attack by more than 60% (23, 24). Many preventive medicine specialists argue that these facts alone are reason enough for engaging in regular physical activity and exercise (7, 18, 26). Chapter 9 provides a detailed discussion of exercise and CVD.

Reduced Risk of Diabetes **Diabetes** is a disease characterized by high blood sugar (glucose) levels. Untreated diabetes can result in numerous health problems, including blindness and kidney dysfunction. Regular physical activity and exercise can reduce the risk of a specific type of diabetes, called type 2, by improving the regulation of blood glucose (9, 27, 28). We will discuss diabetes in more detail in Chapter 6.

Increased Bone Mass The bones of the skeleton provide a mechanical lever system to permit movement and protect internal organs. Clearly, then, it is important to maintain strong and healthy bones. Loss of bone mass and strength is called **osteoporosis,** and it increases the risk of bone fractures. Although osteoporosis can occur in men and women of all ages, it is more common in older adults, particularly women.

Exercise can improve bone health by strengthening your bones. Mechanical force applied by muscular

physical activity Any movement of the body produced by a skeletal muscle that results in energy expenditure, especially through movement of large muscle groups.

exercise Planned, structured, and repetitive bodily movement done to improve or maintain one or more components of fitness.

cardiovascular disease (CVD) Any disease of the heart and blood vessels.

diabetes A metabolic disorder characterized by high blood glucose levels. Chronic elevation of blood glucose is associated with increased incidence of heart disease, kidney disease, nerve dysfunction, and eye damage.

osteoporosis A condition that results from the loss of bone mass and strength.

Regular weight-bearing exercise can prevent loss of bone mass.

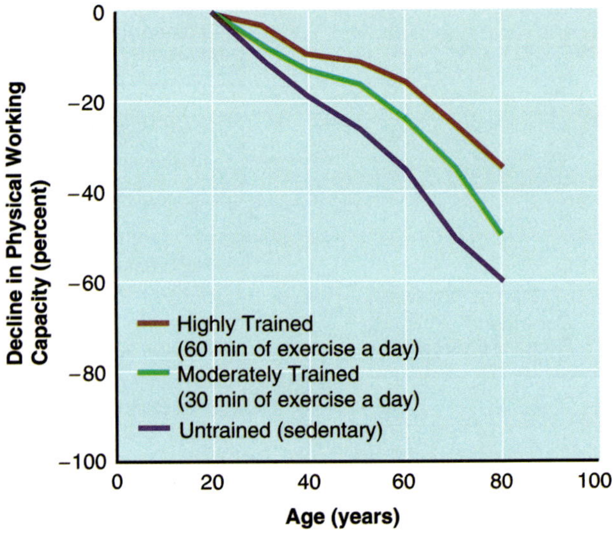

FIGURE 1.4
Regular exercise can reduce the natural decline in working capacity that occurs as we age.

activity is a key factor in regulating bone mass and strength. Numerous studies have demonstrated that regular exercise increases bone mass, density, and strength in young adults (29–31). In particular, weight-bearing activities, such as running, walking, and resistance training, are important for bone health. Further, research on osteoporosis suggests that regular exercise can prevent bone loss in older adults and is also useful in treating osteoporosis (29).

Easier Aging As people age, they gradually lose their physical capacity to do work. As we grow older, our ability to perform strenuous activities (e.g., running, cycling, or swimming) progressively declines. Although this decline may begin as early as the 20s, the most dramatic changes occur after about age 60 (32–34). Regular exercise training can reduce the rate of decline in physical working capacity as we age (32, 35, 36). Notice the differences in physical working capacity among highly trained, moderately trained, and inactive individuals in Figure 1.4. The key point is that although physical working capacity declines with age, regular exercise can reduce the rate of this decline, increasing your ability to enjoy a lifetime of physical recreation and an improved quality of life that comes with it.

Increased Longevity Although controversial, a growing amount of evidence suggests that regular physical activity and exercise (combined with a healthy lifestyle) increase longevity (7, 8, 25, 37–39). For example, a classic study of Harvard alumni over the past 30 years reported that men with a sedentary lifestyle have a 31% greater risk of death from all causes than men who report regular physical activity (8). Studies including women also show that sedentary and low-fit women also have a higher risk of death (40, 41). These findings translate into a longer life span for people who exercise and have more active lifestyles. The primary factor for this increased longevity is thought to be their lower risk of both heart attack and cancer (7, 8).

Improved Psychological Well-Being Strong evidence indicates that regular exercise improves psychological well-being in people of all ages. The mental health benefits of regular exercise include reduced risk for anxiety disorders and depression (42). Also, people report feeling less anxious and stressed after an exercise session, even up to 8 hours afterward. These mental benefits lead to an improved sense of well-being in the physically active individual. We will further discuss the role of exercise as a method for reducing psychological stress in Chapter 10.

Regular physical activity can help you live longer.

Make sure you know...

- Regular physical activity and exercise reduce the risk of both heart disease and diabetes.
- Exercise increases bone mass in young people and strengthens bone in older adults.
- Regular exercise maintains physical working capacity as the person ages.
- Regular physical activity and exercise have been shown to increase longevity and improve quality of life.
- Exercise promotes psychological well-being and reduces risk of depressive and anxiety disorders.

Exercise and Activity for Health-Related Fitness

Exercise conditioning programs can be divided into two broad categories according to their goals: (1) health-related physical fitness and (2) sport or skill-related physical fitness. This textbook focuses on health-related fitness. The overall goal of a total health-related physical fitness program is to optimize the quality of life (1, 42). The specific goals of this type of fitness program are to reduce the risk of disease and to improve total physical fitness so that daily tasks can be completed with less effort and fatigue. In contrast, the single goal of sport and skill-related fitness is to improve physical performance in a specific sport. Note though, that the "weekend warrior" engaged in a total health-related physical fitness program will likely also improve physical performance in many sports.

Most fitness experts agree that there are five major components of total health-related physical fitness:

1. Cardiorespiratory endurance
2. Muscular strength
3. Muscular endurance
4. Flexibility
5. Body composition

In addition to these, some fitness experts include motor skill performance as a sixth component. Motor skills are movement qualities, such as agility and coordination, that help athletes improve their performance. Although motor skills are important for sport performance, they are not directly linked to improving health in young adults and are therefore not considered a major component of health-related physical fitness. However, these motor skills might increase in importance as people age, because good balance, coordination, and agility may help reduce the risk for falls in older adults.

Let's examine each of the five components of fitness in more depth.

Cardiorespiratory Endurance

Cardiorespiratory endurance (sometimes called *aerobic fitness* or *cardiorespiratory fitness*) is often considered the key component of health-related physical fitness. Cardiorespiratory endurance is a measure of the heart's ability to pump oxygen-rich blood to the working muscles during exercise and of the muscles' ability to take up and use the oxygen. The oxygen delivered to the muscles is used to produce the energy needed for prolonged exercise.

In practical terms, cardiorespiratory endurance is the ability to perform endurance-type exercises such as distance running, cycling, and swimming. Someone who has achieved a high measure of cardiorespiratory endurance is generally capable of performing 30 to 60

cardiorespiratory endurance A measure of the heart's ability to pump oxygen-rich blood to the working muscles during exercise and of the muscles' ability to take up and use the oxygen.

Cyclists who bike for long distances exhibit strong cardiorespiratory endurance.

minutes of vigorous exercise without undue fatigue. Chapter 3 discusses the details of exercise training designed to improve cardiorespiratory fitness.

Muscular Strength

Muscular strength is evaluated by how much force a muscle (or muscle group) can generate during a single maximal contraction. Practically, this means how much weight an individual can lift during one maximal effort.

Muscular strength is important in almost all sports. Sports such as football, basketball, and events in track and field require a high level of muscular strength. Even nonathletes require some degree of muscular strength to function in everyday life. For example, routine tasks around the home, such as lifting bags of groceries and moving furniture, require muscular strength. Even modest amounts of weight training (also called resistance training) can improve muscular strength and increase ease of everyday tasks. The principles of developing muscular strength are presented in Chapter 4.

Muscular Endurance

Muscular endurance is the ability of a muscle to generate a submaximal force over and over again. Although muscular strength and muscular endurance are related, they are not the same. These two terms can be best distinguished by examples. A person lifting a 150-pound barbell during one maximal muscular effort demonstrates high muscular strength. If she lifts a 75-pound barbell a dozen times, she demonstrates muscular endurance. As one develops muscular strength, endurance typically improves. However, strength does not generally improve with muscular endurance training.

Most sports require muscular endurance. For instance, tennis players, who must repeatedly swing their racquets during a match, require a high level of muscular endurance. Many everyday activities (e.g., carrying your backpack across campus all day) also require some level of muscular endurance. Techniques of developing muscular endurance are discussed in Chapter 4.

Flexibility

Flexibility is the ability to move joints freely through their full range of motion. Flexible individuals can bend and twist at their joints with ease. Without routine stretching, muscles and tendons shorten and become tight, retarding the range of motion around joints and impairing flexibility.

Individual needs for flexibility vary. Certain athletes (such as gymnasts and divers) require great flexibility to accomplish complex movements. The average individual requires less flexibility than an athlete. However, everyone needs some flexibility for activities of daily living such as reaching for something on the back of the top shelf. Research suggests that flexibility is useful in preventing some types of muscle–tendon injuries and may be useful in reducing low back pain (43, 44). Techniques for improving flexibility are discussed in Chapter 5.

Body Composition

The term **body composition** refers to the relative amounts of fat and lean tissue in your body. The rationale for including body composition as a component of health-related physical fitness is that having a high percentage of body fat (a condition known as obesity) is associated with an increased risk of developing CVD, type 2 diabetes, and some cancers, and it contributes to joint stress during movement. In general, being "overfat" elevates the risk of medical problems.

Lack of physical activity has been shown to play a major role in gaining body fat. Conversely, regular ex-

Swinging a tennis racquet repeatedly during a tennis match requires a high level of muscular endurance.

ercise is an important factor in promoting the loss of body fat. You will learn more about body composition in Chapter 6.

Make sure you know...

> Health-related physical fitness consists of five components: cardiorespiratory endurance, muscular strength, muscular endurance, flexibility, and body composition.

How Can You Make Healthier Behavior Choices?

Remember Maria? She needs to change several behaviors to improve her wellness. Her exercise, eating, sleeping, and time management habits could all be improved. Changing her current behaviors will require some effort on her part, and it will not happen overnight. Unhealthy habits and patterns develop over time, so she cannot expect to change them without time and effort. Fortunately, Maria is committed to improving her health, and she is going to use strategies she learned in her wellness course to make lifestyle behavior changes.

The Stages of Change Model

The **Stages of Change Model** suggests that there are a series of five stages to behavior change:

1. Individuals in the *precontemplation* stage of behavior change do not plan to change their unhealthy behavior. They might not realize the need to change, or they just might not want to change.
2. In the *contemplation* stage, a person is aware of the need to change and intends to do so within the next 6 months. People in these first two stages need information about healthy behaviors and the small steps they can make to get closer to changing.
3. During the *preparation* stage, the person is getting ready to make the change within the next 30 days.

muscular strength The maximal ability of a muscle to generate force.

muscular endurance The ability of a muscle to generate force over and over again.

flexibility The ability to move joints freely through their full range of motion.

body composition The relative amounts of fat and lean tissue (muscle, organs, bone) found in the body.

Stages of Change Model A framework for understanding how individuals move toward adopting and maintaining health behavior changes.

In some cases, the person might already be making some changes (e.g., increasing lifestyle activity before starting an exercise program). People also begin to take practical steps, such as buying a daily planner to list and prioritize daily tasks.

4. In the *action* stage, the behavior change has occurred, but for fewer than 6 months.
5. After sustaining the behavior change for 6 months, the person enters the *maintenance* stage. During this stage, the behavior change is more of a habit and requires less conscious effort. As this stage progresses, the temptation to resume old habits steadily decreases. In the last three stages, it is important to use the behavior modification strategies discussed in the next sections to advance through the stages and to maintain the change long term.

The length of time that one spends in each stage is highly individual, and progression through the stages is not usually linear. Often, people move back and forth between the stages multiple times before they are able to make the behavior change permanent. Note that a setback does not mean failure. If you experience a lapse to an earlier stage, evaluate why you had the setback, and develop a new plan. Learn from this experience, and do not let it discourage you.

The key element in any behavior change plan is the desire to change. Without a genuine desire to make lifestyle changes, the best behavior change plan is doomed to fail. The rest of this section discusses specific strategies and steps to help you adopt and maintain healthy behaviors.

Behavior Modification

Behavior modification is using the cues that precede a behavior or the consequences of the behavior to change it. For example, packing a bag of workout clothes before you go to bed at night and leaving it by your front door is a reminder to take your bag with you the next day so you can stop by the gym after work. If you enjoy the relaxed feeling that results from a good workout, you are likely to keep exercising. Seven commonly used behavior modification strategies are outlined below.

1. *Behavior change contracts* (like the one in the front of this book) include your goals and plans for changing your behavior and are signed by you and a person close to you. Filling out the contract will help you think through your plan, and having another person sign the contract will provide a partner for support and accountability.
2. *Setting realistic short-term and long-term goals* is essential for effective behavior change. The details of goal setting are outlined at length in Chapter 2.
3. *Self-monitoring* involves analyzing your behavior to determine what influences your unhealthy behaviors and patterns. Self-monitoring helps you see the things that trigger and reinforce your unhealthy choices so you can make changes.
4. *Counter conditioning* is replacing an unhealthy behavior choice with a healthier one. Something as simple as keeping fresh fruits and vegetables for snacks instead of potato chips can help you make dietary changes.
5. *Self-reinforcement* is developing a system to reward yourself when you meet your goals.
6. *Decisional balance* involves weighing the positives and negatives of the behavior you want to change. This strategy is usually more helpful for people in the last three stages of change, when they are expecting or experiencing positive outcomes of the new behaviors. In the first two stages, you are more likely to see the negatives of the behavior, so decisional balance might be counterproductive for changing your behavior.
7. *Relapse prevention* is used to keep you from lapsing back to your unhealthy behavior. This strategy involves identifying the "high-risk" situations that are likely to trigger your unhealthy choice and then developing a specific plan of action to avoid or eliminate those situations. If you are trying to drink less alcohol on the weekend and you know that you are likely to drink too much at a campus keg party, you might skip the party and go to a restaurant with your friends instead. Then you might take only enough money for one or two drinks, and rotate the responsibility of being the designated driver.

Assessing Your Habits

Before you can change a wellness-related behavior, you must recognize that the behavior is unhealthy and that you can make changes. You also need to identify alternative behaviors for your unhealthy behavior. A good place to begin is a personal assessment of your health risk status. You can use the lifestyle assessment inventory in Laboratory 1.1 to increase your awareness of factors that affect your health. As you complete the lab, develop a list of your less-than-optimal behaviors. Can you identify where you are in the stages of change? Do you need to gather more information before you initiate your behavior change plan? Remember, to be successful in changing the behavior, you must be ready, physically and mentally. Keep in mind that you can control each of these health behaviors but that being aware of them is not enough to bring about change.

After you determine which behaviors you want to change, you can use self-monitoring to study your

STEPS FOR BEHAVIOR CHANGE

Do you have trouble making healthy behavior changes?

Answer the following questions about your typical efforts to change a health behavior.

Y	N	
☐	☐	Do you have a specific game plan?
☐	☐	Do you get help from your friends and family?
☐	☐	Do you set goals?
☐	☐	Do you reward yourself for your successes?

If you answered no to most or all of the questions, then you should consider using the behavioral contract in the front of the text.

BENEFITS OF USING A BEHAVIORAL CONTRACT

- ☑ Helps you think through and assess your behavior
- ☑ Helps you develop specific plans in writing.
- ☑ Provides you with accountability and support from another person.
- ☑ Shows strong commitment and motivation to change.

habits to make the best plan of action. When you assess your patterns, consider why you make the choices you make and why you want to change. Do you have poor dietary habits because you do not know healthy nutrition recommendations, or do you overeat to deal with stress or emotional problems? Also, you need to assess the things and people in your life that facilitate healthy decisions and that present barriers for healthy decisions.

Lastly when assessing your habits, consider why it is important for you to change. Do you want to change to improve your health and feel better about yourself, or do you want to change to please someone else? Understanding the motivations for your choices will help you develop the best plan to make your changes permanent.

Identifying Behavior Change Barriers

After you have assessed your current behavior patterns, you can focus on the barriers that may prevent you from changing your behavior. For example, you want to start an exercise program, but you have a full load of classes and work part-time in the evening—you may feel that lack of time is a barrier. You want to stop smoking, but all your friends smoke when you hang out together—your barrier would be the social pressure you feel from your friends. Your goal is to reduce or eliminate your barriers, and this is the perfect opportunity to use relapse prevention.

Some barriers are easy to work with. Others are complicated, especially when they are influenced by people who are important to you. To go back to our examples, getting up a half-hour earlier might help you overcome the barrier of a perceived lack of time, but to address the social barrier to your quitting smoking you will need some help from your friends. People who care about you will typically be supportive if they know about your goals, but they cannot help if you do not communicate your desire to change. Telling your friends you want to stop smoking and that you do not want to be with them when they smoke will help them support your decision. Relapse prevention can be very effective in changing behaviors.

CONSUMER CORNER

FINDING CREDIBLE HEALTH INFORMATION

With all of the health information out there, how do you know what to believe? "Experts" endorse products and plans on infomercials and in magazines, but some of the claims seem too good to be true. To avoid becoming overwhelmed—or worse, being scammed—you have to develop a "healthy skepticism." The next time you visit a website, read a supplement label, or watch an infomercial, ask yourself the following questions:

- Do the claims made about this product seem too good to be true?
- Has all of the supporting research been conducted or funded by the company that makes the product or offers the service?
- Are the claims made about the product supported by quality scientific research?
- Is there information available about short- and long-term effects?
- Does the information fit with the information I am learning in class?
- Are potential risks and side effects of products and services mentioned?
- Are the experts endorsing the product or service really experts in that field? (For example, a doctor who is a podiatrist might not be the best source for a weight loss pill.)
- Is there any opposing information available?

Answering yes to the first two questions should always raise a red flag. If you can answer yes to the remaining questions, the product or service might be worth considering. Get the opinion of a trusted professional, such as your instructor or a health care worker at your student health center for further evaluation.

Changing Unhealthy Behaviors

Now you can begin to develop a game plan for changing your behaviors. After you complete Laboratory 1.1, you might see multiple behaviors you could change to improve your wellness. Do not let your results overwhelm you. Recognize that you do not need to change all of your unhealthy behaviors at the same time. Trying to make too many changes at once is usually very difficult and reduces your chances for success. Setbacks can reduce your motivation to change, but keep in mind that a setback does not mean failure.

Before you can develop your plan of action, you need to have accurate information about the behaviors. You will get a lot of information from this book and your instructor. However, you might also need to seek out additional resources, such as counselor at the student health center, a fitness specialist, or a support group. Make sure any outside resources are reputable groups or individuals who are qualified to give you the information and guidance you need (see Consumer Corner for how to identify credible sources of health information).

When deciding which changes you want to make first, consider the number of behaviors you want to change and the effort it will take to change them. Some behaviors, such as flossing your teeth regularly or performing monthly self-exams, are simple and do not require as much effort. However, starting a new exercise program, quitting smoking, or changing your diet require more effort. Most people can successfully make more than one simple change at a time. However, for the more complex behaviors, making them one at a time is recommended. Also, breaking them into smaller steps, or **shaping,** is also recommended to make the change seem less intimidating. Your success with the simple behaviors and the small steps on the way to the complex behavior will increase your confidence and motivate you to work toward total wellness.

Finally, you need to set goals and develop your specific plan for changing the behavior. Something as simple as putting a monthly reminder on your personal digital assistant (PDA) to do a self-exam and hanging a plastic tag on your shower head might do the trick. Or, using counter conditioning by trading a sedentary choice for an active one will increase lifestyle physical activity. However, for many behaviors you will need a more detailed plan of action. For example, changing your eating habits might include meeting with a dietitian, making grocery lists, planning meals ahead of time, and having an accountability partner. Also, these changes will likely be made in stages. Using shaping will make the change seem more manageable.

Make sure you know...

> Knowing your stage of change will help you develop the best plan of action for changing your behavior.

> Behavior modification strategies are very helpful in successfully changing your behavior.

> Assessing your current habits and addressing your barriers are essential before developing your plan for behavior change.

Specific Application of Behavior Modification

Let's apply behavior modification to two common behaviors that can be a challenge to address: quitting smoking and losing weight.

Smoking Cessation

As previously mentioned, cigarette smoking increases the risk of cancer and heart disease. Research shows that smoking is the largest cause of preventable death in the United States (45). Although millions of people have quit smoking, the number of smokers has increased since the late 1960s because of an increase in young smokers, particularly young women. Smoking is a difficult behavior to change because it involves an addiction to nicotine, so outside assistance might be necessary to help overcome the addiction.

CONSIDER THIS!

By grade 12, 54% of students have tried cigarette smoking.

The first step in quitting smoking is having the desire to stop. You may want to quit because you recognize the negative health effects of smoking, or you may have important people in your life who want you to quit. When you analyze your smoking behavior, pay attention to the times you smoke. Think about the reasons you decide to smoke. Is it automatic after a meal, or when you are with certain friends? Note the times you do not have the desire to smoke or when you choose other behaviors over smoking, and note your barriers for quitting smoking.

After you have a good idea of when and why you smoke, it is time to set goals and make a plan. Relapse prevention and counter conditioning can be very helpful. Mobilize your support network by telling your friends and family what you plan to do—and, specifically, how they can help.

When you set your goals, be very specific so you can assess your progress. Also, be sure to set both short-term and long-term goals. Obviously, the long-term goal is to stop permanently, but you should set goals for the things you will do to prepare for and maintain cessation. For example, you might sign a behavioral contract with your roommate and agree to check in after meals to maintain accountability. If you smoke after meals, plan to brush your teeth or chew gum instead of smoking; this is an example of counter conditioning. Relapse prevention might involve eating lunch in a no-smoking restaurant. Planning ahead and having an alternate behavior will decrease the likelihood of smoking at your high-risk times.

Quitting smoking "cold turkey" is the most commonly reported method for smoking cessation (45, 46). Continue using behavior modification strategies to move from the action to the maintenance stage. If you smoke even one cigarette during the action stage, you move back into the preparation or possibly the contemplation stage, but remember that lapse does not mean failure. Reevaluate your behavior and why you had the lapse, and revise your plan. As you maintain your new healthy behavior of not smoking, be sure to reward yourself for accomplishing your goal.

Weight Loss

Losing weight and keeping it off are difficult for many people. Applying behavior modification principles and using behavior change models are essential. Although no single weight-loss program works for all people, the following are common components of most successful efforts:

1. Make sure that you want to lose weight for yourself. If you want to lose weight to please someone else, your chances for success are not as high.
2. Assess your eating habits, including the kind and amount of food you eat and the environmental and social circumstances involved. Also assess your physical activity and exercise patterns.
3. Establish short- and long-term goals. Do not limit your goals to a specific number of pounds to lose; set goals for changing your exercise and eating habits as well.
4. Establish your support network and accountability partners. A behavioral contract can be helpful.
5. Develop your specific plan, including dietary and activity changes. Remember to make it very detailed and to include specific steps. For example, a goal to "prepare healthier meals" is not specific enough. Instead, spell out what you will do to prepare healthier meals. Find recipes for dishes that are low in calories and dense in nutrients. Plan meals for an entire week, and make a grocery list for only the foods needed for your menus. Prepare meals according to

shaping Breaking a behavior or task into small steps to accomplish the larger goal.

the plan, and consider portion size. Each step might seem minor, but each takes effort. With this level of detail, you are using shaping, and you can experience success at each level to increase your confidence. (See Chapter 8 for more on weight management.)

6. Relapse prevention and counter conditioning will help plan for situations that might make you slip from your dietary changes and exercise plans. For example, knowing healthy menu options before you get to the restaurant and planning to exercise as soon you get home instead of watching television can help keep you on track.
7. Use your support network and any other outside assistance.
8. Reward yourself for successes along the way (self-reinforcement). Make sure your rewards do not undermine your success. Rewarding yourself with chocolate cake for a week is not the best choice, but a dessert once in a while is not unreasonable.

There is a lot of good and bad information out there about ways to lose weight. You need to check information for accuracy when you consider a weight-loss plan. Unsound plans often produce rapid weight loss, but they might leave you missing key nutrients and can cause you to gain more weight later. These plans may also lighten your wallet, but not your body. Stay away from products or services that do not have information about long-term effects. Refer to Chapter 8 and your instructor to help you evaluate a plan.

Remember that the key elements in a weight-loss program are the desire to lose weight for oneself, establishing goals, developing a plan, and getting support from your friends and family. As you develop your plan, assess your readiness for change as well as the benefits, barriers, and other factors that will contribute to your success.

Make sure you know...

- Behavior modification can be applied to many health behaviors.
- A detailed plan of action is essential for using behavior modification to change your unhealthy behaviors.

Summary

1. The term *wellness* means "healthy living." Wellness is achieved by practicing a healthy lifestyle, which includes regular physical activity, proper nutrition, eliminating unhealthy behaviors (avoiding high-risk activities such as smoking and drug use), and maintaining emotional and spiritual health.
2. Total wellness can be achieved only by a balance of physical, emotional, intellectual, spiritual, social, and environmental health. The components of wellness do not work in isolation; they interact strongly. For example, poor physical health can lead to poor emotional health.
3. Exercise offers many health benefits. Regular exercise has been shown to reduce risk of CVD and diabetes, increase bone mass, and maintain physical working capacity as one ages.
4. The five major components of "total" health-related physical fitness are cardiorespiratory endurance, muscular strength, muscular endurance, flexibility, and body composition.
5. Used correctly, behavior modification strategies can be very helpful for changing health behaviors.

Study Questions

1. ____________________ is any body movement produced by skeletal muscles that results in energy expenditure.
   a. Exercise
   b. Physical fitness
   c. Physical activity
   d. Health-related fitness
2. ____________________ is *not* a dimension of wellness.
   a. Exercise
   b. Spiritual health
   c. Social health
   d. Mental health

3. Which of the following is *not* a component of health-related fitness?
   a. muscular strength
   b. body composition
   c. agility
   d. flexibility
4. Which of the following is a health benefit of regular physical activity?
   a. reduced risk for osteoporosis
   b. reduced risk for heart disease
   c. improved mental health
   d. all of the above
5. The main goals for *Healthy People 2010* include
   a. increasing quality and quantity of healthy years and eliminating health disparities.
   b. eliminating physical inactivity and reducing obesity.
   c. increasing wellness of all and eliminating smoking.
   d. increasing fitness for all and improving healthy eating.
6. A person in the ________________________ stage of change has been fully participating in the new health behavior for less than 6 months.
   a. maintenance
   b. action
   c. contemplation
   d. new activity
7. Which of the following is an important step in initiating a health behavior change?
   a. making a specific plan
   b. mobilizing your support network
   c. getting outside help if needed
   d. all of the above
8. Which of the following should be considered when you are planning to make a behavior change?
   a. number of behaviors you want to change and effort involved
   b. motive for behavior change
   c. current behavior patterns
   d. all of the above
9. What is wellness?
10. Name at least one behavior associated with each of the six components of wellness.
11. List and discuss the five components of health-related fitness.
12. Outline the strategies for setting exercise goals.
13. Discuss the importance of *Healthy People 2010*.

Suggested Reading

Blair, S., and M. Moore. Surgeon General's report on physical fitness. The inside story. *ACSM's Health and Physical Journal* 1:14–18, 1997.

Brooks, G. A., N. Butte, W. Rand, J. Flatt, and B. Caballero. Chronicle of the Institute of Medicine physical activity recommendation: How a physical activity recommendation came to be among dietary recommendations. *American Journal of Clinical Nutrition* 70:921S 930S, 2004.

Brown, D., D. Brown, G. Heath, L. Balluz, W. Giles, E. Ward, and A. Mokdad. Associations between physical activity dose and health-related quality of life. *Medicine and Science in Sports and Exercise* 36:890–896, 2004.

Franklin, B. Improved fitness = Increased longevity. *ACSM's Health and Fitness Journal* 5:32–33, 2001.

Howley, E., and D. Franks. *Health Fitness Instructor's Handbook*, 4th ed. Champaign, IL: Human Kinetics Publishers, 2003.

Powers, S., and E. Howley. *Exercise Physiology: Theory and Application to Fitness and Performance*, 5th ed. St. Louis, MO: McGraw-Hill, 2004.

Powers, S., S. Lennon, J. Quindry, and J. Mehta. Exercise and cardioprotection. *Current Opinion in Cardiology* 17:495–502, 2002.

Thompson, P., et al. Exercise and physical activity in the prevention and treatment of atherosclerotic cardiovascular disease. *Circulation* 107:3109–3116, 2003.

For links to the websites below, visit The Total Fitness and Wellness Website at www.aw-bc.com/powers.

American Heart Association
Contains latest information about ways to reduce your risk of heart and vascular diseases. Site includes information about exercise, diet, and heart disease.

American College of Sports Medicine
Contains information about exercise, health, and fitness.

WebMD
Contains the latest information on a variety of health-related topics, including diet, exercise, and stress. Links to nutrition, fitness, and wellness topics.

Healthy People
Contains information about the U.S. government's initiative to improve health and wellness for the American people.

References

1. Margen, S., et al., eds. *The Wellness Encyclopedia.* Boston: Houghton Mifflin, 1995.
2. National Institute of Mental Health. The Numbers Count: Mental Disorders in America. Fact Sheet. www.nimh.nih.gov/publicat/numbers.cfm#MajorDepressive
3. Koeing, H. G. Religion, spirituality and medicine: Research findings and implications for clinical practice. *Southern Medical Journal* 97:1194–1200, 2004.
4. Katon, W., E. H. B. Lin, and K. Kroenke. The association of depression and anxiety with medical symptom burden in patients with chronic medical illness. *General Hospital Psychiatry* 29:147–155, 2007.
5. Weaver, A. J., and K. J. Flannelly. The role of religion/spirituality for cancer patients and their caregivers. *Southern Medical Journal* 97:1210–1214, 2004.
6. Caspersen, C. J., K. E. Powell, and G. M. Christenson. Physical activity and exercise: Definitions and distinctions for health related-fitness research. *Public Health Reports* 100:126–130, 1985.
7. Paffenbarger, R., J. Kampert, I-Min Lee, R. Hyde, R. Leung, and A. Wing. Changes in physical activity and other lifeway patterns influencing longevity. *Medicine and Science in Sports and Exercise* 26:857–865, 1994.
8. Paffenbarger, R., R. Hyde, A. Wing, and C. Hsieh. Physical activity, all-cause mortality, longevity of college alumni. *New England Journal of Medicine* 314:605–613, 1986.
9. Helmrich, S., D. Ragland, and R. Paffenbarger. Prevention of non-insulin-dependent diabetes mellitus with physical activity. *Medicine and Science in Sports and Exercise* 26:824–830, 1994.
10. Wood, P. Physical activity, diet, and health: Independent and interactive effects. *Medicine and Science in Sports and Exercise* 26:838–843, 1994.
11. Morris, J. Exercise in the prevention of coronary heart disease: Today's best buy in public health. *Medicine and Science in Sports and Exercise* 26:807–814, 1994.
12. Blair, S. N., M. LaMonte, and M. Nichaman. The evolution of physical activity recommendations: How much is enough? *American Journal of Clinical Nutrition* 79:913S–920S, 2004.
13. Thompson, P., et al. Exercise and physical activity in the prevention and treatment of atherosclerotic cardiovascular disease. *Circulation* 107:3109–3116, 2003.
14. Brooks, G. A., N. Butte, W. Rand, J. Flatt, and B. Caballero. Chronicle of the Institute of Medicine. Physical activity recommendation: How a physical activity recommendation came to be among dietary recommendations. *American Journal of Clinical Nutrition* 79:921S–930S, 2004.
15. Brown, D., D. Brown, G. Heath, L. Balluz, W. Giles, E. Ward, and A. Mokdad. Associations between physical activity dose and health-related quality of life. *Medicine and Science in Sports and Exercise* 36:890–896, 2004.
16. U.S. Department of Health and Human Services. *Physical activity and health: A report of the Surgeon General.* Atlanta, GA: U.S. Department of Health and Human Services, Centers for Disease Control and Prevention, National Center for Chronic Disease Prevention and Health Promotion, 1996.
17. American Heart Association. *Heart and Stroke Facts.* Dallas, TX: American Heart Association, 2004.
18. Barrow, M. *Heart Talk: Understanding Cardiovascular Diseases.* Gainesville, FL: Cor-Ed Publishing, 1992.
19. Williams, P. T. Relationship between distance run per week to coronary heart disease risk factors in 8283 male runners: The National Runners Health Study. *Archives of Internal Medicine* 157:191–198, 1997.
20. Fagard, R. Physical activity in the prevention and treatment of hypertension in the obese. *Medicine and Science in Sports and Exercise* 31:S624–S630, 1999.
21. Williams, P. Physical fitness and activity as separate heart disease risk factors: A meta-analysis. *Medicine and Science in Sports and Exercise* 33:754–761, 2001.
22. Lennon, S., J. Quindry, K. Hamilton, J. French, J. Staib, J. Mehta, and S. K. Powers. Loss of cardioprotection after cessation of exercise. *Journal of Applied Physiology* 96: 299–1305, 2004.
23. Powers, S., M. Locke, and H. Demirel. Exercise, heat shock proteins, and myocardial protection from I-R injury. *Medicine and Science in Sports and Exercise* 33:386–392, 2001.
24. Hamilton, K., J. Staib, T. Phillips, A. Hess, S. Lennon, and S. Powers. Exercise, antioxidants, and HSP72: Protection against myocardial ischemia-reperfusion. *Free Radicals in Biology and Medicine* 34:800–809, 2003.
25. Lee, I. M., and R. Paffenbarger. Associations of light, moderate, and vigorous intensity physical activity with longevity: The Harvard Alumni Health Study. *American Journal of Epidemiology* 151:293–299, 2000.
26. Powell, K., and S. Blair. The public health burdens of sedentary living habits: Theoretical but realistic estimates. *Medicine and Science in Sports and Exercise* 26:851–856, 1994.
27. Rodnick, K., J. Holloszy, C. Mondon, and D. James. Effects of exercise training on insulin-regulatable glucose-transporter protein levels in rat skeletal muscle. *Diabetes* 39:1425–1429, 1990.
28. Pan, X. R., et al. Effects of diet and exercise in preventing NIDDM in people with impaired glucose tolerance. *Diabetes Care* 20:537–544, 1997.
29. Rankin, J. Diet, exercise, and osteoporosis. *Certified News* (American College of Sports Medicine) 3:1–4, 1993.
30. Wheeler, D., J. Graves, G. Miller, R. Vander Griend, T. Wronski, S. K. Powers, and H. Park. Effects of running on the torsional strength, morphometry, and bone mass on the rat skeleton. *Medicine and Science in Sports and Exercise* 27:520–529, 1995.

31. Taaffe, D., T. Robinson, C. Snow, and R. Marcus. High impact exercise promotes bone gain in well-trained female athletes. *Journal of Bone and Mineral Research* 12:255–260, 1997.

32. Hagberg, J. Effect of training in the decline of VO_{2max} with aging. *Federation Proceedings* 46:1830–1833, 1987.

33. Fleg, J., and E. Lakatta. Role of muscle loss in the age-associated reduction in VO_2max. *Journal of Applied Physiology* 65:1147–1151, 1988.

34. Nakamura, E., T. Moritani, and A. Kanetaka. Effects of habitual physical exercise on physiological age in men and women aged 20–85 years as estimated using principal component analysis. *European Journal of Applied Physiology* 73:410–418, 1996.

35. Hammeren, J., S. Powers, J. Lawler, D. Criswell, D. Martin, D. Lowenthal, and M. Pollock. Exercise training–induced alterations in skeletal muscle oxidative and antioxidant enzyme activity in senescent rats. *International Journal of Sports Medicine* 13:412–416, 1992.

36. Powers, S., J. Lawler, D. Criswell, Fu-Kong Lieu, and D. Martin. Aging and respiratory muscle metabolic plasticity: Effects of endurance training. *Journal of Applied Physiology* 72:1068–1073, 1992.

37. Holloszy, J. Exercise increases average longevity of female rats despite increased food intake and no growth retardation. *Journal of Gerontology* 48:B97–B100, 1993.

38. Lee, I., R. Paffenbarger, and C. Hennekens. Physical activity, physical fitness, and longevity. *Aging—Milano* 9:2–11, 1997.

39. Franklin, B. Improved fitness 5 increased longevity. *ACSM's Health and Fitness Journal* 5:32–33, 2001.

40. Blair, S. N., and M. Wei. Sedentary habits, health, and function in older men and women. *American Journal of Health Promotion* 15:1–8, 2000.

41. Blair, S. N., H. W. Kohl, R. Paffenbarger, D. Clark, K. Cooper, and L. Gibbons. Physical fitness and all-cause mortality: A prospective study of healthy men and women. *Journal of the American Medical Association* 262:2395–2401, 1989.

42. Penedo, F. J., and J. R. Dahn. Exercise and well-being: A review of mental and physical health benefits associated with physical activity. *Current Opinion in Psychiatry* 18:198–193, 2005.

43. Jones, M. A., G. Stratton, T. Reilly, and V. B. Unnithan. Biological risk indicators for recurrent non-specific low back pain in adolescents. *British Journal of Sports Medicine* 39:137–140, 2005.

44. Mikkelson, L. O., H. Nupponen, J. Kaprio, H. Kautiainen, and U. M. Kujala. Adolescent flexibility, endurance strength, and physical activity as predictors of adult tension neck, low back pain and knee injury: A 25 year follow up. *British Journal of Sports Medicine* 40:107–113, 2006.

45. Edwards, R. ABC of smoking cessation: The problem of smoking. *British Medical Journal* 328:217–219, 2004.

46. Doran, C. M., L. Valenti, M. Robinson, H. Britt, and R. P. Mattick. Smoking status of Australian general practice patients and their attempts to quit. *Addictive Behaviors* 31:758–766, 2005.

47. Ridner, L. S., and E. J. Hahn. The pros and cons of cessation in college-age smokers. *Clinical Excellence for Nurse Practitioners* 9:81–87, 2005.

2 General Principles of Exercise for Health and Fitness

true or false?

1. Establishing fitness goals is a key part of the exercise prescription.
2. Exercise must be hard and boring to improve physical fitness.
3. Too much exercise can increase your risk of illness.
4. As little as 30 minutes of physical activity per day will have health benefits.
5. Use it or lose it! If you stop exercising, you'll lose fitness.

Answers appear on the next page.

Everyone can improve his or her level of physical fitness. Whether your idea of exercise is getting out of a chair to go grab a soda or going for a daily run, you can improve your fitness level by analyzing your routine and making gradual improvements.

The purpose of this chapter is to discuss the general principles behind improving your physical fitness. The basic concepts presented here apply to both men and women of all ages and fitness levels. You will find out more about the individual components of health-related physical fitness—that is, cardiorespiratory fitness, muscular strength and endurance, flexibility, and body composition—in the next few chapters.

Principles of Exercise Training to Improve Physical Fitness

Although everyone's exercise training program will vary according to personal needs, the general principles of physical fitness are universal. The more you exercise, and the greater the variety of activities you do, the more fit you'll be. In the following sections we describe the training concepts of overload, progression, specificity, recuperation, and reversibility, all of which affect the progress you'll make as you design and carry out your exercise training program.

CONSIDER THIS!

More than 60% of Americans do not get enough physical activity, and 25% engage in almost no physical activity during the day.

Overload Principle

To improve physical fitness, systems of the body (e.g., the muscular and cardiorespiratory systems) must be stressed. For example, for a skeletal muscle to increase in strength, the muscle must work against a heavier load than normal. This concept is part of the **overload principle,** and it's a key component of all conditioning programs (1, 2) (Figure 2.1). We achieve an overload by increasing the intensity of exercise, such as by using heavier weights.

You can also achieve overload by increasing the duration (or time) of exercise. For instance, to increase muscular endurance, a muscle must be worked over a longer duration than normal, such as by performing a higher number of exercise repetitions. To improve flexibility and increase the range of motion at a joint, we must either stretch the muscle to a longer length than normal or hold the stretch for a longer time.

Although overload is important to attaining physical fitness, your workouts should not be exhausting. The often-heard bodybuilding adage "No pain, no gain," is not accurate. In fact, you can improve your physical fitness without punishing training sessions.

Principle of Progression

The **principle of progression** is an extension of the overload principle. It states that overload

Answers

1. **TRUE** **Setting goals is a key part of an exercise prescription because achieving fitness goals motivates you to make a lifetime commitment to exercise.**
2. **FALSE** **You can improve your physical fitness by moderate-intensity and enjoyable forms of exercise.**
3. **TRUE** **High volumes of exercise can impair your immune system and increase your risk of infection.**
4. **TRUE** **Numerous studies reveal that as little as 30 minutes of exercise per day can reduce your risk of developing heart disease and some forms of cancer.**
5. **TRUE** **Cessation of regular exercise training will result in a loss of both muscular strength and endurance.**

FIGURE 2.1
You can use the overload principle to increase your fitness level in each of the key training areas.

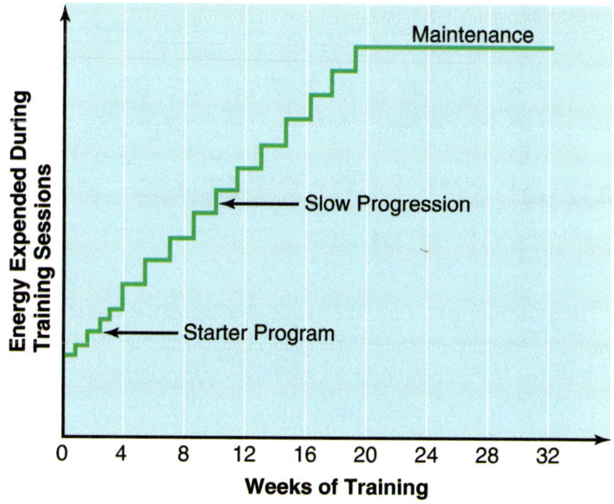

FIGURE 2.2
If you're starting a new exercise training program, you'll begin slowly and progress toward doing more exercise at a greater intensity until you reach your desired fitness level. Then, you'll develop a maintenance program to sustain your new level of fitness.

Source: From Pollack, Wilmore, and Fox, *Health and Fitness through Physical Activity.* Copyright © 1978. Reprinted by permission of Pearson Education, Inc.

should be increased gradually during the course of a physical fitness program. For example, Becky, a sedentary college-aged student who is slightly overweight, might begin her new fitness program with a daily 10-minute walk/jog, then move up to an 11-minute walk/jog in week 2, and by week 5, do a 16-minute jog.

The overload of a training program should generally be increased slowly during the first 4 to 6 weeks of the exercise program. After this initial period, the overload can be increased at a steady but progressive rate during the next 18–20 weeks of training. For best results, the overload should not be increased too slowly or too rapidly. Progressing too slowly may not result in the desired improvement in physical fitness, and progressing too quickly may cause chronic fatigue or injuries.

What is a safe rate of progression during an exercise training program? Although people vary in their tolerance for exercise overload, a commonsense guideline to improve physical fitness and avoid overuse injuries is the **ten percent rule** (2). In short, this rule says that the training intensity or duration of exercise should be increased by no more than 10% per week. For example, a runner running 20 minutes per day could increase his or her daily exercise duration to 22 minutes per day (10% of 20 = 2) the following week.

Once you reach your desired level of physical fitness, you no longer need to increase the training intensity or duration of your physical conditioning. You should instead focus on designing a **maintenance program** to maintain your new fitness level with regular exercise (Figure 2.2).

Specificity of Exercise

Another key concept of training is the **principle of specificity,** which states that the exercise training effect is specific to those muscles involved in the activity (3). If you perform leg curls, for example, you wouldn't expect your upper arms to benefit, and likewise, your

overload principle A basic principle of physical conditioning that states that in order to improve physical fitness, the body or specific muscles must be stressed.

principle of progression A principle of training that states that overload should be increased gradually.

ten percent rule The training intensity or duration of exercise should not be increased by more than 10% per week.

maintenance program Exercising to sustain a desired level of physical fitness.

principle of specificity The effect of exercise training is specific to those muscles involved in the activity.

CONSUMER CORNER

BUYING THE BEST RUNNING SHOE FOR YOU

Choosing the correct running or exercise shoe is an important decision. All runners need flexible, durable shoes that protect the foot. Moreover, good running shoes should absorb shock and control foot motion. In selecting running shoes, remember that there is no best running shoe for all people. Every individual is different, and each model of running shoe is different. Because of the complexity of individual foot shapes and biomechanics (i.e., running style), it usually is a good idea to buy running shoes at a specialty shoe store with a well-trained, expert staff that can help you find the best shoe to meet your exercise needs.

Here are some tips for choosing your optimal running shoe:

- Shop for shoes late in the day. The swelling your feet experience by the end of the day is similar to the swelling they experience during running (swelling is due to increased blood flow and fluid collection). Trying on shoes at the end of the day will help you find the best-fitting shoe.
- Wear the socks that you will wear when running. This will also help you find the best-fitting shoes.
- Bring an old pair of running shoes with you to the store so that the running shoe expert can see where your shoes wear the most. The salesperson will use this information to recommend the types of running shoes that you should consider.

Here are some tips on how to make sure the shoe fits:

- Make sure that there is a full thumb length between the end of your longest toe and the end of the shoe. This ensures that the shoe is long enough for your foot.
- Make sure the front section of the shoe (the "toe box") allows the toes to move around.
- The shoe should not feel too tight, but the foot should not slide around in the shoe.
- Many running shoe specialty stores will have a treadmill so you can try walking or running in the shoes you're thinking of buying. If your shoe store has a treadmill, use it. This will help you see the shoes in action.
- Do not rely on a break-in period for your shoes to stretch—running shoes should feel good on the day you buy them.
- If in doubt about the correct size, buy the larger size.

Because running involves the use of the leg muscles, doing it regularly will improve the endurance of those muscles. This is an example of specificity of training.

biceps curls aren't going to improve your calf muscles. This is part of the reason why a varied set of exercises is so important to overall physical fitness improvement.

Specificity of training also applies to the types of adaptations that occur in the muscle. For example, strength training, such as with free weights, results in an increase in muscle strength but does not greatly improve the endurance of the muscle. Therefore, strength training is specific to improving muscular strength (4). Similarly, endurance exercise training, such as distance running, results in improved muscular endurance without altering muscular strength much (5). Suppose you want to improve your ability to run a distance of 3 miles. In this case, specific training should include running 3 or more miles several times a week. This type of training would improve muscular endurance in your legs but would not result in large improvements in leg strength (3).

Principle of Recuperation

Overloading your muscles means stressing them, and they need a period of rest before your next workout. During the recovery period, the body adapts to the exercise stress by increasing endurance or becoming

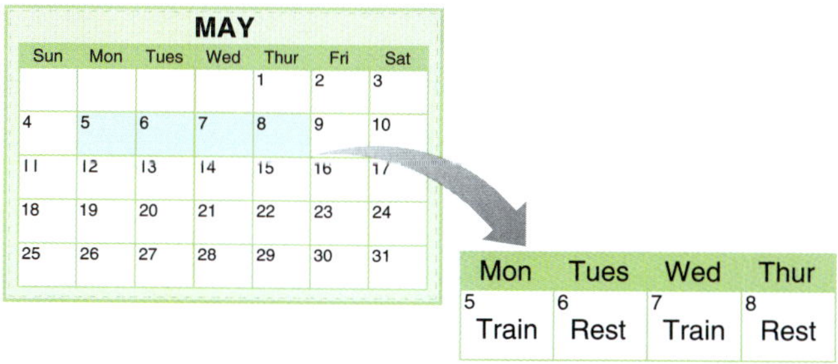

FIGURE 2.3
To avoid injury and maximize benefits, allow adequate rest periods between sessions in your exercise training program.

stronger. In fact, a rest period, usually 24 hours or more, is essential for achieving maximal benefit from exercise. This needed rest period between exercise training sessions is called the **principle of recuperation** (2) (Figure 2.3).

Failure to get enough rest between sessions may result in a fatigue syndrome referred to as **overtraining.** Overtraining may lead to chronic fatigue and/or injuries. Common symptoms of overtraining include sore and stiff muscles or a feeling of general fatigue the morning after an exercise training session, sometimes called a "workout hangover." The cure is either to increase the duration of rest between workouts, to reduce the intensity of workouts, or both. Although too much exercise is the primary cause of the overtraining syndrome, an inadequate diet, particularly if it's short on carbohydrates, can also contribute (we will cover more about the effects of good nutrition on exercise in Chapter 7).

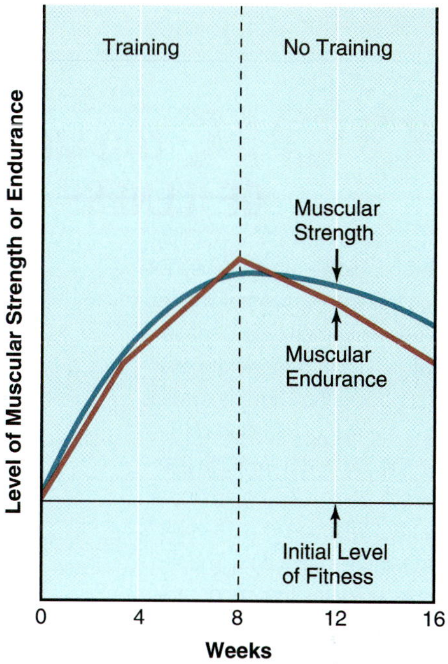

FIGURE 2.4
Stopping exercise training will reverse gains made in both muscular strength and muscular endurance.

CONSIDER THIS!

Among people who start an exercise program, 50% will drop out within 6 months.

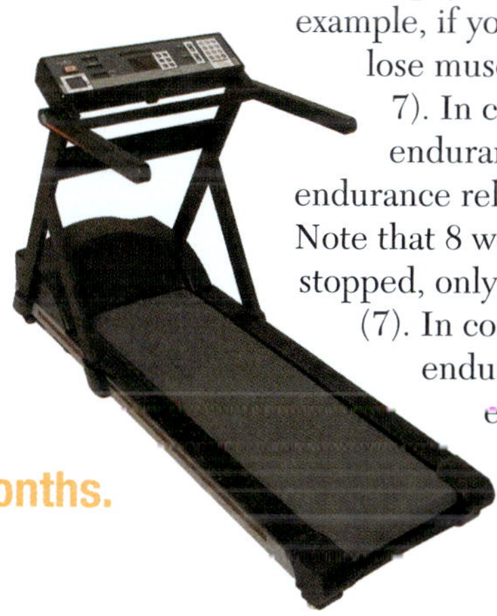

How quickly is fitness lost after training has stopped? The answer depends on which component of physical fitness you are referring to. For example, if you stop strength training, you will lose muscular strength relatively slowly (4, 7). In contrast, after you stop performing endurance exercise, you will lose muscular endurance relatively rapidly (6) (Figure 2.4). Note that 8 weeks after strength training is stopped, only 10% of muscular strength is lost (7). In contrast, 8 weeks after cessation of endurance training, 30–40% of muscular endurance is lost (6).

Reversibility of Training Effects

Although rest periods are important to maximizing your benefits from exercise, going too long between exercise sessions (such as days or weeks), or being too inconsistent in your routine, can result in losing the progress you've made (6). To maintain physical fitness, you need to exercise regularly. In other words, physical fitness cannot be stored. The loss of fitness due to inactivity is an example of the **principle of reversibility.**

principle of recuperation The body requires recovery periods between exercise training sessions to adapt to the exercise stress. Therefore, a period of rest is essential for achieving maximal benefit from exercise.

overtraining The result of failure to get enough rest between exercise training sessions.

principle of reversibility The loss of fitness due to inactivity.

A CLOSER LOOK TOO MUCH EXERCISE INCREASES YOUR RISK OF ILLNESS

Research indicates that intense exercise training (or overtraining) reduces the body's immunity to disease (14). In contrast, light to moderate exercise training boosts the immune system and reduces the risk of infections (15). The relationship between exercise training and the risk of developing an upper respiratory tract infection (e.g., a cold) is shown in the figure in this box. The J-shaped curve indicates that moderate exercise training reduces the risk of infection, whereas high-intensity and long-duration exercise training increase the risk of infection.

The explanation for this relationship is complex, but it appears that too much exercise increases levels of stress hormones in the body that weaken the immune system. Depressed immune function increases your risk for developing an infection when you are exposed to bacteria or viruses.

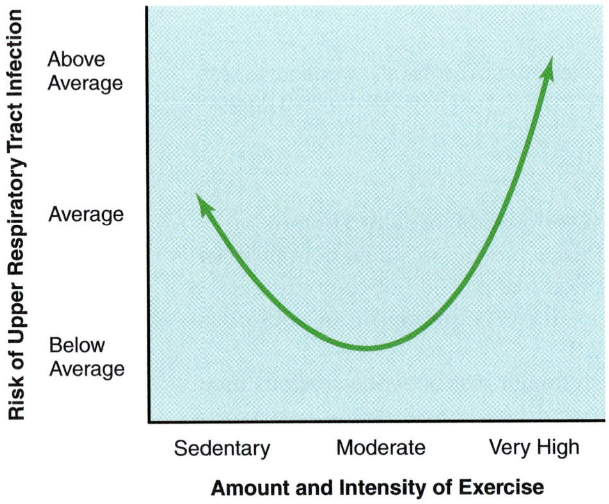

This J-shaped curve illustrates the relationship between physical activity and colds. Note that moderate physical activity reduces your risk of infection, whereas long-duration or high-intensity exercise increases your risk of disease.

Source: Redrawn from Nieman, D. Moderate exercise boosts the immune system: Too much exercise can have the opposite effect. *ACSM's Health and Fitness Journal* 1(5):14–18, 1997. Reprinted by permission of Lippincott Williams & Wilkins, http://lww.com.

Make sure you know . . .

- Five key principles of exercise training are overload principle, principle of progression, specificity of exercise, principle of recuperation, and reversibility of training effects.
- The overload principle states that to improve physical fitness, the body or the specific muscle group used during exercise must be stressed.
- The principle of progression is an extension of the overload principle and states that overload should be increased gradually over the course of a physical fitness training program.
- The principle of specificity refers to the fact that exercise training is specific to those muscles involved in the activity.
- The requirement for a rest period between training sessions is called the principle of recuperation.
- The principle of reversibility refers to loss of physical fitness due to inactivity.

Designing Your Exercise Program

If you go to a doctor with a bacterial infection and she prescribes you an antibiotic as treatment, chances are good that the dose she asks you to take is going to be different from the dose she might prescribe for your 10-year-old brother. Similarly, for each individual there is a correct "dose" of exercise to effectively promote physical fitness, called an **exercise prescription** (6). Exercise prescriptions should be tailored to meet the needs of the individual (3, 6, 9). They should include fitness goals, mode of exercise (or type of activity), a warm-up, a primary conditioning period, and a cool-down. The following sections provide a general introduction to each of these components.

Setting Goals

If you don't know what you're working toward, you are not likely to achieve it. Thus, setting goals (both short-term and long-term goals) is an essential part of an exercise prescription. Visualizing your leaner, stronger body or your improved competitive performance (if these were your goals, for example) would help motivate you to begin your exercise program. Further, attaining your fitness goals improves self-esteem and provides the incentive needed to make a lifetime commitment to regular exercise.

One common type of fitness goal is a performance goal. You can establish performance goals in each component of health-related physical fitness. Figure 2.5 illustrates a hypothetical example of how Susie Jones might establish short-term and long-term performance goals using fitness testing to determine when she has reached her objective. The column labeled "current status" contains Susie's fitness ratings based on tests performed prior to starting her exercise program. After consulting with her instructor, Susie has established short-term goals that she hopes to achieve within the first 8 weeks of training. Note that the short-term goals are not "fixed in stone" and can be modified if the need arises. Susie's long-term goals are fitness levels that she hopes to reach within the first 18 months of training. Similar to short-term goals, long-term goals can be modified to meet changing needs or circumstances.

In addition to performance goals, consider establishing exercise adherence goals. That is, set a goal to exercise a specific number of days per week. Exercise adherence goals are important because fitness will improve only if you exercise regularly!

The following guidelines can help you set achievable fitness goals:

- *Be realistic.* This is perhaps the most important rule in goal setting—set goals that you can reach. Consider your current fitness level, consult with your instructor, and write down goals you know you can achieve. Setting goals that are unachievable is likely to frustrate you and may result in your giving up on your program.
- *Establish short-term goals first.* Reaching short-term fitness goals will motivate you to continue exercising. Therefore, establishing realistic short-term goals is critical. After you reach a short-term goal, pat yourself on the back, and then establish a new one.
- *Set realistic long-term goals.* When setting your long-term goals, take into account your physical limitations and any hereditary factors that may affect your fitness limits. Set goals that are realistic for you and not based on performance scores of other people.

Name: Susie Jones

FITNESS GOALS

FITNESS CATEGORY	CURRENT STATUS	SHORT-TERM GOAL (8 weeks)	LONG-TERM GOAL (18 months)
Cardiorespiratory fitness	Poor	Average	Excellent
Muscular strength	Poor	Average	Excellent
Muscular endurance	Very poor	Average	Good
Flexibility	Poor	Average	Good
Body composition	High fat	Moderately high	Optimal

FIGURE 2.5
As you begin thinking about your short-term and long-term goals for each of the five fitness components, fill out a worksheet like this so you can track your progress.

- *Establish lifetime maintenance goals.* In addition to short-term and long-term goals, consider establishing a fitness maintenance goal. The purpose of this goal will be to maintain your new fitness level by remaining physically active.
- *Put goals in writing.* A key to meeting goals (and to not forgetting them) is to write them down and post them where you will see them every day. You should revisit and revise your goals periodically as your routine or schedule changes so that they continue to be realistic and up-to-date. Remember, just because goals are in writing does not mean that they cannot be changed.

exercise prescription The individualized amount of exercise that will effectively promote physical fitness for a given person.

Swimming and volleyball are both excellent for the cardiovascular system. Swimming puts less stress on the joints and is considered a low-impact activity, whereas volleyball puts more stress on joints and is considered a high-impact activity.

- *Make your goals specific and measurable.* You need a way to determine whether you met your goal. Be sure to avoid unfocused goals, such as, "I want to lose weight by spring break. To lose weight I will eat healthy and exercise regularly." Establish focused goals instead: "I want to lose 15 pounds by spring break. I will exercise 3 times a week for at least 20 minutes and follow the healthy eating plan outlined by my dietitian. With these changes I should lose 1.5 pounds a week for 10 weeks."
- *Establish a time frame.* Setting a date for reaching the goal will help you stay focused.
- *Use a reward system.* Reaching a goal is an accomplishment that you should acknowledge with a reward that is meaningful to you.
- *Recognize obstacles to achieving goals.* Once you begin your fitness program, be prepared for setbacks (such as skipping workouts and losing motivation) and to backslide a bit (and have your fitness level decline temporarily). This is normal. However, once you realize that you have stopped making progress toward your goals, you must get back on track and start making progress again as soon as you can.

The importance of fitness goals cannot be overemphasized. Goals provide structure and motivation for a personal fitness program. Keys to maintaining a lifelong fitness program are discussed again in Chapter 16.

Selecting Activities

Every exercise prescription includes at least one **mode of exercise**—that is, a specific type of exercise to be performed. For example, to improve cardiorespiratory fitness, you could select from a wide variety of activities, such as running, swimming, or cycling. To ensure that you'll engage in the exercise regularly, you should choose activities that you will enjoy doing, that are available to you, and that carry little risk of injury.

Physical activities can be classified as being either high impact or low impact, based on the amount of stress placed on joints during the activity. Low-impact activities put less stress on the joints than high-impact activities. Because of the strong correlation between high-impact activities and injuries, many fitness experts recommend low-impact activities for fitness beginners or for people susceptible to injury (such as people who are older or overweight). Examples of low-impact activities include walking, cycling, swimming, and low-impact aerobic dance. High-impact activities include running, basketball, and high-impact aerobic dance.

The Importance of a Warm-Up

A **warm-up** is a brief (5- to 15-minute) period of exercise that precedes a workout. It generally involves light calisthenics or a low-intensity form of the exercise and

An Example of the FIT Principle

Frequency	3–5 times per week
Intensity	Moderate
Time (Duration)	30 minutes

often includes stretching exercises. The purpose of a warm-up is to elevate muscle temperature and increase blood flow to those muscles that will be engaged in the workout (1). A warm-up can also reduce the strain on the heart imposed by rapidly engaging in heavy exercise and may reduce the risk of muscle and tendon injuries. You can find specific some warm up exercises in Laboratory 2.1.

THE WORKOUT

Regardless of the activity, the major components of the exercise prescription that make up the workout (also called the primary conditioning period) are frequency, intensity, and duration (time) of exercise (see box above), often called the *FIT principle.* The **frequency of exercise** is the number of times per week that you intend to exercise. The recommended frequency of exercise to improve most components of health-related physical fitness is 3 to 5 times per week (10–12).

The **intensity of exercise** is the amount of physiological stress or overload placed on the body during the exercise. The method for determining the intensity of exercise varies with the type of exercise performed. For example, as you use more energy during exercise, your heart rate will increase, so measuring heart rate has become a standard means to determine exercise intensity during cardiorespiratory fitness training.

Whereas heart rate can also be used to gauge exercise intensity during strength training, the number of repetitions performed before muscular fatigue occurs is more useful for monitoring intensity during weight lifting. For instance, a load that can be lifted only 5 to 8 times before complete muscular fatigue is an example of high-intensity weight lifting. In contrast, a load that can be lifted 50 to 60 times without resulting in muscular fatigue is an illustration of low-intensity weight training.

Finally, flexibility is improved by stretching muscles beyond their normal lengths. Intensity of stretching is monitored by the degree of tension felt during the stretch. Low-intensity stretching results in only minor tension on the muscles and tendons. In contrast, high-intensity stretching places great tension or moderate discomfort on the muscle groups being stretched.

A key aspect of the primary conditioning period is the **duration of exercise**—that is, the amount of time invested in performing the primary workout. Note that the duration of exercise does not include the warm-up or cool-down. Research has shown that 30 minutes per exercise session (performed 3 or more times per week) is the minimum amount of time required to significantly improve physical fitness. Figure 2.6 shows a physical activity pyramid that can help you identify types of physical activities that increase your fitness level, and how frequently you should perform them.

The Importance of the Cool-Down

The **cool-down** is a 5- to 15-minute period of low-intensity exercise that immediately follows the primary conditioning period. For instance, a period of slow walking might be used as a cool-down following a running workout. A cool-down period accomplishes several goals. In addition to lowering body temperature after exercise, the cool-down allows blood to return from the muscles toward the heart (3–6). During exercise, large amounts of blood are pumped to the working muscles. Once exercise stops, blood tends to pool in large blood vessels located around the exercised muscles. Failure to redistribute pooled blood after exercise could result in your feeling lightheaded or even fainting. You can prevent blood pooling by doing low-intensity exercise that uses the same muscles you used during the workout.

Personalizing Your Workout

Although the same general principles of exercise training apply to everyone, no two people are the same, and everyone's exercise prescription will be slightly different. Your exercise prescription should be based on your

mode of exercise The specific type of exercise to be performed.

warm-up A brief (5- to 15-minute) period of exercise that precedes a workout.

frequency of exercise The number of times per week that one exercises.

intensity of exercise The amount of physiological stress or overload placed on the body during exercise.

duration of exercise The amount of time invested in performing the primary workout.

cool-down A 5- to 15-minute period of low-intensity exercise that immediately follows the primary conditioning period; sometimes called a *warm-down.*

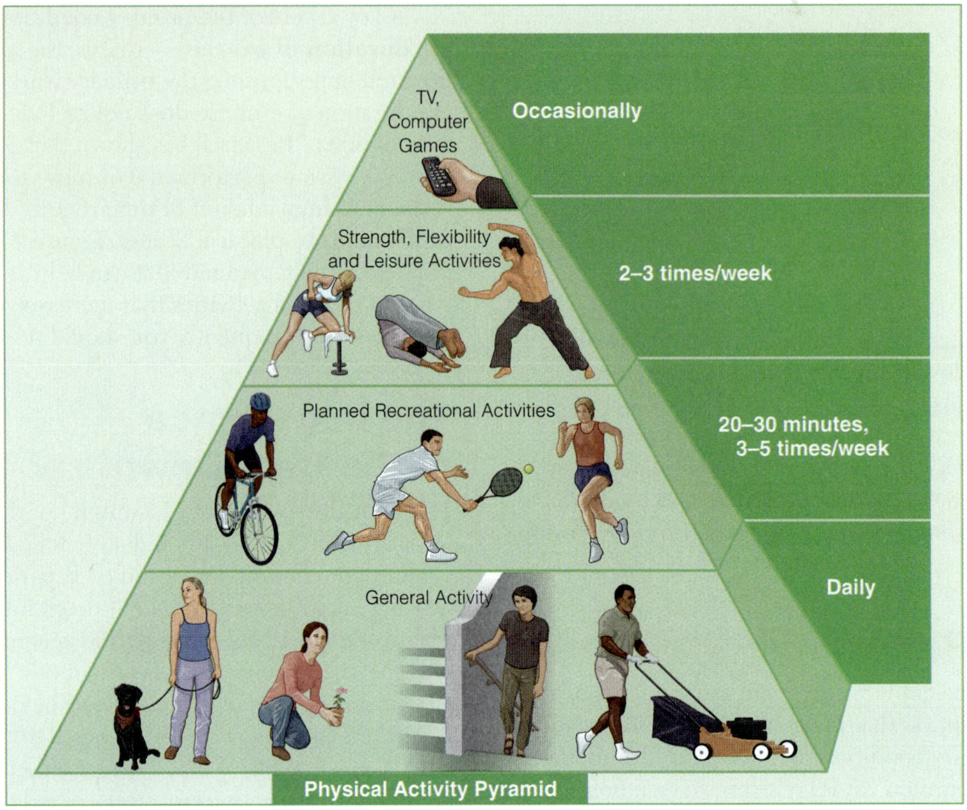

FIGURE 2.6
A physical activity pyramid like this one shows examples of activities you can incorporate into your fitness program and can help guide the frequency and time you plan for each activity.

Source: Corbin, C. B., and R. D. Pangrazi. Physical activity pyramid rebuffs peak experience. *ACSM's Health and Fitness Journal* 2(1), 1998. Copyright © 1998. Used with permission.

general health, age, fitness status, musculoskeletal condition, and body composition. You will learn more about individualizing workouts in the next several chapters.

Make sure you know . . .

- The "dose" of exercise required to effectively promote physical fitness is called the exercise prescription.
- The components of the exercise prescription include fitness goals, mode of exercise, the warm-up, the workout, and the cool-down. You can use the FIT principle (frequency, intensity and type of exercise) to help you design your fitness program.
- Exercise training programs should be individualized by considering such factors as age, health, and fitness status of the individual.

Health Benefits of Exercise: How Much Is Enough?

As discussed in Chapter 1, exercise training to improve sport performance differs from exercise performed to achieve health benefits. Exercise training for sport performance typically includes long workouts (60–180 minutes/day) involving high-intensity exercise. In contrast, exercising to obtain health benefits does not need to be as high in intensity, or performed as long, as exercise to improve performance.

Although even low levels of physical activity can provide some health benefits, evidence indicates that moderate-to-high levels of physical activity are required to provide major health benefits (10, 12–14, 16, 19, 20). The theoretical relationship between physical activity and health benefits is illustrated in Figure 2.7. Note that the minimum level of exercise required to achieve some of the health benefits is the **threshold for health benefits.** Most experts believe that 30–60

STEPS FOR BEHAVIOR CHANGE

Are you a couch potato?

Answer the following questions to find out whether you could use more daily physical activity.

Y	N	
☐	☐	Do you usually drive to your destinations, even for short trips to the corner store?
☐	☐	Do you tend to take the elevator instead of the stairs?
☐	☐	Does your evening routine involve hours of inactivity (e.g., sitting in front of the computer or television)?
☐	☐	When you drive to a store for shopping, do you tend to park as close to the store entrance as possible?
☐	☐	Do you always use a remote control to adjust the volume on your stereo or change the channel on your television?

If you answered "yes" to more than one question, you may be a bit too sedentary.

TIPS TO INCORPORATE MORE PHYSICAL ACTIVITY INTO YOUR DAILY ROUTINE

- ☑ Walk or ride your bike for short trips and errands; walk to class if you live close to or on campus.
- ☑ Get off the bus a stop early, and walk the rest of the way.
- ☑ Forgo an hour of Internet time every day to walk the dog, or play a round of basketball or tennis with a friend.
- ☑ Take the stairs instead of the elevator.
- ☑ Instead of settling in with the television after dinner, go for a bike ride with a friend or family member.

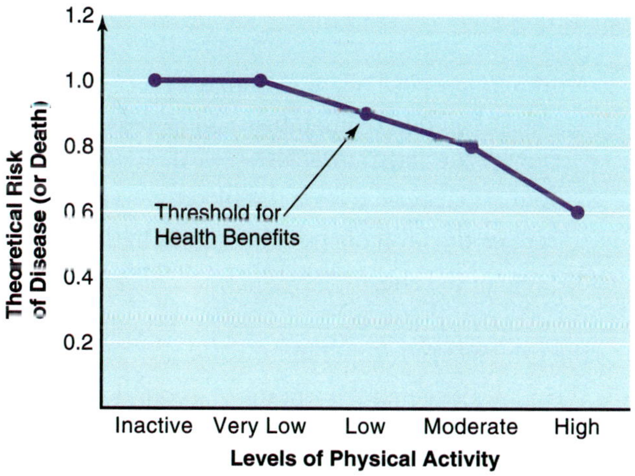

FIGURE 2.7
The relationship between physical activity and improved health benefits. Note that as the level of regular physical activity increases, the theoretical risk of disease (or death) decreases.

Source: Data are from References 17–19.

minutes of moderate-to-high-intensity exercise performed 3–5 days per week will surpass the threshold for health benefits and will reduce risk of all causes of death (19–22, 24–26). (See Laboratory 2.3 for one way to determine whether you're engaging in enough physical activity to achieve health benefits—counting your steps with a pedometer).

Current public health recommendations for physical activity are a minimum of 30 minutes of moderate-intensity activity each day (22–27). Fortunately, the activity doesn't need to be done all at once and can be divided into two to three segments of exercise throughout the day (24). If you walk briskly for 15 minutes to

threshold for health benefits The minimum level of physical activity required to achieve some of the health benefits of exercise.

get to your class in the morning and then take a 15-minute bike ride to get to your job in the afternoon, you've attained the goal of incorporating 30 minutes of moderate exercise into your day.

However, this dose of exercise may be insufficient to prevent weight gain in some individuals who need additional exercise and calorie restriction to prevent weight gain (see Chapter 8 for more details). Further, people who get 30 minutes of moderate intensity exercise per day are likely to achieve additional health benefits if they exercise for longer periods of time (24).

Are some forms of exercise better than others for obtaining health benefits? There is no short answer to this question. Nonetheless, numerous activities, including running, swimming, cycling, and walking, can help achieve exercise-related health benefits. Details on how to achieve health-related aspects of physical fitness will be discussed in Chapters 4 through 6.

Make sure you know . . .

> Although low levels of physical activity can provide some health benefits, moderate-to-high levels of physical activity are required to provide major health benefits.

> The threshold for health benefits is the minimum level of exercise required to achieve some health benefits of exercise.

Summary

1. The overload principle, which is the most important principle of exercise training, states that to improve physical fitness, the body or muscle group used during exercise must be stressed.
2. The principle of progression states that overload should be increased gradually during the course of a physical fitness program.
3. The need for a rest period between exercise training sessions is called the principle of recuperation.
4. Physical fitness can be lost due to inactivity; this is often called the principle of reversibility.
5. The components of the exercise prescription include fitness goals, type of activity, the warm-up, the workout, and the cool-down.
6. All exercise training programs should be tailored to meet the objectives of the individual. Therefore, the exercise prescription should consider the individual's age, health, fitness status, musculoskeletal condition, and body composition.
7. The minimum level of physical activity required to achieve some of the health benefits of exercise is called the threshold for health benefits.

Study Questions

1. Which one of the following is NOT a key principle of exercise training?
   a. overload principle
   b. principle of progression
   c. principle of recuperation
   d. principle of supercompensation
2. The current public health recommendation is for adults to achieve a minimum of _____ minutes of moderate intensity physical activity each day.
   a. 15
   b. 20
   c. 30
   d. 60
3. A primary purpose of a warm-up is to
   a. elevate muscle temperature and increase blood flow to the active muscles.
   b. remove lactic acid from the blood.
   c. reduce the level of stress hormones in the blood.
   d. none of the above.
4. What is the difference between overtraining and the principle of recuperation?
5. What are the general purposes of a cool-down and a warm-up?
6. What are the components of the exercise prescription?
7. How does the principle of progression apply to the exercise prescription?

8. What is the overload principle, and what is one practical example?
9. Why is the threshold for health benefits an important concept?
10. What happens to physical fitness if you stop training?
11. Why should the exercise prescription be individualized?
12. Why is goal setting important when beginning an exercise program?

Suggested Reading

ACSM's Resource Manual for Exercise Testing and Prescription. Philadelphia: Lippincott Williams and Wilkins, 2005.

Blair, S., M. LaMonte, and M. Nichman. The evolution of physical activity recommendations: How much exercise is enough? *American Journal of Clinical Nutrition* 79:913S–920S, 2004.

Humphrey, R. Activity and fitness in health risk. *ACSM's Health and Fitness Journal* 11:36–37, 2007.

Powers, S., and E. Howley. *Exercise Physiology: Theory and Application to Fitness and Performance,* 6th ed. St. Louis, MO: McGraw-Hill, 2007.

Swain, D. Moderate or vigorous-intensity exercise: What should we prescribe? *ACSM's Health and Fitness Journal* 10:42–43, 2006.

Warburton, D., C. Nicol, and S. Bredin. Prescribing exercise as preventative therapy. *Canadian Medical Association Journal* 28:961–974, 2006.

For links to the websites below, visit The Total Fitness and Wellness Website at www.aw-bc.com/powers.

American Heart Association

Contains the latest information about ways to reduce your risk of heart and vascular diseases. Includes information about exercise, diet, and heart disease.

American College of Sports Medicine

Contains information about exercise, health, and fitness.

WebMD

Contains the latest information on a variety of health-related topics, including diet, exercise, and stress. Includes links to nutrition, fitness, and wellness topics.

References

1. Howley, E., and B. D. Franks. *Health Fitness: Instructors Handbook.* Champaign, IL: Human Kinetics, 2003.
2. Powers, S., and E. Howley. *Exercise Physiology: Theory and Application to Fitness and Performance,* 6th ed. St. Louis, MO: McGraw-Hill, 2007.
3. Stone, M., S. Plisk, and D. Collins. Training principles: Evaluation of modes and methods of resistance training—A coaching perspective. *Sports Biomechanics* 1:79–103, 2002.
4. Abernethy, P., J. Jurimae, P. Logan, A. Taylor, and R. Thayer. Acute and chronic response of skeletal muscle to resistance exercise. *Sports Medicine* 17:22–28, 1994.
5. Powers, S., D. Criswell, J. Lawler, L. Ji, D. Martin, R. Herb, and G. Dudley. Influence of exercise and fiber type on antioxidant enzyme activity in rat skeletal muscle. *American Journal of Physiology* 266:R375–R380, 1994.
6. Coyle, E., W. Martin, D. Sinacore, M. Joyner, J. Hagberg, and J. Holloszy. Time course of loss of adaptations after stopping prolonged intense endurance training. *Journal of Applied Physiology* 57:1857–1864, 1984.
7. Costill, D., and A. Richardson. *Handbook of Sports Medicine: Swimming.* London: Blackwell Publishing, 1993.
8. Lamb, D., and M. Williams. *Ergogenics: Enhancement of Performance in Exercise and Sport.* Vol. 4. Madison, WI: Brown and Benchmark, 1991.
9. McGlynn, G. *Dynamics of Fitness: A Practical Approach.* Dubuque, IA: Wm. C. Brown, 1996.
10. Bouchard, C., R. Shephard, T. Stephens, J. Sutton, and B. McPherson, eds. *Exercise, Fitness, and Health: A Consensus of Current Knowledge.* Champaign, IL: Human Kinetics, 1990.
11. Barrow, M. *Heart Talk: Understanding Cardiovascular Diseases.* Gainesville, FL: Cor-Ed Publishing, 1992.
12. Morris, J. Exercise in the prevention of coronary heart disease: Today's best buy in public health. *Medicine and Science in Sports and Exercise* 26:807–814, 1994.
13. Warburton, D., C. Nicol, and S. Bredin. Prescribing exercise as preventative therapy. *Canadian Medical Association Journal* 28:961–974, 2006.
14. Nieman, D. Immune response to heavy exertion. *Journal of Applied Physiology* 82:1385–1394, 1997.
15. Nieman, D. Moderate exercise boosts the immune system: Too much exercise can have the opposite effect. *ACSM's Health and Fitness Journal* 1(5):14–18, 1997.
16. Paffenbarger, R., J. Kampert, I-Min Lee, R. Hyde, R. Leung, and A. Wing. Changes in physical activity and other lifeway patterns influencing longevity. *Medicine and Science in Sports and Exercise* 26:857–865, 1994.
17. Blair, S., H. W. Kohl, N. Gordon, and R. Paffenbarger. How much physical activity is good for health? *Annual Review of Public Health* 13:99–126, 1992.

18. Lee, I., and R. Paffenbarger. Associations of light, moderate, and vigorous intensity physical activity with longevity. *American Journal of Epidemiology* 151:293–299, 2000.

19. Williams, P. Physical fitness and activity as separate heart disease risk factors: A meta-analysis. *Medicine and Science in Sports and Exercise* 33:754–761, 2001.

20. Pollock, M., G. Gaesser, J. Butcher, J. P. Despres, R. Dishman, B. Franklin, and C. Garber. The recommended quantity and quality of exercise for developing and maintaining cardiorespiratory fitness, muscular fitness, and flexibility in healthy adults. *Medicine and Science in Sports and Exercise* 30:975–991, 1998.

21. Howley, E. T. You asked for it: Is rigorous exercise better than moderate activity in achieving health-related goals? *ACSM's Health and Fitness Journal* 4(2):6, 2000.

22. Thompson, P. et al. Exercise and physical activity in the prevention and treatment of atherosclerotic cardiovascular disease. *Circulation* 107:3109–3116, 2003.

23. Swain, D. Moderate or vigorous intensity exercise: What should we prescribe? *ACSM's Health and Fitness Journal* 10:21–27, 2006.

24. Blair, S., M. LaMonte, and M. Nichman. The evolution of physical activity recommendations: How much exercise is enough? *American Journal of Clinical Nutrition* 79: 913S–920S, 2004.

25. Brooks, G., N. Butte, W. Rand, J.P. Flatt, and B. Caballero. Chronicle of the institute of medicine physical activity recommendation: How a physical activity recommendation came to be among dietary recommendations. *American Journal of Clinical Nutrition* 79:921S–930S, 2004.

26. Brown, D., D. Brown, G. Heath, L. Balluz, W. Giles, E. Ford, and A. Mokdad. Associations between physical activity dose and health-related quality of life. *Medicine and Science in Sports and Exercise* 36:890–896, 2004.

27. Ishikawa-Takata, K., T. Ohta, and H. Tanaka. How much exercise is required to reduce blood pressure in essential hypertensive: A dose-response study. *American Journal of Hypertension* 16:629–633, 2003.

NAME ______________________________ DATE ________________

Warming Up

Use the following activities to warm up your body for aerobic activities such as jogging, walking, or cycling. Perform the exercises slowly, holding each stretch for 20 to 30 seconds. Do not bounce or jerk the muscle. Do each stretch at least once and up to three times.

Cardiovascular Warm-Up

Walk briskly or jog slowly for 5 minutes.

Stretches

Calf Stretch for Gastrocnemius and Soleus

Stand with your right foot about 1 to 2 feet in front of your left foot, with both feet pointing forward. Keeping your left leg straight, lunge forward by bending your right knee and pushing your left heel backward. Hold this position. Then pull your left foot in slightly and bend your left knee. Shift your weight to your left leg and hold. Repeat this entire sequence with the left leg forward.

Sitting Toe Touch for Hamstrings

Sit on the ground with your right leg straight and your left leg tucked close to your body. Reach toward your outstretched right foot as far as possible with both hands. Repeat with the left leg.

Step Stretch for Quadriceps and Hip

Step forward and bend your front knee about 90 degrees, keeping your knee directly above your ankle. Stretch the opposite leg back so that it is parallel to the floor. Rotate your hips forward and slightly down to stretch. Your arms can be at your sides or resting on top of your forward thigh. Repeat on the other side.

Leg Hug for the Hip and Back Extensors

Lie flat on your back with both legs straight. Bending your knees, bring your legs up to your torso, and grasp both legs behind the thighs. Pull both legs in to your chest and hold.

Side Stretch for the Torso

Stand with feet shoulder-width apart, knees slightly bent, and pelvis tucked under. Raise one arm over your head, and bend sideways from the waist. Support your torso by placing the hand of your resting arm on your hip or thigh for support. Repeat on the other side.

You can also repeat these same exercises after a workout to cool down.

1. Did you notice an increase in heart rate during the cardiovascular warm-up? ____________________
2. In which stretch did you feel the most tightness? ______________________________
3. Do you think the sample warm-up is adequate for the activities you plan to do as part of your exercise program? If not, what exercises would you add?

   ____

   ____

NAME ______________________________ DATE ______________

Which Physical Activities Work Best for You?

As you design your personal fitness program, think about the activities you currently enjoy most and least and about new activities you would like to try. Which can you incorporate into your program?

Answer the following questions in the spaces provided.

1. List the fitness/wellness activities in which you have participated or are currently participating. Examples include recreational tennis, high school basketball, or yoga classes.

   ____

2. Which of these activities did you enjoy the most? Why?

   ____

3. What are some new activities you might enjoy? (See the list at the end of the lab for additional options)

   ____

   ____

4. What components of physical fitness do you think these activities affect? For instance, jogging improves cardiovascular fitness, whereas weight lifting increases muscular strength.

   ____

   ____

5. What areas of physical and mental health would you like to improve? Can you think of any physical activities that would aid in this goal?

   ____

   ____

Examples of Exercise and Physical Activity

- Walking or jogging on a treadmill
- Walking to work instead of driving
- Cycling on an upright or recumbent exercise bike
- Cycling to work instead of driving
- Outdoor walking or jogging
- Outdoor cycling
- Aerobics class
- Kickboxing class
- Weight or resistance training
- Yoga
- Martial arts
- Pilates
- Hiking
- Rock climbing
- Elliptical trainer
- Sport activities (e.g., soccer, basketball, tennis, racquetball)

NAME ______________________ DATE ______________

Using a Pedometer to Count Your Steps

One way to determine your level of daily physical activity is to use a pedometer to measure the number of steps you take in a day. A pedometer is a small portable device that contains a sensor and, often, software applications to estimate the distance walked and the number of calories expended. The accuracy of pedometers can vary from device to device, but many pedometers are reasonably accurate if they are worn in the optimal position (such as on a belt clip). However, carrying a pedometer in a pocket or handbag tends to reduce its accuracy. Moreover, some pedometers record movement other than walking (e.g., bending to tie your shoes), and therefore some "false steps" may show up on your daily step count.

Experts currently recommend 10,000 steps per day to reach a level of physical activity that is considered to be an active lifestyle with positive health benefits. Do you think you meet this goal?

A pedometer worn at the waist.

Directions:

Wear a pedometer for a day and note your number of steps. Write in the total number below. Then, set a goal for the number of steps you want to take per day, and list some strategies for incorporating more steps into your day. Track the number of steps you take every day for the next 2 weeks, and note your progress toward your goal.

Number of steps for day 1: ______________ Goal number of steps/day: _____

Number of steps for day 2: ______________

Number of steps for day 3: ______________

Number of steps for day 4: ______________

Number of steps for day 5: ______________

Number of steps for day 6: ______________

Number of steps for day 7: ______________

Number of steps for day 8: ______________

Number of steps for day 9: ______________

Number of steps for day 10: ______________

Number of steps for day 11: ______________

Number of steps for day 12: ______________

Number of steps for day 13: ______________

Number of steps for day 14: ______________

Analysis

1. Did you meet your goal for number of daily steps on most days? Yes/No
2. Are you walking at least the recommended 10,000 steps per day? Yes/No
3. If not, think about how you can incorporate more steps into your daily routine. List below four ways to increase the amount of walking you do daily:

   ____

   ____

   ____

   ____

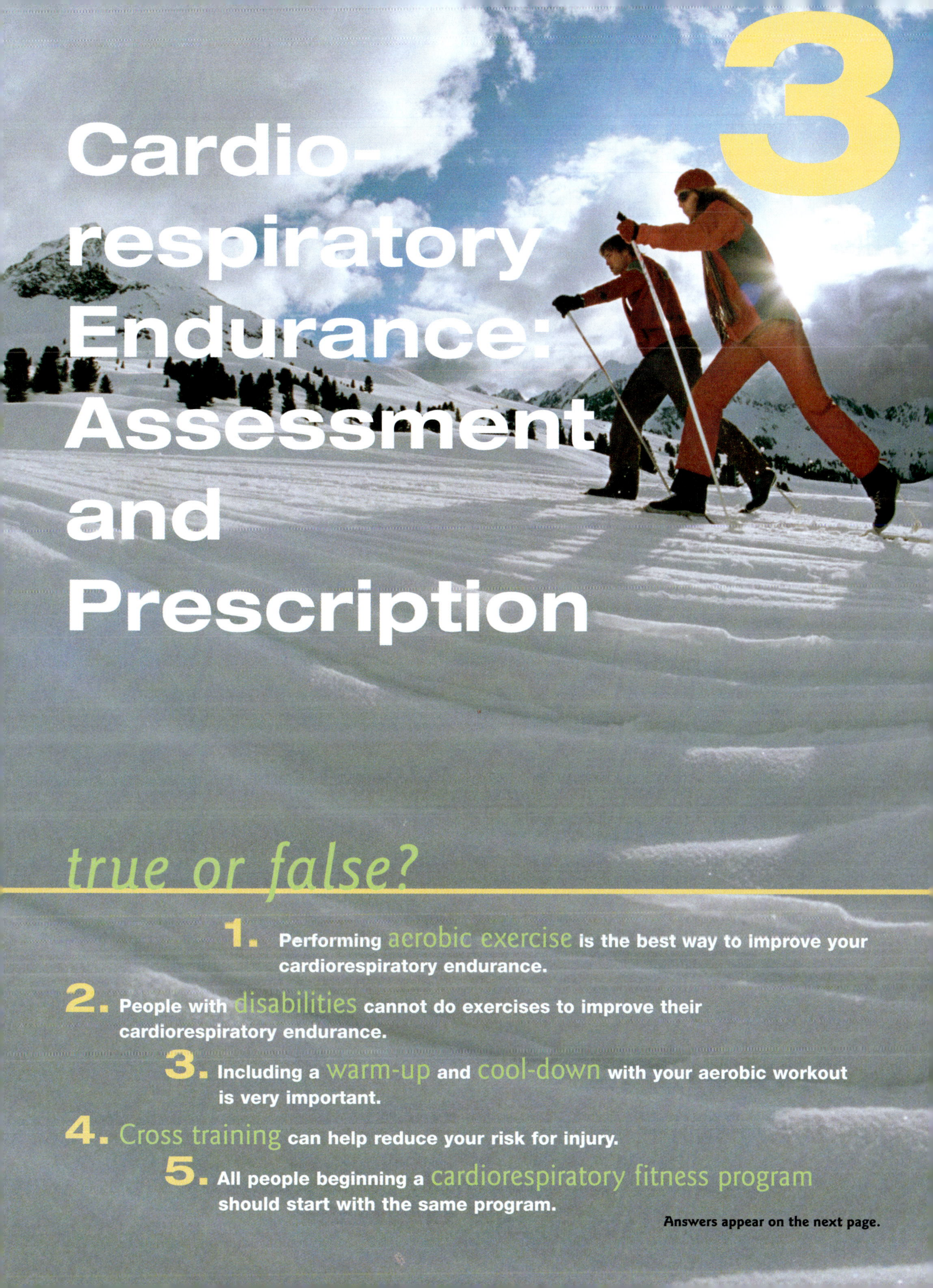

3

Cardiorespiratory Endurance: Assessment and Prescription

true or false?

1. Performing aerobic exercise is the best way to improve your cardiorespiratory endurance.
2. People with disabilities cannot do exercises to improve their cardiorespiratory endurance.
3. Including a warm-up and cool-down with your aerobic workout is very important.
4. Cross training can help reduce your risk for injury.
5. All people beginning a cardiorespiratory fitness program should start with the same program.

Answers appear on the next page.

Are there any hills on your campus? Have you ever trudged up one of them, only to be winded and out of breath by the time you got to the top? Do you notice that some of your fellow students, and probably many of your professors, can perform the activity without exertion? If you answered yes to these questions, you are already familiar with the concept of cardiorespiratory endurance. The low cardiorespiratory endurance that often accompanies a lack of regular exercise can make even common everyday tasks difficult. In this chapter, we will explore the basics of cardiorespiratory endurance and the types of exercise that will improve it.

In Chapters 1 and 2, we discussed the health benefits of exercise and the general principles of exercise training. In this and the next three chapters, we describe how to assess your level of each health-related fitness component and how to design a comprehensive, scientifically based exercise program to meet your health and fitness goals. Before we discuss the assessment and prescription for cardiovascular fitness, we need to define cardiorespiratory endurance and to cover some basic cardiovascular physiology.

The Need for Cardiorespiratory Endurance in Daily Living

Developing cardiorespiratory endurance is beneficial for a number of everyday activities. Walking around your campus to get to class or the library requires cardiorespiratory fitness. Other everyday activities, such as cleaning your dorm room or apartment, or yard work if you live in a house, are easier when you have a higher level of cardiorespiratory fitness. Your leisure time and social activities, such as a weekend hiking or camping trip with friends or a night out dancing, are more enjoyable with higher cardiorespiratory fitness.

What Are Cardiorespiratory Endurance and the Cardiovascular System?

Cardiorespiratory endurance is the ability to perform **aerobic exercises,** such as swimming, jogging and cycling, for a prolonged period of time, and is effective in promoting weight loss and reducing the risk of cardiovascular disease. Because of this, many exercise scientists consider cardiorespiratory endurance to be the most important component of health-related physical fitness (2, 3).

The most valid measurement of cardiorespiratory fitness is **$\dot{V}O_2$max,** or maximal aerobic capacity, which is the maximum amount of oxygen the body can take in and use during exercise. In simple terms, $\dot{V}O_2$max is a measure of the endurance of both the cardiorespiratory system and exercising skeletal muscles.

The cardiorespiratory system is made up of the cardiovascular system (the heart and blood vessels) and the respiratory system (the lungs and muscles involved in respiration). Together these systems deliver oxygen and nutrients throughout the body and remove waste products (e.g., carbon dioxide) from tissues. Exercise challenges the cardiorespiratory system because it in-

Answers

1. TRUE Aerobic exercises such as walking, participating in aerobics classes, and swimming will improve or maintain cardiorespiratory endurance.
2. FALSE There are many activities that persons with disabilities can do to improve their cardiorespiratory fitness. The Closer Look box on page 63 and the Appreciating Diversity box on page 69 discuss some exercise options for people with temporary or permanent disabilities.
3. TRUE A warm-up and cool-down will help reduce your risk for injury and muscle soreness. Both should be included with your workouts even if you are exercising for a short duration or at moderate intensity.
4. TRUE Cross training means using multiple types of exercise, and this practice can reduce the risk for overuse injuries, especially if you perform high-impact exercises.
5. FALSE Your program should be based on your initial fitness level. The boxes on pages 66, 67, and 68 provide examples for beginners of initial low, average, and high fitness levels.

Cycling, whether outside or at the gym, is one popular type of exercise that will improve cardiorespiratory endurance.

creases the demand for oxygen and nutrients in the working muscles.

The Cardiovascular System

The heart is a pump, about the size of your fist, that contracts and generates pressure to move blood through the blood vessels throughout the body. Actually, the heart is considered two pumps in one. The right side pumps oxygen-depleted (deoxygenated) blood to the lungs in a pathway called the **pulmonary circuit,** and the left side pumps oxygen-rich (oxygenated) blood to tissues throughout the body through a pathway called the **systemic circuit.** Figure 3.1 illustrates the path of blood through the heart and lungs.

There are different types of blood vessels in the circulatory system. With the exception of the pulmonary artery (which carries oxygen-depleted blood from the heart to the lungs), **arteries** carry oxygen-rich blood away from the heart and to the rest of the body. Except for the pulmonary vein (which carries oxygen-rich blood from the lungs to the heart), **veins** carry oxygen-depleted blood from the body's tissues back to the heart.

Blood is pumped from the left side of the heart into the aorta, the largest artery in the body. From the aorta, arteries branch into smaller vessels called *arterioles*, which further branch into **capillaries.** The capillaries have walls that are one cell thick through which oxygen and nutrients can easily pass. Through capillaries, oxygen and nutrients are delivered to the tissues, and carbon dioxide and waste are picked up from the tissues and taken back to the heart. The capillaries branch into bigger vessels called *venules*, and then into veins. From the veins the blood enters the right side of the heart and is pumped to the lungs.

Every time your heart pumps (or beats), you can feel a pulse. People often measure the number of times their heart beats per minute (commonly called the *heart rate*), to gauge their exercise intensity (more on this later in the chapter). When people say they are "taking their pulse," they are referring to their heart rate. The easiest places to take your heart rate are your radial and carotid arteries. The radial artery is located on the inside of your wrist just below your thumb, and the carotid artery can be found along the neck (Figure 3.2). The amount of blood that is pumped with each heartbeat is called **stroke volume.** The product of heart rate and stroke volume is **cardiac output,** which is the amount of blood that is pumped per minute.

The Respiratory System

The respiratory system controls our breathing. In the lungs, carbon dioxide and waste from the oxygen-depleted blood pass into tiny air sacs called **alveoli.** When we exhale, the carbon dioxide and waste are released into the air. Then, as we inhale, we bring oxygen into the lungs, where oxygen enters the alveoli and passes into the capillaries. From the lungs the oxygen-rich blood travels to the left side of the heart to start the process again.

Make sure you know...

> Cardiorespiratory endurance, which refers to how well you can perform aerobic exercises, is considered one of the most important health-related fitness components.

cardiorespiratory endurance The ability to perform aerobic exercises for a prolonged period of time.

aerobic exercise A common term to describe all forms of exercises that primarily use the aerobic energy system and that are designed to improve cardiorespiratory fitness.

$\dot{V}O_2$max The maximum amount of oxygen the body can take in and use during exercise.

pulmonary circuit The vascular system that circulates blood from the right side of the heart, through the lungs, and back to the left side of the heart.

systemic circuit The vascular system that circulates blood from the left side of the heart, throughout the body, and back to the right side of the heart.

arteries The blood vessels that carry blood away from the heart.

veins Blood vessels that transport blood toward the heart.

capillaries Thin-walled vessels that permit the exchange of gases (oxygen and carbon dioxide) and nutrients between the blood and tissues.

stroke volume The amount of blood pumped per heartbeat (generally expressed in milliliters).

cardiac output The amount of blood the heart pumps per minute.

alveoli Tiny air sacs in the lungs that receive carbon dioxide and other wastes from oxygen-depleted blood.

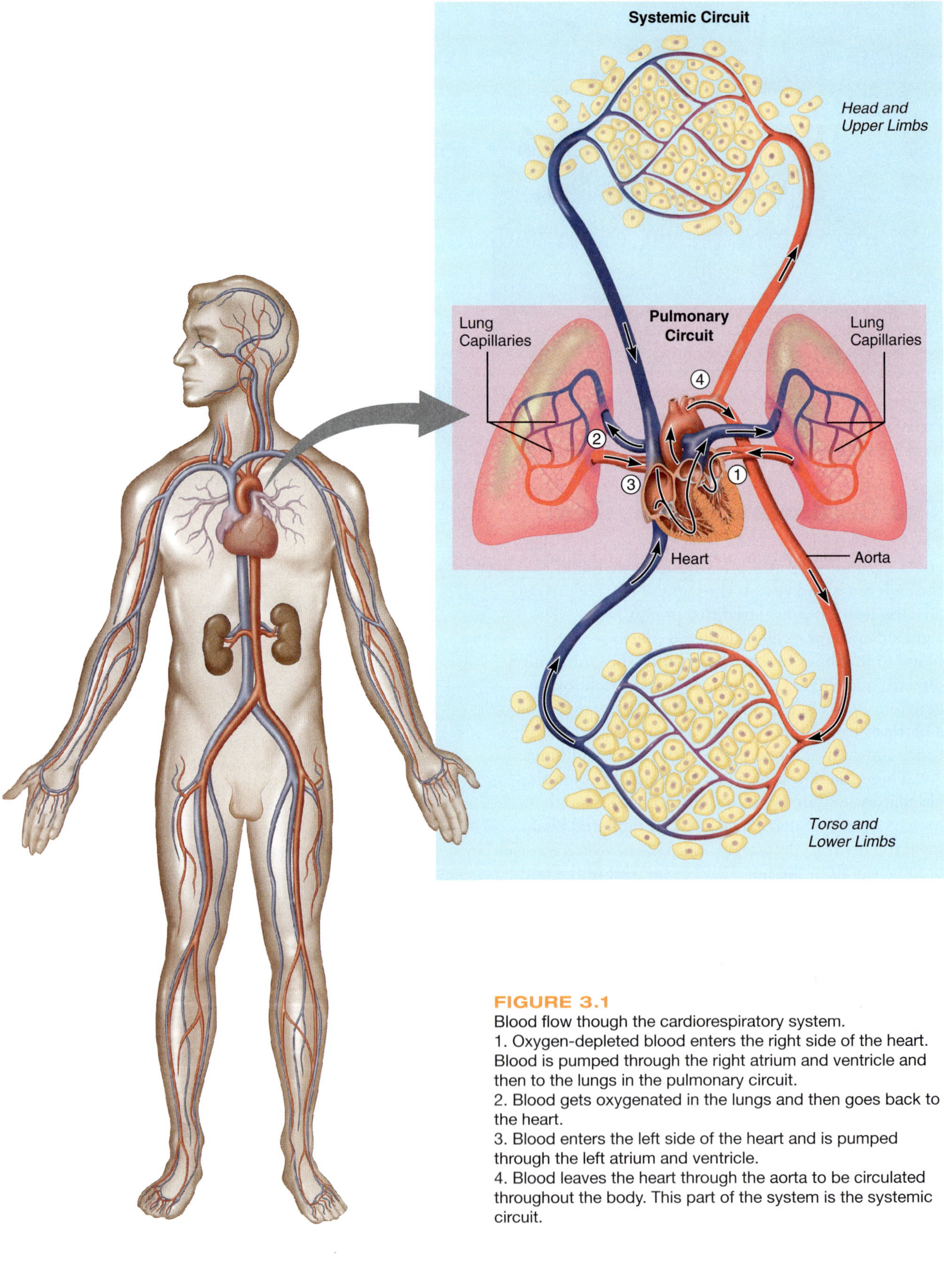

FIGURE 3.1
Blood flow though the cardiorespiratory system.
1. Oxygen-depleted blood enters the right side of the heart. Blood is pumped through the right atrium and ventricle and then to the lungs in the pulmonary circuit.
2. Blood gets oxygenated in the lungs and then goes back to the heart.
3. Blood enters the left side of the heart and is pumped through the left atrium and ventricle.
4. Blood leaves the heart through the aorta to be circulated throughout the body. This part of the system is the systemic circuit.

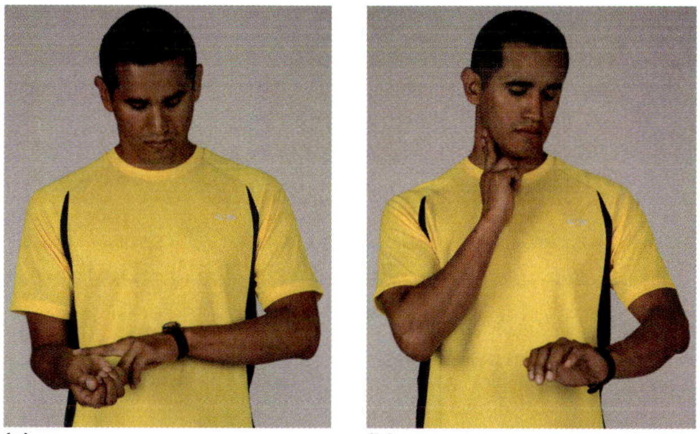

(a) (b)

FIGURE 3.2
You can measure heart rate at either the radial artery in the wrist **(a)** or at the carotid artery in the neck **(b).**

- $\dot{V}O_2$max is a measure of cardiorespiratory endurance.
- The cardiorespiratory system consists of the cardiovascular and respiratory systems.
- The heart and blood vessels make up the cardiovascular system, and the lungs and muscles used for breathing make up the respiratory system.
- The pulmonary circuit pumps blood to the lungs, and the systemic circuit pumps blood throughout the body.

How Do We Get Energy for Exercise?

We have discussed the importance of getting oxygen to the muscles and having energy for prolonged exercise. But why is it important to get more oxygen to the muscles, and what do we mean by *energy*? Energy is the fuel needed to make the muscles move for activity, and we get that energy from the breakdown of food. However, food energy cannot be used directly by the muscles. Instead, the energy released from the breakdown of food is used to make a biochemical compound, called **adenosine triphosphate (ATP).** ATP is made and stored in small amounts in muscle and other cells. The breakdown of ATP releases energy that your muscles can use to contract and make you move. ATP is the only compound in the body that can provide this immediate source of energy. Therefore, for muscles to contract during exercise, a supply of ATP must be available.

The body uses two "systems" in muscle cells to produce ATP. One system does not require oxygen and is called the **anaerobic** ("without oxygen") system. The second system requires oxygen and is called the **aerobic** ("with oxygen") system. The aerobic system is the primary system for developing cardiorespiratory endurance, which is why we need to get oxygen to the muscles.

Anaerobic Energy Production

Most of the anaerobic ATP production in muscle occurs during **glycolysis,** the process that breaks down carbohydrates in cells. In addition to ATP production, glycolysis often results in the formation of **lactic acid.** Because of this lactic acid by-product, this pathway for ATP production is often called the *lactic acid system*. This system can use only carbohydrates as an energy source. Carbohydrates are supplied to muscles from blood sugar (glucose) and from muscle stores of glucose called *glycogen*.

The anaerobic energy pathway provides ATP at the beginning of exercise and for short-term (30–60 seconds) high-intensity exercise. Exercise that is intense and less than 2 minutes in duration, such as a 60- to 80-second 400-meter sprint, primarily relies on this system. During this type of intense exercise, muscles produce large amounts of lactic acid because the lactic acid system is operating at high speed.

Aerobic Energy Production

After about a minute of high-intensity exercise, anaerobic production of ATP begins to decrease, and aerobic production of ATP starts to increase. The aerobic system needs oxygen for the chemical reactions to make ATP. Activities of daily living and many types of exercise depend on ATP production from the aerobic system.

Whereas the anaerobic system uses only carbohydrates as a food source, aerobic metabolism can use fats, carbohydrates, and protein to produce ATP. However, for a healthy person who eats a balanced diet,

adenosine triphosphate (ATP) A high-energy compound that is synthesized and stored in small quantities in muscle and other cells. The breakdown of ATP results in a release of energy that can be used to fuel muscular contraction.

anaerobic "Without oxygen"; in cells, pertains to biochemical pathways that do not require oxygen to produce energy.

aerobic "With oxygen"; in cells, pertains to biochemical pathways that use oxygen to produce energy.

glycolysis A process during which carbohydrates are broken down in cells. Much of the anaerobic ATP production in muscle cells occurs during glycolysis.

lactic acid A by-product of glucose metabolism, produced primarily during intense exercise (i.e., greater than 50–60% of maximal aerobic capacity).

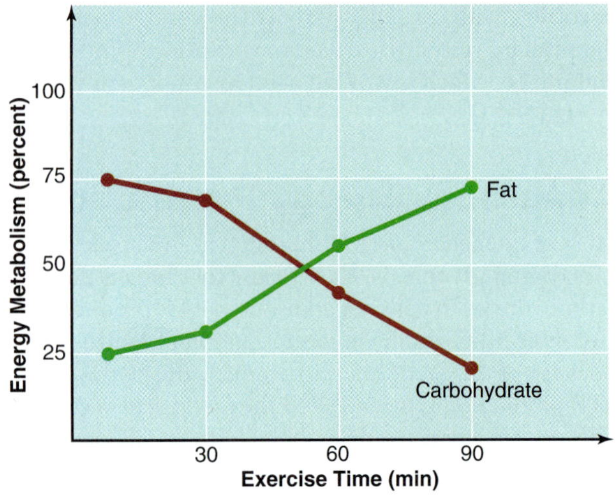

FIGURE 3.3
After about 60 minutes of exercise, the body begins to use more fat and fewer carbohydrates for ATP production.

proteins have a limited role during exercise—carbohydrates and fats are the primary sources. In general, at the beginning of exercise, carbohydrates are the main fuel broken down during aerobic ATP production. During prolonged exercise (i.e., longer than 20 minutes), there is a gradual shift from carbohydrates to fat as an energy source (Figure 3.3).

The Energy Continuum

Although we often speak of aerobic versus anaerobic exercise, in reality many types of exercise use both systems. Figure 3.4(a) illustrates the anaerobic–aerobic energy continuum as it relates to exercise duration. Anaerobic energy production is dominant during short-term exercise, and aerobic energy production is greatest during long-term exercise. For example, a 100-meter dash sprint uses anaerobic energy sources almost exclusively. At the other end of the energy spectrum, running a marathon uses mostly aerobic production of ATP, because the exercise involves 2 or more hours of continuous activity. Running a maximal-effort 800-meter race (exercise of 2–3 minutes' duration) is an example of an exercise duration that uses almost an equal amount of aerobic and anaerobic energy sources.

Figure 3.4(b) applies the anaerobic–aerobic energy continuum to various sports activities. Weight lifting, gymnastics, and wrestling are examples of sports that use anaerobic energy production almost exclusively. Boxing and skating (1500 meters) require an equal contribution of anaerobic and aerobic energy production. Finally, during cross-country skiing and jogging, aerobic energy production dominates.

Make sure you know...

- ATP is used for energy during exercise.
- Anaerobic energy production does not require oxygen, uses carbohydrates for fuel, and supplies energy for short-term and high-intensity exercises.
- Aerobic energy production requires oxygen to make ATP; can use carbohydrates, fats, or proteins for fuel; and is used for longer-duration exercises.
- Many activities use both energy systems at some level.

What Happens to the Cardiorespiratory System with Exercise and Training?

You have probably noticed that when you go for a run or spend more than a few minutes on an exercise bike, your heart rate increases and you start to sweat. These reactions are due to specific needs of your body during exercise. We'll discuss these next.

During an exercise session and after a regular exercise program, your cardiorespiratory system undergoes several **responses** and **adaptations.** Responses are the changes that occur during and immediately after exercise. For example, your increased heart rate and heavy breathing after you walk up a hill is a response. Adaptations are the changes you will see if you stick with a regular exercise program. Your ability to walk up that hill without getting winded after a few weeks of regular aerobic exercise is the result of adaptations to the cardiorespiratory system. As the cardiorespiratory system gets stronger, it does not have to work as hard for the same level of exercise.

Responses to Exercise

When you exercise, the exercising muscles need more oxygen and nutrients to maintain their activity, so your cardiac output has to increase. The faster heart rate you experience during exercise contributes to the increased cardiac output. Stroke volume also increases to increase cardiac output, enabling your working muscles to get enough oxygen to produce energy. The arteries going to the working muscles dilate (or expand) to deliver the increased blood and oxygen to the exercising muscles.

The respiratory system also has to respond to the demand of exercise by maintaining constant levels of oxygen and carbon dioxide in the blood. Exercise increases the amount of oxygen the body uses and the amount of carbon dioxide produced. Therefore,

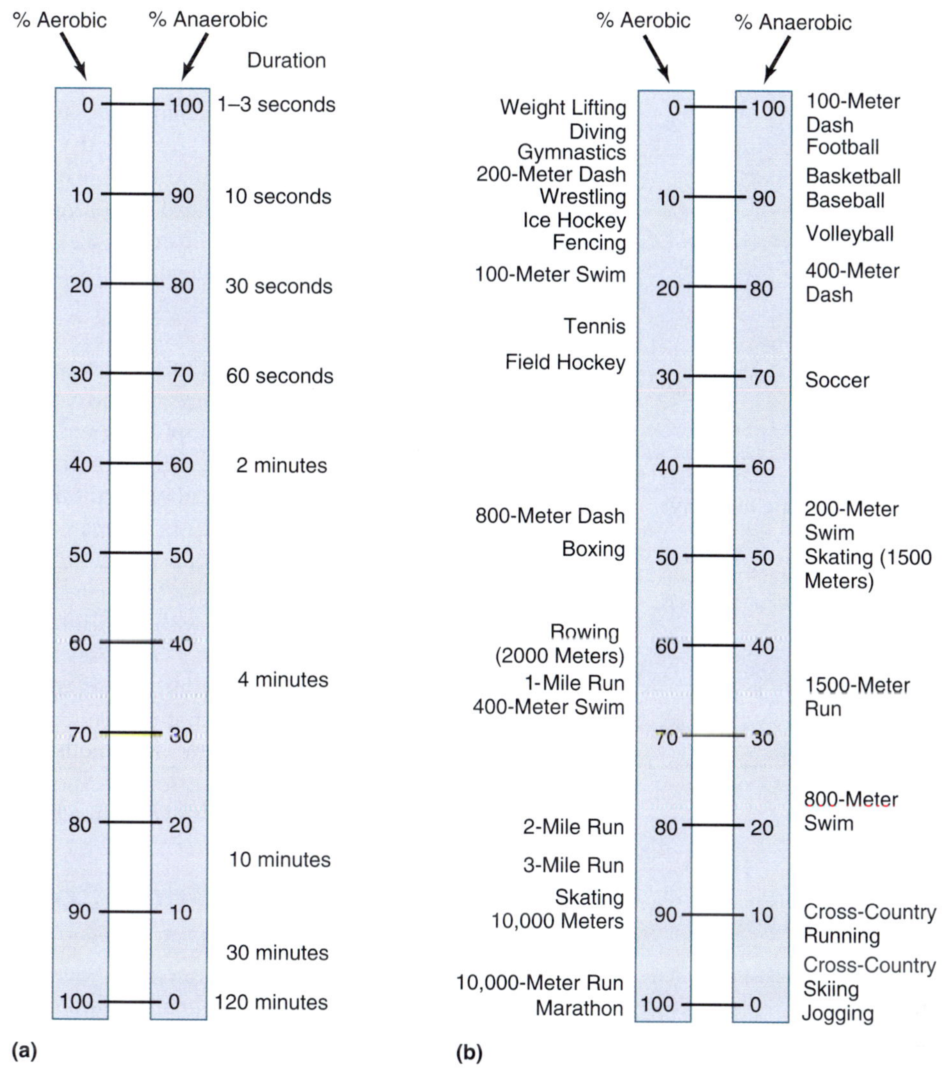

FIGURE 3.4
Contributions of aerobically and anaerobically produced ATP to energy metabolism during exercise. **(a)** Contributions as a function of exercise duration. **(b)** Contributions for various sport activities.

breathing rate increases to bring more oxygen into the body and to remove the carbon dioxide. As you exercise at higher intensities, breathing increases rapidly to enhance removal of carbon dioxide.

Adaptations to Exercise

Regular endurance exercise training results in adaptations in the cardiovascular and respiratory systems, skeletal muscles, and the energy-producing systems.

Endurance training results in several adaptations in the cardiovascular system (4). One thing you will notice as your cardiorespiratory fitness level increases is that your resting heart rate decreases. This occurs because your heart is able to pump more blood per heartbeat, so it does not have to beat as many times per minute to get the same amount of blood throughout the body. The maximum number of times your heart beats per minute does not increase with aerobic exercise training, but your maximal stroke volume does. As maximal stroke volume increases, maximal cardiac output increases. Remember that cardiac output is the amount of blood that is pumped through the body per

responses The changes that occur during exercise to help you meet the demand of the exercise session. These changes return to normal levels shortly after the exercise session.

adaptations Semipermanent changes that occur over time with regular exercise. Adaptations can be reversed when a regular exercise program is stopped for an extended period of time.

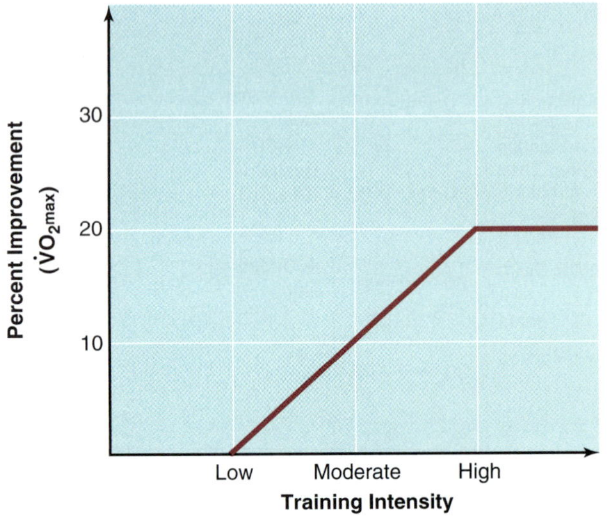

FIGURE 3.5
The relationship between training intensity and improvements in $\dot{V}O_2max$ following a 12-week training period.

minute. Because the maximal amount of blood your heart can pump per minute increases, the maximal amount of oxygen you can use during exercise, or your $\dot{V}O_2max$ increases.

Aerobic exercise training does not alter the structure or function of the respiratory system, but it does increase the endurance of the muscles involved in the breathing process (5). The diaphragm, located below the lungs, and other key muscles of respiration can work harder and longer without fatigue. This improvement in respiratory muscle endurance may reduce the feeling of being out of breath during exercise and eliminate the pain in the side (often called a stitch) that people sometimes experience when beginning an aerobic exercise program.

Endurance training also increases the muscles' capacity to produce aerobic energy. The practical results of this adaptation are that the body is better able to use fat to produce energy and that muscular endurance increases (4). Note that these changes occur only in those muscles used for exercise or activity. For example, endurance training using a stationary exercise cycle results in improved muscular endurance in leg muscles, but it has little effect on arm muscles. Also, although endurance training improves muscle tone, you will not see significant increases in muscle size or strength.

Recall that many exercise physiologists consider $\dot{V}O_2max$ to be the best single measure of cardiorespiratory fitness. Therefore, improved $\dot{V}O_2max$ is an important adaptation of regular aerobic exercise training. In general, 12 to 15 weeks of endurance exercise produce a 10–30% improvement in $\dot{V}O_2max$ (4). A combination of the adaptations of the cardiorespiratory system, improved aerobic capacity of the aerobic muscles, and increased maximal cardiac output produce the increase in $\dot{V}O_2max$. The benefits of the increase are that your body can deliver and use more oxygen during exercise, muscular endurance improves, and you experience less fatigue during routine daily activities.

In general, a person with an initial low $\dot{V}O_2max$ will have greater increases than a person who starts an aerobic exercise program with a high $\dot{V}O_2max$. The increase in $\dot{V}O_2max$ is directly related to the intensity of the training program, with high-intensity training programs producing greater increases than low-intensity and short-duration programs (6) (Figure 3.5). Note though, that poor nutritional habits will impede improvements in $\dot{V}O_2max$. You will learn more about developing a healthy diet in Chapter 7.

CONSIDER THIS!

$\dot{V}O_2max$ begins to decrease around the age of 25 and decreases at a rate of approximately 1% per year.

Body Composition

Endurance training generally produces a loss of body fat and healthier body composition (4). However, a loss of body fat is not guaranteed. If you begin an aerobic exercise program with the goal of losing weight, you also need to consider the amount of exercise you do and your dietary habits. You will learn more about body composition and weight management in Chapters 6 and 8.

Make sure you know...

- Responses are the short-term changes that occur during exercise, and adaptations are the changes that occur over time as a result of regular exercise.
- Responses to exercise include increases in heart rate, stroke volume, cardiac output, and breathing rate.
- Adaptations to regular aerobic exercise include decreased resting heart rate, increased stroke volume and $\dot{V}O_2max$, improved ability to use fat for fuel, and improved body composition.

What Are the Health Benefits of Cardiorespiratory Endurance?

As you learned in Chapter 1, health and fitness are not the same. You also learned the differences between physical activity and exercise. Regular physical activity can lead to health improvements (e.g., reduced risk for heart disease) even if you do not have a structured exercise program. However, without a structured exercise program, you probably will not see significant changes in your cardiorespiratory endurance level.

Among the most significant health benefits of cardiorespiratory fitness are a lower risk of cardiovascular disease (CVD) and increased longevity. Also, people who exercise to improve their cardiorespiratory fitness have a reduced risk of type 2 diabetes, lower blood pressure, and increased bone density in weight-bearing bones (7).

In addition to physical health benefits, there are also psychological health benefits associated with regular aerobic exercise training, including higher self-esteem and a more positive body image (8). This relationship is due to multiple factors. First, there is a sense of accomplishment that comes from starting and maintaining a regular exercise program and meeting personal goals. Regular exercise also improves muscle tone and helps with weight management, both of which can have positive impact on appearance. Improved sleep quality is another psychological benefit of regular exercise (9). Fit individuals tend to sleep longer without interruptions (i.e., they enjoy more restful sleep) than do less-fit people. A better night's rest will likely translate to a more complete feeling of being mentally restored.

Benefits of cardiorespiratory endurance also extend to activities of daily living. More energy for work and play is a commonly reported benefit; fit individuals can perform more work with less fatigue. People with high levels of cardiorespiratory fitness often say they exercise because it makes them feel better. The box on this page summarizes the benefits you can expect to experience from the improved cardiovascular fitness that results from a regular exercise program.

Make sure you know...

> Regular exercise is needed to improve your cardiorespiratory endurance.

> There are numerous physical and psychological health benefits of regular aerobic exercise, including reduced risk of CVD, increased longevity, and improved self-esteem and body image.

Benefits of Improved Cardiorespiratory Fitness

- Lower risk of heart disease
- Reduced risk of type 2 diabetes
- Lower blood pressure
- Increased bone density
- Increased energy for work and play
- Increased feeling of well-being
- Improved self-esteem
- Increased muscle tone and endurance
- Easier weight control
- Improved sleep

Evaluation of Cardiorespiratory Endurance

The most accurate means of measuring cardiorespiratory fitness is the laboratory assessment of $\dot{V}O_2max$ (4,10). However, direct measurement of $\dot{V}O_2max$ requires expensive equipment and is very time-consuming, so it is not practical for general use. Fortunately, there are numerous field tests for estimating $\dot{V}O_2max$ (11–13). Each of these tests has a margin of error, but they are valid measures, and the practical advantages outweigh the disadvantages. This section will explain some of the common ways you can easily estimate your $\dot{V}O_2max$. You can also use Laboratory 3.1C at the end of the chapter to estimate your $\dot{V}O_2max$.

One of the simplest and most accurate assessments of cardiorespiratory fitness is the **1.5-mile run test.** This test is based on the idea that people with a higher level of cardiorespiratory fitness can run 1.5 miles faster than those with a lower level of cardiorespiratory fitness (11, 12).

The objective of the test is to complete a 1.5-mile run in the shortest possible time. Regular exercisers and people with active lifestyles can probably complete the 1.5-mile distance running or jogging. Because this test requires you to run the 1.5 miles as fast as you can, it is not the best option for sedentary people over age 30, for people who have a very low fitness level due to medical reasons, for individuals with joint problems, or for obese individuals. For less active individuals, a

1.5-mile run test One of the simplest and most accurate assessments of cardiorespiratory fitness.

FIGURE 3.6
A cycle ergometer can be used to assess cardiorespiratory endurance.

1.5 mile run/walk test is better suited. Laboratory 3.1A at the end of the chapter provides instructions for performing the test and recording the score.

The 1-mile walk test is another common field test to estimate cardiorespiratory fitness. The walk test is based on the same idea as the 1.5-mile run test: that people who have higher cardiorespiratory fitness will be able to complete the test faster than those with low cardiorespiratory fitness. This test is particularly good for sedentary individuals (14–16). However, people with joint problems should consider a non-weight-bearing test, such as the cycle test described next. See Laboratory 3.1B for instructions on how to perform the 1-mile walk test and how to determine your score.

Two other tests that can be used to assess your cardiorespiratory endurance are the cycle ergometer test and the step test. A **cycle ergometer** test (Figure 3.6) is ideal for people with joint problems because, unlike walking or jogging, it does not involve weight bearing. The cycle ergometer test is a submaximal cycle test based on the principle that individuals with high cardiorespiratory fitness levels have a lower exercise heart rate at a standard workload than less-fit individuals (13, 17). You can use Laboratory 3.1C to estimate your $\dot{V}O_2max$ according to your heart rate and the workload used during the cycle ergometer test.

Finally, the step test can be performed by people at all fitness levels. Additionally, this test does not require expensive equipment, and it can be performed in a short amount of time. However, the step test is not recommended for overweight individuals or for people with joint problems. The step test is based on the principle that your heart rate "recovers," or returns to resting levels, faster after exercise when you have a high level of cardiorespiratory fitness. Therefore, individuals with a higher cardiorespiratory fitness will have a lower heart rate during a 3-minute period immediately following the test compared to less-fit individuals (4). Also, be aware that this test requires stepping at a consistent rate and accurately taking your heart rate multiple times, so there is more chance for error. You can use Laboratory 3.1D to perform the step test and to find the norms for step test results in a college-aged population (18–25 years).

Make sure you know...

- Common tests to assess cardiorespiratory fitness include the 1.5-mile run, the 1-mile walk, the cycle ergometer test, and the step test.
- Obese individuals and people with joint problems should avoid weight-bearing cardiorespiratory assessment tests. Sedentary individuals should avoid the 1.5-mile run test.

Designing Your Aerobic Exercise Program

After you know your level of cardiorespiratory fitness, you can design an appropriate exercise plan to meet your goals. As we discussed in Chapter 1, setting long- and short-term goals is key to making a healthy behavior change. Starting and maintaining your aerobic exercise program will be much easier if you set goals first and then plan your program specifically to meet your goals. Many fitness experts agree that lack of goals is a major contributor to the high dropout rates seen in many organized fitness programs (18).

As you learned from Chapter 2, each exercise session will include the warm-up, workout, and cool-down phases. Within the workout phase you need to consider the frequency, intensity, time, and type (mode) of exercise. Also, it is important to consider the stage of the program, the initial conditioning, progression, and maintenance phases.

The Warm-Up

Every workout should begin with a warm-up of 5 to 10 minutes of low-intensity exercise and some light stretching. If you take a class such as step aerobics or spinning, your instructor will lead you though an appropriate warm-up. If you do other aerobic exercises, such as jogging or swimming, then you will need to plan your own warm-up. Typically, the warm-up will include a lower-intensity activity that is similar to or the same as your activity of choice for your workout. For example, you might walk or jog as warm-up for a run or swim a couple of laps more slowly than you would for the rest of your swim workout. You might also include some light stretching (see Chapter 5). Then, as you start the workout phase, you will gradually increase your intensity to the desired level.

CONSIDER THIS!

Up to 50% of college students do not get the recommended amount of exercise.

The Workout

The components of an exercise prescription to improve cardiovascular fitness include the components of the FITT principle: frequency, intensity, time (or duration), and type of exercise.

Frequency The general recommendation for exercise frequency is 3 to 5 sessions per week to achieve near-optimal gains in cardiorespiratory fitness with minimal risk of injury. However, cardiorespiratory fitness gains can be achieved with as few as 2 exercise sessions per week (10). You typically will not see significantly greater improvements in your cardiorespiratory fitness if you exercise more than 5 days per week. Additionally, greater exercise frequency entails a greater risk for injury, which generally does not outweigh any added benefit of a greater frequency.

You might have to start with 2 or 3 days per week and increase the frequency as you progress through your program. You should also consider the rest between exercise sessions. A general rule is to exercise no more than 3 days in a row and to rest no more than 3 days in a row, especially if you are doing the same exercise each session.

Intensity Cardiorespiratory fitness improves when the training intensity is at least 50% of $\dot{V}O_2max$ (this level is often called the **training threshold**). Training at exercise intensities close to $\dot{V}O_2max$ does not produce significantly greater benefits and increases risk for injury. Therefore, the recommended range of exercise intensity for improving health-related physical fitness is between 50% and 85% $\dot{V}O_2max$.

You cannot readily assess your percent $\dot{V}O_2max$ during exercise, but you can use heart rate to monitor exercise intensity. $\dot{V}O_2max$ and heart rate both increase linearly as exercise intensity increases. We also know that maximal heart rate is reached at $\dot{V}O_2max$. This relationship, coupled with the fact that heart rate is easily monitored, make heart rate a practical way to monitor exercise intensity.

How do you know what your heart rate should be during exercise? We can calculate a **target heart rate (THR)** range. Figure 3.7 illustrates the pattern of heart rate during an exercise session in the THR. Because the tests we described to assess cardiorespiratory endurance are submaximal tests, we have to estimate maximal heart rate. *Maximal heart rate* (HR_{max}) decreases with age and can be estimated by this formula:

$$HR_{max} = 220 - \text{age (in years)}$$

For example, we can estimate a 20-year-old college student's maximal heart rate by the formula

$$HR_{max} = 220 - 20 = 200 \text{ beats/min}$$

To determine your THR, we next have to determine your **heart rate reserve (HRR)**. Heart rate reserve is the difference between your maximal heart rate and resting heart rate:

$$HRR = HR_{max} - \text{resting HR}$$

Let's assume that our 20-year-old college student's resting heart rate is 60 beats per minute (bpm). Then,

$$HRR = 200 - 60 = 140 \text{ beats/min}$$

After determining the HRR, we can calculate 50% and 85% of his HRR. This range will place him at the desired percentage of his $\dot{V}O_2max$.

$$0.50 \times 140 = 70 \text{ bpm}$$
$$0.85 \times 140 = 119 \text{ bpm}$$

cycle ergometer A stationary exercise cycle that provides pedaling resistance so the amount of work can be measured.

training threshold The training intensity above which there is an improvement in cardiorespiratory fitness. This intensity is approximately 50% of $\dot{V}O_2max$.

target heart rate (THR) The range of heart rates that corresponds to an exercise intensity of approximately 50–85% $\dot{V}O_2max$. This is the range of training heart rates that results in improvements in aerobic capacity.

heart rate reserve (HRR) The difference between your maximal heart rate and resting heart rate.

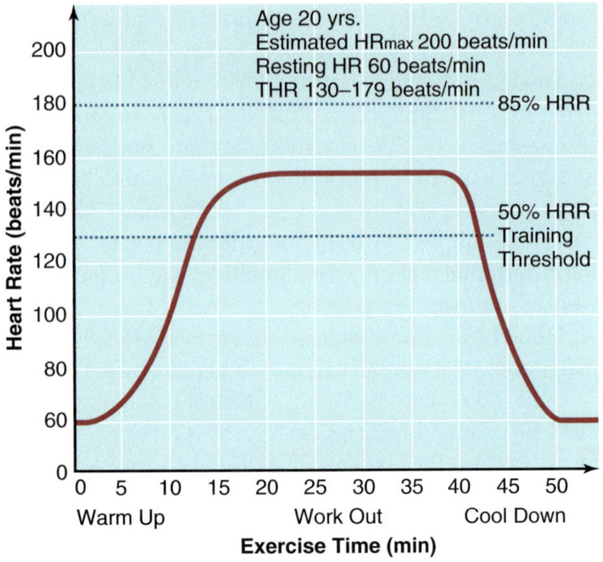

FIGURE 3.7
Sample workout in the target heart rate range.

The final step in determining the THR is to add your resting heart rate back to the values you just calculated. This step is done because your resting heart rate is the starting point. Our student's THR is calculated as follows:

$$70 + 60 = 130 \text{ bpm}$$
$$119 + 60 = 179 \text{ bpm}$$
$$\text{THR} = 130 - 179 \text{ bpm}$$

You can calculate your THR using Laboratory 3.3 at the end of the chapter. Because your maximal heart rate decreases with age, your THR will change as you get older (Figure 3.8). Also, remember that a lower resting heart rate is an adaptation of aerobic exercise

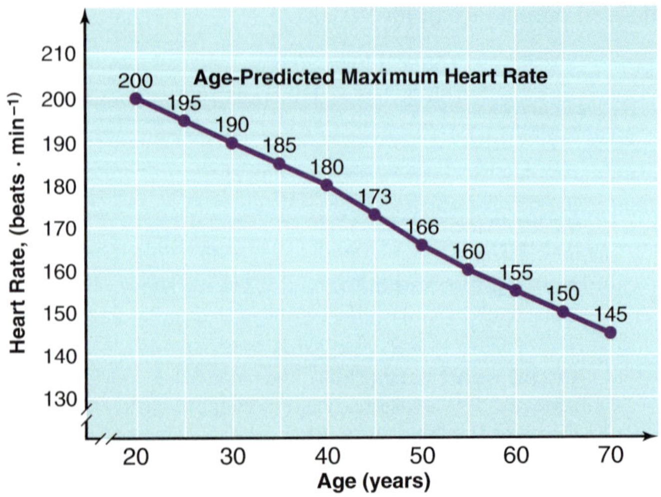

FIGURE 3.8
As you age, your maximal heart rate will decrease.

	6	No exertion at all
	7	Extremely light
	8	
	9	Very light
	10	
	11	Light
	12	
	13	Somewhat hard
Target Heart Rate for Most People —	14	
	15	Hard (heavy)
	16	
	17	Very hard
	18	
	19	Extremely hard
	20	Maximal exertion

FIGURE 3.9
Borg's Rating of Perceived Exertion (RPE) scale. The perception of exertion depends mainly on the strain and fatigue in your muscles and on your feelings of breathlessness or aches in the chest. Try to appraise your feeling of exertion as honestly as possible, without thinking about what the actual physical load is. Don't underestimate it, but don't overestimate it either.

Source: Borg-RPE-scale® from G. Borg, (1998), *Borg's Perceived Exertion and Pain Scales.* Champaign, IL: Human Kinetics. © Gunnar Borg, 1970, 1985, 1994, 1998. Used with permission of Dr. G. Borg. For correct usage of the scale the exact design and instructions given in Borg's folders must be followed: The BORG-RPE SCALE®, a method for measuring perceived exertion. © G. Borg, 1994, 2003. Order folders and scales from: Borg Products, Inc., "BPU," Joseph V. Myers III, 1579F, Monroe Drive, #416, Atlanta, GA 30324.

training. As you get older and see changes in your resting heart rate, you should recalculate your THR.

Another way to estimate exercise intensity is the **Borg Rating of Perceived Exertion (RPE)** scale in Figure 3.9.(19). Perceived exertion is how hard you think you are working during exercise. To determine your RPE, take into consideration your efforts of breathing, how much you are sweating, and feelings in your muscles. Because your heart rate increases as your exercise intensity increases, your perception of effort assessed by the RPE scale typically correlates with heart rate during exercise. An RPE value between 12 and 16 will correspond with the target heart rate range for most people.

Time (Duration) Recall that the duration of exercise does not include the warm-up or cool-down. In general, exercise durations most effective in improving cardiorespiratory fitness are between 20 and 60 minutes (10). The time you need to obtain your desired benefits will be specific to your initial level of fitness and your training intensity. For example, a poorly conditioned individual may see improvement in his cardiorespiratory endurance with 20 to 30 minutes of exercise 3 to 5 days per week at his THR. In contrast, a highly trained person may need regular exercise sessions of 40 to 60 minutes' duration to improve cardiorespiratory fitness.

When determining your exercise duration, you also have to consider your exercise intensity. If you choose

A CLOSER LOOK

AEROBIC WORKOUTS—FAQS

Which is better, exercising for a brief period several times, or exercising for one longer period?
Both approaches can work. You do need to warm up for 5 to 10 minutes and cool down for 5 to 10 minutes, regardless of the session length. Short sessions last typically at least 10 minutes for the workout phase. After you add the time for the warm-up and cool-down, you are looking at a 20-minute session. Keep in mind that if you choose multiple sessions, your total workout time should be the same as with one longer session. Also, shorter sessions should not be less intense. You still have to maintain your prescribed exercise intensity to maximize the benefits.

What is the best time of day to exercise?
It doesn't matter whether you exercise in the morning or afternoon, but it does matter that you stick with your routine. So, the best time of day to exercise is whenever you're most likely to do it consistently.

Should I train if I'm sick?
Generally, if the sickness is above the neck (e.g., sinus problem, headache, sore throat), light exercise might not be a problem. Just take it easy, and be sure to respect others who are not sick by wiping off any equipment that you use and by washing your hands frequently. If you are not sure whether you should exercise, listen to your body. If you feel you need to rest, then you should take the day off.

Can I do aerobic exercise if I have asthma?
People with asthma can, in general, safely participate in all types of exercise. However, it is important to have a prescribed medication program to control your asthma (21). When asthma is under control, your exercise prescription need not be different from those for individuals without asthma. Exercise with other people present, and keep your inhaler readily available while exercising in case of an asthma attack. Additionally, you should avoid exercise in cold weather and in polluted environments. If you live in an area with a high level of pollution, exercising in a place with properly filtered indoor air may be preferable to exercising outdoors.

lower-intensity exercise rather than higher-intensity exercise, you will need to factor in a longer duration. For example, training at the lower end of your target heart rate range, around 50% of HRR, might require an exercise duration of 40 to 50 minutes to improve cardiorespiratory fitness. However, if you exercise at a moderate or higher intensity, such as 70% of HRR, you might see similar improvements with only 20 to 30 minutes.

Type Any type of aerobic activities that you enjoy enough to do consistently will help improve and maintain your cardiorespiratory fitness. Also, any activity that uses a large muscle mass (e.g., the legs) in a slow, rhythmic pattern can improve cardiorespiratory endurance. These activities can be performed at a duration and intensity that will use the aerobic energy system. The box at right lists several activities that have been shown to improve cardiorespiratory fitness.

Because there are many exercises and activities that will improve your cardiorespiratory endurance, it is important to select activities you will enjoy. Another consideration is the risk of injury associated with high-impact activities, such as running. Listen to your body when it comes to choosing a high-impact exercise. If

Exercises and Activities That Can Improve Cardiorespiratory Fitness

- Aerobics classes
- Bicycling
- Cross-country skiing
- Hiking
- Skipping rope
- Rowing
- Running
- Skating (ice or roller)
- Spinning classes
- Stair climbing
- Swimming
- Brisk walking

Borg Rating of Perceived Exertion A subjective way of estimating exercise intensity based on a numerical scale of 6 to 20.

Frequency	3–5 times per week
Intensity	50–85% of HR_{max}
Time	20–60 minutes per session
Type	Jogging

FIGURE 3.10
An example of the FITT principle for improving cardiorespiratory fitness.

you experience joint pain or discomfort with high-impact activities, you should see a physician. You might need to find lower-impact exercises, such as swimming or cycling. Cross training, discussed later in the chapter, is another option to reduce your risk for injury if you enjoy a high-impact exercise. For an example of how to use the FITT principle in designing an exercise program, see Figure 3.10.

Consumer CORNER

HOW GOOD ARE EXERCISE GADGETS?

Trends and fads come and go in the fitness industry, and right up with diet trends and workout fads are the gadgets that tend to get sold on late-night infomercials and in fitness magazines. Some gadgets work, and others do not. Before buying a new gadget, do your homework. If you have not used the equipment before, try to find someone who has to get an honest opinion. If you are concerned with which modality burns the most calories, the best piece is the one that you use consistently and for the longest amount of time.

For home exercise, treadmills and exercise bikes are excellent choices, but they can be very expensive. The most expensive is not always the best, but you often get what you pay for. Lower-priced treadmills or exercise bikes might not be sturdy enough for long-term use. For outside exercise, bicycles or rollerblades/inline skates are great options. You can usually get good assistance from the sporting goods staff to determine the most appropriate bike or skates for your fitness goals.

Don't forget what you learned in this chapter about aerobic exercise. Abdominal machines or equipment that promise great results in "just 5 minutes" per day are not going to give you an aerobic workout. Keep in mind no gadget will work if you do not use it, so make sure whatever you are considering is something you will put to good use.

The Cool-Down

Every training session should conclude with a cool-down of light exercises and stretching. Allowing your cardiovascular system to slow down gradually is important: Stopping your workout abruptly can cause blood to pool in the arms and legs, which could result in dizziness and/or fainting. A cool-down may also decrease the muscle soreness and cardiac irregularities that sometimes appear after a vigorous workout. Although cardiac irregularities are rare in healthy individuals, a cool-down period is still wise to minimize the risk.

A general cool-down of at least 5 minutes (e.g., light exercise such as walking, or a lighter intensity of the activity you did for your exercise session) should be followed by 5 to 30 minutes of flexibility exercises. If you take an exercise class, your instructor will lead you through the cool-down. In general, stretching exercises should focus on the muscles used during training. The type and duration of the stretching session depends on your flexibility goals (Chapter 5).

Make sure you know...

> Establishing both short-term and long-term fitness goals is essential before beginning a fitness program.
> Each workout should include warm-up, workout, and cool-down phases.
> You need to consider the exercise frequency, intensity, time (duration), and type (mode) for the workout phase.
> Intensity can be monitored using the target heart rate range or Rating of Perceived Exertion.
> Aerobic exercise performed 3 to 5 days per week at 50–85% of your heart rate reserve for 20–60 minutes is recommended to improve your cardiorespiratory endurance.

Developing an Individualized Exercise Prescription

As we discussed in Chapter 2, anyone beginning a new aerobic exercise program, regardless of initial fitness level or exercise mode, will usually go through three stages: initial conditioning, improvement, and maintenance. In this section we will show you how you can individualize these stages to meet your specific needs and goals.

Initial Conditioning Phase

The initial conditioning stage is to your program what the warm-up is to your workout. Starting slowly will allow the body to adapt gradually to exercise and to avoid soreness, injury, and discouragement. Generally this stage lasts 4 weeks, but it can be as short as 2 weeks or as long as 6 weeks, depending on your initial fitness level (10). For example, if your cardiorespiratory fitness is poor, this stage will likely last closer to 6 weeks, but if you start at a relatively high cardiorespiratory fitness level, a 2-week initial conditioning stage might be sufficient.

You should include 10- to 15-minute warm-up and cool-down phases with each workout. In the initial conditioning period of your workout, exercise intensity will be low, typically 40–60% HRR or RPE of 11–13 (10). For people who have never been involved in a regular exercise program or who have very low fitness, the initial intensity might even be less than the 50% HHR we calculated earlier. It is acceptable to start at an intensity of 40–50% HRR if that is comfortable for you (10). The duration of the session will likely be short. Initial sessions for a person with very low fitness might be as short as 10 to 15 minutes. At these intensity and duration recommendations, an exercise frequency of 3 or 4 days is ideal (10).

Here are some key points to remember for your initial conditioning stage:

- Start at an exercise intensity that is comfortable for you.
- Increase your training duration or intensity when you are comfortable, but do not increase intensity and duration at the same time. Gradually increase your duration, and then work on increasing the intensity. Your goal should be 20 to 30 minutes of continuous low to moderate (40–60% HHR) activity at the end of the initial conditioning phase (10).
- Be aware of new aches or pains. Pain is a symptom of injury and indicates that the body needs rest to repair itself. (See Chapter 12 for a discussion of injury prevention and treatment.)

Improvement Phase

The improvement phase can range from 12 to 40 weeks, and your program will progress more rapidly during this period than in the initial conditioning phase (10). The duration and frequency are increased first, and then the intensity is increased toward the upper end of the THR (60–85% HRR or RPE of 13–16). The changes should be gradual, with increases in the duration of no more than 20% per week until you can do 20 to 30 minutes at a moderate to vigorous intensity (10). Frequency of 3 to 4 days might still be appropriate, but if you want greater changes in your cardiorespiratory endurance, increasing to 5 days might be necessary. A general recommendation is to increase the intensity by no more than 5% of your HRR every sixth exercise session (10). If you are exercising 3 days per week, that means an increase every 2 weeks. As you can see, the changes are gradual, and you should not feel pressure to make increases faster than you feel comfortable doing so.

Maintenance Phase

The average college-aged student will generally reach the maintenance phase of the exercise prescription after 16 to 28 weeks of training, but it might take longer for those who started at a low fitness level. In the maintenance stage, you have achieved your fitness goal, and your new goal is to maintain this level of fitness. You still need to exercise regularly, but you do not need to keep increasing all of the components of your exercise prescription.

Several studies have shown that the key factor in maintaining cardiorespiratory fitness is exercise intensity (6). If you keep your intensity at the same level you reached in the final weeks of the improvement stage, you can reduce your frequency. Exercising as little as 2 days per week can still maintain your fitness level. If you keep to the same frequency and intensity as you achieved during the final weeks of the improvement stage, you can reduce duration to 20 to 25 minutes per session. However, if you hold frequency and duration constant, decreasing intensity by even one-third can significantly decrease your cardiorespiratory endurance. So, if you keep up your exercise intensity, you can cut back the duration or frequency to keep your hard-earned benefits.

Sample Exercise Prescriptions

Your exercise program should be tailored to your individual needs to meet the goals you set. An important consideration in designing a personal training program is your current fitness level. People with good or excellent cardiorespiratory fitness can start at a higher level and progress more rapidly than people with low cardiorespiratory endurance. The boxes on pages 66–68 illustrate three sample cardiorespiratory training programs designed for college-aged people with varying initial cardiorespiratory fitness levels. Note that these programs are sample programs to give you an idea of how to start and develop your program. You can use Laboratory 3.4 at the end of this chapter to develop your personal exercise prescription.

Make sure you know...

> Regardless of your initial fitness level, an exercise prescription to improve cardiorespiratory fitness has three phases: initial conditioning, improvement, and maintenance.

Sample Exercise Program for Someone with an Initial Low Level of Cardiorespiratory Fitness

General guidelines:

1. Begin each session with a warm-up.
2. Don't progress to the next level until you feel comfortable with your current level of exercise.
3. Monitor your heart rate during each training session.
4. End each session with a cool-down.
5. Be aware of aches and pains. If you are injury prone, choose a low-impact activity mode, and limit your exercise duration to 20 to 30 minutes per day.

Week No.	Phase	Duration (min/day)	Intensity (% of HR_{max})	Frequency (days/wk)
1	Initial conditioning	10	60	3
2	Initial conditioning	10	60	3
3	Initial conditioning	12	60	3
4	Initial conditioning	12	70	3
5	Initial conditioning	15	70	3
6	Initial conditioning	15	70	3
7	Improvement	20	70	3
8	Improvement	20	70	3
9	Improvement	25	70	3
10	Improvement	25	70	3
11	Improvement	30	70	3
12	Improvement	30	70	3
13	Improvement	35	70	3
14	Improvement	35	70	3
15	Improvement	40	70	3
16	Improvement	40	70	3
17	Improvement	40	75	3
18	Improvement	40	75	3
19	Improvement	40	75	3
20	Improvement	40	75	3–4
21	Improvement	40	75	3–4
22	Improvement	40	75	3–4
23	Maintenance	30	75	3–4
24	Maintenance	30	75	3–4
25	Maintenance	30	75	3–4
26	Maintenance	30	75	3–4

> Your exercise program should be tailored to your individual needs and should take into account your current fitness level.

Training Techniques

Endurance training is a generic term that refers to any type of exercise aimed at improving cardiorespiratory endurance. However, there are numerous endurance training methods that you can use to improve your cardiorespiratory endurance. Most common is the use of a continuous activity, such as walking or jogging at a constant exercise intensity. Cross training and interval training are two techniques for people who need some variety or want to make faster gains.

Cross Training

Cross training is the use of multiple training modes. To cross-train, you might take an aerobic class one day, run one day, and swim another day. Some people use cross training to reduce the boredom of performing the same kind of exercise day after day. Cross training also

Sample Exercise Program for Someone with an Initial Average Level of Cardiorespiratory Fitness

General guidelines:

1. Begin each session with a warm-up.
2. Don't progress to the next level until you feel comfortable with your current level of exercise.
3. Monitor your heart rate during each training session.
4. End each session with a cool-down.
5. Be aware of aches and pains. If you are injury prone, choose a low-impact activity mode, and limit your exercise duration to 20 to 30 minutes per day.

Week No.	Phase	Duration (min/day)	Intensity (% of HR_{max})	Frequency (days/wk)
1	Initial conditioning	10	70	3
2	Initial conditioning	15	70	3
3	Initial conditioning	15	70	3
4	Initial conditioning	20	70	3
5	Improvement	25	70	3
6	Improvement	25	75	3
7	Improvement	25	75	3
8	Improvement	30	75	3
9	Improvement	30	75	3
10	Improvement	35	75	3
11	Improvement	35	75	3
12	Improvement	40	75	3
13	Improvement	40	75	3
14	Improvement	40	75	3
15	Improvement	40	80	3
16	Improvement	40	80	3–4
17	Improvement	40	80	3–4
18	Improvement	40	80	3–4
19	Maintenance	30	80	3–4
20	Maintenance	30	80	3–4
21	Maintenance	30	80	3–4
22	Maintenance	30	80	3–4

might reduce the risk and occurrence of overuse injuries. However, cross training does not provide training specificity. Your cardiorespiratory endurance will improve, but jogging will not improve your swimming, because jogging does not train the arm muscles. Cross training might not be ideal if you are looking to improve your ability in a specific activity, but if you like variety and simply want to increase your cardiorespiratory fitness, cross training is a great option.

Interval Training

Interval training is typically used by athletes and others who are at a higher fitness level. This type of training includes repeated sessions, or intervals, of relatively intense exercise alternated with lower-intensity periods to rest or recover. Runners, swimmers, and cyclists use interval training to improve their times in competition. People exercising to improve fitness might use interval training to make more rapid increases in their exercise intensity during the improvement stage. Interval workouts are intense training sessions and should not be used on a daily basis: rather, they should be alternated with continual moderate-intensity exercise sessions.

cross training The use of a variety of activities for training the cardiorespiratory system.

interval training Type of training that includes repeated sessions or intervals of relatively intense exercise alternated with lower-intensity periods to rest or recover.

Sample Exercise Program for Someone with an Initial High Level of Cardiorespiratory Fitness

General guidelines:

1. Begin each session with a warm-up.
2. Don't progress to the next level until you feel comfortable with your current level of exercise.
3. Monitor your heart rate during each training session.
4. End each session with a cool-down.
5. Be aware of aches and pains. If you are injury prone, choose a low-impact activity mode, and limit your exercise duration to 20 to 30 minutes per day.

Week No.	Phase	Duration (min/day)	Intensity (% of HR_{max})	Frequency (days/wk)
1	Initial conditioning	15	75	3
2	Initial conditioning	20	75	3
3	Improvement	25	75	3
4	Improvement	30	75	3
5	Improvement	35	75	3
6	Improvement	40	75	3
7	Improvement	40	75	3–4
8	Improvement	40	75	3–4
9	Improvement	40	80	3–4
10	Improvement	40	80	3–4
11	Improvement	40	80	3–4
12	Improvement	40	80–85	3–4
13	Improvement	40	80–85	3–4
14	Improvement	40	80–85	3–4
15	Maintenance	30	80–85	3–4
16	Maintenance	30	80–85	3–4
17	Maintenance	30	80–85	3–4
18	Maintenance	30	80–85	3–4

The duration of the intervals can vary, but a 1- to 5-minute duration is common. Each interval is followed by a rest period, which should be equal to or slightly longer than the interval duration. For example, if you are running 400-meter intervals on a track and it takes you approximately 90 seconds to complete each run, your rest period between efforts should be at least 90 seconds. An "active rest" period is recommended. If you are running, your rest would be an easy jog or brisk walk to prevent muscle tightness. You do not have to use a track for interval training. You can use a stop watch and do an interval workout anywhere you usually train.

Make sure you know...

- Cross training can prevent you from becoming bored with an exercise program and reduce your risk for injury.
- Interval training is used by athletes and more advanced exercisers to produce faster gains in cardiorespiratory endurance.

How Can You Get Motivated to Be Active?

Every year, millions of people make the decision to start an exercise program. Unfortunately, over half of those who begin an aerobic exercise program quit within the first 6 months (18). There are many reasons for this high dropout rate, but lack of time is the most commonly cited reason (18). Although finding time for exercise in a busy schedule is difficult, it is not impossible. The key is to schedule a regular time for exercise and to stick with it. A small investment in time to exercise can reap large improvements in fitness and health.

Think about how much time you have in a week and how much of that time is needed to improve your cardiorespiratory endurance. There are 168 hours in every week, and all you need is three 30-minute workouts to improve cardiorespiratory fitness. Of course you need to

APPRECIATING DIVERSITY

DON'T LET A DISABILITY STOP YOU!

A temporary or permanent disability can discourage you from exercising, but you can take comfort in knowing that even with most disabilities you can obtain all of the benefits of cardiovascular exercise. If you have an injury that temporarily keeps you from performing your exercise of choice, your physical therapist or physician can help you find suitable alternative exercises to maintain your fitness level. Consulting a physical therapist, physician, or exercise specialist for the best exercise options is also recommended if you have a permanent disability. Additionally, these health professionals will be able to make you aware of any medical complications associated with your disability and how you can address them.

In general, swimming and other water activities are excellent ways to decrease the need to support your body weight and safely exercise capable muscle groups. Other benefits of water exercise include the following:

- They pose little to no risk of falling.
- Flexibility exercises are much easier to do in water.
- Water provides resistance to capable muscle groups. This resistance enables you to progressively overload the intensity and improve the cardiorespiratory system.
- A variety of water aids, including hand paddles, pull-buoys, flotation belts, and kickboards can be used to help maintain buoyancy and balance as well as help you work in the water.

Basic water safety rules still apply, so be sure to perform water activities with a workout partner or with a lifeguard present.

A CLOSER LOOK

SPINNING—REV IT UP?

Do you like to exercise with a group? Do you like biking but find it hard to do around campus or in your city? Find a spinning class! Spinning is an aerobic exercise performed on stationary bikes in an indoor group ride led by an instructor. The bike is specially designed so you can quickly change the speed and resistance of pedaling. Being able to make the quick changes enables you to mimic cycling in outdoor settings, such as a long country road or up a mountain. The spinning bikes also are designed to be much more comfortable than typical stationary bikes and feature multiple ways to adjust the seats and handlebars.

Spinning is led by an instructor, so you have the benefit of someone guiding you through your session. The instructor's direction is especially important if you are a beginner, because the instructor can tell you how to make the changes in intensity to fit your experience and fitness level. The classes usually last 30 to 60 minutes, have music for motivation, and use visualization techniques so you can feel as though you were cycling over hills and through valleys.

Spinning is an excellent exercise for improving cardiorespiratory endurance. You can burn up to 600 calories in an hour depending on the speed and resistance, and it is a low-impact activity that is easy on your joints. Additional benefits of spinning include a group setting for support and encouragement and an indoor setting so weather is not a barrier.

STEPS FOR BEHAVIOR CHANGE

How good is your level of cardiorespiratory fitness?

Answer the following questions to assess your level of cardiorespiratory fitness.

Y	N	
☐	☐	Do you participate in recreational or competitive sports?
☐	☐	Can you perform at least 20 minutes of continuous aerobic exercise?
☐	☐	Can you do your regular household chores without getting out of breath (e.g., cleaning your apartment, walking your dog, mowing the lawn)?
☐	☐	Can you walk across campus to your classes with little effort?

If you answered yes to either of the first two questions, your cardiorespiratory fitness level is probably above average. If you answered yes only to the last two questions or to none of the questions, you might need to make some improvements.

TIPS TO BECOME MORE ACTIVE

- ☑ Take the stairs when possible.
- ☑ Walk to class instead of driving or taking the bus.
- ☑ Find a friend to take a walk with you.
- ☑ Join a club or intramural sport team.
- ☑ Visit your campus recreation center for options for activity and exercise programs.
- ☑ Get a pedometer to see how many steps per day you walk. Fewer than 5000 per day indicates a sedentary lifestyle.

add warm-ups, cool-downs, and showers, which still totals only about 3 hours per week. That leaves you with 165 hours per week to accomplish all of the other things you need to do. The bottom line is that with proper time management, anyone can find time to exercise.

Consider the strategies you learned for behavior change in Chapter 1, and apply them to your aerobic exercise program. Setting long- and short-term goals is important. Changes happen slowly, and short-term goals will help you monitor your progress to stay on track. Keeping a record of your training program will help you see the small changes that occur on the way to your long-term goal. Keeping your program enjoyable also is important. Exercising with a partner can make your workout more fun and maintain your commitment to a regular exercise routine. Just make sure you choose a partner who is committed and a good exercise role model.

Finally, some discomfort and soreness after your first several exercise sessions is normal. Do not let these feelings discourage you. In a short time the soreness will fade, and the discomfort associated with exercise will disappear. As your fitness level improves, you will feel better and look better. Although reaching and maintaining a healthy level of cardiorespiratory fitness requires time and effort, the rewards are well worth the labor.

Make sure you know...

- > You should apply the behavior strategies you learned in Chapter 1 to help maintain your new aerobic exercise program.
- > Discomfort and soreness are normal with a new exercise routine but will last only for a brief period.

Summary

1. Benefits of cardiorespiratory fitness include a lower risk of disease, feeling better, increased capacity to perform everyday tasks, and improved self-esteem and body image.
2. Adenosine triphosphate (ATP) provides the energy muscles need to move. It is produced by two systems: anaerobic (without oxygen) and aerobic (with oxygen).
3. Anaerobic energy production is the primary source of energy for short-term exercise, and aerobic energy production dominates during prolonged exercise.
4. The term *cardiorespiratory system* refers to the cooperative work of the circulatory and respiratory systems. The primary function of the circulatory system is to transport blood carrying oxygen and nutrients to body tissues. The principal function of the respiratory system is to load oxygen into and remove carbon dioxide from the blood.
5. Responses to exercise are the short-term changes that occur during exercise to meet the immediate demand of exercise. Adaptations are developed over the long term through regular exercise training and will remain if you continue your exercise program.
6. Many exercise physiologists consider $\dot{V}O_2max$ (which is the maximum capacity of the cardiorespiratory system to transport and use oxygen during exercise) to be the most valid measurement of cardiorespiratory endurance.
7. Cardiac output, stroke volume, and heart rate increase as a function of exercise intensity. Breathing rate also increases in proportion to exercise intensity.
8. There are many field tests that can be used to estimate $\dot{V}O_2max$. These tests are practical and can be performed with little equipment.
9. Establishing both short-term and long-term fitness goals is essential before beginning a fitness program.
10. These primary elements make up the exercise prescription: warm-up, workout (primary conditioning period), and cool-down.
11. The components of the workout are the frequency, intensity, time (duration), and type (mode) of exercise (FITT).
12. In general, the FITT principle for improving cardiorespiratory endurance calls for a type of exercise that uses large-muscle groups in a slow, rhythmic pattern for 20 to 60 minutes 3 to 5 times per week.
13. The target heart rate is the range of exercise heart rates that lie between 50% and 85% of heart rate reserve.
14. Regardless of your initial fitness level, an exercise prescription for improving cardiorespiratory fitness has three phases: initial conditioning, improvement, and maintenance.
15. Cross training and interval training provide alternatives to a continuous workout of the same mode. Cross training can be done by individuals of all fitness levels, but interval training is for those who are more experienced with exercise.
16. Maintaining a regular exercise routine requires proper time management and choosing physical activities that you enjoy.

Study Questions

1. Which of the following is not an example of an aerobic exercise?
   a. running
   b. swimming
   c. abdominal toning class
   d. spinning class
2. The anaerobic energy pathway is predominantly responsible for production of ATP during which of the following activities?
   a. wrestling
   b. 800-meter run
   c. 400-meter swim
   d. 30-minute brisk walk

3. __________ is an adaptation of a regular aerobic exercise program.
   a. Lower maximal heart rate
   b. Lower resting heart rate
   c. Faster breathing rate
   d. All of the above
4. Exercise intensity should be at least ________ % of heart rate reserve to improve cardiorespiratory endurance.
   a. 85
   b. 70
   c. 50
   d. 25
5. __________ is a response during exercise.
   a. Faster heart rate
   b. Increased cardiac output
   c. Faster breathing
   d. All of the above
6. __________ are the blood vessels that take blood away from the heart.
   a. Arteries
   b. Veins
   c. Capillaries
   d. Venules
7. What is meant by the term *cardiorespiratory system*?
8. List the major functions of the circulatory and respiratory systems.
9. Why is the heart considered "two pumps in one"?
10. Define the following terms:
    adenosine triphosphate (ATP)
    cross training
    target heart rate

Suggested Reading

American College of Sports Medicine. American College of Sports Medicine position stand: The recommended quantity and quality of exercise for developing and maintaining cardiorespiratory and muscular fitness and flexibility in healthy adults. *Medicine and Science in Sports and Exercise* 30:975–991, 1998.

Blair, S. N., M. J. LaMonte, and M. Z. Nichaman. The evolution of physical activity recommendations: How much is enough? *American Journal of Clinical Nutrition* 79(5):913S–920S, 2004.

Brisswalter J., M. Collardeau, and A. Rene. Effects of acute physical exercise characteristics on cognitive performance. *Sports Medicine* 32(9):555–566, 2002.

Chobanian, A. V., G. L. Bakris, H. R. Black, W. C. Cushman, L. A. Green, J. L. Izzo Jr, D. W. Jones, B. J. Materson, S. Oparil, J. T. Wright Jr, and E. J. Roccella. National Heart, Lung, and Blood Institute Joint National Committee on Prevention, Detection, Evaluation, and Treatment of High Blood Pressure; National High Blood Pressure Education Program Coordinating Committee. The seventh report of the Joint National Committee on Prevention, Detection, Evaluation, and Treatment of High Blood Pressure: The JNC 7 report. *Journal of the American Medical Association* 289(19):2560–2572, 2003.

Pollock, M. L., and J. H. Wilmore. *Exercise in Health and Disease*, 3rd ed. Philadelphia: W. B. Saunders, 1998.

Powers, S., and E. Howley. *Exercise Physiology: Theory and Application to Fitness and Performance*, 4th ed. Dubuque, IA: McGraw-Hill, 2004.

Robertson, Robert. *Perceived Exertion for Practitioners: Rating Effort With the OMNI Picture System.* Champaign, IL: Human Kinetic Publishers, 2004.

Spriet, L. L., and M. J. Gibala. Nutritional strategies to influence adaptations to training. *Journal of Sports Science* 22(1):127–141, 2004.

Warburton, D. E., N. Gledhill, and A. Quinney. Musculoskeletal fitness and health. *Canadian Journal of Applied Physiology* 26(2):217–237, 2001.

For links to the websites below, visit The Total Fitness and Wellness Website at www.aw-bc.com/powers.

WebMD.com
General information about exercise, fitness, and wellness. Great articles, instructional information, and updates.

ACSM.org
Comprehensive website providing information, articles, equipment recommendations, how-to articles, books, and position statements about all aspects of health and fitness.

FitnessOnline
Provides information, tools, and support to achieve health and fitness goals.

Sympatico: Health
Includes numerous articles, book reviews, and links to nutrition, fitness, and wellness topics.

The Running Page
Contains information about racing, running clubs, places to run, running-related products, magazines, and treating running injuries.

Meriter Fitness
Contains information on injury prevention and treatment, weight training, flexibility, exercise prescriptions, and more.

References

1. Cooper, K. H. *Aerobics*. New York: Bantam Books, 1968.
2. Ross, R., and I. Janssen. Physical activity, total and regional obesity: Dose-response considerations. *Medicine and Science in Sports and Exercise* 33(6):S345–S641, 2001.
3. Kohl, H. W. Physical activity and cardiovascular disease: Evidence for a dose response. *Medicine and Science in Sports and Exercise* 33(6):S472–S483, 2001.
4. Powers, S., and E. Howley. *Exercise Physiology: Theory and Application to Fitness and Performance*, 4th ed. St. Louis, MO: McGraw Hill, 2004.
5. Powers, S., S. Grinton, J. Lawler, D. Criswell, and S. Dodd. High intensity exercise training–induced metabolic alterations in respiratory muscles. *Respiration Physiology* 89:169–177, 1992.
6. Laursen, P. B., and D. G. Jenkins. The scientific basis for high-intensity interval training: Optimising training programmes and maximising performance in highly trained endurance athletes. *Sports Medicine* 32(1):53–73, 2002.
7. Kesaniemi, Y. A., E. Danforth, M. D. Jensen, P. G. Kopelman, P. Lefebvre, and B. A. Reeder. Dose-response issues concerning physical activity and health: An evidence-based symposium. *Medicine and Science in Sports and Exercise* 33(6):S351–S358, 2001.
8. Dunn, A. L., M. H. Trivedi, and H. A. O'Neal. Physical activity dose-response effects on outcomes of depression and anxiety. *Medicine and Science in Sports and Exercise* 33(6):S587–S597, 2001.
9. Gambelunghe, C., R. Rossi, G. Mariucci, M. Tantucci, and M. V. Ambrosini. Effects of light physical exercise on sleep regulation in rats. *Medicine and Science in Sports and Exercise* 33(1):57–60, 2001.
10. American College of Sports Medicine. *ACSM's Guidelines for Exercise Testing and Prescription*, 7th ed. Philadelphia: Lippincott Williams, & Wilkins, 2006.
11. Cooper, K. *The Aerobics Program for Total Well-Being*. New York: M. Evans, 1982.
12. Cooper, K. *The Aerobics Way*. New York: Bantam Books, 1977.
13. Fox, E. A simple technique for predicting maximal aerobic power. *Journal of Applied Physiology* 35:914–916, 1973.
14. Rippe, J., A. Ward., J. Porcari, and P. Freedson. Walking for fitness and health. *Journal of the American Medical Association* 259:2720–2724, 1988.
15. Rippe, J. Walking for fitness: A roundtable. *Physician and Sports Medicine* 14:144–159, 1986.
16. Ward, A., and J. Rippe. *Walking for Health and Fitness*. Philadelphia: J. B. Lippincott, 1988.
17. Pollock, M., J. Wilmore, and S. Fox. *Health and Fitness Through Physical Activity*. New York: John Wiley and Sons, 1978.
18. Mullineaux, D. R., C. A. Barnes, and E. F. Barnes. Factors affecting the likelihood to engage in adequate physical activity to promote health. *Journal of Sports Sciences* 19(4):279–288, 2001.
19. Borg, G. *Borg's Perceived Exertion and Pain Scales*. Champaign, IL: Human Kinetics, 1998.
20. Keating, X. D., J. Guan, J. C. Pinero, D. M. Bridges. A meta-analysis of college students' physical activity behaviors. *Journal of American College Health* 54(2):116–125, 2005.
21. Storms, W. W. Review of exercise-induced asthma. *Medicine and Science in Sports and Exercise* 35 (9):1464–1470, 2003.

NAME ______________________________ DATE ______________

Measuring Cardiorespiratory Fitness: The 1.5-Mile Run Test

The objective of the test is to complete the 1.5-mile distance as quickly as possible. You can complete the run on an oval track or any properly measured course. If the run will take place outside, the test is best conducted in moderate weather conditions; avoid running it on very hot or very cold days. A good strategy is to try to keep a steady pace during the entire distance. Performing a practice test is a good way to get familiar with the distance and determine the ideal pace you can maintain. You should use a stopwatch to get an accurate time. You should attempt this test only if you have met the medical clearance criteria discussed in Chapter 1 of this text.

Before the test, perform a 5- to 10-minute warm-up. If you become extremely fatigued during the test, slow your pace or walk—do not overstress yourself! If you feel faint or nauseated or experience any unusual pains in your upper body, stop and notify your instructor.

After you complete the test, cool down and record your time and fitness category from Table 3.1 included in this lab. Find your age group along the top of the table, and then locate your time range according to your sex. The fitness classifications are along the left of the table.

Test date: ____________

Finish time: ____________

Fitness category: ____________

1. Is your fitness classification what you expected based on your current level of activity? If not, why do you think it was higher or lower than expected?

____

____

2. Write fitness goals for maintaining or improving your cardiorespiratory endurance. You might have to refer to Chapter 1 for a reminder on how to set goals.

____

____

TABLE 3.1
Fitness Categories for Cooper's 1.5-Mile Run Test

Fitness Category	Age (years) 13–19	20–29	30–39	40–49	50–59	60+
Men						
Very poor	>15:30	>16:00	>16:30	>17:30	>19:00	>20:00
Poor	12:11–15:30	14:01–16:00	14:46–16:30	15:36–17:30	17:01–19:00	19:01–20:00
Average	10:49–12:10	12:01–14:00	12:31–14:45	13:01–15:35	14:31–17:00	16:16–19:00
Good	9:41–10:48	10:46–12:00	11:01–12:30	11:31–13:00	12:31–14:30	14:00–16:15
Excellent	8:37–9:40	9:45–10:45	10:00–11:00	10:30–11:30	11:00–12:30	11:15–13:59
Superior	<8:37	<9:45	<10:00	<10:30	<11:00	<11:15
Women						
Very poor	>18:30	>19:00	>19:30	>20:00	>20:30	>21:00
Poor	16:55–18:30	18:31–19:00	19:01–19:30	19:31–20:00	20:01–20:30	20:31–21:31
Average	14:31–16:54	15:55–18:30	16:31–19:00	17:31–19:30	19:01–20:00	19:31–20:30
Good	12:30–14:30	13:31–15:54	14:31–16:30	15:56–17:30	16:31–19:00	17:31–19:30
Excellent	11:50–12:29	12:30–13:30	13:00–14:30	13:45–15:55	14:30–16:30	16:30–18:00
Superior	<11:50	<12:30	<13:00	<13:45	<14:30	<16:30

Times are given in minutes and seconds. (> = greater than; < = less than)

Source: From Cooper, K. *The Aerobics Program for Total Well-Being.* Bantam Books, New York, 1982. Copyright © 1982 by Kenneth H. Cooper. Used by permission of Bantam Books, a division of Random House, Inc.

NAME ______________________________ DATE ______________

Measuring Cardiorespiratory Fitness: The 1-Mile Walk Test

The objective of the test is to walk the 1-mile distance as quickly as possible. You can complete the walk on an oval track or any properly measured course. You should attempt this test only if you have met the medical clearance criteria discussed in Chapter 1 of this text.

Before the test, perform a 5- to 10-minute warm-up. If you become extremely fatigued during the test, slow your pace—do not overstress yourself! If you feel faint or nauseated or experience any unusual pains in your upper body, stop and notify your instructor.

After you complete the test, cool down and record your time and fitness category from Table 3.2 included in this lab. Find your age group along the top of the table, and then locate your time range according to your sex. The fitness classifications are along the left of the table.

Test date: ____________

Finish time: ____________

Fitness category: ____________

1. Is your fitness classification what you expected based on your current level of activity? If not, why do you think it was higher or lower than expected?

____

____

2. Write fitness goals for maintaining or improving your cardiorespiratory endurance. You might have to refer to Chapter 1 for a reminder on how to set goals.

____

____

TABLE 3.2
Fitness Classification for 1-Mile Walk Test

Fitness Category	*Age (years)* 13–19	20–29	30–39	40+
Men				
Very poor	>17:30	>18:00	>19:00	>21:30
Poor	16:01–17:30	16:31–18:00	17:31–19:00	18:31–21:30
Average	14:01–16:00	14:31–16:30	15:31–17:30	16:01–18:30
Good	12:30–14:00	13:00–14:30	13:30–15:30	14:00–16:00
Excellent	<12:30	<13:00	<13:30	<14:00
Women				
Very poor	>18:01	>18:31	>19:31	>20:01
Poor	16:31–18:00	17:01–18:30	18:01–19:30	19:31–20:00
Average	14:31–16:30	15:01–17:00	16:01–18:00	18:01–19:30
Good	13:31–14:30	13:31–15:00	14:01–16:00	14:31–18:00
Excellent	<13:30	<13:30	<14:00	<14:30

Because the 1-mile walk test is designed primarily for older or less conditioned individuals, the fitness categories listed here do not include a "superior" category.

Source: Modified from *Rockport Fitness Walking Test.* Copyright © 1993. The Rockport Company, Inc. All rights reserved. Reprinted by permission of The Rockport Company, Inc.

3.1C

LABORATORY

NAME ______________________ DATE ______________

Measuring Cardiorespiratory Fitness: Submaximal Cycle Test

This lab test is performed with a partner. While you are exercising, your partner will help by setting the workload for the test, checking your pedal rate, and taking your heart rate. The work performed on a cycle ergometer is commonly expressed either in *kilopond meters per minute (KPM)* or in watts. Your instructor will explain how to use the KPM and watts settings to adjust the workload.

Warm up for 3 minutes without using any resistance (unloaded pedaling). Your instructor will tell you how to adjust the workload. Set the appropriate load for your age, sex, and level of conditioning (Table 3.3), and begin pedaling at the rate of 50 revolutions per minute (RPM). Your instructor will set a metronome so you know how fast to pedal. Exercise for a 5-minute period. Your partner will take your heart rate during a 15-second period between minutes 4.5 and 5 of the test.

Cool down for 3 to 5 minutes without resistance. Record your heart rate (15-second count) below, and calculate your relative $\dot{V}O_2$max using Table 3.4. After calculating your relative $\dot{V}O_2$max, locate your fitness category in Table 3.5.

Test date: __________

Heart rate (15-second count) during minute 5 of test: __________

Fitness category: __________

1. Is your fitness classification what you expected based on your current level of activity? If not, why do you think it was higher or lower than expected?

____

____

2. Write fitness goals for maintaining or improving your cardiorespiratory endurance. You might have to refer to Chapter 1 for a reminder on how to set goals.

____

____

TABLE 3.3
Work Rates for Submaximal Cycle Ergometer Fitness Test

Gender	Age (years)	Pedal Speed (RPM)	Load	(watts)
Men				
	Up to 29	50	150	(900 KPM)
	30 and up	50	50	(300 KPM)
Women				
	Up to 29 (or well conditioned)	50	100	(600 KPM)
	30 and up (or poorly conditioned)	50	50	(300 KPM)

TABLE 3.4

Cycle Ergometer Fitness Index for Men and Women

Locate your 15-second heart rate in the left-hand column; then find your estimated $\dot{V}O_2max$ in the appropriate column on the right. For example, the second column from the left contains the absolute $\dot{V}O_2max$ (expressed in mL/min) for male subjects using the 900-KPM work rate. The third column from the left contains the absolute $\dot{V}O_2max$ (expressed in mL/min) for women using the 600-KPM work rate, and so on. After determination of your absolute $\dot{V}O_2max$, calculate your relative $\dot{V}O_2max$ (mL/kg/min) by dividing your $\dot{V}O_2max$ expressed in mL/min by your body weight in kilograms (1 kilogram = 2.2 pounds). For example, if your body weight is 70 kilograms and your absolute $\dot{V}O_2max$ is 2631 mL/min, your relative $\dot{V}O_2max$ is approximately 38 mL/kg/min (i.e., 2631 divided by 70 = 37.6). After computing your relative $\dot{V}O_2max$, use Table 3.5 to identify your fitness category.

	Estimated Absolute $\dot{V}O_2max$ (mL/min)		
15-Second Heart Rate	Men: 900-KPM Work Rate (mL/min)	Women: 600-KPM Work Rate (mL/min)	Men or Women: 300-KPM Work Rate (mL/min)
28	3560	2541	1525
29	3442	2459	1475
30	3333	2376	1425
31	3216	2293	1375
32	3099	2210	1325
33	2982	2127	1275
34	2865	2044	1225
35	2748	1961	1175
36	2631	1878	1125
37	2514	1795	1075
38	2397	1712	1025
39	2280	1629	—
40	2163	1546	—
41	2046	1463	—
42	1929	1380	—
43	1812	1297	—
44	1695	1214	—
45	1578	1131	—

TABLE 3.5

Cardiorespiratory Fitness Norms for Men and Women Based on Estimated $\dot{V}O_2max$ Values Determined by the Cycle Ergometer Fitness Test

After determining your relative $\dot{V}O_2max$ (mL/kg/min) in Table 3.4, find your appropriate fitness category.

Age Group (years)	*Fitness Categories Based on $\dot{V}O_2max$ (mL/kg/min)*					
	Very Poor	Poor	Average	Good	Excellent	Superior
Men						
18–25	<30	30–39	40–45	46–60	61–64	>64
26–35	<29	29–38	39–43	44–55	56–59	>59
36–45	<27	27–35	36–40	41–49	50–55	>55
46–45	<25	25–31	32–35	36–45	46–49	>49
56–65	<22	22–28	29–33	34–40	41–43	>43
>65	<20	20–25	26–28	29–34	35–38	>38
Women						
18–25	<30	30–38	39–43	44–54	55–58	>58
26–35	<28	28–33	34–41	42–53	54–58	>58
36–45	<24	24–32	33–36	37–46	47–50	>50
46–55	<22	22–28	29–31	32–41	42–45	>45
56–65	<19	19–25	26–29	30–36	37–40	>40
>65	<17	17–21	22–25	26–30	31–34	>34

Source: Data reprinted from Golding, L., (ed.). *YMCA Fitness Testing and Assessment Manual,* 4th Edition. With permission of the YMCA of the USA, Chicago IL. Copyright © 2000.

NAME ______________________________ DATE ____________

Measuring Cardiorespiratory Fitness: Step Test

To complete this test, you need a step or bench that is approximately 18 inches high, such as a locker room bench or a sturdy chair. The step test lasts for 3 minutes, and then heart rate is assessed in the 3.5 minutes following the test. You will need a metronome to help you maintain the step rate.

To perform this test, you will step up and down at a rate of 30 complete steps per minute. If you set the metronome to 60 tones per minute, you will step with each tone making a complete step (up, up, down, down) every 2 seconds. Note that it is important that you straighten your knees during the "up" phase of the test (see the figure). After you complete the test, sit quietly in a chair or on the step bench, and take your heart rate for 30 seconds at the following times:

1 to 1.5 minutes post exercise

2 to 2.5 minutes post exercise

3 to 3.5 minutes post exercise

Maintaining the 30-step-per-minute cadence and accurately taking your heart rate are very important for getting a good estimate from the step test. To determine your fitness category, add the three 30-second heart rates obtained during the period after exercise.

(a) (b)

Step test to evaluate cardiorespiratory fitness. (a, b) Subject steps up onto an 18-inch surface and then down (c, d) once every 2 seconds.

(c) (d)

Step test to evaluate cardiorespriatory fitness. (continued)

Record your heart rates below, and use Table 3.6 on the next page to determine your fitness category.

Test date: ____________

Recovery heart rate post exercise (bpm)

1–1.5 min: ____________

2–2.5 min: ____________

3–3.5 min: ____________

Total (recovery index): ____________

Fitness category: ____________

TABLE 3.6
Norms for Cardiorespiratory Fitness Using the Sum of Three Recovery Heart Rates Obtained Following the Step Test

	3-Minute Step Test Recovery Index	
Fitness Category	Women	Men
Superior	95–120	95–117
Excellent	121–135	118–132
Good	136–153	133–147
Average	154–174	148–165
Poor	175–204	166–192
Very Poor	205–233	193–217

Fitness categories are for college-aged men and women (aged 18–25 years) at the University of Florida who performed the test on an 18-inch bench.

1. Is your fitness classification what you expected based on your current level of activity? If not, why do you think it was higher or lower than expected?

____

____

2. Write fitness goals for maintaining or improving your cardiorespiratory endurance. You might have to refer to Chapter 1 for a reminder on how to set goals.

____

____

NAME ______________________ DATE ______________

Assessing Cardiorespiratory Fitness for Individuals with Disabilities

This test uses arm exercise and is for people who cannot perform exercise that requires use of the legs (people in wheelchairs or with leg or foot injuries). To perform this assessment, you will need an arm crank ergometer. Your instructor will adjust the ergometer to the correct height and position for the test.

First, do a warm-up with no resistance. Then your instructor will increase the resistance, and you will perform a 2-minute stage. Rest 5 to 10 minutes. Then, after your instructor increases the workload, perform another 2-minute period of arm exercise. Repeat this cycle until you cannot complete 2 minutes of exercise at a given workload. Your instructor will tell you the workload for the last stage in which you completed the full 2 minutes of exercise. You can use that number, along with Table 3.7 included in this lab, to determine your $\dot{V}O_2max$. After you find your weight and workload on the table, find the corresponding number and multiple that value by 3.5 to get your $\dot{V}O_2max$. If your weight is not on the table, you can use the following equation to calculate your $\dot{V}O_2max$:

$$\dot{V}O_2max = 3 \times (\text{work rate*})/\text{body weight in kg}\dagger + 3.5$$

Table 3.5 in Laboratory 3.1C has the fitness classifications that correspond to your $\dot{V}O_2max$. Because this test uses arm exercise, which involves a smaller muscle mass than leg or whole body exercise, your $\dot{V}O_2max$ estimate will be a slight underestimate.

Fitness category: ___________

1. Is your fitness classification what you expected based on your current level of activity? If not, why do you think it was higher or lower than expected?

   ____

   ____

2. Write fitness goals for maintaining or improving your cardiorespiratory endurance. You might have to refer to Chapter 1 for a reminder on how to set goals.

   ____

   ____

* Your instructor will give you this value.

† Weight in kg = weight in lbs ÷ 2.2

TABLE 3.7
Approximate Energy Requirements in METs* during Arm Ergometry

Body Weight		Power Output (kg/g/min and W†)					
kg	lb	150 25	300 50	450 75	600 100	750 125	900 (kg/m/min) 150 (W)
50	110	3.6	6.1	8.7	11.3	13.9	16.4
60	132	3.1	5.3	7.4	9.6	11.7	13.9
70	154	2.8	4.7	6.5	8.3	10.2	12.0
80	176	2.6	4.2	5.8	7.4	9.0	10.6
90	198	2.4	3.9	5.3	6.7	8.1	9.6
100	220	2.3	3.6	4.9	6.1	7.4	8.7

* 1 MET=3.5 ml/kg/min. This value is your $\dot{V}O_2$ at rest.

† W = watts.

Source: From American College of Sports Medicine. *ACSM's Guideline for Exercise Testing and Prescription,* 7th ed. Philadelphia: Lippincott, Williams, & Wilkins, 2006.

NAME ______________________ DATE ______________

Developing Your Personal Exercise Prescription

Using the boxes on pages 66–68 as models, develop your personal exercise program based on your current fitness level and goals. Record the appropriate information in the spaces provided below.

Week No.	Phase	Duration (min/day)	Intensity (% of HHR or RPE)	Frequency (days/week)	Exercise Mode	Comments
1						
2						
3						
4						
5						
6						
7						
8						
9						
10						
11						
12						
13						
14						
15						
16						

NAME ______________________ DATE ______________

Determining Rate of Perceived Exertion

Rate of perceived exertion (RPE) was originally developed to correspond to heart rates. Adding a zero to the numerical rating produces the expected heart rate range for that rating. However, people perceive exertion differently, so ratings do not always match heart rate values. The important thing to learn is the RPE number that corresponds to your threshold of training heart rate and the RPE that represents the upper-limit heart rate of your target heart rate (THR) range. Typically, numerical RPE ratings for exercise in the THR zone will fall between 12 and 16. With practice, you can learn to make accurate ratings.

Use the following RPE scale to rate your exertion.

Scale	Verbal Rating
6	No exertion at all
7	Extremely light
8	
9	Very light
10	
11	Light
12	
13	Somewhat hard
14	
15	Hard (heavy)
16	
17	Very hard
18	
19	Extremely hard
20	Maximal exertion

Perform the following exercises:

1. Walk for 3 minutes at a brisk pace.
2. Jog for 3 minutes at a slow pace.
3. Jog for 3 minutes at a pace that will elevate your heart rate to your threshold level.

LABORATORY 3.5 *(continued)*

After each exercise bout, take your heart rate. Also, rate the intensity of the exercise at the end of minute 3 using the RPE scale above. Record these values on the table that follows.

Next, perform a more intense 3-minute run that elevates your heart rate to the upper one-third of your THR zone. After the run, take your heart rate and give an RPE value.

Activity	Heart Rate (bpm)	Rating of Perceived Exertion
Walk		
Slow jog		
Faster jog (to reach training threshold)		
Intense run		

After you've completed your slow and faster jogs, answer the following questions:

1. Did you reach your heart rate training threshold with the walk or slow jog? ___ Yes ___ No
2. Was your RPE less than 12 for the walk or slow jog? ___ Yes ___ No
3. Was your RPE for the faster jog in the range of 12 to 16? ___ Yes ___ No
4. Did your heart rate reach the upper end of your THR for the run? ___ Yes ___ No
5. Was your RPE in the intense run in the range of 12 to 16? ___ Yes ___ No
6. Was your heart approximately 10 times your RPE? ___ Yes ___ No
7. With practice, do you think you could learn to use the RPE scale to assess your exercise intensity?

   ___ ___________

8. What are the limitations for using heart rate to assess your exercise intensity?

   ____

   ____

9. What are the limitations for using RPE to assess your exercise intensity?

   ____

   ____

4 Improving Muscular Strength and Endurance

true or false?

1. Women who lift weights will quickly develop "bulky" muscles.
2. Increasing muscle endurance will always increase muscle strength.
3. Muscle turns to fat if you don't use it regularly.
4. Weight lifters should take protein or other supplements to get bigger faster.
5. Strength training is important only when you are young.

Answers appear on the next page.

Can you imagine running the 26 continuous miles of a marathon or biking the 2241 miles in the Tour de France? Or would you consider competing in the Iron Man triathlon, in which you swim 2.4 miles, bike 112 miles, and then run 26.2 miles, all in less than 9 hours? These extraordinary feats of human performance are all possible because of the human body's great capacity for muscular strength and endurance. And although not everyone will compete in a bike race, marathon, or triathalon, improved muscular strength and endurance offers numerous everyday benefits for everyone.

In this chapter you'll learn about the everyday benefits of muscle strength and endurance, the anatomy and physiology behind them, how to assess your own level of muscle fitness, and how to develop an exercise plan to improve your strength and endurance.

The Need for Muscular Strength and Endurance in Daily Living

When you climb a flight of stairs or carry a heavy book bag across campus, you're relying on your muscular strength and endurance to perform the task without becoming exhausted. If you've ever worked in a job that required you to shuttle loaded trays of food among tables or move boxes from points A to B, you've relied on strength and endurance to earn your living. And if you play competitive or recreational sports, your skill level is determined in large part by the strength and reliability of your muscles. Whether we're aware of it or not, the strength and endurance of our muscles affects our physical performance numerous times every day.

Recall from Chapter 1 that muscular strength and endurance are related but are not the same thing. Muscular strength is the ability of a muscle to generate maximal force. In simple terms, muscular strength is the amount of weight that an individual can lift during one maximal effort. In contrast, muscular endurance is the ability to generate force over and over again. In general, increasing muscular strength by exercise training will also increase muscle endurance. However, training to improve muscular endurance does not significantly improve muscular strength.

Muscle strength and endurance can be increased and maintained with strength-training and endurance-training programs. In addition, regular strength training promotes numerous health benefits. For example, incidence of low back pain, a common problem in both men and women, can be reduced with the appropriate strengthening exercises for the lower back and abdominal muscles (1). Further, studies demonstrate that muscle-strengthening exercises may reduce the occurrence of joint and/or muscle injuries that occur during physical activity (2). Strength training can also delay the decrease in muscle strength experienced by sedentary older individuals (3) and may help prevent osteoporosis.

Another important benefit of strength training is that it increases **resting energy expenditure** in larger muscles. (4). Resting energy expenditure (also called *resting metabolic rate*) includes the energy required to drive the heart and respiratory muscles and to build

Answers

1. **FALSE** The male sex hormone testosterone affects muscle size. With the same amount of training, men will gain more muscle mass than women because they produce more testosterone.
2. **FALSE** The intensity and number of exercises you do to improve muscular endurance will not necessarily improve muscular strength.
3. **FALSE** Fat and muscle are two different types of tissue, and one cannot convert to the other. However, if you stop exercise and consume more calories than you expend, you may build up more fat tissue, and you will probably notice it in your physical appearance.
4. **FALSE** Buying supplements such as protein powders or pills is mostly a waste of your hard-earned funds. Although athletes do need slightly higher amounts of protein than less active people, their needs can be easily met through a healthy diet, so supplements are unnecessary.
5. **FALSE** Muscle strength and endurance are needed throughout the life span. Strength training for older individuals has been shown to help prevent falls and allow for independent living.

and maintain body tissues. An elevated metabolic rate allows the body to burn more calories throughout the day. Conversely, a lower metabolic rate burns fewer calories, thereby leading to weight gain.

How does strength training influence resting metabolic rate? One of the primary results of strength training is an increase in muscle mass in relation to body fat. An increase of 1 pound of muscle elevates resting metabolism by approximately 2–3%. This increase can be magnified with larger gains in muscle. For instance, a 5-pound increase in muscle mass results in a 10–15% increase in resting metabolic rate. Changes in resting metabolic rate of this magnitude can play an important role in helping you lose weight or maintaining desirable body composition throughout life. Although overall body weight may increase slightly as muscle mass increases, fat mass should decrease. Clothing may fit better, and self-image is likely to improve.

You now know that strength training will increase muscle mass. But how does this work, and how do muscles, in general work? We'll discuss this next.

Make sure you know...

> Muscular strength and endurance are important for numerous daily tasks. Strength training can reduce low back pain, reduce the incidence of exercise-related injuries, decrease the incidence of osteoporosis, and help maintain functional capacity that normally decreases with age.

> Muscular strength is the ability to generate maximal force, whereas muscular endurance is the ability to generate force over and over again.

> Strength training can improve a muscle's resting energy expenditure.

How Muscles Work: Structure and Function

There are about 600 skeletal muscles in the human body, and their primary function is to provide force for physical movement. When the muscles shorten or lengthen during a **muscle action**, they apply force to the bones, causing the body to move.

The skeletal muscles also are responsible for maintaining posture and help regulate body temperature through the mechanism of shivering (which results in heat production). Because all fitness activities require the use of skeletal muscles, anyone beginning a physical fitness program should understand basic muscle structure and function.

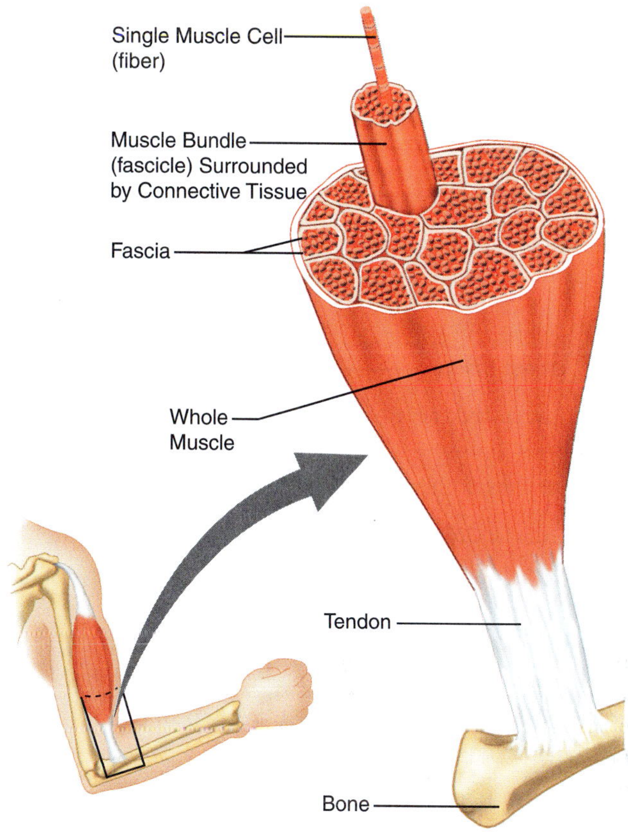

FIGURE 4.1
The structure of skeletal muscle.
Source: Johnson, M. *Human Biology,* 4th ed. San Francisco: Benjamin Cummings, 2008.

Muscle Structure

Skeletal muscle is a collection of long, thin cells called *fibers*. These fibers are surrounded by a dense layer of connective tissue called **fascia** that holds the individual fibers together and separates muscle from surrounding tissues (Figure 4.1).

Muscles are attached to bones by connective tissues known as **tendons.** Muscular action causes the tendons to pull on the bones, thereby causing movement. Muscles cannot push the bones; they can only

resting energy expenditure The amount of energy expended during all sedentary activities. Also called *resting metabolic rate*.

muscle action The shortening of a skeletal muscle (causing movement) or the lengthening of a skeletal muscle (resisting movement).

fascia A thin layer of connective tissue that surrounds the muscle.

tendon A fibrous connective tissue that attaches muscle to bone.

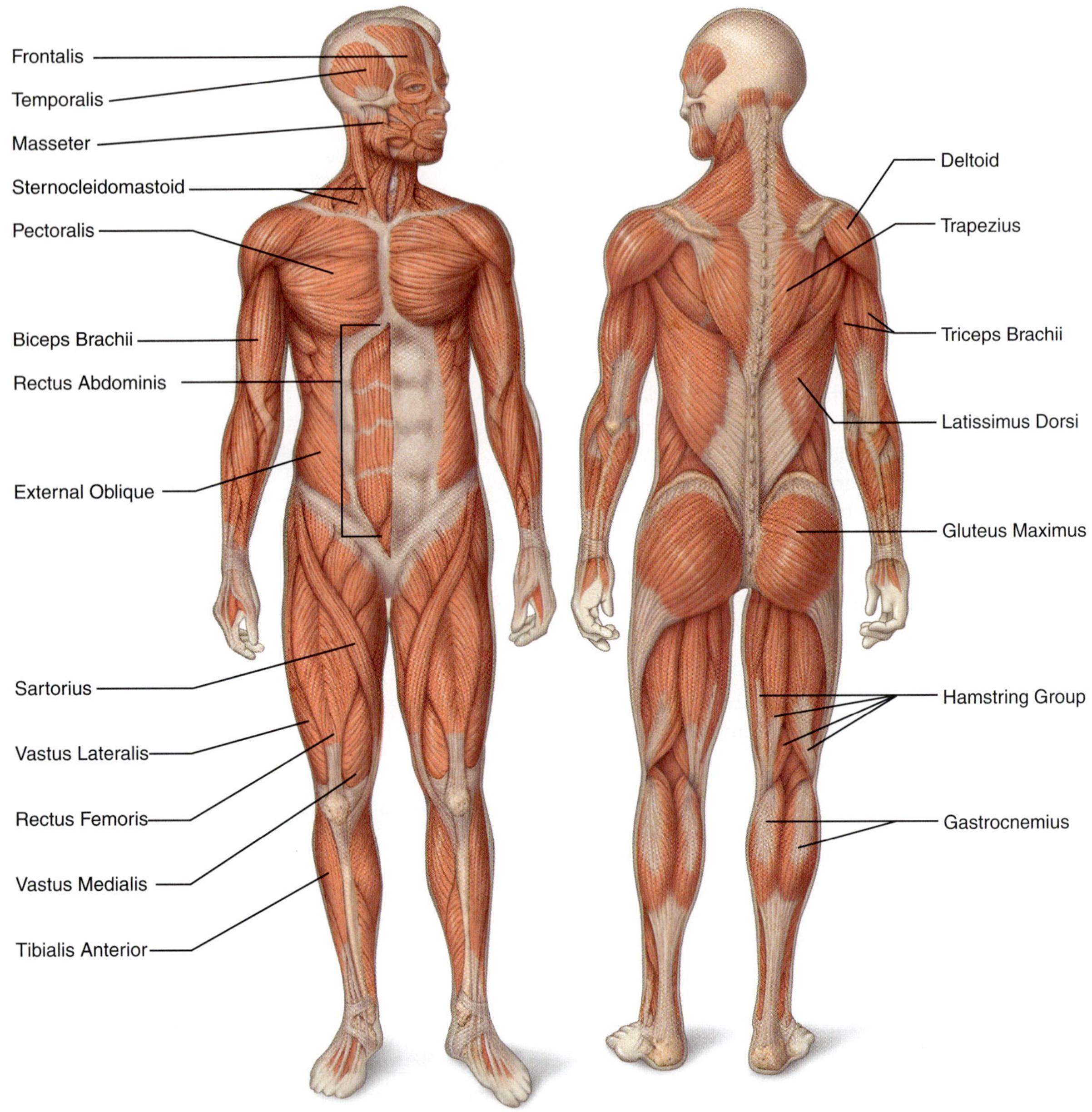

FIGURE 4.2
Major muscles of the human body.
Source: Johnson, M. *Human Biology,* 4th ed. San Francisco: Benjamin Cummings, 2008.

pull them. Many of the muscles involved in movement are illustrated in Figure 4.2.

Muscle Function

Muscle actions are regulated by electrical signals from motor nerves. Motor nerves originate in the spinal cord and send messages to individual muscles throughout the body. A motor nerve and an individual muscle fiber make contact at a neuromuscular junction (Figure 4.3). Note from the figure that each motor nerve branches and then connects with numerous individual muscle fibers.

The motor nerve and all of the muscle fibers it controls comprise a **motor unit.** Motor units come in various sizes, depending on how many muscle fibers they contain. A motor nerve can innervate a few muscle fibers for fine motor control, such as blinking the eye, or it can innervate many muscle fibers for gross motor movement, such as kicking a ball.

A muscle action begins when a message to develop tension (called a nerve impulse) reaches the neuromus-

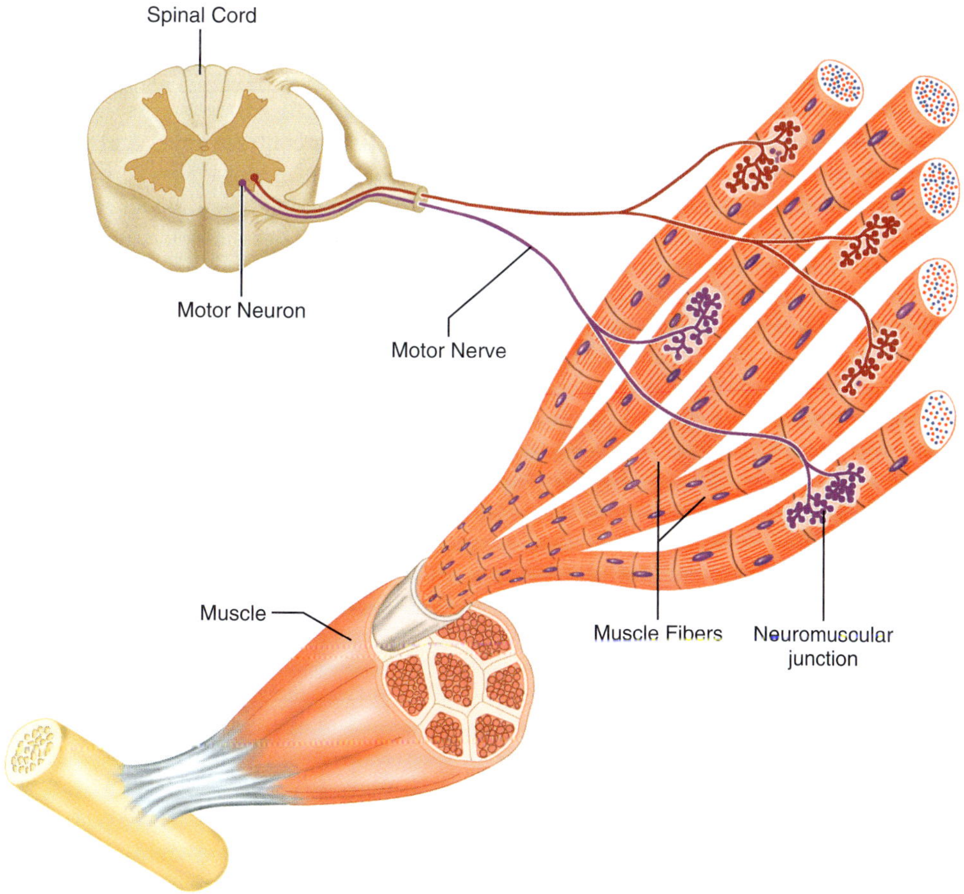

FIGURE 4.3
A motor unit. Two motor nerves from the central nervous system are shown innervating several muscle fibers. With one impulse from the motor nerve, all fibers respond.

cular junction. The arrival of the nerve impulse triggers the action process by permitting the interaction of contractile proteins in muscle. Just as the nerve impulse initiates the contractile process, the removal of the nerve signal from the muscle "turns it off." That is, when a motor nerve ceases to send signals to a muscle, the muscle action stops. Occasionally, however, an uncontrolled muscular action occurs, which results in a muscle cramp or a muscle twitch.

Muscle Exercise and Muscle Actions

Skeletal muscle exercise is classified into three major categories: **isotonic, isometric,** and **isokinetic.** Isotonic (also called *dynamic*) exercise results in movement of a body part at a joint. Most exercise or sports activities are isotonic. For example, lifting a dumbbell involves movement of the forearm and is therefore classified as an isotonic exercise.

An isometric (also called *static*) exercise requires the development of muscular tension but results in no movement of body parts. A classic example of isometric exercise is pressing the palms of the hands together. Although there is tension within the muscles of the arms and chest, the arms do not move. Isometric exercises are an excellent way to develop strength during the early stages of an injury rehabilitation program.

Isokinetic exercises are performed at a constant velocity; that is, the speed of muscle shortening or lengthening is regulated at a fixed, controlled rate. This is generally accomplished by using a machine

motor unit A motor nerve and all of the muscle fibers it controls.

isotonic A type of exercise in which there is movement of a body part. Most exercise or sports skills are isotonic exercise. Also called *dynamic* exercise.

isometric A type of exercise in which muscular tension is developed but the body part does not move. Also called *static* exercise.

isokinetic A type of exercise that can include concentric or eccentric muscle actions performed at a constant speed using a specialized machine.

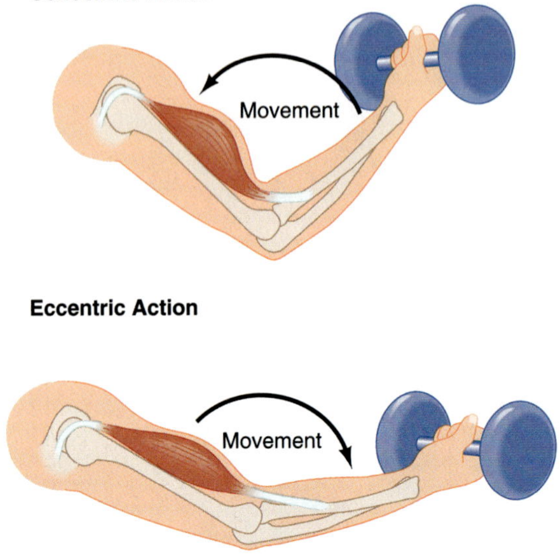

FIGURE 4.4
Concentric and eccentric muscle actions in an isotonic exercise. The muscle shortens during a concentric action and lengthens during an eccentric action.
Source: Adapted from Powers, S., and E. Howley. *Exercise Physiology: Theory and Application to Fitness and Performance,* 5th ed. Copyright 2003. Reprinted by permission of McGraw-Hill Companies.

that provides an accommodating resistance throughout the full **range of motion.**

Muscle actions can similarly be classified as isometric, concentric, or eccentric, depending on the activity the muscle needs to perform. Like isometric exercise, isometric muscle actions are static and do not involve any joint movement. An isometric muscle action occurs during isometric exercises.

A **concentric muscle action** causes movement of the body part against resistance or gravity and occurs when the muscle shortens. Concentric muscle actions (also called *positive work*) can be performed during isotonic or isokinetic exercise. For example, the upward movement of the arm during a bicep curl (Figure 4.4, top) is an example of a concentric muscle action.

In contrast, **eccentric muscle actions** (also called *negative work*) control movement with resistance or gravity and occur when the muscle lengthens. The downward or lowering phase of the bicep curl is controlled as the biceps muscle lengthens (Figure 4.4, bottom). Here, the muscle is developing tension, but the force developed is not great enough to prevent the weight from being lowered.

Types of Muscle Fibers

There are three types of skeletal muscle fibers: slow-twitch, intermediate, and fast-twitch. These fiber types differ in their speeds of action and in fatigue resistance (5). Because most human muscles contain a mixture of all three fiber types, it is helpful to understand each of them before beginning the strength-training process.

Slow-Twitch Fibers

As the name implies, **slow-twitch fibers** contract slowly and produce small amounts of force; however, these fibers are highly resistant to fatigue. Slow-twitch fibers appear red or darker in color because of the numerous capillaries that supply the fibers. They have the capacity to produce large quantities of adenosine triphosphate (ATP) aerobically, which makes them ideally suited for a low-intensity, prolonged exercise, such as walking or slow jogging. Because of their resistance to fatigue, most postural muscles are composed primarily of slow-twitch fibers.

Fast-Twitch Fibers

Fast-twitch fibers contract rapidly and generate great amounts of force, but fatigue quickly. These fibers have a low aerobic capacity and appear white because they are supplied by only a few capillaries. Fast-twitch fibers are well equipped to produce ATP anaerobically, but only for a short time. With their ability to shorten rapidly and produce large amounts of force, fast-twitch fibers are used during activities requiring rapid or forceful movement, such as jumping, sprinting, and weight lifting. In strenuous exercise, these fibers are most easily damaged and cause soreness.

Intermediate Fibers

Intermediate fibers have a combination of characteristics found in fast- and slow-twitch fibers. They contract rapidly, produce great force, and resist fatigue because they have a well-developed aerobic capacity. Intermediate fibers contract more quickly and produce more force than slow-twitch fibers, but they contract more slowly and produce less force than fast-twitch fibers. They are slightly redder in appearance than fast-twitch fibers but are not as red as the slow-twitch fibers. Table 4.1 summarizes the properties of all three fiber types.

You can see the differences in fiber types during your next chicken or turkey dinner. The dark meat of a chicken drumstick contains primarily slow-twitch fibers. Because these fibers are slow to fatigue, a living bird is able to walk around most of the day. The white meat in the chicken breast is composed of mostly fast-twitch fibers. Fast-twitch fibers allow the bird to fly, but only for short distances before fatiguing. The intermediate fibers found in the bird's wings exhibit the beneficial characteristics of each fiber type—they resist fatigue and generate high force.

Individual Variations in Fiber Type

People vary in the number of slow-twitch, intermediate, and fast-twitch fibers their muscles contain; however, the average nonathlete generally has equal num-

TABLE 4.1
Properties of Human Skeletal Muscle Fiber Types

	Fiber Type		
Property	**Slow-Twitch**	**Intermediate**	**Fast-Twitch**
Contraction speed	Slow	Intermediate	Fast
Resistance to fatigue	High	Intermediate	Low
Predominant energy system	Aerobic	Combination aerobic and anaerobic	Anaerobic
Force generation	Low	Intermediate	High
Color	Red	White (pink)	White
Best suited for	Endurance events (marathon)	Middle-distance events (5–10 K)	Fast events (100-m sprint)

bers of all three fiber types. Research has shown a relationship between muscle fiber type and athletic success. For example, champion endurance athletes, such as marathon runners, have a predominance of slow-twitch fibers. This finding is logical, because endurance sports require muscles with high fatigue resistance. In contrast, elite sprinters, such as 100-meter runners, have more fast-twitch fibers.

Muscle fiber type has also been suggested as a link to obesity and diabetes (6, 7). Individuals with a predominance of fast-twitch muscle fibers may be more susceptible to obesity and developing diabetes than those with a predominance of slow-twitch muscle fibers.

Some evidence has shown that fibers can be converted from one type to another. For example, endurance training has been shown to cause some fiber conversion between the intermediate- and fast-twitch fibers. However, there is limited evidence to support that fast- or intermediate-twitch fibers convert to slow-twitch fibers (8). This means that athletes that do well in short distances can stretch their careers by moving to intermediate distances, and athletes that do well at long distances can also move to the intermediate distances. But a long-distance athlete would not be able to switch to a short-distance event. Lance Armstrong, for example, started doing Iron Man for Kids triathlons when he was 13. He had a great career as a long-distance bicyclist. He is now training for the marathon.

Although endurance exercise training has been shown to cause some fiber conversion, the number and percentage of skeletal muscle fiber types are strongly influenced by genetics (5).

Recruitment of Muscle Fibers during Exercise

Many types of exercise use only a small fraction of the muscle fibers available in a muscle group. For example, walking at a slow speed may use fewer than 30% of the muscle fibers in the legs. More intense types of exercise, however, require more force. To generate more force, a greater number of muscle fibers must be called into play. The process of involving more muscle fibers to produce increased muscular force is called **fiber recruitment.** Figure 4.5 illustrates the order in which muscle fibers are recruited as the intensity of exercise increases. Note that during low-intensity exercise, only slow-twitch fibers are used. As the exercise intensity increases, fibers are progressively recruited, from slow-twitch to intermediate fibers and finally to fast-twitch fibers. High-intensity activities, such as weight training, recruit large numbers of fast-twitch fibers.

range of motion The amount of movement possible at a joint.

concentric muscle action Action in which the muscle develops tension as it shortens against resistance and/or gravity. Also called *positive work*.

eccentric muscle action Action in which the muscle develops tension as it lengthens while controlling the movement with gravity. Also called *negative work*.

slow-twitch fibers Red muscle fibers that contract slowly and are highly resistant to fatigue. These fibers have the capacity to produce large quantities of ATP aerobically.

fast-twitch fibers White muscle fibers that contract rapidly but fatigue quickly. These fibers have a low aerobic capacity and produce ATP anaerobically.

intermediate fibers Muscle fibers with a combination of the characteristics of fast- and slow-twitch fibers. They contract rapidly and are fatigue resistant because they have a well-developed aerobic capacity.

fiber recruitment The process of involving more muscle fibers to increase muscular force.

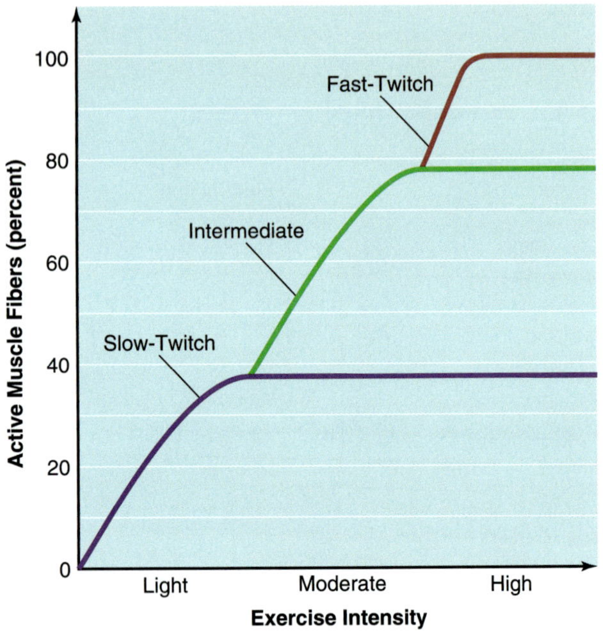

FIGURE 4.5
The relationship between exercise intensity and recruitment of muscle-fiber type.
Source: Adapted from Powers, S., and E. Howley. *Exercise Physiology: Theory and Application to Fitness and Performance*. Copyright 2003. Reprinted by permission of McGraw-Hill Companies.

Muscular Strength

Two physiological factors determine the amount of force that a muscle can generate: the size of the muscle and the number of fibers recruited during the contraction. Muscle size is the primary factor. The larger the muscle, the greater the force it can produce.

Although there is no difference in the chemical makeup of muscle in men and women, men tend to have more muscle mass and are therefore generally stronger. The larger muscle mass is due to higher levels of the hormone testosterone in men, which helps build muscle. The fact that testosterone promotes an increase in muscle size has led some athletes to use drugs in an attempt to improve muscular strength (see A Closer Look below).

The other significant factor that determines how much force is generated is the number of fibers recruited for a given movement. The more muscle fibers that are stimulated, the greater the total muscle force generated, because the force generated by individual fibers is additive (Figure 4.6).

Muscle fiber recruitment is regulated voluntarily through the nervous system. That is, we decide how much effort to put into a particular movement. For instance, when we choose to make a minimal effort to lift an object, we recruit only a few motor units, and the muscle develops limited force. However, if we decide to exert maximal effort to lift a heavy object, many muscle fibers are recruited, and a larger force is generated. Have you ever tried to open a locked door? If you didn't know the door was locked, your first attempt might involve minimal effort and few muscle fibers, because you hadn't anticipated having to use much force. However, once your first attempt didn't work, you might try again and recruit more muscle fibers to call upon more force to open the door. This process might continue until you either exerted enough force to yank the door open or gave up to go look for the key.

A CLOSER LOOK: ANABOLIC STEROID USE INCREASES MUSCLE SIZE BUT HAS SERIOUS SIDE EFFECTS

The abuse of *anabolic steroids* (synthetic forms of the hormone testosterone) and their precursors has mushroomed over the past several decades. The fierce competition in body building and other sports that require strength and power has driven both men and women to risk serious health consequences in the quest to develop large muscles.

The large doses of steroids needed to increase muscle mass produce several health risks. A partial list of the side effects caused by abusing steroids and their precursors includes liver cancer, increased blood pressure, increased levels of "bad" cholesterol, severe depression, and prostate cancer. Prolonged use and high doses of steroids can be lethal.

One of the most popular chemical precursors to testosterone, androstenedione, is used to increase blood testosterone with the intent to increase strength, lean body mass, and sexual performance. However, research indicates that androstenedione does not significantly increase strength and/or lean body mass.

Another precursor to testosterone production in the body, dehydroepiandrosterone (DHEA), has also been used to increase testosterone in the body. DHEA is also advertised as a weight-loss and anti-aging supplement capable of improving libido, vitality, and immunity levels. However, the best evidence demonstrates that DHEA supplementation does not increase testosterone concentrations or increase strength in men, and it may have masculinizing effects in women.

Make sure you know...

- Skeletal muscle is composed of various types of fibers that are attached to bone by tendons.
- Skeletal muscle actions are regulated by signals coming from motor nerves. A motor unit consists of a motor nerve and all the muscle fibers it controls.
- Exercise can be isometric, isotonic, or isokinetic. Isometric actions do not result in movement, whereas isotonic actions move a body part.
- Isometric exercise involves isometric muscle actions. Isotonic and isokinetic exercises use concentric actions (muscle shortens) and eccentric actions (muscle lengthens).
- Slow-twitch muscle fibers shorten slowly but are fatigue resistant. Fast-twitch fibers shorten rapidly but fatigue rapidly. Intermediate fibers shorten quickly but fatigue slowly.
- The process of involving more muscle fibers to produce increased muscular force is called fiber recruitment.
- Two factors determine muscle force: the size of the muscle and the number of fibers recruited.

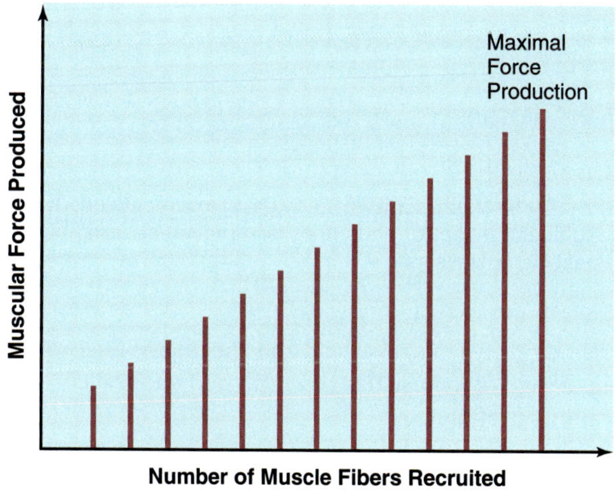

FIGURE 4.6
The relationship between recruitment of motor units and production of muscular force.

Evaluation of Muscular Strength and Endurance

Muscular strength can be assessed by the **one-repetition maximum (1 RM) test,** which measures the maximum amount of weight that can be lifted one time. Although the 1 RM test for muscular strength is widely accepted, it has been criticized as unsuitable for use by older individuals or highly deconditioned people (9). The major concern is the risk of injury. The 1 RM test should therefore be attempted only after several weeks of strength training, which will improve both skill and strength and will reduce the risk of injury. An older or sedentary individual would probably require 6 weeks of exercise training prior to the 1 RM test, whereas a physically active college-aged student could probably perform the 1 RM test after 1 to 2 weeks of training. See Laboratory 4.1 for a step-by-step walk through of the 1 RM test.

To further reduce the possibility of injury during strength testing, researchers have also developed a method to estimate the 1 RM using a series of submaximal lifts. Although this method is slightly less accurate, it does reduce the risk of injury. You can read instructions for performing this test in Laboratory 4.2.

Muscular endurance is usually evaluated with two simple tests: the **push-up test** and either the **sit-up test** or **curl-up test.** Push-ups require endurance of the shoulder, arm, and chest muscles, whereas sits-ups and curl-ups primarily require endurance of the abdominal muscles. To learn how to perform these tests and assess your own muscular endurance, turn to Laboratory 4.3 at the end of the chapter.

Make sure you know...

- The 1 RM test can be used to evaluate muscular strength.
- To reduce the possibility of injury, the estimated 1 RM test can be performed instead of the 1 RM test.
- The push-up and sit-up (or curl-up) tests are used to evaluate muscular endurance.

Principles for Designing a Strength and Endurance Program

In Chapter 2 we discussed the general principles for developing training programs to improve physical fitness. Before we discuss the specifics of how to develop a strength-training program, let's discuss how two

one-repetition maximum (1 RM) test Measurement of the maximum amount of weight that can be lifted one time.

push-up test A fitness test designed to evaluate endurance of shoulder and arm muscles.

sit-up test A test to evaluate abdominal and hip muscle endurance.

curl-up test A test to evaluate abdominal muscle endurance.

High Resistance + Low Repetitions = Increased Strength

Low Resistance + High Repetitions = Increased Endurance

FIGURE 4.7
Muscular strength is improved by using low repetitions/high weight, and muscular endurance is improved by using high repetitions/low weight.

training principles, overload and specificity, factor in the design of a muscular strength- and endurance-training program.

Progressive Resistance Exercise

The concept of **progressive resistance exercise (PRE)** is an application of the overload principle to strength and endurance exercise programs. If your goal is to develop strong biceps muscles, you must progressively increase the resistance that you lift. For example, you may begin your program using 10-pound dumbbells and perform one set of 8 repetitions 3 times a week. As this exercise becomes easier, you can progressively increase the workload by increasing the weight, increasing the number of sets up to 3, and/or increasing the number of repetitions up to 12.

Specificity of Training

The principle of **specificity of training** states that development of muscular strength and endurance is specific to both the muscle group that is exercised and the training intensity. Only those muscles that are trained will improve in strength and endurance. To improve the strength of the back muscles, for example, you need to train the specific muscles involved with movement of the lower back.

The intensity of training will determine whether the muscular adaptation is primarily an increase in strength or in endurance (Figure 4.7). High-intensity training (e.g., lifting heavy weights 6 to 8 times) increases muscular strength but yields only limited improvements in muscular endurance. Conversely, high-repetition, low-intensity training (e.g., lifting light weights 20–25 times or more) increases muscular endurance but yields only limited improvements in muscular strength.

Make sure you know...

> In the context of strength and endurance training, the PRE principle means you need to progressively increase the amount of resistance with which you train.

> The intensity of training determines whether you primarily increase muscular strength or endurance. High-intensity training will increase muscle strength and size; low-intensity training will increase muscular endurance.

Strength Training: How the Body Adapts

What physiological changes result from strength training? How quickly can you gain muscular strength? Do men and women differ in their responses to weight-training programs? Let's address these questions next.

Physiological Changes Due to Weight Training

You now know that programs designed to improve muscular strength can do so only by increasing muscular size and/or by increasing the number of muscle fibers recruited. Strength training alters both these factors (10). Research has shown that strength-training programs increase muscular strength first by altering fiber recruitment patterns, and then by increasing muscle size.

Increase in muscle size is due primarily to an increase in fiber size, called **hypertrophy** (10). Most research has shown that strength training has little effect on the formation of new muscle fibers, a process called **hyperplasia.** The role that hyperplasia plays in the increase in muscle size due to strength training remains controversial (11). Regardless, the increase in muscle size depends on diet, the muscle fiber type (fast-twitch fibers may hypertrophy more than slow-twitch fibers), blood levels of testosterone, and the type of training program.

Although strength training does not result in significant improvements in cardiorespiratory fitness (12), a regular weight-training program can provide positive changes in both body composition and flexibility. For most men and women, rigorous weight training results in an increase in muscle mass and in loss of body fat, both of which decrease the percentage of body fat.

Performing weight-training exercises over the full range of motion at a joint can improve flexibility (9). In fact, many diligent weight lifters have excellent flexibility. Therefore, the notion that weight lifting causes inflexibility is generally incorrect.

Rate of Strength Improvement with Weight Training

How rapidly does strength improvement occur? The answer depends on your initial strength level. Strength gains occur rapidly in untrained people, whereas gains are more gradual in individuals with relatively higher strength levels. In fact, for a novice lifter, strength gains can occur very quickly (13). These rapid strength gains tend to motivate the lifter to stick with a regular weight-training program.

Gender Differences in Response to Weight Training

Men and women do not differ in their initial responses to weight training programs (14). On a percentage basis, women gain strength as rapidly as men during the first 12 weeks of a strength-training program. However, as a result of long-term weight training, men generally exhibit a greater increase in muscle size than do women. The reason is that men have 20 to 30 times more testosterone than do women.

Make sure you know...

> Muscle size increases primarily because of hypertrophy (increase in size) of muscle fibers.
> Strength training promotes positive changes in both body composition and flexibility.
> The rate of improvement in weight training depends on initial strength level.
> Early in a weight-training program, women gain strength as fast as men.

Designing a Training Program for Increasing Muscle Strength

There are numerous approaches to designing weight-training programs. Any program that adheres to the basic principles described earlier will improve strength and endurance. However, the type of weight-training program that you develop for yourself depends on your goals and the types of equipment available to you. There are several other factors to consider in developing a weight-training program: we discuss those next.

Safety Concerns

Before beginning any weight-training program, you need to think about safety. Follow these safety guidelines when weight training:

- When using free weights (such as barbells), have spotters (helpers) help you perform the exercises. The purpose of a spotter is to help you complete a lift if you are unable to do it on your own. Using weight machines reduces the need for spotters.
- Be sure that the collars on the end of the bars of free weights are tightly secured to prevent the weights from falling off. Dropping weight plates on toes and feet can result in serious injuries. Again, many weight machines have safety features that reduce the risk of dropping weights.
- Warm up properly before doing any weight-lifting exercise. Stretching the intended muscles and lifting very light weight is a good way to start.
- Do not hold your breath during weight lifting. To prevent breath holding, follow this breathing pattern: Exhale while lifting the weight, and inhale while lowering it. Also, breathe through both your nose and mouth.
- Although debate continues as to whether high-speed weight lifting yields greater strength gains than slow-speed lifting, slow movements may reduce the risk of injury. A general rule of thumb is to lift the weight on the count of 2 and to lower the weight on the count of 4.
- Use light weights in the beginning so that you can maintain the proper form through the full range of motion in each exercise. This is particularly important when you are lifting free weights.

Types of Weight-Training Programs

Weight-training programs specifically designed to improve strength and programs designed to improve muscular endurance differ mainly in the number of repetitions and the amount of resistance (10). The combination of low repetition and high resistance appears to be the optimal training method to increase strength; moreover, this type of training improves muscular endurance as well. In contrast, weight training using high repetition and low resistance improves endurance but results in only small strength increases, particularly in less fit individuals.

As with types of weight-training exercise, weight-training programs can be divided into three general categories: isotonic, isometric, and isokinetic.

progressive resistance exercise (PRE) Application of the overload principle to strength and endurance exercise programs.

specificity of training The concept that the development of muscular strength and endurance, as well as cardiorespiratory endurance, is specific to both the muscle group exercised and the training intensity.

hypertrophy An increase in muscle fiber size.

hyperplasia An increase in the number of muscle fibers.

STEPS FOR BEHAVIOR CHANGE

Are you reluctant to strength train?

Answer the following questions to assess the barriers that prevent you from starting a strength-training program.

Y	N	
☐	☐	I feel intimidated by other people in the strength-training facility.
☐	☐	I cannot find time in my schedule to exercise.
☐	☐	I do not know how to use the various machines or free weights.
☐	☐	I do not know how to begin a strength-training program.

If you answered yes to more than one question, check out the following tips to help you break through the barriers.

TIPS TO EASE YOURSELF INTO A STRENGTH-TRAINING ROUTINE

☑ Fitness facilities cater to a wide range of clients, from beginners to professional body builders. Do your homework and find a facility that makes you feel welcome and comfortable.

☑ Make a commitment to set aside 30–60 minutes a day for training, and do not allow others to interfere with your personal time. Personal fitness does require a time commitment, but you are worth the investment.

☑ Take an orientation tour through a fitness facility to familiarize yourself with the machines and equipment. If you feel you need more individualized instruction, hire a personal trainer at the facility.

☑ Most facilities have fitness professionals that will assess your overall strength and suggest a starting program. The facility may also provide personal trainers for a reasonable hourly rate.

Isotonic Programs Isotonic programs involve contracting a muscle against a movable load (usually a free weight or weights on a weight machine). The load is lifted on the up phase using concentric muscle actions and then lowered on the down phase using eccentric muscle actions. Isotonic programs are the most common type of weight-training program in use today.

Weight-training machines are ideal for the beginning exerciser because the weight is mounted to a cable or chain. If you were unable to complete a lift using a heavy weight and accidentally let go of the bar, the weights would slam down on the weight stack without injuring you or someone else. In addition, machines allow a single joint to be isolated and exercised.

Free weights are preferred by many serious weight lifters because they can be used to exercise multiple joints. For example, the squat exercise involves muscles at the hip, knee, and ankle, thus allowing three joints to be exercised during one movement.

Isometric Programs An isometric strength-training program is based on the concept of contracting a muscle at a fixed angle against an immovable object, using an isometric muscle action. Interest in strength training increased dramatically during the 1950s with the finding that maximal strength could be increased by contracting a muscle for 6 seconds at two-thirds of maximal tension once per day for 5 days per week. Although subsequent studies suggested that these claims were exaggerated, it is generally agreed that isometric training can increase muscular strength and endurance (9).

Two important aspects of isometric training make it different from isotonic training. First, in isometric training, the development of strength and endurance is specific to the joint angle at which the muscle group is trained (15). Therefore, if you use isometric techniques, you will need to perform isometric contractions at several different joint angles if you want to gain strength and endurance throughout a full range of motion. In contrast, because isotonic contractions generally involve the full range of joint motion, strength is developed over the full movement pattern.

Second, the static nature of isometric muscle actions can lead to breath holding (called a **Valsalva maneuver**), which can reduce blood flow to the brain and cause dizziness and fainting. In an individual at high risk for coronary disease, the maneuver could be extremely dangerous and should always be avoided. Remember: Continue to breathe during any type of isometric or isotonic exercise.

Isokinetic Programs Recall that isokinetic exercise involves concentric or eccentric muscle actions performed at a constant speed (*isokinetic* refers to constant speed of movement). Isokinetic training is a relatively underused strength-training method, so limited research exists to describe its strength benefits compared with those of isometric and isotonic programs.

Isokinetic exercises require the use of machines that govern the speed of movement during muscle actions. The first isokinetic machines available were very expensive and were used primarily in clinical settings for injury rehabilitation. Recently, less expensive machines use a piston device (much like a shock absorber on a car) to limit the speed of movement throughout the range of the exercise.

Make sure you know...

- The greatest strength gains are made with a training program using low repetitions and high resistance, whereas the greatest improvement in endurance is made using high repetitions and low resistance.
- Isotonic programs include exercises with movable loads. Isometric training includes exercises in which a muscle contracts at a fixed angle against an immovable object. Isokinetic exercises involve machines that govern speed of movement during muscle contraction.

Exercise Prescription for Weight Training

We introduced in Chapter 2 the general concepts of the frequency, intensity, and duration (or time) of exercise required to improve physical fitness. Although these same concepts apply to improving muscular strength and endurance through weight training, the terminology used to monitor the intensity and duration of weight training is unique. For example, the intensity of weight training is measured not by heart rate but by the number of *repetition maximums*. Similarly, the duration of weight training is monitored not by actual time but by the number of sets performed. Let's discuss these two concepts briefly.

The intensity of exercise in both isotonic and isokinetic weight-training programs is measured by the repetition maximum (RM). Recall from earlier in the chapter that 1 RM is the maximal load that a muscle group can lift one time. Similarly, 6 RM is the maximal load that can be lifted six times. Therefore, the amount of weight lifted is greater when you perform a low

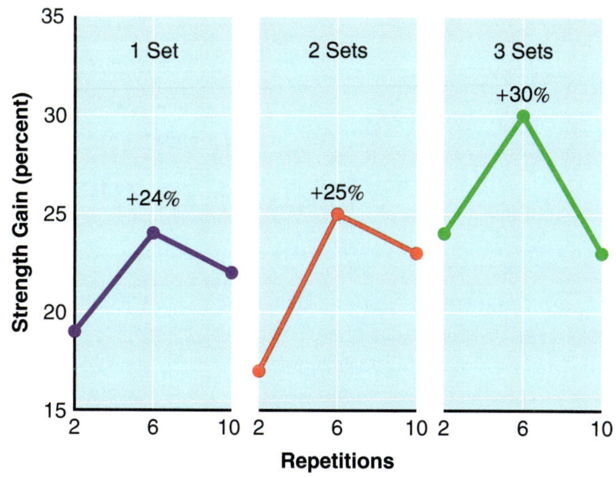

FIGURE 4.8
Strength gains from a resistance-training program consisting of various sets and repetitions. All programs were performed 3 days a week for 12 weeks. Note that the greatest strength gains (+30% improvement) were obtained using 3 sets of 6 reps per set.
Source: Adapted from Fox, E., R. Bowers, and M. Foss. *Fox's Physiological Basis of Exercise and Sports.* Copyright 1998, McGraw-Hill.

number of RM than a high number of RM; that is, the weight lifted while you perform 4 RM is greater than the weight lifted while you perform 15 RM.

The number of repetitions (reps) performed consecutively without resting is called a **set.** For example, if you lift 6 RM, 1 set = 6 reps. Because the amount of rest required between sets will vary among individuals depending on how fit they are, the duration of weight training is measured by the number of sets performed, not by actual time.

Although some experts disagree as to the optimum number of reps and sets required to improve strength and endurance, they do agree on some general guidelines. To improve strength, 3 sets of 6 reps for each exercise are generally recommended. Applying the concept of progressive resistance to a strength-training program involves increasing the amount of weight to be lifted a specific number of reps. For example, suppose that 3 sets of 6 reps were selected as your exercise prescription for increasing strength. As the training progresses and you become stronger, the amount of weight you lift must be increased. A good rule of thumb is that once you can perform 10 reps easily, you should increase the load to a level at which 6 reps are again maximal. Figure 4.8 illustrates the relationship between strength improvement and various combinations of reps and sets.

Valsalva maneuver Breath holding during an intense muscle contraction; can reduce blood flow to the brain and cause dizziness and fainting.

set The number of repetitions performed consecutively without resting.

A CLOSER LOOK DO WEIGHT LIFTERS NEED LARGE AMOUNTS OF PROTEIN IN THEIR DIETS?

Although many nutritional supplement companies claim that weight lifters require large quantities of protein in their diets, organizations such as the American College of Sports Medicine (ACSM), American Dietetic Association (ADA), and Dietitians of Canada (DC) have concluded that athletes have only slightly higher protein requirements than nonathletes. These organizations have also found that most athletes consume protein far in excess of any increased protein requirement. Provided that sound nutrition principles are followed and energy intake is sufficient to maintain body weight, athletes require about 10–15% of their total caloric intake from protein and do not need to fortify their diets with expensive protein powders or amino acid supplements. The table at right illustrates the daily energy and protein requirements for the average endurance or strength athlete.

Daily Protein Requirement for a 154-lb Active Individual*

Type of Athlete	Energy (Calories per day)	Grams of Protein per lb Body Weight per Day	Total Grams of Protein per Day	% of Daily Calories
Endurance	3800	0.55–0.64	84–98	9–10
Strength	3200	0.73–0.77	112–119	14–15

*Values assume a resting energy expenditure equivalent to 40 Kcal per kilogram (18 Kcal/lb) of body weight per day; a male runner who runs 10 miles per day at a pace of 6 minutes per mile with an energy expenditure for running of 0.11 Kcal per minute per pound of body weight; and an additional cost of 2.7 Kcal per pound body weight per day for heavy resistance training.

Source: Data are from American College of Sports Medicine, American Dietetic Association, and Dietitians of Canada. Joint position statement: Nutrition and athletic performace. *Medicine and Science in Sports and Exercise* 32:2130–2145, 2000.

A key point in Figure 4.8 is that programs involving 3 sets result in the greatest strength gains. The reason is that the third set requires the greatest effort and thus is the greatest overload for the muscle. Although it may seem that adding a fourth set would elicit even greater gains, most studies suggest that performing 4 or more sets results in overtraining and decreased benefits.

To improve muscular endurance, 4 to 6 sets of 18 to 20 reps for each exercise are recommended. Note that you can improve endurance by either increasing the number of reps progressively while maintaining the same load, or by increasing the amount of weight while maintaining the same number of reps. The advantage of the latter program is that it would also improve muscular strength.

Most research suggests that 2 to 3 days of exercise per week is optimal for strength gains (16). However, studies have also shown that once the desired level of strength has been achieved, one high-intensity training session per week is sufficient to maintain the new level of strength. Finally, although limited research exists regarding the optimal frequency of training to improve muscular endurance, 3 to 5 days per week appear adequate (13).

Make sure you know...

- Progressively overloading a muscle can be accomplished by changing the frequency, intensity, and or duration of the activity. Increasing the weight lifted will increase the intensity of the exercise. Increasing repetitions will increase the duration of the exercise.
- Exercising 2 to 3 days per week is optimal for strength gains; however, one high-intensity session per week is sufficient to maintain new strength levels; exercising 3 to 5 days per week is adequate to improve muscular endurance.

Starting and Maintaining a Weight-Training Program

As with any plan for behavior change, you should begin your weight-training program with both short- and long-term goals. Be sure to establish realistic short-term goals that you can reach in the first several weeks

TABLE 4.2
Suggested Isotonic Strength-Training Routine to Be Included in a Basic Fitness Program
The durations of the starter and slow progression phases will depend on your initial strength level.

Week	Phase	Frequency	Sets	Reps	Weight
1–3	Starter	2/week	2	15	15 RM
4–20	Slow progression	2–3/week	3	6	6 RM
20+	Maintenance	1–2/week	3	6	6 RM

Guidelines and Precautions to Follow Prior to Beginning a Strength-Training Program

- Warm up before beginning a workout. This involves 5 to 10 minutes of movement (calisthenics) using all major muscle groups.
- Start slowly. The first several training sessions should involve limited exercises and light weight!
- Use the proper lifting technique, as shown in the isotonic strength-training exercises in this chapter. Improper technique can lead to injury.
- Follow all safety rules (see the section on safety concerns on page 105).
- Always lift through the full range of motion. This not only develops strength throughout the full range of motion but also helps you maintain flexibility.

of training. Reaching these goals will help motivate you to continue training.

Developing an Individualized Exercise Prescription

An exercise prescription for strength training has three stages: the starter phase, the slow progression phase, and the maintenance phase.

The primary objective of the **starter phase** is to build strength gradually without developing undue muscular soreness or injury. You can accomplish this by starting your weight-training program slowly—beginning with light weights, a high number of repetitions, and only 1 set per exercise, gradually working up to 2 sets per exercise. The recommended frequency of training during this phase is twice per week. The duration of this phase varies from 1 to 3 weeks, depending on your initial strength fitness level. A sedentary person might spend 3 weeks in the starter phase, whereas a relatively well-trained person may spend only 1 to 2 weeks.

The **slow progression phase** may last 4 to 20 weeks, depending on your initial strength level and your long-term strength goal. The transition from the starter phase to the slow progression phase involves three changes in the exercise prescription: increasing the frequency of training from 2 to 3 days per week; increasing the amount of weight lifted (and decreasing the number of repetitions); and increasing the number of sets performed from 2 to 3 sets. The objective of the slow progression phase is to gradually increase muscular strength until you reach your desired level.

After reaching your strength goal, your long-term objective is to maintain this level of strength by entering the **maintenance phase** of the strength-training exercise prescription. Maintaining strength will require a lifelong weight-training effort. You will lose strength if you do not continue to exercise. The good news is that the effort required to maintain muscular strength is less than the initial effort needed to gain strength. Research has shown that as little as one workout per week is required to maintain strength (17).

Sample Exercise Prescription for Weight Training

As with training to improve cardiorespiratory fitness, the exercise prescription for improving muscular strength must be tailored to the individual. Before starting a program, review the guidelines and precautions listed in the box on this page.

Table 4.2 illustrates the stages of a suggested strength-training exercise prescription. When

starter phase The beginning phase of an exercise program. The goal of this phase is to build a base for further physical conditioning.

slow progression phase The second phase of an exercise program. The goal of this phase is to increase muscle strength beyond the starter phase.

maintenance phase The third phase of an exercise program. The goal of this phase is to maintain the increase in strength obtained during the first two phases.

TABLE 4.3
Total-Body Resistance-Training Program

Target Area	Muscles	Without Weights	With Weights
Arms	Biceps	Pull-up	Biceps curl
	Triceps	Push-up	Triceps extension
Chest	Pectoralis major	Push-up, dip	Fly, chest press, bench press
Upper back	Trapezius, rhomboids	Push-up	Upright row
Abdomen	Rectus abdominis, obliques	Curl-up, plank	Abdominal curl
Lower back	Latissimus dorsi	Pull-up	Lateral pulldown, back extension
Legs	Gluteus maximus	Lunge	Leg press
	Quadriceps	Lunge	Leg extension, leg press
	Hamstrings	Lunge	Hamstring curl
	Gastrocnemius, soleus	Heel raise	Calf raise

you reach the strength goals of the program, the maintenance phase begins. You will use the same routine as you used during the progression phase, but you'll need to perform the routine only once per week.

The isotonic strength-training program contains exercises that are designed to provide a whole-body workout. Although you can perform some exercises using either machines or free weights, keep in mind that safety and proper lifting techniques are especially important when using free weights.

Follow the exercise routines described and illustrated on the following pages, and develop your program using the guidelines provided in Table 4.2. This selection of exercises is designed to provide a comprehensive strength-training program that focuses on the major muscle groups. You can also use Table 4.3 to help you plan a program that works the total body. Be aware of which muscle groups are involved in an exercise to avoid overtraining any one muscle group. Note that it is not necessary to perform all exercises in one workout session; you can perform half of the exercises on one day and the remaining exercises on an alternate day.

Make sure you know...

> As you develop your strength-training program, divide it into three phases: a starter phase, a slow progression phase, and a maintenance phase.

Motivation to Maintain Strength Fitness

The problems associated with starting and maintaining a weight-training program are similar to those associated with cardiorespiratory training. You must find time to train regularly, so good time management is critical.

Another key feature of any successful exercise program is that training must be fun. You can make weight training fun in a variety of ways. First, find an enjoyable place to work out. Locate a facility which contains the type of weights that you want to use and in which you feel comfortable and motivated. Second, develop a realistic weight-training routine. Designing a training routine that is too hard may be good for improving strength but does not increase your desire to train. Therefore, design a program that is challenging, but fun. Weight training is often more enjoyable with a partner. When looking for a workout buddy, ask a friend who is highly motivated to exercise and has strength abilities similar to yours.

Although the benefits of weight training are numerous, recent studies have shown that improved appearance, elevated self-esteem, and the overall feeling of well-being that result from regular weight training are the most important factors in motivating people to continue to train regularly. Looking your best and feeling good about yourself are excellent reasons to maintain a regular weight-training program. In addition, your elevated resting metabolic rate can help you burn calories more efficiently throughout the day, so even if you put on a few extra pounds of muscle mass, your clothes will fit better, and you will look better.

Some Isotonic Exercises for Increasing Muscular Strength

EXERCISE 4.1 BICEPS CURL

Purpose: To strengthen the **elbow flexor muscles** (biceps, brachialis, brachioradialis)

Position: Hold the grips with palms up and arms extended.

Movement: Curl up as far as possible and slowly return to the starting position.

EXERCISE 4.2 TRICEPS EXTENSION

Purpose: To strengthen the muscles on the **back of the upper arm** (triceps)

Position: Sit upright with elbows bent.

Movement: With the little-finger side of the hand against the pad, fully extend the arms and then slowly return to the original position.

Some Isotonic Exercises for Increasing Muscular Strength

EXERCISE 4.3 DUMBBELL FLY

Purpose: To strengthen the muscles of the **chest** (pectoralis major) and **shoulder** (anterior deltoid)

Position: Lie on an incline bench set at an angle between 45–60 degrees. Hold the dumbbells in front of your body with arms slightly flexed at the elbows.

Movement: Inhale, then lower the dumbbell until your elbows are at shoulder height. Raise the dumbbell while exhaling.

EXERCISE 4.4 UPRIGHT ROW

Purpose: To strengthen the muscles of the **upper back** (rhomboids, middle trapezius, posterior deltoid, latissimus dorsi)

Position: Stand with your weight equally distributed on both feet and bend legs slightly. Bend forward at the waist to a 45-degree angle with head up, looking straight ahead. Grasp the bar with an overhand grip and keep hands shoulder width apart.

Movement: Pull the bar to the chest on the count of 2. Lower the bar to the starting position on the count of 4.

Caution: Beginners and people with lower back problems should use very light weight or a dumbbell at first.

EXERCISE 4.5 LUNGE

Purpose: To strengthen the muscles of the **hip** (gluteus maximus, hamstrings), **knee** (quadriceps), and **lower back** (erector spinae)

Position: Stand with your feet hip-width apart.

Movement: Lunge forward, putting all of the weight on your leading leg. Do not let the knee of your leading leg move in front of toes. Keep your knee in line with your ankle. Vary the stride length by taking a simple step forward to involve the quadriceps, or a large step forward to place more stress on the hamstrings and gluteals while stretching the quadriceps and hip flexors.

Some Isotonic Exercises for Increasing Muscular Strength

EXERCISE 4.6 LEG EXTENSION

Purpose: To strengthen the muscles in the **front of the upper leg** (quadriceps [rectus femoris, vastus lateralis, vastus intermedius, vastus medialis])

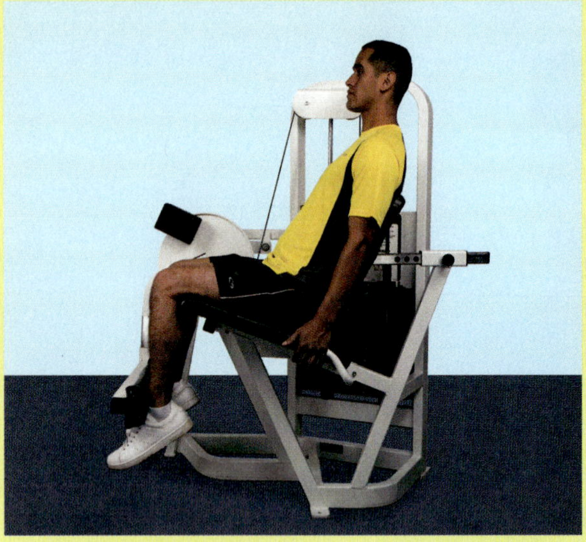

Position: Sit in a nearly upright position and grasp the handles on the side of the machine. Position your legs so the pads of the machine are against the lower shin.

Movement: Extend the legs until they are completely straight and then slowly return to the starting position.

EXERCISE 4.7 HAMSTRING CURL

Purpose: To strengthen the muscles on the **back of the upper leg** and **buttocks** (hamstrings [biceps femoris, semimembranosus, semitendinosis])

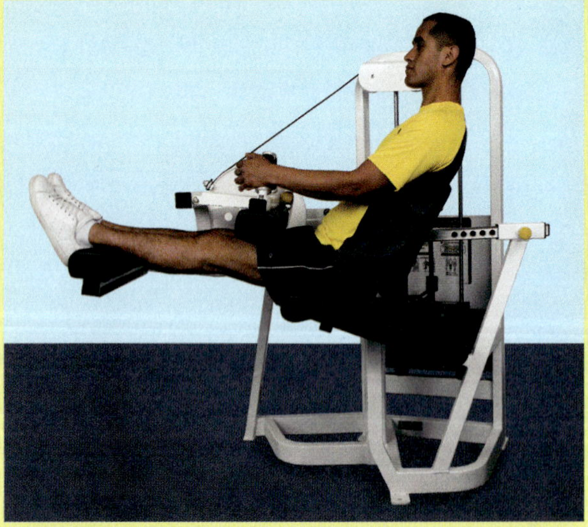

Position: In a seated position, extend legs so the pads of the machine are just below the calf muscles.

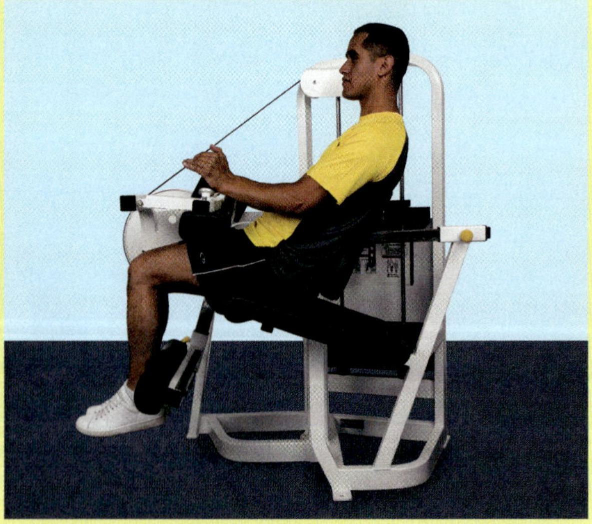

Movement: Curl the legs by pushing down on the pads to at least a 90-degree angle and then slowly return to the original position.

EXERCISE 4.8 ABDOMINAL CURL

Purpose: To strengthen the **abdominal muscles** (rectus abdominis, external oblique, internal oblique)

Position: Sit on the bench and place crossed arms on the padded armrest.

Movement: Bend forward until you feel the abdominals engage. Slowly return to starting position.

EXERCISE 4.9 BACK EXTENSION

Purpose: To strengthen the muscles of the **lower back** (erector spinae, quadratus lumborum)

Position: Sit with your upper back positioned against the back pads, and your feet flat on the platform. Push back against the pads until the spine is straight. Cross your arms over your chest and straighten your spine.

Movement: Press backward against the back pad and slowly extend at the hip, keeping your spine straight. Slowly return to the starting position, keeping the spine straight.

Some Isotonic Exercises for Increasing Muscular Strength

EXERCISE 4.10 BENCH PRESS

Purpose: To strengthen the muscles in the **chest**, the **front of the shoulders** (pectoralis major, anterior deltoid), and the **back of the upper arm** (triceps)

Position: Sit on the bench with the bench press hand grips level with your chest and your feet flat on the floor.

Movement: Grasp the bar handles and press outward until your arms are completely extended. Return slowly to the original position.

Caution: Do not arch your back while performing this exercise.

EXERCISE 4.11 PULLOVER

Purpose: To strengthen the muscles of the **chest** (pectoralis major) and **shoulder** (triceps, latissimus dorsi, teres major)

Position: Sit with your elbows against the padded ends of the movement arm and grasp the bar behind your head.

Movement: Press forward and down with your arms, pulling the bar overhead and down to your abdomen. Slowly return to the original position.

EXERCISE 4.12 DIP

Purpose: To strengthen the muscles of the **upper back, chest** (pectoralis major), and **shoulder** (triceps, deltoid)

Position: Stand in front of a platform or a box, facing forward. Place both hands on the platform behind you.

Movement: Dip down until the elbows are at 90-degree angles. Return to starting position.

EXERCISE 4.13 TOE RAISE

Purpose: To strengthen the **calf muscles** (gastrocnemius, soleus).

Position: Stand with your feet flat on the floor, or on the edge of a step.

Movement: Raise yourself up using the ankle joint only, and lower yourself back to starting position.

APPRECIATING DIVERSITY STRENGTH TRAINING FOR OLDER ADULTS

According to the Centers for Disease Control and Prevention (CDC), about 1.9 million people aged 65 and older were treated in emergency rooms for injuries due to falls in 2004. Almost 15,000 people over age 65 died from falls. In an effort to combat the number and minimize the severity of the falls, the American Academy of Orthopedic Surgeons (AAOS) and the National Athletic Trainers Association (NATA) are teaming up to help older Americans avoid falls and reduce the severity of injuries when falls do occur. The two organizations have established guidelines that call for older adults to keep muscles and bones strong by strength training with weight-bearing and resistive exercise.

Weight-bearing exercises increase bone density and help prevent osteoporosis. Research has shown that resistance training can enhance muscle mass and function even in 90-year-old subjects. Seniors can increase their lean muscle mass, improve dynamic balance, and increase their strength by participating in a well–designed strength training program 2 or 3 days a week.

Sources: Frontera, W. R., V. A. Hughes, R. A. Fielding, M. A. Fiatarone, W. J. Evans, and R. Roubenoff, Aging of skeletal muscle: A 12-yr longitudinal study. *Journal of Applied Physiology* 88: 1321–1326, 2000; McComas, A. J *Skeletal Muscle: Form and Function*, 2nd ed. Champaign, IL: Human Kinetics, 2005.

Summary

1. Strength training can reduce low back pain, reduce the incidence of exercise-related injuries, decrease the incidence of osteoporosis, and help maintain functional capacity, which normally decreases with age.
2. Muscular strength is the ability of a muscle to generate maximal force. In simple terms, this refers to the amount of weight that an individual can lift during one maximal effort. Muscular endurance is the ability of a muscle to generate force over and over again. In general, increasing muscular strength by exercise training will also increase muscular endurance. In contrast, training to improve muscular endurance does not always result in improved muscular strength.
3. Skeletal muscle is composed of a collection of long thin cells (fibers). Muscles are attached to bone by thick connective tissue (tendons). Muscle actions result in the tendons pulling on bone, causing movement.
4. Muscle action is regulated by signals coming from motor nerves. Motor nerves originate in the spinal cord and branch out to individual muscles throughout the body. The motor nerve plus all of the muscle fibers it controls make up a motor unit.
5. Isotonic exercises result in movement of a body part. Isometric exercises involve developing tension within the muscle but result in no movement of body parts. Concentric muscle actions (positive work) involve muscle shortening. In contrast, eccentric muscle actions (negative contractions) involve muscle lengthening.
6. Human skeletal muscle can be classified into three major fiber types: slow-twitch, fast-twitch, and intermediate fibers. Slow-twitch fibers shorten slowly but are highly fatigue resistant. Fast-twitch fibers shorten rapidly but fatigue rapidly. Intermediate fibers possess a combination of the characteristics of fast- and slow-twitch fibers.
7. The process of involving more muscle fibers to produce increased muscular force is called fiber recruitment.
8. The percentages of slow-twitch, intermediate, and fast-twitch fibers vary among individuals. There is a relationship between predominant muscle fiber type and success in athletics. For example,

champion endurance athletes (e.g., marathon runners) have a high percentage of slow-twitch fibers.

9. Two primary physiological factors determine the amount of force that can be generated by a muscle: the size of the muscle and the number of fibers recruited.
10. Muscle size is increased primarily because of an increase in fiber size (hypertrophy).
11. The overload principle states that a muscle will increase in strength and/or endurance only when it works against a workload that is greater than normal. The concept of progressive resistance exercise (PRE) is the application of the overload principle to strength and endurance exercise programs.
12. A weight-training program using low repetitions and high resistance results in the greatest strength gains, whereas a weight-training program using high repetitions and low resistance results in the greatest improvement in muscular endurance.
13. Isotonic exercises involves contracting a muscle against a movable load (usually a free weight or weights on a weight machine). An isometric strength-training program is based on the concept of contracting a muscle at a fixed angle against an immovable object (using isometric muscle action). Isokinetic exercises require the use of machines that govern the speed of movement during muscle contraction throughout the range of motion.
14. To begin a strength-training program, divide the program into three phases: starter phase—2 to 3 weeks, with 2 workouts per week using 2 sets at 8 reps; slow progression phase—20 weeks, with 2 to 3 workouts per week using 3 sets at 6 reps; and maintenance phase—continues for life with 1 workout per week using 3 sets at 6 reps.

Study Questions

1. What type of muscle action occurs as the muscle lengthens and controls the movement with resistance and/or gravity?
   a. concentric action
   b. eccentric action
   c. isometric action
2. A slow-twitch muscle fiber
   a. contracts slowly and produces small amounts of force.
   b. contracts rapidly and generates great amounts of force.
   c. contracts rapidly, produces great force, and fatigues rapidly.
   d. fatigues rapidly and is ideal for short bursts of activity.
3. Muscular strength is defined as
   a. the ability of a muscle to generate force over and over again.
   b. the ability of a muscle to generate maximal force.
   c. the ability of a muscle to shorten as it moves a resistance.
   d. the ability of a muscle to increase in size.
4. Which of the following is a benefit of a regular strength training program?
   a. reduces the incidence of a back pain
   b. increases $\dot{V}O_2$max
   c. reduces the incidence of colds
   d. increases endurance exercise capacity
5. Which of the following should be the general rule to follow to increase strength in a weigh training program?
   a. high resistance — high repetitions
   b. low resistance — low repetitions
   c. low resistance — high repetitions
   d. high resistance — low repetitions
6. Define the following terms:
   hypertrophy
   hyperplasia
   isotonic exercise
   isometric exercise
   isokinetic exercise
   motor unit
   progressive resistance exercise
   static contraction
   Valsalva maneuver
7. List at least three reasons why training for strength and endurance is important.
8. List and discuss the characteristics of slow-twitch, fast-twitch, and intermediate skeletal muscle fibers.
9. Discuss the pattern of muscle fiber recruitment with increasing intensities of contraction.

10. Discuss the relationship of muscle fiber type to success in various types of athletic events.
11. What factors determine muscle strength?
12. What physiological changes result from strength training?
13. Describe the concept of progressive resistance exercise.
14. Discuss the concept of specificity of training.
15. Compare and contrast the differences in training to increase strength versus training to increase endurance.
16. Define the concept of 1 RM.
17. List the phases of a strength- and endurance-training program, and discuss how they differ.
18. Distinguish isometric, concentric, and eccentric muscle actions.
19. Describe each of the following types of exercise: isokinetic, isometric, and isotonic.

Suggested Reading

American College of Sports Medicine. The recommended quantity and quality of exercise for developing and maintaining cardiorespiratory and muscular fitness, and flexibility in healthy adults. *Medicine and Science in Sports and Exercise* 30:975–991, 1998.

Blair, S. N., M. J. LaMonte, M. Z. Nichaman. The evolution of physical activity recommendations: How much is enough? *American Journal of Clinical Nutrition* 79(5):913S–920S, 2004.

Fleck, S. J., and W. J. Kraemer. *Designing Resistance Training Programs*. Champaign, IL: Human Kinetics, 2004.

Komi, P. *Strength and Power in Sport*. Oxford: Blackwell Publishers, 2002.

Kraemer, W. J., N. A. Ratamess, and D. N. French. Resistance training for health and performance. *Current Sports Medicine Report* 1(3):165–171, 2002.

Lemon, P. W., J. M. Berardi, and E. E. Noreen. The role of protein and amino acid supplements in the athlete's diet: Does type or timing of ingestion matter? *Current Sports Medicine Report* 1(4):214–221, 2002.

Phillips, S. M. Assessment of protein status in athletes. In *Nutritional Assessment of Athletes*, ed. J. A. Driskell and I. Wolinsky, pp. 283–316. Boca Raton, FL: CRC Press, 2002.

Sandler, D. *Weight Training Fundamentals*. Champaign, IL: Human Kinetics, 2003.

For links to the websites below, visit The Total Fitness and Wellness Website at www.aw-bc.com/powers.

ACSM.org

Comprehensive website that provides equipment recommendations, how-to articles, book recommendations, and position statements about all aspects of health and fitness.

Women's Fitness

Provides basic information and programs, current articles, and exercises for beginner-level strength training.

WebMD.com

General information about exercise, fitness, wellness. Great articles, instructional information, and updates.

Meriter Fitness

Discusses injury prevention and treatment, weight training, flexibility, exercise prescriptions, and more.

Muscle Physiology

Includes in-depth discussions of how muscle works, as well as recent research articles from a world-renowned muscle physiology lab.

References

1. Mannion, A. F., A. Junge, S. Taimela, M. Muntener, K. Lorenzo, and J. Dvorak. Active therapy for chronic low back pain. Part 3: Factors influencing self-rated disability and its change following therapy. *Spine* 26(8):920–929, 2001.
2. Buckwalter, J. A. Sports, joint injury, and posttraumatic osteoarthritis. *Journal of Orthopedics Sport and Physical Therapy* 33(10):578–588, 2003.
3. Seguin, R., and M. E. Nelson. The benefits of strength training for older adults. *American Journal of Preventive Medicine* 25(3 Suppl 2):141–149, 2003.
4. Winett, R. A., and R. N. Carpinelli. Potential health-related benefits of resistance training. *Preventive Medicine* 33(5):503–513, 2001.
5. Pette, D. Perspectives: Plasticity of mammalian skeletal muscle. *Journal of Applied Physiology* 90(3):1119–1124, 2001.
6. Lillioja, S., A. A.Young, C. L. Culter, J. L. Ivy, W. G. Abbott, et al. Skeletal muscle capillary density and fiber type are possible determinants of in vivo insulin resistance in man. *Journal of Clinical Investigation* 80:415–424, 1987.
7. Tanner, C. J., H. A. Barakat, G. Lynis Dohm, W. J. Pories, K. G. MacDonald, P. R. G. Cunningham, M. S. Swanson, and J. A. Houmard. Muscle fiber type is associated with obesity and weight loss. *American Journal of Physiology—Endocrinology and Metabolism* 282:E1191–E1196, 2002.

8. Wang, Y., C. Zhang, R. T. Yu, H. K. Cho, M. C. Nelson, C. R. Bayuga-Ocampo, J. Ham, H. Kang, and R. M. Evans. Regulation of muscle fiber type and running endurance by PPARδ. *PLoS Biology* 10: e294, 2004.
9. Kraemer, W. L., N. D. Duncan, and J. S. Volek. Resistance training and elite athletes: Adaptations and program considerations. *Journal of Orthopedic Sports and Physical Therapy* 28(2):110–119, 1998.
10. Fleck, S. J., and W. J. Kraemer. *Designing Resistance Training Programs*. Champaign, IL: Human Kinetics, 2004.
11. Folland, J. P., and A. G. Williams. The adaptations to strength training : Morphological and neurological contributions to increased strength. *Sports Medicine* 37(2):145–168, 2007
12. Hakkinen, K., M. Alen, W. J. Kraemer, E. Gorostiaga, M. Izquierdo, H. Rusko, J. Mikkola, A. Hakkinen, H., Valkeinen, E. Kaarakainen, S. Romu, V. Erola, J. Ahtiainen, and L. Paavolainen. Neuromuscular adaptations during concurrent strength and endurance training versus strength training. *European Journal of Applied Physiology* 89(1):42–52, 2003.
13. Duchateau, J., and R. M. Enoka. Neural adaptations with chronic activity patterns in able-bodied humans. *American Journal of Physical Medicine Rehabilitation*. 81(11 Suppl):S17–27, 2002.
14. Shephard, R. J. Exercise and training in women. Part 1: Influence of gender on exercise and training responses. *Canadian Journal of Applied Physiology* 25(1):19–34, 2000.
15. Kitai, T. A. Specificity of joint angle in isometric training. *European Journal of Applied Physiology* 58:744, 1989.
16. Powers, S., and E. Howley. *Exercise Physiology: Theory and Application to Fitness and Performance,* 4th ed. Dubuque, IA: McGraw-Hill, 2003.
17. Gabriel, D. A., G. Kamen, and G. Frost. Neural adaptations to resistive exercise: Mechanisms and recommendations for training practices. *Sports Medicine* 36(2): 133–49, 2006.

NAME ______________________ DATE ______________

Evaluating Muscular Strength: The 1 RM Test

The 1 RM test is used to measure muscular strength. You can use the following procedure to determine your 1 RM:

1. Begin with a 5- to 10-minute warm-up using the muscles to be tested.
2. For each muscle group, select an initial weight that you can lift without undue stress.
3. Gradually add weight until you reach the maximum weight that you can lift at one time. If you can lift the weight more than once, add additional weight until you reach a level of resistance such that you can perform only one repetition. Remember that a true 1 RM is the maximum amount of weight that you can lift one time.

The seated chest press and the leg press are two common methods for the 1 RM test. The seated chest press measures upper body muscular strength, and the leg press measures muscular strength in the lower body.

The seated chest press can be used to evaluate upper body muscular strength.

A leg press can be used to evaluate lower-body muscular strength.

Your muscle strength score is your percentage of body weight lifted in each exercise. To compute your strength score, divide your 1 RM weight in pounds by your body weight in pounds, and then multiply by 100. For example, suppose a 150-pound man has a bench press 1 RM of 180 pounds. This individual's muscle strength score for the bench press is computed as

$$\frac{\text{1 RM weight}}{\text{body weight}} \times 100 = \text{muscle strength score}$$

Therefore,

$$\text{muscle strength score} = \frac{\text{180 pounds}}{\text{150 pounds}} \times 100 = 120$$

Table 4.4 and Table 4.5 on pages 125 and 126 list strength score norms for college-aged men and women for the seated chest press and leg press, respectively. According to Table 4.4, a muscle strength score of 120 on the seated chess press places a college-aged man in the "good" category.

In the spaces below, record your muscular strength score and fitness category for the 1 RM tests for the leg press and seated chess press.

Age: 18 Body weight: 146 lb

Date: 10/18/10

Exercise	1 RM (lb)	Muscular Strength	Fitness Category
Seated chest press			
Leg press			

Goal Setting

1. Based on your results, write a goal to maintain or improve your current fitness level. For example, if you scored "fair" on this test, your goal might be to improve your fitness level to a "good" rating. If your fitness level indicated a score of "excellent," your goal might be to maintain your current fitness status.

   Goal: I want to lose belly fat and get bigger arms

2. Write three strategies for how you intend to achieve the goal you wrote. For example, one strategy for improving your current fitness status might be to perform 1 set of 10 repetitions at 50% of your 1 RM, 3 times a week. To progressively overload the muscles, increase the number of sets, and increase the weight load by 5–10 lb.

   - ______________________
   - ______________________
   - ______________________

TABLE 4.4

Strength Score Norms for the Seated Chest Press

Locate your fitness level for upper body muscular strength using your seated chest press score.

Fitness Level	Age 20–29	Age 30–39	Age 40–49	Age 50–59	Age 60+
Men					
Superior	>148	>124	>110	>97	>89
Excellent	132–148	112–124	100–110	90–97	82–89
Good	114–131	98–111	88–99	79–89	72–81
Average	99–113	88–97	80–87	71–78	66–71
Poor	89–98	79–87	73–79	64–70	58–65
Very poor	<89	<79	<73	<64	<58
Women					
Superior	>90	>76	>71	>61	>64
Excellent	80–90	70–76	62–71	55–61	54–64
Good	70–79	60–69	54–61	48–54	47–53
Average	59–69	53–59	50–53	44–47	43–46
Poor	52–58	48–52	44–49	40–43	39–42
Very poor	<52	<48	<44	<40	<39

1 RM seated bench press with bench press weight ratio = weight pushed ÷ body weight × 100.

TABLE 4.5
Strength Score Norms for the Leg Press
Locate your fitness level for lower body muscular strength using your seated leg press score.

Fitness Level	Age 20–29	Age 30–39	Age 40–49	Age 50–59	Age 60+
Men					
Superior	>227	>207	>191	>179	>172
Excellent	213–227	193–207	182–191	171–179	162–172
Good	197–212	177–192	168–181	158–170	149–161
Average	183–196	165–176	157–167	146–157	138–148
Poor	164–182	153–164	145–156	133–145	126–137
Very poor	<164	<153	<145	<133	<126
Women					
Superior	>181	>160	>147	>136	>131
Excellent	168–181	147–160	137–147	125–136	118–131
Good	150–167	133–146	123–136	110–124	104–117
Average	137–149	121–132	113–122	99–109	93–103
Poor	123–136	110–120	103–112	89–98	86–92
Very poor	<123	<110	<103	<89	<86

1 RM seated leg press with leg press weight ratio = weight pushed ÷ body weight × 100.

NAME ______________________________ DATE ____________________

Evaluating Muscular Strength: The Estimated 1 RM Test

You can use the following procedure to determine your estimated 1 RM for any particular lift (e.g., chest press):

1. First, perform a set of 10 repetitions using a light weight.
2. Next, add additional weight and perform another set of 10 repetitions.
3. Repeat this process until you reach a weight that you can lift only 10 times (called the 10 RM).

Be sure to have an experienced instructor supervise the process so that your 10 RM weight can be discovered in fewer than five trials. Rest about 5 minutes after each trial to recover.

After determining the 10 RM, you can use Table 4.6 on page 128 to estimate your 1 RM. For example, if your 10 RM for a particular lift is 100 pounds, then the estimate for the 1 RM would be about 135 pounds.

You can determine your muscle strength score from the estimated 1 RM using the same formula used for the 1 RM test. That is,

$$\text{muscle strength score} = \frac{\text{1 RM weight}}{\text{body weight}} \times 100$$

Record your muscular strength scores below, and use Table 4.4 or Table 4.5 in Laboratory 4.1 to determine your fitness category.

Age: ________ Body weight: _________ lb

Date: ________________

Exercise	1 RM (lb)	Muscular Strength	Fitness Category
Seated chest press			
Leg press press			

Goal Setting

1. Based on your results, write a goal to maintain or improve your current fitness level. For example, if your score was "fair" on this test, your goal might be to improve your fitness level to a "good" rating. If your fitness level indicated a score of "excellent," your goal might be to maintain your current fitness status.

   Goal: ____

2. Write three strategies for how you intend to achieve the goal you wrote. For example, one strategy for improving your current fitness status could be to perform 1 set of 10 repetitions at 50% of your 1 RM, 3 times a week. To progressively overload the muscles, increase the number of sets, and increase the weight load by 5–10 lb.

   - ____

     ____

- ____
____
- ____
____

Source: Roitman, J. (ed). *ACSM's Resource Manual for Guidelines for Exercise Testing and Prescription.* Philadelphia: Lippincott Williams & Wilkins, 2001.

TABLE 4.6
Estimating the 1 RM from the 10 RM

Estimated 1 RM (lb)	Lifted during 10 Repetitions (lb)	Estimated 1 RM (lb)	Lifted during 10 Repetitions (lb)
5.0	3.7	145.0	106.6
10.0	7.4	150.0	110.3
15.0	11.0	155.0	113.9
20.0	14.7	160.0	117.6
25.0	18.4	165.0	121.3
30.0	22.1	170.0	125.0
35.0	25.7	175.0	128.6
40.0	29.4	180.0	132.3
45.0	33.1	185.0	136.0
50.0	36.8	190.0	139.7
55.0	40.4	195.0	143.3
60.0	44.1	200.0	147.0
65.0	47.8	205.0	150.7
70.0	51.5	210.0	154.4
75.0	55.1	215.0	158.0
80.0	58.8	220.0	161.7
85.0	62.5	225.0	165.4
90.0	66.2	230.0	169.1
95.0	69.8	235.0	172.7
100.0	73.5	240.0	176.4
105.0	77.2	245.0	180.1
110.0	80.9	250.0	183.8
115.0	84.5	255.0	187.4
120.0	88.2	260.0	191.2
125.0	91.9	265.0	194.8
130.0	95.6	270.0	198.5
135.0	99.2	275.0	202.1
140.0	102.9		

Source: Axler, C., and S. McGill. Low back loads over a variety of abdominal exercises: Searching for the safest abdominal challenge. *Medicine and Science in Sports and Exercise* 29: 804–810, 1997.

NAME ______________________ DATE ______________

Tracking Your Progress

Use the log below to chart your strength-training progress. Record the date, number of sets, reps, and the weight for each of the exercises listed in the left column.

Date				
Exercise	St/Rp/Wt*	St/Rp/Wt	St/Rp/Wt	St/Rp/Wt
Biceps curl (see Exercise 4.1)				
Triceps extension (see Exercise 4.2)				
Abdominal curl (see Exercise 4.8)				
Quadriceps extension (see Exercise 4.6)				
Hamstring curl (see Exercise 4.7)				
Bench press or chest press (see Exercise 4.10)				
Upright rows (see Exercise 4.4)				
Lunges (with or without weights) (see Exercise 4.5)				
Dumbbell fly (see Exercise 4.3)				

* St/Rp/Wt = Sets/Reps/Weight. *Example:* 2/6/80 = 2 sets of 6 reps each with 80 lb.

NAME ______________________________ DATE ______________

Measuring Muscular Endurance: The Push-Up, Sit-Up, and Curl-Up Tests

The Standard Push-Up Test

Perform the standard push-up test as follows:

1. Position yourself on the ground in push-up position (Figure a). (Note that you can instead use the modified push-up position shown in Figures c and d.) Place your hands about shoulder width apart, and extend your leg in a straight line with your weight on your toes.
2. Lower your body until your chest is within 1 to 2 inches off the ground (Figure b), and raise yourself back to the up position. Be sure to keep your back straight and to lower your entire body as a unit.
3. Select a partner to count your push-ups and time your test (test duration is 60 seconds). Warm up with a few push-ups, and rest for 2 to 3 minutes after the warm-up to prepare for the test.
4. When your partner says "Go," start performing push-ups. Have your partner count your push-ups aloud, and ask him or her to let you know periodically how much time remains.
5. Record your score in the chart on page 133.

The standard push-up

(a)

(b)

The modified push-up

(c)

(d)

The Sit-up Test

You can perform the bent-knee sit-up test as follows:

1. Lie on your back with your arms crossed on your chest. Bend your knees so that they're approximately 90-degree angles, with your feet flat on the floor (Figure a).
2. Bring your chest up to touch your knees (Figure b), and then return to the original lying position. The entire movement counts as one full sit-up. Be sure to let your abdominal muscles do the work of the movement (avoid stress on your neck), and be careful not to hit your head on the floor when returning to the lying position. Performing the test on a mat is helpful.
3. Select a partner to count your sit-ups and hold your feet on the floor by grasping your ankles, and to time the test.
4. Warm up with a few sit-ups. Rest for 2 to 3 minutes after your warm-up before starting the test.
5. When you partner says "Go," start performing sit-ups and continue for 60 seconds. Have your partner count your sit-ups aloud, and ask him or her to let you know periodically how much time remains.
6. Record your score in the chart on page 133.

(a)

(b)

The Curl-Up Test

The curl-up differs from the sit-up in that the trunk is not raised more than 30 to 40 degrees above the floor. The advantages of curl-ups are that they use only the abdominal muscles (whereas the sit-up also involves the hip flexors), and they put less stress on the lower back than do the conventional sit-ups.

You can perform the curl-up test as follows:

1. Lie on your back with your legs shoulder-width apart, your knees bent 90 degrees, your arms straight at your sides, and your palms flat on the mat (Figure a).
2. Extend your arms so that your fingertips touch a strip of tape perpendicular to your body. A second strip of tape is located toward the feet and parallel to the first (10 centimeters apart).
3. Use the cadence provided on a metronome set to 50 beats per minute. Slowly curl up your upper spine until your fingers touch the second strip of tape. Then slowly return to the lying position with your head and shoulder blades touching the mat and your fingertips touching the first strip of tape. Breathe normally throughout, exhaling during the curling up stage.
4. Have your partner count the number of consecutive curl-ups you do in 1 minute, maintaining the metronome cadence and without pausing, to a maximum of 25, and record your score in the chart on page 133.

TABLE 4.8
Norms for Muscular Endurance Using the Sit-Up Test

Fitness Level	Age 20–29	Age 30–39	Age 40–49	Age 50–59	Age 60+
Men					
Superior	>49	>45	>41	>35	>31
Excellent	44–49	40–45	35–41	29–35	25–31
Good	39–43	35–39	30–34	25–28	21–24
Average	35–38	31–34	27–29	22–24	17–20
Poor	25–35	22–30	17–26	13–21	9–16
Very poor	<25	<22	<17	<13	<9
Women					
Superior	>43	>39	>33	>27	>24
Excellent	37–43	33–39	27–33	22–27	18–24
Good	33–36	29–32	23–26	18–21	13–17
Average	29–32	25–28	19–22	14–17	10–12
Poor	18–28	13–24	7–18	5–13	3–9
Very poor	<18	<13	<7	<5	<3

Source: Norms are adapted from Golding, L. A., C. R. Myers, and W. E. Sinning. *Y's Way to Physical Fitness: The Complete Guide to Fitness Testing and Instruction,* 3rd ed. Champaign, IL: Human Kinetics, 1989.

TABLE 4.9
Norms for Muscular Endurance Using the Curl-Up Test

Fitness Level	Age 15–19	Age 20–29	Age 30–39	Age 40–49	Age 50–59	Age 60–69
Men						
Excellent	25	25	25	25	25	25
Very Good	23–24	21–24	18–24	18–24	17–24	16–24
Good	21–22	16–20	15–17	13–17	11–16	11–15
Fair	16–20	11–15	11–14	6–12	8–10	6–10
Needs Improvement	≤15	≤10	≤10	≤5	≤7	≤5
Women						
Excellent	25	25	25	25	25	25
Very Good	22–24	18–24	19–24	19–24	19–24	17–24
Good	17–21	14–17	10–18	11–18	10–18	8–16
Fair	12–16	5–13	6–9	4–10	0–9	3–7
Needs Improvement	≤11	≤4	≤5	≤3	≤5	≤2

Source: From "Canadian Physical Activity, Fitness and Lifestyle Approach: CSEP–Health and Fitness Program's Appraisal & Counseling Strategy," Third Edition © 2003. Reprinted with permission from the Canadian Society for Exercise Physiology.

5

Improving Flexibility

True or false?

1. **Bouncing is the best way to stretch the muscles.**
2. **Stretching should always be done when the muscle is warm.**
3. **The purpose of stretching is to lengthen the ligaments that cross the joints.**
4. **For maximum results, you need to stretch to the point of pain.**
5. **Stretching the neck muscles throughout the day will help prevent neck aches.**

Answers appear on the next page.

Abby is a 22-year-old college junior whose biology major requires a lot of paper writing. She finds herself at the library at least four nights a week, conducting hours of research about cell behavior and gene function. Often, by the time she looks up from her textbook, her eyes are blurry, and her neck aches. Abby's fitness instructor advised her to take periodic breaks during her study time and to stretch her neck muscles to alleviate the kink in her neck. Although she knows this is probably good advice, she hasn't tried it yet because she's not sure how to properly stretch her neck muscles, and she forgets to look it up when she has a chance. Hence, the stiffness in her neck continues.

What do you think is causing Abby's stiff neck? Do you think her instructor's advice to stretch her neck will help alleviate the problem? Do you know how to properly stretch your neck muscles? In this chapter we'll discuss what causes muscle tightness and how stretching can improve flexibility. We'll also discuss the proper way to do various stretches and to target specific areas of the body for improved flexibility.

The Need for Flexibility in Daily Living

Gymnasts and ice skaters are not the only people who need to maintain adequate **flexibility.** When you bend down to tie your shoes or reach up to pull a sweatshirt over your head, you're relying on your body's flexibility to perform these tasks. In fact, any movement that requires you to stretch, reach, or twist your body without pain or stiffness is possible because you enjoy a range of motion around your joints. Unfortunately, you may not appreciate the importance of flexibility as a fitness component until you experience an injury that keeps you from performing these routine movements.

People vary in their degrees of flexibility because of differences in body structure, and the range of motion of most joints can decline with disuse. Tightness of the muscle, tendon, and connective tissue surrounding a joint can limit your range of motion; however, this restriction can be eliminated through proper stretching.

Make sure you know...

- Flexibility is the range of motion of a joint, and it allows you to bend, twist, and reach without experiencing pain or stiffness.
- Stretching can alleviate tightness at a joint.

How Flexibility Works: Muscles, Joints, and Stretching

The range of motion around a joint is determined partly by the shapes and positions of the bones that make up the joint and partly by the composition and arrangement of muscles, tendons, and connective tissue around the joint (1, 2). Although the structure of the bones cannot be altered, the soft tissues can be lengthened to allow for greater range of motion.

Of course, there are some movements that you will not be able to do, no matter how much you stretch, without causing yourself harm. You can't bend your fingers backward, for example, or rotate your arm 360 degrees at the elbow. The reason is that you are limited in the range of motion at your joints by your body's anatomy. Let's take a closer look at how this works.

Answers

1. **FALSE Bouncing can lead to a strained or torn muscle. For most people, slow static stretching will allow muscles to lengthen gradually.**
2. **TRUE A "cold" muscle is more reluctant to stretch than a warm muscle.**
3. **FALSE The purpose of stretching is to stretch muscle and tendon. Stretching the ligaments will cause injury and affect the stability of the joint.**
4. **FALSE Although stretching to the point of discomfort will help improve flexibility, a sharp pain during stretching can indicate that a ligament, muscle, or tendon has been torn.**
5. **TRUE Holding a muscle in one position for a long period of time, such as by staring at a computer screen for several hours, can result in muscle stiffness. Stretching can help alleviate this.**

Structural Limitations to Movement

There are five primary anatomical factors that limit movement (Figure 5.1):

1. *The shape of the bones* determines the amount of movement possible at each joint. For example, because of the way they are structured, ball and socket joints, such as the shoulder and hip, have greater range of motion than hinge joints, such as the elbow and knee.
2. *A stiff muscle* will limit the range of motion at a joint; likewise, a warmed up muscle will be flexible and allow a greater range of motion.
3. *The connective tissue* within the joint capsule provides stability at the joint. **Ligaments,** for example, are positioned around the joint to prevent the bone ends from coming apart, as in a dislocation injury. They prevent movements that a normal, healthy joint is not supposed to do. **Cartilage** covers the ends of the bones and creates a better fit between the bones, which helps eliminate unnecessary movements.
4. *Tendons,* which connect muscle to bones and to connective tissue surrounding joints, are extensions of the muscle tissue. If the muscle is tight, the tendon will also be tight.
5. *Tight skin* can limit the range of motion at a joint.

Exercise aimed at improving flexibility does not change the structure of bone, but it alters the soft tissues (muscle, joint connective tissue, and tendons) that contribute to flexibility. Table 5.1 lists the resistance of the various soft tissues to total joint flexibility. Note that the structures associated with the joint capsule, muscles, and tendons provide most of the body's resistance to movement. Therefore, flexibility exercises must alter the resistance of one of these three to increase the range of motion around a joint. Stretching the muscle and tendon is desirable because these soft tissues can lengthen over time and improve flexibility. Stretching the ligaments in the joint capsule, in contrast, is undesirable because it can lead to a loose joint that would be highly susceptible to injury.

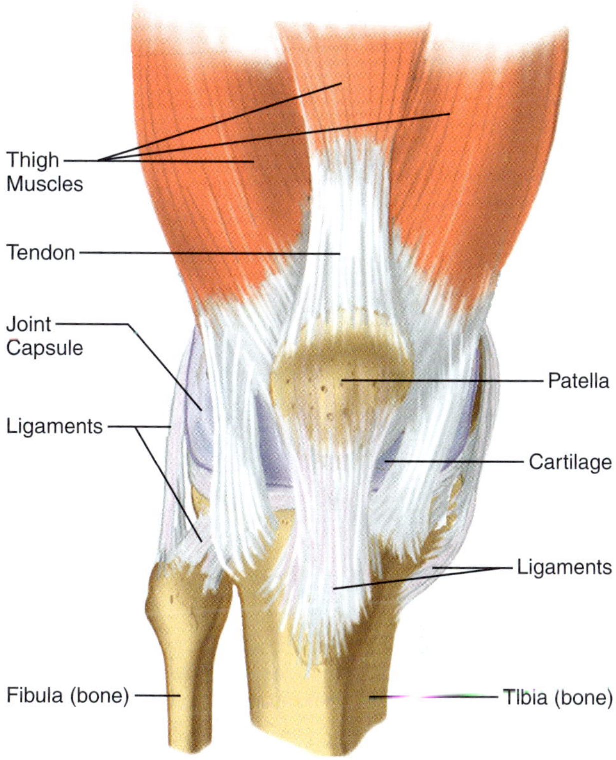

FIGURE 5.1
A view of the knee joint and the anatomical structures that influence movement.

Source: Johnson, M., *Human Biology*, 4th ed. San Francisco: Benjamin Cummings, 2008, 114.

Before we examine specific stretching exercises, let's find how stretching works.

Stretching and the Stretch Reflex

When a doctor taps you on the knee with a rubber hammer, your knee extends. This is a **stretch reflex** caused by the rapid stretching of the **muscle spindles**

TABLE 5.1
Soft-Tissue Resistance to Joint Movement

Structure	Limitation to Flexibility (% of total resistance)
Joint capsule	47
Muscle	41
Tendon	10
Skin	2

flexibility The ability to move joints freely through their full range of motion.

ligaments Connective tissue within the joint capsule that holds bones together.

cartilage A tough connective tissue that forms a pad on the end of long bones, such as the femur, tibia, and humerus. Cartilage acts as a shock absorber to cushion the weight of one bone on another and to provide protection from the friction due to joint movement.

stretch reflex Involuntary contraction of a muscle due to rapid stretching of that muscle.

muscle spindles The type of proprioceptor found within muscle.

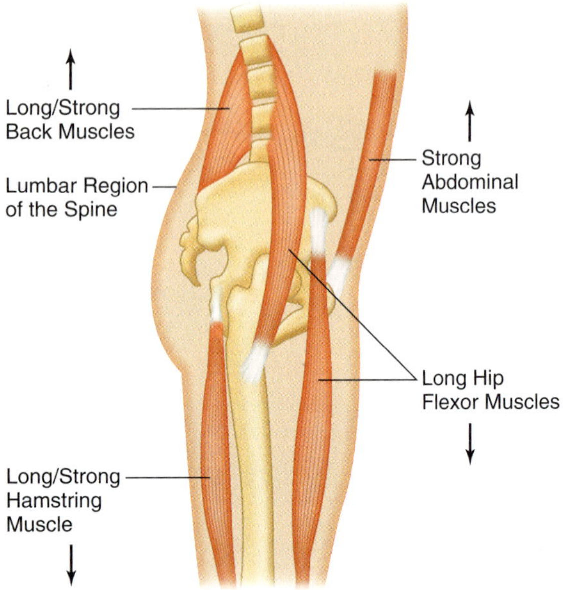

FIGURE 5.2
Strong abdominal and hip flexor muscles, balanced with strong back and hamstring muscles, help keep the spine and pelvis in neutral alignment, thereby lowering the risk of LBP.

within the quadriceps muscles that move the knee joint. Activating the stretch reflex is counterproductive to flexibility, because during the stretch the muscle shortens rather than lengthens. (Remember that the goal of stretching is to lengthen the muscle). Fortunately, you can avoid the stretch reflex if you stretch the muscles and tendons very slowly. In fact, if you hold a muscle stretch for several seconds, the muscle spindles allow the muscle being stretched to further relax and permit an even greater stretch (2, 3). Therefore, stretching exercises are most effective when they avoid promoting a stretch reflex.

Muscle spindles are one type of **proprioceptor,** specialized receptors in muscles and tendons that provide feedback to the brain about the position of the body parts. When you were learning to catch a ball, you had to look at the position of your arms and hands to make sure they were in line with the path of the ball. As your catching skills improved, you no longer had to look at the arm position to know that it was lined up with the ball. The proprioceptors in your muscles and tendons provided feedback to your brain about where the arm was positioned. The proprioceptors within the muscles are muscle spindles, and the proprioceptors within the tendons are **Golgi tendon organs.**

Make sure you know...

- The structural and physiological limits to flexibility are due to the characteristics of bone; muscle; connective tissue within the joint capsule, such as ligaments and cartilage; the tendons, which connect muscle to bones and to connective tissue surrounding joints; and skin.
- If muscle spindles are stretched suddenly, they initiate a stretch reflex that causes the muscle to contract and shorten. However, if muscles are stretched slowly, the stretch reflex can be avoided.
- The proprioceptors (muscle spindles and Golgi tendon organs) monitor the muscles and tendons and report their positions to the brain.

Benefits of Flexibility

Although increased flexibility provides numerous benefits, including increased joint mobility, efficient body movement, and good posture (1, 3, 4), there is no research evidence to support the idea that it reduces the incidence of muscle injury during exercise. In fact, one critical review article suggests that stretching may contribute to injury (5). The only studies suggesting that stretching offers protection from muscle injury combined the stretching with a general warm-up.

However, improved flexibility does help keep your joints healthy and can prevent lower back pain. Let's look at these benefits more closely.

Keeping Joints Healthy

Joints will suffer from lack of movement if you do not regularly engage them. If a joint is not moved enough or has a limited range of motion, scar tissue can form that further restricts the joint motion and can be painful to the point that you may not be able to move the joint. The shoulder joint is particularly susceptible to this scar tissue formation. Mild stretching on a daily basis can prevent a joint from becoming immobile.

Joint mobility is also important for keeping the joint lubricated. Joints contain synovial fluid, which is needed to reduce friction and decrease wear and tear. Moving the joint helps circulate the synovial fluid, which in turn reduces the friction on the cartilage between the bones. Too much friction can damage cartilage, setting the stage for arthritis. Mild stretching can improve the mobility of the joint and promote normal wear on the cartilage covering the ends of the bones.

Stretching also directly affects the joints by reducing tension within the fibers of a muscle. When a muscle is stretched, these fibers are free to slide past one another, and the tension is literally worked out of the muscle. Reduced muscle tension reduces the tension exerted by the tendon as it crosses the joint. The force of the muscle exerted through the tendon on the bone can cause the bone ends of the joint to be pulled closer together, thus limiting the joint range of motion. In essence, stretching can have the same effects on muscle tension as a manual muscle massage, at a much lower cost.

Preventing Lower Back Pain

Another benefit of improved flexibility is that it can help prevent low back problems. Low back pain (LBP) is sometimes called a **hypokinetic disease,** that is, a disease associated with a lack of exercise. The weak abdominal muscles commonly seen in sedentary individuals and the lack of flexibility in the hip flexor muscles are two common causes of LBP.

The abdominal muscles play a significant role in keeping the pelvic girdle in a neutral alignment with the spine (Figure 5.2). When the abdominal muscles are weak, the pelvis tilts forward and creates an increased hyperextension (forward curve), called *lordosis*, in the lower back. The muscles that flex the hip can affect the pelvis in the same way; however, they pull the pelvis forward when they are tight. Stretching these muscles and strengthening the abdominal muscles are important to keep the pelvis in a neutral alignment.

In addition to the abdominal muscles and the hip flexor muscles, the hamstrings and the lower back muscles also attach to the posterior side of the pelvis and can affect its alignment. The hamstring muscles exert a downward pull on the pelvis, whereas the low back muscles exert an upward pull. Keeping all four muscle groups in balance helps keep the pelvis in a neutral alignment with the lumbar region of the spine and therefore diminishes the likelihood for LBP.

Up to 80% of people will experience LBP, and approximately 15% of Americans will be disabled by LBP in their lifetime (6). Men and women are affected equally by back pain, usually between the ages of 25 and 60. Most pain in the lower back goes away in a few days or weeks. Low back pain that lasts for longer than 6 months is considered chronic.

People who regularly carry heavy backpacks are at increased risk of lower back problems. In one study (7), curvature of the spine significantly increased as subjects wearing backpacks became fatigued. Interestingly, after the subjects rested for several minutes, both trunk and head angles were not significantly different from the fatigued condition. Although this study did not examine resulting back problems from the chronic wearing of a backpack, the findings certainly suggest that long-term backpack use can result in misalignment in the lower back.

The psychological, social, and physical costs of lower back pain are high, as are the economic costs. The medical, insurance, and business/industry costs are generally considered to be in the billions of dollars per year. Developing and maintaining healthy low back function requires a balance of flexibility, strength, and endurance.

Focus on the following stretches (shown later in this chapter) to help you maintain a healthy back: thigh stretch (Exercise 5.3), leg stretch (Exercise 5.4), hip and gluteal stretch (Exercise 5.7), lower back stretch (Exercise 5.8), and the trunk twister (Exercise 5.10). Leg pulls, sitting hamstring stretches, curl-ups, and knee-to-toe touches will also help. Also see Laboratory 5.3.

Top Potential Contributors to Lower Back Pain

- *Poor low back lumbar flexibility*. Tight low back muscles exert an uneven pull on the pelvis, resulting in a hyperextended lumbar spine.
- *Poor hamstring flexibility.* Weak hamstring muscles allow the pelvis to tilt forward.
- *Poor hip flexor flexibility.* Tight hip flexors exert a forward and downward pull on the pelvis and lumbar vertebrae.
- *Poor strength and endurance of the forward and lateral abdominals.* Weak abdominal muscles allow the pelvis to tilt forward.
- *Poor flexibility and endurance of the back extensor muscles.* Back extensor muscles must have the endurance to exert a pull on the pelvis for the duration of exercise.

Make sure you know...

> Improved flexibility increases joint mobility and joint health, increases resistance to muscle injury, helps prevent low back problems, allows for efficient body movement, and improves posture and personal appearance.

> Flexibility of the hamstrings and lower back and strong abdominal muscles are important for a healthy back.

Evaluating Flexlbility

Flexibility is joint specific. That is, you might be flexible in one joint but lack flexibility in another. You may also notice that you are more flexible on one side of your body than the other. This disparity is often due to the greater usage of the dominant side of the body.

proprioceptor Specialized receptor in muscle or tendon that provides feedback to the brain about the position of body parts.

Golgi tendon organ The type of proprioceptor found within tendons.

hypokinetic disease Disease associated with a lack of exercise.

Although no single test is representative of total body flexibility, measurements of trunk and shoulder flexibility are commonly evaluated. The **sit-and-reach test** measures the ability to flex the trunk, which means stretching the lower back muscles and the muscles in the back of the thigh (hamstrings). The figure in Laboratory 5.1 on page 163 illustrates the sit-and-reach test using a sit-and-reach box.

The **shoulder flexibility test** evaluates the range of motion at the shoulder. See Laboratory 5.1 at the end of the chapter for a walk-through of the sit-and-reach test and shoulder flexibility tests.

Once you complete the sit-and-reach test and the shoulder flexibility test, you will better understand how flexible or inflexible you are. Both active and inactive individuals are often classified as average or below average for trunk and shoulder flexibility. In fact, only individuals who regularly perform stretching exercises are likely to possess flexibility levels that exceed the average. Regardless of your current flexibility classification, your flexibility goal should be to reach a classification of above average (i.e., good, excellent, or superior).

CONSIDER THIS!

Contrary to popular belief, weight lifting does not decrease flexibility. In fact, the use of proper form during weight lifting (lifting through the full range of motion) can actually increase flexibility.

Make sure you know...

- Flexibility measurements are joint specific.
- Two popular tests to evaluate flexibility are the sit-and-reach test and the shoulder flexibility test.

Designing a Flexibility Training Program

Because flexibility training is a key part of any fitness program, you'll want to include stretching exercises in your fitness routine. As with designing programs for the other fitness components, your first step will be to set short- and long-term goals. Do you want to become more flexible in the shoulders, or is your aim more to improve your hamstring and low back flexibility? No matter what your goal, you will want to think about how you will get there before you begin your new flexibility training routine. Also consider keeping a record of your workouts and improvements to follow your progress and plan your future training schedule.

Once you've set your goals, you can consider the types of stretches to include in your program. Three kinds of stretching techniques are commonly used to increase flexibility: **dynamic stretching, ballistic stretching,** and **static stretching.** A fourth type of stretching called **proprioceptive neuromuscular facilitation (PNF)** is often used in rehabilitation settings (2, 8).

Dynamic stretching can be useful for athletes whose events involve quick changes of direction. The fluid, exaggerated movements in dynamic stretches mimic the movements that an athlete engages in during competition. Ballistic stretching, in contrast, involves rapid and forceful bouncing movements to stretch the muscles. The movements of ballistic stretching are more likely to cause injury, so exercises to warm up the muscles prior to stretching are helpful. Ballistic stretches may be most beneficial to individuals involved in quick, explosive movements. With dynamic and ballistic stretching, the athlete trains the nervous system and the muscles to adapt to the movements that she routinely performs. However, for the average fitness enthusiast seeking to increase flexibility, ballistic movements may activate the stretch reflex, injuring muscles and tendons. For this reason, ballistic stretching techniques are not usually incorporated into a nonathlete's fitness program.

Most people will benefit from incorporating static and proprioceptive neuromuscular facilitation techniques into their fitness program. We'll discuss these two types of stretching next.

Static Stretching

Static stretching is extremely effective for improving flexibility (2, 4). Static stretching involves slowly lengthening a muscle to a point at which further movement is limited (slight discomfort is felt) and holding this position for a fixed period of time. Holding the stretch for 20 to 30 seconds, and repeating it 3 to 4 times, improves flexibility (4). Compared with ballistic stretching, the risk of injury to the muscle or tendon associated with static stretching is minimal. When performed during the cool-down period, static stretching may reduce the muscle stiffness associated with some exercise routines (2, 4).

You can perform static stretches at home, and you don't need any special equipment to do them. You can even do them while watching television or sitting at your computer. See Exercises 5.1 through 5.12 for examples of static stretches.

STEPS FOR BEHAVIOR CHANGE

Are you too stiff?

Answer the following questions to help determine whether you would benefit from increased flexibility.

Y	N	
☐	☐	Do you often feel as though you have a stiff neck?
☐	☐	Is your mobility impaired when you turn your head to the left or right?
☐	☐	Do you have difficulty washing your own back?
☐	☐	Does your lower back feel stiff when you sit at your desk for prolonged periods of time?
☐	☐	Do your ankles and feet feel stiff when you get out of bed in the morning?

If you answered yes to more than one question, check out the following tips.

TIPS TO IMPROVE FLEXIBILITY

- ☑ If your neck feels stiff when you are working at your desk, perform 5 minutes of gentle neck stretches and shoulder rolls at the top of every hour.
- ☑ Next time you shower, let the warm water hit the back of your neck, shoulders, and upper back. Perform 10 shoulder rolls forward, 10 backward, and 10 neck tilts to the left and right while the shower spray is aimed at your neck and shoulders.
- ☑ To increase the flexibility in your shoulders, try holding a washcloth in your right hand as you reach behind your head. Grasp the washcloth with your left hand as you reach behind your back. Try pulling the washcloth up and down as you grasp it in both hands, increasing your range of motion with each up-and-down movement.
- ☑ If your low back is stiff after sitting for prolonged periods of time, try sitting on a physioball instead of a desk chair. The smaller muscles of the spine will be exercised as you balance on the physioball.
- ☑ Every morning when you wake up, sit on the edge of your bed and make 10 small and 10 large circles to the right and then to the left with your right foot. Switch and repeat circling motion with your left foot.

Proprioceptive Neuromuscular Facilitation

Proprioceptive neuromuscular facilitation (PNF) combines stretching with alternating contraction and relaxation of muscles. There are two common types of PNF stretching: *contract-relax (CR) stretching* and *contract-relax/antagonist contract (CRAC) stretching*. The CR stretch technique calls for first contracting the muscle to be stretched. Then, after the muscle is relaxed, it is slowly stretched. The CRAC method calls for the same contract-relax routine but adds to this the contraction of the **antagonist** muscle, the muscle on the opposite side of the joint. The purpose of contracting the antag-

sit-and-reach test A fitness test that measures the ability to flex the trunk.

shoulder flexibility test A fitness test that measures the ability of the shoulder muscles to move through their full range of motion.

dynamic stretching Stretching that involves moving the joints through the full range of motion to mimic a movement used in a sport or exercise.

ballistic stretching A type of stretch that involves sudden and forceful bouncing to stretch the muscles.

static stretching Stretching that slowly lengthens a muscle to a point where further movement is limited.

proprioceptive neuromuscular facilitation (PNF) A series of movements that combines stretching with alternating contraction and relaxation of muscles.

antagonist The muscle on the opposite side of the joint.

FIGURE 5.3
An example of a partner-assisted CRAC procedure for stretching the calf muscles. The exerciser contracts the calf muscles against resistance provided by the assistant. Then, unassisted, the exerciser contracts the shin (antagonist) muscles, thereby relaxing the calf muscles. Finally, while the exerciser continues contracting the shin muscles, the assistant stretches the calf muscles.

onist muscle is to promote a reflex relaxation of the muscle to be stretched.

How do PNF techniques compare with ballistic and static stretching? First, PNF has been shown to be safer and more effective in promoting flexibility than ballistic stretching (8). Further, studies have shown PNF programs to be equal to, or in some cases superior to, static stretching for improving flexibility (9).

Passive and Active Stretching

Some PNF stretches cannot be done alone — that is, they require a partner. The partner supplies resistance to the body part during the contraction of the antagonist muscles, thus preventing the body part from moving. This sequence of movements allows the muscle to relax more than in a static stretch, and greater range of motion can be achieved. The only drawback to this type of stretch is that the partner must provide resistance, which can be very tiring over a short period of time.

The following steps illustrate how a CRAC procedure can be done with a partner (Figure 5.3):

1. After the assistant moves the limb in the direction necessary to stretch the desired muscles to the point of tightness (where mild discomfort is felt), the exerciser isometrically contracts the muscle being stretched for 3 to 5 seconds and then relaxes it.
2. The exerciser then moves the limb in the opposite direction of the stretch by isometrically contracting the antagonist muscles. The exerciser holds this isometric contraction for approximately 5 seconds, during which time the muscles to be stretched relax. While the desired muscles are relaxed, the assistant may increase the stretch of the desired muscles.
3. The exerciser then isometrically contracts the antagonist muscles for another 5 seconds, which relaxes the desired muscles, and the assistant again stretches the desired muscles to the point of mild discomfort.

This cycle of three steps is repeated 3 to 5 times.

Some PNF stretches can also be done without a partner (Figure 5.4). Using a towel or other object to provide resistance can achieve the same benefits without fatiguing an assistant.

Applying the FIT Principle

So what are the best frequency, intensity, and time (duration) for your stretching routine (the FIT principle)? The answers vary according to your present level of flexibility, among other factors. However, a good rule of thumb is that the first week, or starter phase, of a stretching regimen should include one stretching session. During the next 4 weeks, or the slow progression phase, of the program, one stretching session should be added per week. Initially, the duration of each training session should be approximately 5 minutes and should increase gradually to 20 to 30 minutes following 6 to 12 weeks of stretching during the slow progression phase.

The physiological rationale for increasing the duration of stretching is that each stretch position is held for progressively longer durations as the program continues. For example, begin by holding each stretched position for 15 seconds, then add 5 seconds each week up to 30 seconds. Start by performing each of the exercises once (1 rep), and progress to 4 reps. The frequency and duration of a stretching exercise prescription should be 2 to 5 days per week for 10 to 30 minutes each day. Table 5.2 illustrates a sample exercise prescription for a flexibility program.

What about the intensity of stretching? In general, a limb should not be stretched beyond a position of mild discomfort. The intensity of stretching is increased by extending the stretch to the limits of your range of motion. Your range of motion will gradually increase as your flexibility improves during the training program.

To improve overall flexibility, all major muscle groups should be stretched. Just because you have good flexibility in the shoulders does not mean your flexibility will be good in the hamstrings. Exercises 5.1 through 5.12 illustrate the proper methods of performing 12 different stretching exercises. Integrate these exercises into the program outlined in Table 5.2.

These exercises are designed to be used in a regular program of stretching to increase flexibility. For safety reasons, all flexibility programs should consist of either PNF or static stretching exercises. The exercises presented involve the joints and major muscle groups for which range of motion tends to decrease with age and disuse. The exercises include both static and PNF movements and may require a partner. To avoid injury, be sure to follow the guidelines in the box on page 149.

Some stretches that were once thought to improve flexibility are now known to be potentially damaging to the musculoskeletal system. The photos starting on page 157 show some common exercises that may cause injury, and provide substitute exercises that help accomplish the same goals.

FIGURE 5.4
You can use a towel to do some PNF stretches without a partner.

Make sure you know...

> Ballistic stretching involves sudden, forceful bouncing. Dynamic stretching involves moving the joints through a range of motion that is specific to a sport or activity. Static stretches involve stretching a

TABLE 5.2
Sample Flexibility Program Using the FIT Principle

Week	Phase	Duration of Stretch Hold	Repetitions	Frequency (times/wk)
1	Starter	15 sec	1	1
2	Slow progression	20 sec	2	2
3	Slow progression	25 sec	3	3
4	Slow progression	30 sec	4	3
5	Slow progression	30 sec	4	3–4
6	Slow progression	30 sec	4	4–5
7+	Maintenance	30 sec	4	4–5

A CLOSER LOOK

PILATES—MORE THAN STRETCHING?

Pilates (pronounced Puh-**lah**-teez) is a widely used form of exercise among professional dancers, gymnasts, recreational exercisers, and rehabilitation specialists. It involves gentle, subtle stretching and contracting of muscles to produce very fluid, controlled movements that emphasize a mind–body interaction.

This body conditioning routine improves flexibility, strength, endurance and coordination without increasing muscle bulk. There are two forms of exercise in Pilates. The first form focuses on mat exercises that use your body weight as the resistance force. The other form involves using specialized machines to tone and strengthen the body. One piece of Pilates equipment, called the Reformer, consists of a moving carriage on a horizontal frame. There is a series of up to 100 exercises that can be performed on it without stopping.

Pilates emphasize the following basic principles:

- *Concentration*—The mind–body connection. This stresses that conscious control of movement enhances body awareness.
- *Control/precision*—It's not about intensity or multiple "reps"; it's more about proper form.
- *Centering*—A mental focus within the body calms the spirit, and a particular focus on the torso develops a strong core and enables the rest of the body to function efficiently. All action initiates from the trunk and flows outward to the extremities.
- *Stabilizing*—Before you move, you have to be still. This helps provide a safe starting place for mobility.
- *Breathing*—Deep, coordinated, conscious diaphragmatic patterns of inhalation and exhalation initiate movement, help activate deep muscles, and keep you focused.
- *Alignment*—Proper alignment is key to good posture. You'll be aware of the position of your head and neck on the spine and pelvis, right down through the legs and toes.
- *Fluidity*—Smooth, continuous motion rather than jarring repetitions.
- *Integration*—Several different muscle groups are engaged simultaneously to control and support movement. All principles come together, making for a holistic mind–body workout.

muscle to the limit of movement and holding the stretch for an extended period of time. Proprioceptive neuromuscular facilitation (PNF) combines stretching with alternating contraction and relaxation of muscles to improve flexibility.

> Stretching exercises should be performed 2 to 5 days per week for 10 to 30 minutes each day.

> The intensity of a stretch is considered to be maximal where "mild discomfort" is felt.

> You can minimize your risk of injury during stretches by avoiding hazardous exercises and making sure to perform stretches correctly.

Avoiding Hazardous Exercises

To avoid injury during stretching exercises, follow these guidelines:

- Don't hold your breath. Try to breathe as normally as possible during the exercise.
- Do not fully extend the knee, neck, or back.
- Do not stretch muscles that are already stretched.
- Do not stretch to the point that joint pain occurs.
- Avoid stretching ligaments by avoiding unnatural movements at the joint.
- Use caution when having someone help you with passive stretches. Make sure you communicate about the end of the range of motion.
- Avoid forceful extension and flexion of the spine.

Motivation to Maintain Flexibility

Maintaining flexibility requires a commitment to performing regular stretching. Just as in other types of fitness training, good time management is critical if you are going to succeed. Set aside time for 3 to 5 stretching periods per week, and stick to your schedule. Remember that you can stretch almost anywhere, because you don't need special equipment. So take advantage of "windows" of free time in your day and plan stretching workouts.

You are not likely to maintain a lifetime stretching program if you do not enjoy your workouts. One suggestion for making stretching more fun is to perform stretching workouts while listening to music or during a television program you enjoy.

A CLOSER LOOK

WHEN MUSCLES CRAMP

A muscle cramp is one of the most common problems encountered in sports and exercise. For many years, the primary causes of muscle cramps were thought to be dehydration and/or electrolyte imbalances. Accordingly, drinking enough fluids and ensuring that the diet contains sufficient amounts of sodium (from table salt, for example) and potassium (e.g., from bananas) have long been encouraged as preventive measures. When muscles cramp, stretching and/or massage have been used to relieve the cramping until electrolyte balance can be restored.

More recent research, however, suggests that cramping may be due to abnormal spinal control of motor neuron activity, especially when a muscle contracts while shortened (9). For example, the cramping that often occurs in the calf muscles of recreational swimmers when their toes are pointed may occur because those calf muscles are contracting while they are shortened.

The most prevalent risk factors for cramps during exercise are muscle fatigue and poor stretching habits (failure to stretch regularly and long enough during each session). Other risk factors include older age, higher body mass index, and a family history of muscle cramps.

If cramping occurs, you should do the following:

- Passively stretch the muscle. Such stretching induces receptors that sense the stretch to initiate nerve impulses that inhibit muscle stimulation.
- Drink plenty of water to avoid dehydration or electrolyte imbalances. Sports drinks can help replenish glucose and electrolytes, but do not use salt tablets or drink fluids containing caffeine.
- Seek medical attention if multiple muscle groups are involved, because this could be a sign of more serious problems.

Although no strategies for preventing muscle cramping during exercise have been proven effective, regular stretching using PNF techniques, correcting muscle balance and posture, and proper training for the exercise activity involved may be beneficial.

Sample Flexibility Exercises

EXERCISE 5.1 LOWER LEG STRETCH

Purpose: To stretch the **calf** muscles (gastrocnemius, soleus) and the **Achilles' tendon**.

Position: Stand on the edge of a surface that is high enough to allow your heel to drop lower than your toes. Have a support nearby to hold for balance.

Movement: Rise up on your toes as far as possible for several seconds, then lower your heels as far as possible. Shift your body weight from one leg to the other for added stretch of the muscles.

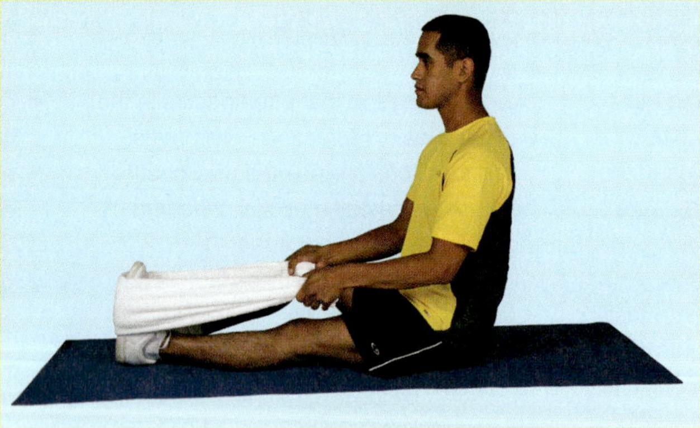

Variation: Sit on the floor with leg outstretched, loop a towel under the ball of your foot, and gently pull your foot upward so that the top of the foot moves closer to your shin. Another variation (not pictured) is to sit on the floor with one leg outstretched, and the other leg flexed with the sole of your foot along the knee of your other leg. Reach down, grasp the toes of the outstretched leg, and gently pull the foot upward so that the top of the foot is moving closer to the shin.

EXERCISES

EXERCISE 5.2 SHIN STRETCH

Purpose: To stretch the muscles of the **shin** (tibialis anterior, extensor digitorum longus, extensor hallucis longus).

Position: Kneel on both knees, with your trunk rotated to one side and the hand on that side pressing down on your ankle.

Movement: While pressing down on your ankle, move your pelvis forward; hold for several seconds. Repeat on the other side.

EXERCISE 5.3 THIGH STRETCH

Purpose: To stretch the muscles in the front of the **thigh** (quadriceps) of the extended (rear) leg.

Position: Kneel on one knee, resting your rear shin and foot flat on the floor. Place both hands on the forward knee. *Note*: If you need more stability, you can place your hands on the floor on either side of the forward foot.

Movement: Slide your rear leg backward so that the knee is slightly behind your hips; then press your hips forward and down, and hold for several seconds. While stretching, maintain approximately a 90-degree angle at the knee of the front leg. Switch the positions of the legs to stretch the other thigh.

Sample Flexibility Exercises

EXERCISE 5.4 LEG STRETCH

Purpose: To stretch the muscles on the **back of the hip** (gluteus maximus), the **back of the thigh** (hamstrings), and the **calf** (gastrocnemius and soleus).

Position: Lying on your back, bring one knee toward your chest, and grasp your toes with the hand on the same side. Place the opposite hand on the back of the leg just below the knee.

Movement: Pull your the knee toward your chest while pushing your heel toward the ceiling and pulling your toes toward your shin. Straighten your knee until you feel sufficient stretch in the muscles of the back of the leg, and hold for several seconds. Repeat for the other leg.

EXERCISE 5.5 MODIFIED HURDLER'S STRETCH

Purpose: To stretch the **lower back muscles** (erector spinae) and muscles in the **back of the thigh** (hamstrings).

Position: Sit on a level surface with one leg out in front, bend the other knee, and place the sole of the foot alongside the knee of the outstretched leg.

Movement: Reach down, and grab the ankle of the outstretched leg. Keeping your head and trunk straight, lean your trunk forward, and attempt to touch your chest to your knee. Hold for several seconds. Return to the upright position, and alternate legs.

Variation: Grasp the toes of the extended leg, and pull your toes toward your shin while stretching. This will also stretch the calf muscles (gastrocnemius and soleus).

EXERCISE 5.6 INSIDE LEG STRETCH

Purpose: To stretch the muscles on the **inside of the thighs** (adductors and internal rotators).

Position: Sit with the bottoms of your feet together and place your hands just below your knees.

Movement: Try to raise your knees while pushing down with your hands and forearms. Then relax, and, using your hands, press your knees toward the floor; hold for several seconds.

EXERCISE 5.7 HIP AND GLUTEAL STRETCH

Purpose: To stretch the muscles at the **hip** (gluteals, tensor fasciae latae).

Position: Lie on your back, with one leg crossed over the other and both shoulders and both arms on the floor.

Movement: Grasp behind the knee of the leg that is not crossed over, and pull the thigh toward your chest. Hold for several seconds. Reverse the positions of the legs, and repeat the stretch.

Sample Flexibility Exercises

EXERCISE 5.8 LOWER BACK STRETCH

Purpose: To stretch the muscles of the **lower back** (erector spinae) and **buttocks** (gluteals).

Position: Lie on your back with your hips and knees bent, your feet flat on the floor, and your arms positioned along your sides.

Movement: First, arch your back, and lift your hips off the floor; hold for several seconds. Then relax and return to starting position. Place your hands behind your knees, and pull the knees to your chest. Hold for several seconds.

EXERCISE 5.9 SIDE STRETCH

Purpose: To stretch the muscles of the **upper arm** (triceps) and **side of the trunk** (latissimus dorsi).

Position: Sit on the floor with your legs crossed.

Movement: Stretch one arm over your head while bending at your waist in the same direction. With the opposite arm, reach across your chest as far as possible; hold for several seconds. Do not rotate your trunk; try to stretch the muscle on the same side of the trunk as the overhead arm. Alternate arms to stretch the other side of the trunk.

EXERCISE 5.10 TRUNK TWISTER

Purpose: To stretch the muscles of the **trunk** (obliques and latissimus dorsi) and **hip** (gluteus maximus).

Position: Sit with your left leg extended, your right leg bent and crossed over your left knee, and your right foot on the floor. Place your right hand on the floor behind your buttocks.

Movement: Placing your left arm on the right side of your right thigh, and your right hand on the floor, use your left arm to push against your right leg while twisting your trunk to the right; hold for several seconds. Then assume the starting position with your right leg extended, and stretch the opposite side of the body.

Sample Flexibility Exercises

EXERCISE 5.11 CHEST STRETCH

Purpose: To stretch the muscles across the **chest** (pectoralis major) and **shoulder** (anterior deltoid and biceps).

Position: Stand in a doorway, and grasp the frame of the doorway at shoulder height.

Movement: Press forward on the frame for 5 seconds. Then relax, and shift your weight forward until you feel the stretch of muscles across your chest; hold for several seconds.

EXERCISE 5.12 NECK STRETCH

Purpose: To stretch the muscles that rotate the **head** (sternocleidomastoid).

Position: After turning your head to one side, place your hand against your cheek with your fingers toward the ear, and your elbow pointing forward.

Movement: Try to turn your head and neck against the resistance of your hand; hold for a few seconds. Remove your hand and relax, then turn your head as far as possible in the same direction. Repeat the stretch, turning in the other direction.

Alternatives for Unsafe Exercises

Purpose: To stretch the **lower back** and **buttocks**.

May Cause Injury:
KNEE PULL

This position places undue stress on the knee joint.

Try This Instead:
LEG PULL

Lie on your back, and pull your knee toward your chest by pulling on the back of your leg just below the knee. Then extend the knee joint, and point the sole of your foot straight up. Continue to pull your leg toward your chest. Repeat several times with each leg.

Purpose: To strengthen the **upper leg** and stretch the **lower leg**.

May Cause Injury:
DEEP KNEE BEND

This movement hyperflexes the knee and "opens" the joint while stretching the ligaments.

Try This Instead:
LUNGE

From a standing position, step forward with either foot and touch the opposite knee to the ground. Repeat with the opposite leg.

Alternatives for Unsafe Exercises

Purpose: To stretch the **lower back**, **buttocks**, and **hamstrings**.

May Cause Injury:
STANDING TOE TOUCH

This movement could damage the lower back.

Try This Instead:
SITTING HAMSTRING STRETCH

Sit at leg-length from a wall. With your foot on the wall and the other knee bent with the foot between the wall and your buttocks, bend forward, keeping your lower back straight. The bent knee can fall to the side.

Purpose: To strengthen the **abdominal muscles**.

May Cause Injury:
SIT-UP (HANDS BEHIND HEAD)

This movement could cause hyperflexion of the neck and strain the neck muscles.

Try This Instead:
CURL-UP

Lie on your back with your knees bent, and cross your arms over your chest. Using your abdominal muscles, curl up until the upper half of your back is off the floor, and then return to the starting position.

Purpose: To stretch the **neck muscles**.

May Cause Injury: NECK CIRCLES

This movement hyperextends the neck, which can pinch arteries and nerves, as well as damage disks in the spine.

Try This Instead: NECK STRETCHES

Sit with your head and neck straight. Move your head down to flex your neck, and return your head upright. Then, slowly turn your head from side to side as far as possible; attempt to point your chin at each shoulder.

Purpose: To stretch and strengthen the **buttocks**.

May Cause Injury: DONKEY KICK

When kicking the leg back, most people hyperextend the neck and/or back.

Try This Instead: KNEE-TO-NOSE TOUCH

While on your hands and knees, lift one knee toward your nose and then extend that leg to the horizontal position. Alternate legs. Do not lift your leg higher than your hips, and keep your neck in line with your back.

Summary

1. Flexibility is the range of motion of a joint.
2. Improved flexibility results in the following benefits: increased joint mobility, prevention of low back problems, efficient body movement, and improved posture and personal appearance.
3. The five structural and physiological limits to flexibility are the shape of bone; muscle; connective tissue within the joint capsule; the tendons, which connect muscle to bones and to connective tissue that surrounds joints; and skin.
4. Proprioceptors are constantly monitoring the tension of the muscles and tendons and providing feedback to the brain. If muscle spindles are suddenly stretched, they respond by initiating a stretch reflex that causes the muscle to contract. However, if the muscles and tendons are stretched slowly, the stretch reflex can be avoided.
5. Designing your flexibility program involves setting short-term and long-term goals and selecting stretches that will help you meet your goals. Static stretches involve stretching a muscle to the limit of movement and holding the stretch for an extended period of time. Dynamic stretches involve fluid, exaggerated movements designed to mimic the movements of a given sport or activity.
6. Proprioceptive neuromuscular facilitation (PNF) combines stretching with alternating contraction and relaxation of muscles to improve flexibility. Ballistic stretches may be appropriate for some athletes but are not safe for the general public.

Study Questions

1. Which of the following is not an anatomical factor that can limit movement at a joint?
   a. shape of the bones
   b. tight skin
   c. tight tendons
   d. length of the bone
2. Proprioceptors include which of the following?
   a. motor units
   b. Golgi organs
   c. muscle spindles
   d. a and b
   e. b and c
3. Static stretching is not advisable for nonathletes.
   a. True
   b. False
4. To avoid injury, most stretching should be done
   a. only at night.
   b. after the muscles have been warmed up.
   c. while watching television.
   d. to the point of pain.
5. Lower back pain is the result of
   a. weak abdominal muscles.
   b. weak hamstring muscles.
   c. hyperextension of the lower back.
   d. all of the above.
6. Define the following terms:
   flexibility
   range of motion
   cartilage
   ligament
   tendon
   proprioceptive neuromuscular facilitation
   antagonist
7. Describe the difference in function between ligaments and tendons.
8. Compare static and ballistic stretching.
9. List three primary reasons why maintaining flexibility is important.
10. List the factors that limit flexibility. Which factors place the greatest limitations on flexibility?
11. Briefly outline the exercise prescription to improve flexibility.
12. Describe why the stretch reflex should be avoided.

Suggested Reading

Bishop, D. Warm up II: Performance changes following active warm up and how to structure the warm up. *Sports Medicine* 33(7):483–498, 2003.

Blair, S. N., M. J. LaMonte, and M. Z. Nichaman. The evolution of physical activity recommendations: How much is enough? *American Journal of Clinical Nutrition* 79(5):913S–920S, 2004.

Guissard, N., and J. Duchateau. Effect of static stretch training on neural and mechanical properties of the human plantar-flexor muscles. *Muscle Nerve* 29(2):248–255, 2004.

Weldon, S. M., and R. H. Hill. The efficacy of stretching for prevention of exercise-related injury: A systematic review of the literature. *Manual Therapy* 8(3):141–150, 2003.

Wilmore, J., and D. Costill. *Physiology of Sport and Exercise*, 3rd ed. Champaign, IL: Human Kinetics, 2004.

For links to the websites below, visit The Total Fitness and Wellness Website at www.aw-bc.com/powers.

WebMD.com

General information about exercise, fitness, wellness. Great articles, instructional information, and updates.

ACSM.org

Comprehensive website of the American College of Sports Medicine. Provides information, articles, equipment recommendations, books, and position statements about all aspects of health and fitness.

References

1. Kubo, K., H. Kanehisa, Y. Kawakami, and T. Fukunaga. Influence of static stretching on viscoelastic properties of human tendon structures in vivo. *Journal of Applied Physiology* 90(2):520–526, 2001.
2. Guissard, N., and J. Duchateau. Effect of static stretch training on neural and mechanical properties of the human plantar-flexor muscles. *Muscle Nerve* 29(2): 248–255, 2004.
3. McGill, S. M. Low back stability: From formal description to issues for performance and rehabilitation. *Exercise and Sport Sciences Review* 29(1):26–31, 2001.
4. American College of Sports Medicine. The recommended quantity and quality of exercise for developing and maintaining cardiorespiratory and muscular fitness, and flexibility in healthy adults. *Medicine and Science in Sports and Exercise* 30(6):975–991, 1998.
5. Thacker, S. B., J. Gilchrist, D. F. Stroup, and C. D. Kimsey. The impact of stretching on sports injury risk: A systematic review of the literature. *Medicine and Science in Sports Exercise* 36(3):371–378, 2004.
6. Plowman, S. A. Physical fitness and healthy low back function. *Research Digest: The President's Council on Physical Fitness*, 1(3): 2004.
7. Orloff, H. A., and C. M. Rapp. The effects of load carriage on spinal curvature and posture. *Spine* 29(12): 1325–1329, 2004.
8. McAtee, R. *Facilitated Stretching*, 3rd ed. Champaign, IL: Human Kinetics, 2007.
9. Chalmers, G. Re-examination of the possible role of Golgi tendon organ and muscle spindle reflexes in proprioceptive neuromuscular facilitation muscle stretching. *Sports Biomechanics* 3(1):159–183, 2004.

NAME ______________________________ DATE ______________

Assessing Flexibility: Trunk Flexion (Sit-and-Reach) Test and the Shoulder Flexibility Test

The Sit-and-Reach Test

To perform the sit-and-reach test, start by sitting upright with your feet flat against a sit-and-reach box. Keeping your feet flat on the box and your legs straight, extend your hands as far forward as possible, and hold this position for 3 seconds. Repeat this procedure 3 times. Your score on the sit-and-reach test is the distance, measured in inches, between the edge of the sit-and-reach box closest to you and the tips of your fingers during the best of your three stretching efforts.

Note that you should warm up by stretching for a few minutes before you perform the test. To reduce the possibility of injury, avoid rapid or jerky movements during the test. It is often useful to have a partner help by holding your legs straight during the test and by measuring the distance. After completing the test, consult Table 5.3 on page 164 to locate your flexibility fitness category, and record your scores on the following page.

The sit-and-reach test.

The shoulder flexibility test.

The Shoulder Flexibility Test

To perform the shoulder flexibility test follow these steps. While standing, raise your right arm, and reach down your back as far as possible. At the same time, extend your left arm behind your back, and reach upward toward your right hand. The objective is to try to overlap your fingers as much as possible. Your score on the shoulder flexibility test is the distance, measured in inches, of finger overlap.

Measure the distance of finger overlap to the nearest inch. For example, an overlap of $\frac{3}{4}$ inch would be recorded as 1 inch. If your fingers fail to overlap, record this score as −1. Finally, if your fingertips barely touch, record this score as 0. After completing the test with the right hand up, repeat the test in the opposite direction (left hand up).

As with the sit-and-reach test, you should warm up with a few minutes of stretching prior to performing the shoulder flexibility test. Again, to prevent injury, avoid rapid or jerky movements during the test. After completion of the test, consult Table 5.4 on page 164 to locate your shoulder flexibility category, and record your scores on the following page.

LABORATORY 5.1 *(continued)*

Date: __________

Sit-and-reach score (inches): ________   Fitness category: __________

Shoulder flexibility (inches)

Left side: ________________   Fitness category: ____________

Right side: ________________   Fitness category: ____________

Goal Setting

1. Based on your results for the flexibility testing, write a goal to either improve or maintain your fitness category.
2. Write three objectives to help you achieve your goal.
   - ______________________________
   - ______________________________
   - ______________________________

TABLE 5.3

Physical Fitness Norms for Trunk Flexion

Note that these norms are from the YMCA's sit-and-reach test. Units for the sit-and-reach are inches.

	Fitness Category Based on Sit and Reach		
Age Group	Excellent	Average	Poor
Men			
18–25	22	16	13
26–35	21	15	12
36–45	21	15	11
Women			
18–25	24	19	16
26–35	23	18	14
36–45	22	17	13

Source: Modified from Golding, L., ed. *YMCA Fitness Testing and Assessment Manual,* 4th edition. With permission of the YMCA of the USA, Chicago, IL. Copyright © 2000.

TABLE 5.4

Physical Fitness Norms for Shoulder Flexibility

Note that these norms are for both men and women of all ages. Units for the shoulder flexibility test score are inches and indicate the distance between the fingers of your right and left hands.

Right Hand up Score	Left Hand Up Score	Fitness Classification
<0	<0	Very poor
0	0	Poor
+1	+1	Average
+2	+2	Good
+3	+3	Excellent
+4	+4	Superior

Source: From Fox, El L., T. E. Kirby, and A. R. Fox. *Bases of Fitness.* Copyright © 1987. All rights reserved. Adapted by permission of Allyn and Bacon. Norms from Gretchell, B. *Physical Fitness: A Way of Life,* 5th ed. Needham Heights, MA: Allyn and Bacon, 1998.

5.2

LABORATORY

NAME ______________________________ DATE ______________

Flexibility Progression Log

Use this log to record your progress in increasing flexibility in selected joints. Record the date, hold time, and sets for each of the exercises listed in the left column.

St/Hold = sets and hold time
Example: 2/30 = 2 sets held for 30 seconds each.

Date: ______________

Exercise	St/Hold	St/Hold	St/Hold	St/Hold	St/Hold	St/Hold	St/Hold
Lower leg stretch (see Exercise 5.1)							
Shin stretch (see Exercise 5.2)							
Thigh stretch (see Exercise 5.3)							
Leg stretch (see Exercise 5.4)							
Modified hurdler's stretch (see Exercise 5.5)							
Inside leg stretch (see Exercise 5.6)							
Hip and gluteal stretch (see Exercise 5.7)							
Lower back stretch (see Exercise 5.8)							

Exercise	St/Hold	St/Hold	St/Hold	St/Hold	St/Hold	St/Hold	St/Hold
Side stretch (see Exercise 5.9)							
Trunk twister (see Exercise 5.10)							
Chest stretch (see Exercise 5.11)							
Neck stretch (see Exercise 5.12)							

NAME ______________________________ DATE ______________

Stretching to Prevent or Reduce Lower Back Pain

Stretching exercises are important in maintaining a flexible and healthy back. Our daily activities often result in overuse and tightening of back muscles. Chronic overuse and straining can cause significant back pain and increase your risk for back injury.

In this lab, you will learn exercises to stretch the lower muscles of your back to help in maintaining flexibility. Performing these stretches will help prevent back pain and may help reduce back aches.

Back Extension — Prone

1. Lie on your stomach.
2. Prop yourself up on your elbows, extending your back.
3. Start straightening your elbows, further extending your back.
4. Continue straightening your elbows until you feel a gentle stretch.
5. Hold for 15 seconds.
6. Return to the starting position.
7. Repeat 10 more times.

Cat Stretch

1. Get down on the floor on your hands and knees.
2. Push your back up toward the ceiling (like a cat arching its back).
3. Continue arching until you feel a gentle stretch in your back.
4. Hold for 15 seconds.
5. Return to the starting position.
6. Repeat 10 more times.

The Pelvic Tilt

1. Lie on your back, with your knees bent and feet flat on the floor.
2. Exhale, and press the small of your back against the floor.
3. Hold for 15 seconds.
4. Return to the starting position.
5. Repeat 10 more times.

6

Body Composition

true or false?

1. An overweight person can be fit.
2. Over half of the U.S. adult population is overweight or obese.
3. Body mass index (BMI) is the best way to estimate body composition.
4. Moderate weight loss in an obese person can reduce the risk for heart disease and diabetes.
5. Being underweight can increase the risk for certain health problems.

Answers appear on the next page.

Josh is a 19-year-old college sophomore who is a sprinter on his school's track team. His training routine involves track workouts and short-distance runs 5 days a week, and weight lifting 3 days a week. At 5 feet, 10 inches and 190 pounds, Josh is solid and hefty and considers himself to be in pretty good shape. Jason, meanwhile, is his 20-year-old roommate who makes it to the gym once in a while but spends most of his free time studying in the student lounge or meeting with friends at a favorite local hangout. Jason is also 5 feet 10 inches and weighs in at 168 pounds, which is about 15 pounds more than he weighed when he graduated from high school 2 years ago.

Would you be surprised to learn that Josh's higher weight is healthier than Jason's lower one? In this chapter, we will find out how to assess your level of body fat, how much body fat is considered healthy, and the health benefits and problems associated with having too much or too little body fat.

What Is Body Composition and What Does It Tell Us?

Body composition refers to the relative amounts of fat and fat-free tissues (e.g., bone, muscle, and internal organs) in the body. When body composition is assessed, it is typically expressed as a percentage of fat in the body. So, if a person has 20% body fat, 20% of his body weight is fat mass, and the remaining 80% of his body weight is fat-free or lean body mass. A high percentage of body fat is associated with an increased risk of heart disease, diabetes, and other conditions, whereas too low a percentage is also associated with health problems, such as malnutrition and osteoporosis.

Measuring percentage of body fat can help determine whether a person is at a healthy weight, **overweight,** or **obese.** Someone who is overweight has a body fat percentage above the recommended level that is considered to be "healthy." The "overweight" classification is based on research examining the relationship between body fatness and rates of disease. A person classified as obese has a very high percentage of body fat, generally over 25% for men and over 30% for women (1–5).

Make sure you know...

- Body composition refers to the relative amounts of fat and fat-free mass in the body and is generally reported in terms of the percentage of fat in the body.
- Measuring percentage body fat can help determine whether someone is overweight or obese.

Answers

1. **TRUE** Research has shown that individuals who are overweight, but active or fit, have lower risk for heart disease than both low-active, low-fit overweight individuals and low-active, low-fit normal-weight individuals.
2. **TRUE** It is estimated that approximately 65% of U.S. adults are overweight or obese.
3. **FALSE** BMI can provide information about whether a person is at a healthy weight, and BMI is related to body fat percentage. However, there are limitations for BMI in assessing body fat percentage, because it can overestimate body fat for muscular individuals.
4. **TRUE** A weight loss of as little as 5–10% can reduce the risk of heart disease and diabetes in overweight and obese individuals.
5. **TRUE** The relationship between weight and health follows what is referred to as a J-shaped curve. Although disease risk is greater for obese individuals, people at the lowest end of range are also at increased risk for disease.

How Is Body Composition Related to Health?

You need to consider percentage of body fat when determining a healthy body weight because a person can be "overweight" (i.e., based on height/weight charts) without being over-fat. Consider an athlete who is very muscular, like Josh. The athlete might weigh the same or even more than an individual who is clearly overweight because of a high percentage of body fat. The opposite is also true. A person can be over-fat, like Jason, without being considered "overweight." A sedentary person who appears to be at a healthy weight based on height and weight charts might have a percentage of body fat that is considered unhealthy or even obese.

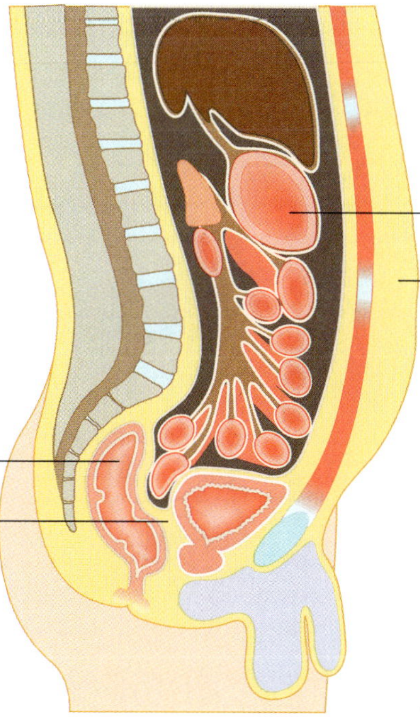

FIGURE 6.1
Storage fat can be visceral or subcutaneous. Visceral fat is stored around the organs; subcutaneous fat is stored between the skin and muscle layers.

Some muscular athletes can be "overweight" without being over-fat.

We Need Some Fat

Although we worry about having too much body fat, a certain amount is necessary. **Essential fat** is necessary for body functions such as facilitating nerve impulses. Some locations of this fat include nerves, the heart, mammary glands, and liver. Men have approximately 3% of their body weight as essential fat, and women—who carry more fat in their breasts, uterus, and other sex-specific sites—have approximately 12%.

The fat we have in addition to the essential fat, called **storage fat,** is contained within **adipose tissue** in the body. This fat may be **visceral fat,** which means it is located around internal organs, or **subcutaneous fat,** which is located just below the skin (Figure 6.1).

body composition The relative amounts of fat and fat-free mass in the body.

overweight A weight above the recommended level for health.

obese An excessive amount of fat in the body; typically above 25% for men and 30% for women.

essential fat Body fat that is necessary for physiological functioning.

storage fat Excess fat reserves stored in the body's adipose tissue.

adipose tissue Tissue where fat is stored in the body.

visceral fat Fat stored in the abdomen and around the organs.

subcutaneous fat Fat stored just beneath the skin.

Women tend to store fat in the lower body, around the hips and thighs.

Men tend to store fat in the upper body, around the abdomen.

Storage fat provides energy for activity, insulates the body to retain heat, and protects against trauma to the body.

In general a healthy percentage body fat for men can range from 8–22%, and for women, from 20–35% (1). However, many fitness experts recommend levels at the lower end of these ranges for young adults, 12–15% and 22–25% for men and women, respectively (1). For most people, a body fat percentage outside these ranges indicates an unhealthy body weight. However, athletes or very active individuals might have lower values. Some athletic men have as little as 5–13% fat, and athletic women can have as little as 12–22% (1). Keep in mind that these values are not recommended for the general population and that you can be healthy if your body fat percentage falls within the earlier mentioned ranges. See Figure 6.2 for ranges according to sex and age.

It is not just *how much* body fat a person carries that can greatly affect his risk for several chronic diseases; *where* he carries it also matters. Fat cells are unequally distributed throughout the body, and the distribution of body fat is determined largely by genetics. We inherit specific fat storage traits that determine the regional distribution of fat. For example, many men have a high number of fat cells in the upper body and as a result store more fat within the abdominal area (e.g., around the waist). This is referred to the **android pattern** of obesity. In contrast, women tend to carry more fat cells in the waist, hips, and thighs of the lower body. This is called

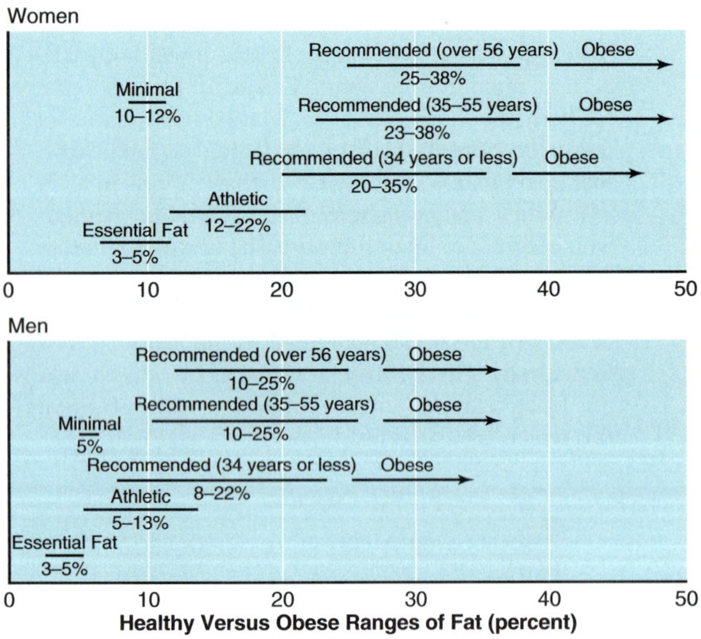

FIGURE 6.2

Recommended levels of body fat for men and women according to age. Note the differences for athletes and the general population.

Source: American College of Sports Medicine. *Resource Manual for Guidelines of Exercise Testing and Prescription*, 5th ed. Philadelphia: Lippincott Williams & Wilkins, 2006, p. 204.

APPRECIATING DIVERSITY THE SEARCH FOR OBESITY-RELATED GENES

Even though obese individuals are found in every segment of the U.S. population, certain subsets of Americans experience the greatest prevalence of obesity. For example, compared to the U.S. population as a whole, the risk of becoming obese is greatest among Mexican American women, African American women, some Native Americans (for example, Pima Indians), and children from low-income families. The high prevalence of obesity in these populations places individuals in those groups at the greatest risk of developing obesity-related diseases.

Research efforts to understand the roles of genetics in the high prevalence of obesity in these populations are expanding. One large investigation, called the Heritage Family Study, is searching for the genes responsible for both obesity and weight loss. Results from this and other genetics studies are expected to provide important information for developing programs that can prevent and treat obesity in high-risk populations.

Source: Changnon, Y. C., et al. Genomic scan for genes affecting body composition before and after training in Caucasians from HERITAGE. *Journal of Applied Physiology* 90:1777–1787, 2001.

the **gynoid pattern** of obesity. People who carry body fat primarily in the abdominal or waist area are at greater risk for developing heart disease and diabetes than are those who store body fat in the hips or lower part of the body (6, 7).

Mental and Physical Health Benefits of a Healthy Weight

Maintaining a healthy weight is important for physical health, and it is also associated with certain aspects of mental health. People who are overweight or obese are more likely to have poor body image and low self-esteem compared to people of normal weight. An unhealthy body image and poor self-esteem are associated with poor health behavior choices and increased risk for physical and mental health problems, such as depression and increased anxiety (8, 9). Maintaining a healthy body weight will make physical activity and everyday activities easier. Individuals who maintain a healthy body weight have a lower risk for developing major chronic conditions such as cardiovascular disease, type 2 diabetes, and certain types of cancers. Cardiovascular disease and all-cause death rates are also lower in people at their recommended body weights compared to overweight and obese individuals (10–11).

CONSIDER THIS!

On average, college students gain 4–9 pounds during their first year of college.

Overweight and Obesity in the United States

Obesity is often defined as a fat percentage body greater than 25% for men and greater than 30% for women. Current estimates for the United States suggest that over 65 million people meet the criteria for obesity (6, 12). Obesity is a major health problem in the United States, and numerous diseases have been linked to being too fat. Because of a strong link between obesity and disease, the National Institutes of Health has estimated that obesity directly accounts for 15–20% of the deaths in the United States (13).

The burden of obesity also has had a significant effect on health care costs. An estimated 9.1% of medical costs, or about $80 billion, were attributed to overweight- and obesity-related health problems in 1998, and estimates reached almost $100 billion

android pattern A pattern of fat distribution characterized by fat stored in the abdominal region; more common in men.

gynoid pattern A pattern of fat distribution characterized by fat stored in the hips and thighs; more common in women.

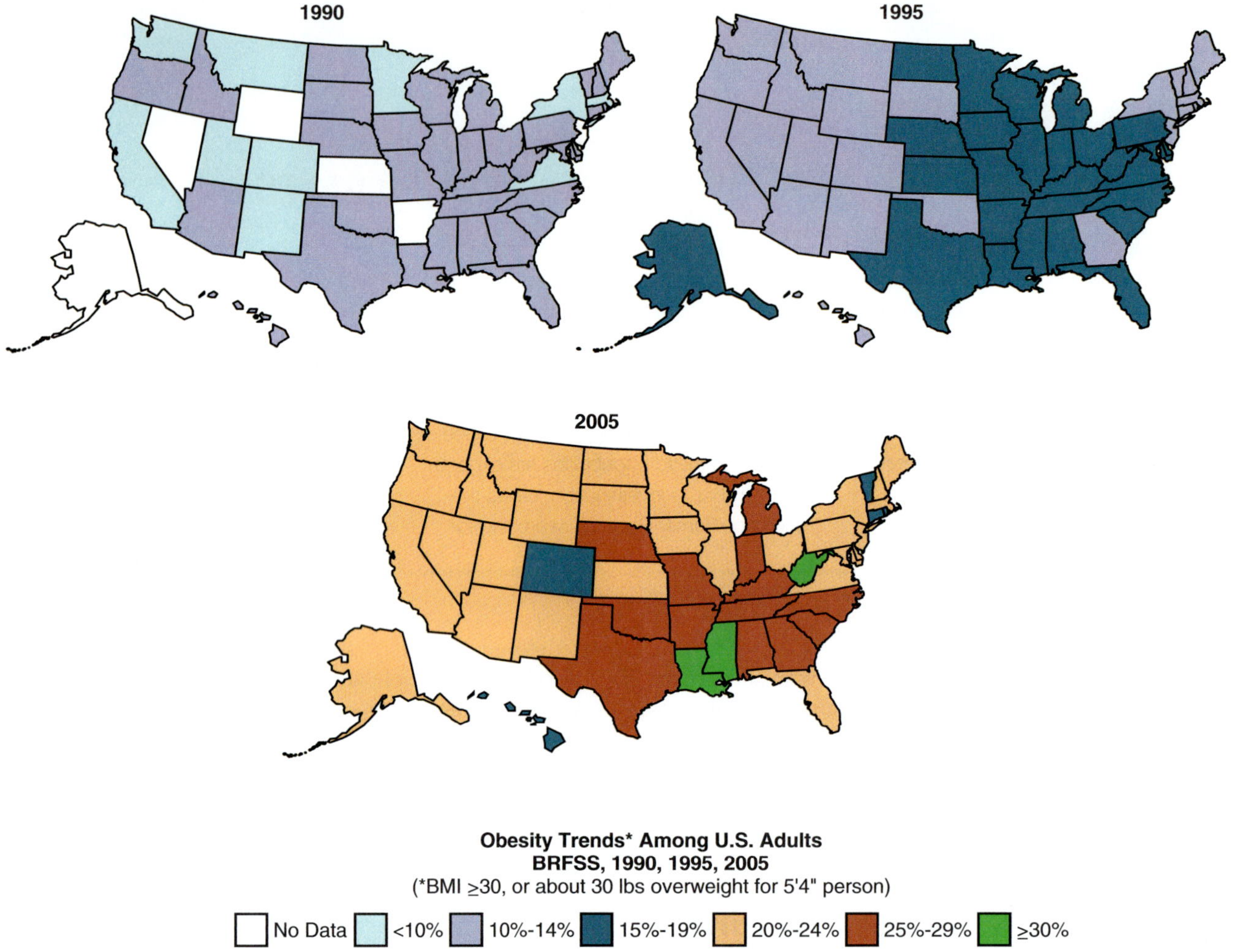

FIGURE 6.3
Obesity rates in the United States increased dramatically in the 15 years between 1990 and 2005.
Source: Centers for Disease Control and Prevention, "U.S. Obesity Trends: 1985–2005, Obesity Trend Maps," www.cdc.gov/nccdphp/dnpa/obesity.

dollars by 2002 (14). However, total health care costs were an estimated $117 billion in the United States for the direct *and* indirect costs of overweight and obesity (15).

News sources frequently report that the obesity rates in America are the highest in the world and continue to climb. The reports are based on studies indicating that the number of obese or overweight people in the United States has increased by 40% in the last 20 years (16). In 1980, 46% of Americans were obese or overweight; by 2000, the number had increased to 65%. You can see the changes in obesity across the United States from 1990 to 2005 in Figure 6.3. Despite the sounding of the alarm in recent years, a new study reveals that the level of obesity has remained steady since 1999 (17). This is the good news. The bad news is that 65% of all Americans are either obese or overweight, and there is no evidence that the rate of obesity is decreasing in adults or children (17). Therefore, obesity continues to be a major threat to wellness in the United States.

Why are so many Americans obese? There is no single answer. Obesity is related to both genetic traits and lifestyle (18, 19). These influences will be discussed more in Chapter 8. Many individuals, such as Jason (introduced at the beginning of the chapter), who put on 15 pounds over 3 years, experience **creeping obesity** by gradually adding fat over a period of time.

This type of weight gain is usually attributed to poor diet (including increased food intake) and a gradual decline in physical activity (20). The woman in Figure 6.4 is gaining one-half pound of fat per month (6 pounds per year), and after five years, she will have gained 30 pounds! The weight gain is so gradual that it typically does not become a concern until years later, when the total weight is more noticeable.

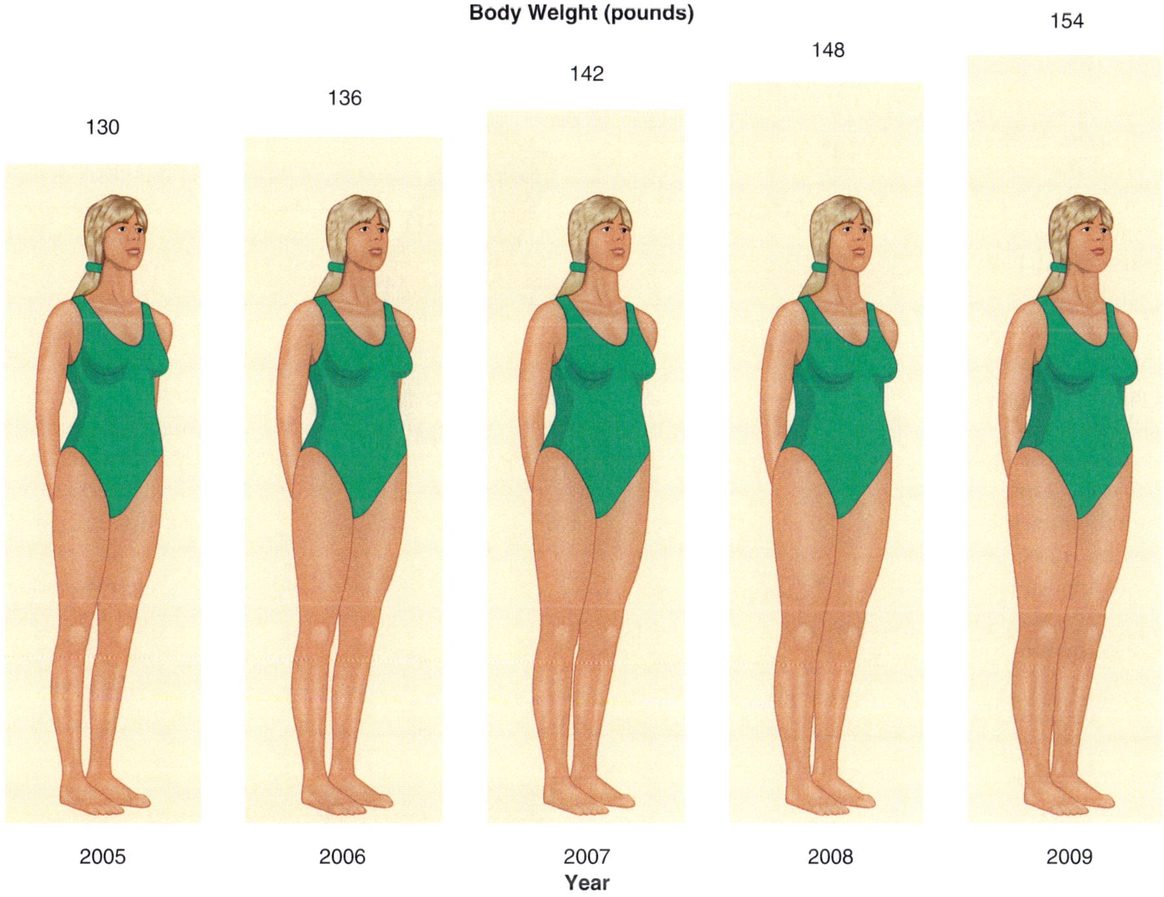

FIGURE 6.4
The concept of creeping obesity.

Chronic Conditions Associated with Overweight and Obesity

Obesity increases the risk of developing at least 26 diseases. Heart disease, colon cancer, hypertension (high blood pressure), kidney disease, arthritis, and diabetes are among the most serious (12, 13, 20).

Heart Disease

Heart disease (also called *cardiovascular disease*, or *CVD*) is the leading cause of death in the United States for both men and women. Obesity is considered a major independent risk factor for coronary heart disease, which happens to be the leading cause of heart attacks. Obesity has been shown to increase the risk of heart attack by 60–80% (21).

Hypertension (high blood pressure) is more common among overweight and obese individuals. However, on a positive note, blood pressure is usually reduced with weight loss. Obesity is linked to elevated cholesterol levels and unhealthy blood lipid profiles. As with hypertension, the cholesterol profile typically improves with weight loss. High blood pressure and cholesterol levels are also independent risk factors for coronary heart disease, so the combination of obesity with these risk factors poses a significantly greater risk for a heart attack. Heart disease will be discussed in much greater detail in Chapter 9.

Diabetes

Diabetes is a metabolic disorder characterized by high blood glucose levels that affects over 18 million people. Chronic elevation of blood glucose is associated with increased incidence of heart disease, kidney disease, nerve dysfunction, and eye damage. In fact, diabetes is one of the leading causes of death and disability in the United States, and its incidence is increasing.

There is a strong relationship between the onset of type 2 diabetes and body fatness; over 80% of people with type 2 diabetes are obese. Type 2 diabetes has

creeping obesity A slow increase in body weight and percentage of body fat over several years.

diabetes A metabolic disorder characterized by high blood glucose levels that is associated with increased risk for heart disease, kidney disease, nerve dysfunction, and eye damage.

traditionally been referred to as *adult-onset diabetes* because its risk increases after age 45. However, this type of diabetes is largely associated with behavioral factors, such as poor dietary habits, physical inactivity, and obesity. As obesity among young people has increased, so has the incidence of type 2 diabetes among adolescents and young adults.

Type 2 diabetes is also known as non–insulin-dependent diabetes, because insulin is not always required as treatment. In type 2 diabetes, the body can produce insulin, but there is a reduced ability of insulin to transport glucose from the blood to the cells. This problem, called *decreased insulin sensitivity*, results in elevated blood glucose levels. People can have decreased insulin sensitivity but not have blood glucose levels high enough to be diagnosed with diabetes. In this case, a person has *pre-diabetes*, which is also more common among obese individuals. As with heart disease, weight loss can significantly reduce the risk of diabetes and help manage diabetes. In fact, research has indicated that modest weight loss of 5–10% can reduce the risk of heart disease and type 2 diabetes (22, 23).

Other Conditions Obesity is a risk factor for some of the most prevalent types of cancers, including breast, prostate, and colon cancer. Overweight and obese individuals are at higher risk for joint problems and osteoarthritis. Sleep apnea, a condition in which a person stops breathing for brief periods while sleeping, and gallbladder disease are more common among obese individuals. Additionally, obese women are more likely to experience menstrual abnormalities, difficulty conceiving, and complications during pregnancy than women of normal weight.

Health Effects of Underweight

Although the current rates of overweight and obesity among U.S. adults indicate there is an obesity epidemic, a small percentage of people in the country suffers from health problems associated with being underweight. As with overweight, underweight can be determined by measuring height, weight, and body fat percentage. However, just as with determining overweight and obesity, it is best to use a measure of body composition to determine whether one is underweight. Getting close to or below the level of essential body fat is an indicator that an individual might be too thin.

Health problems associated with being underweight are typically related to malnutrition, because the person is likely not eating enough to get all the necessary nutrients. Severe and prolonged malnutrition can result in a loss of muscle mass and strength. Further, underweight individuals are at increased risk for osteoporosis, and under-

CONSIDER THIS!

Sedentary adults are over 2.5 times more likely to experience significant weight gain over 10 years compared to those who report that they exercise vigorously 2 or more times per week.

Being underweight can also lead to significant health problems.

STEPS FOR BEHAVIOR CHANGE

Are you at risk for developing diabetes?

Does your body composition, or other factors, put you at increased risk for developing diabetes? To find out whether you are at increased risk, respond true or false to the following statements.

T	F	
☐	☐	I have a BMI that puts me in the overweight or obese category.
☐	☐	I am under 65 years of age AND I get little or no exercise.
☐	☐	I have a sister or brother with diabetes.
☐	☐	I have a parent with diabetes.
☐	☐	I am a woman who has had a baby weighing more than 9 pounds at birth.

In general, the more "true" answers you have, the higher your risk.

TIPS TO REDUCE YOUR RISK OF DIABETES

☑ Determine whether you are overweight, and if so, lose weight. If you have a BMI above the healthy range, get a body composition assessment to determine your level of fat. If your percentage of body fat is above the healthy range, talk to your instructor or a health educator at your campus health center about setting goals and preparing a plan for weight loss.

☑ Get more exercise. Be more active most days of the week. See Chapter 1 for tips to change your health behavior.

☑ Incorporate more fresh fruits and vegetables and whole grains into your diet, and cut back on the salt and high-fat foods.

☑ See your health care provider. A lot of people have diabetes and pre-diabetes without knowing it.

Source: American Diabetes Association. Diabetes risk test. www.diabetes.org.

weight women are at increased risk for menstrual abnormalities that can lead to infertility. People with eating disorders, such as anorexia nervosa and bulimia, can experience many other health problems. Heart problems, digestive disorders, kidney damage, anemia, lethargy, muscle weakness, dry skin, and poor immune function are some of the common problems associated with anorexia nervosa or bulimia nervosa.

Eating disorders are complex conditions that involve much more than just being underweight. We will discuss these conditions in greater detail in Chapter 8.

Make sure you know...

- Overweight refers to a weight above the recommended level, and obesity refers to a high percentage of body fat.
- A certain amount of fat is needed for normal physiological functioning, and excess storage fat is associated with increased risk for numerous conditions.
- Physical and mental health are affected by unhealthy levels of body fat.
- Rates of obesity in the United States are high and contribute significantly to health care costs.
- The amount and distribution of excess storage fat can lead to increased risk of illness and death associated with heart disease and diabetes.
- Having too little body fat can lead to significant health problems.

A CLOSER LOOK

CAN YOU BE FIT AND FAT?

Although overweight and obesity are associated with numerous unhealthy conditions, and people should always strive for a healthy body weight, it is possible to be fit and overweight. Think about watching your favorite football team. Do all the players look thin and healthy? Probably not. However, because of their intense workouts even those players with the seemingly unhealthy looking physiques can still be healthy.

Multiple research studies have found that overweight individuals can be healthy if they are physically active or fit. The strongest evidence comes from longitudinal studies conducted at the Cooper Clinic in Dallas, Texas. Researchers examined heart disease and death risk and overall death rates in men and women. Death risk was 1.5 times greater for low-fit participants compared to highly fit participants across both normal and overweight BMI classifications. Those with the highest fitness levels and the lowest BMIs had the lowest risk for disease and death. However, overweight highly fit men and women had lower risk for death than their overweight low-fit counterparts and than low-fit weight men and women of normal weight. Others have found reduced risk for heart disease and death in active and fit overweight and obese individuals.

These findings support the fact that efforts to incorporate regular physical activity into one's lifestyle are not in vain, because active overweight individuals do enjoy the benefits of lower risk of heart disease. People who are inactive but at a recommended weight still should consider a regular exercise program to minimize their risk of chronic disease.

Sources: Lohman, T., et al. Body fat measurement goes high-tech: Not all are created equal. *ACSM'S Health and Fitness Journal* 1(1):30–35, 1997; Lee, C. D., S. N. Blair, and A. S. Jackson. Cardiorespiratory fitness, body composition, and all-cause cardiovascular disease mortality in men. *American Journal of Clinical Nutrition* 69:373–380, 1999; Lee, C. D., A. S. Jackson, and S. N. Blair. U.S. weight guidelines: Is it also important to consider cardiorespiratory fitness? *International Journal of Obesity and Related Metabolic Disorders* 22 (suppl 2):S2–S7, 1998.

Assessing Body Composition

Several field and laboratory methods for assessing body composition have been developed. Field methods require little equipment and can be easily administered at a fitness center or gym to determine weight status or body composition. The laboratory measures are used more frequently in research or medical settings. Each measure has strengths and limitations.

Field Methods

Several quick and inexpensive field techniques are used to evaluate body composition and the risk for disease (24–26). The procedures discussed in this section have been validated and can provide good estimates of your level of body fat or level of disease risk.

Body Mass Index One of the easiest techniques used to determine whether someone is overweight or obese is the **body mass index (BMI).** The BMI is simply the ratio of the body weight (in kilograms; kg) divided by height (in meters squared; m^2):

$$\text{BMI} = \text{weight (kg)} \div \text{height (m)}^2$$

(*Note*: 1 kg = 2.2 lb, and 1 m = 39.25 in.)

For example, for an individual who weighs 64.5 kg and is 1.72 m tall, the BMI would be computed as follows:

$$64.5\ \text{kg}/(1.72\ \text{m})^2 = 64.5 \div 2.96 = 21.8\ \text{kg/m}^2$$

The concept behind the BMI is that individuals with low percentage of body fat will have a low BMI. For example, men and women with a BMI of less than 25 kg/m^2, respectively, are classified as having optimal body fat (Table 6.1). In contrast, men and women with a BMI of greater than 30 kg/m^2 are considered obese. Additionally, research has indicated that individuals classified as overweight or obese according to BMI are at increased risk for cardiovascular disease and death.

BMI is a simple and inexpensive method for determining your weight status, but it has limitations. For example, BMI does not give you a direct measure of fat percentage. In fact, in some cases the method can over- or underestimate body fatness. An individual with

TABLE 6.1
Ranges and Classification for BMI and Waist Circumference

	BMI	*Disease Risk* Relative to Normal Weight and Waist Circumference* Men, ≤102 cm Women, ≤88 cm	Men, >102 cm Women, >88 cm
Underweight	<18.5	—	—
Normal	18.5–24.9	—	—
Overweight	25.0–29.9	Increased	High
Obesity			
Class I	30.0–34.9	High	Very high
Class II	35.0–39.9	Very high	Very high
Class III	≥40	Extremely high	Extremely high

*Disease risk for type 2 diabetes, hypertension, and cardiovascular disease. Dashes (—) indicate that no additional risk at these levels of BMI was assigned. Increased waist circumference can also be a marker for increased risk even in persons of normal weight.

Source: Modified from American College of Sports Medicine. *ACSM's Guidelines for Exercise Testing and Prescription,* 7th ed. Philadelphia: Lippincott Williams & Wilkins, 2006, p. 58.

a low percentage of body fat but a high level of muscularity would typically have a relatively high BMI, which would incorrectly suggest a high percentage of body fat. If you calculate BMI values for Josh and Jason, for example, you might be surprised to learn that, based on BMI guidelines, Josh is "overweight" and Jason is in the normal-weight category.

BMI is best used to obtain an initial estimate of whether one's weight is at a healthy level. You should follow up a BMI calculation with a measure of body fat percentage, especially if you feel you are at a healthy weight and your BMI indicates otherwise.

Skinfold Assessment Because more than 50% of body fat is subcutaneous fat that lies just beneath the skin, a **skinfold test** can be used to estimate a person's overall body fatness (20, 27). In a skinfold test, subcutaneous fat is measured using an instrument called a skinfold caliper. To be accurate, skinfold tests to estimate body fat for both men and women require at least three skinfold measurement sites (20). The anatomical sites to be measured in men (abdominal, chest, thigh skinfolds) and in women (suprailium, triceps, and thigh skinfolds) are illustrated in Laboratory 6.1. Note that for standardization, all measurements should be made on the right side of the body.

Skinfold measurements to determine body fat are reliable but generally have a ± 3–4% margin of error (27, 28). Using calibrated metal calipers (instead of plastic) and having a skilled technician do the test are two ways to increase accuracy. If you are having a skinfold measure taken, it is very important that you follow the instructions given by the fitness professional to ensure the most accurate readings.

Skinfold assessment is an easy measure to obtain and can provide good estimates when done properly. However, it is not necessarily a good measure to assess body composition for very obese individuals, because it is often difficult to obtain accurate readings. Inaccurate estimates can be misleading and discouraging and can interfere with setting an appropriate goal weight. Bioelectrical impedance (discussed later in this chapter) may be preferred for obese individuals.

Waist Measurement and Waist-to-Hip Ratio Waist measurements and the **waist-to-hip ratio** can be used to determine the risk of disease associated with high body fat. These techniques do not provide an estimate of body fat percentage. However, they are excellent indicators of whether the body fat distribution is unhealthy. Waist measurements greater or equal to 40 inches (102 cm) for men and 35 inches (88 cm) for women are considered high risk and

body mass index (BMI) A ratio of body weight (kg) divided by height squared (m^2) used to determine whether a person is at a healthy body weight; BMI is related to the percentage of body fat.

skinfold test A field test used to estimate body composition; representative samples of subcutaneous fat are measured using calipers to estimate the overall level of body fat.

waist-to-hip ratio A ratio of the waist and hip circumferences used to determine the risk for disease associated with the android pattern of obesity.

indicate the android pattern of obesity. You can better evaluate your risk according to waist measurement by also considering your BMI (see Table 6.1). A high waist measurement alone might not indicate increased risk. For example, a high waist measurement for someone who is tall might be proportional to his height, and the level of BMI and body fat might be well within the healthy ranges.

Another way to estimate disease risk according to body fat distribution is the waist-to-hip ratio. An individual with a large fat deposit in the abdominal region would have a high waist-to-hip ratio and would have a higher risk of disease than someone with a lower waist-to-hip ratio.

Both waist and hip circumference measurements should be made while the person is standing, using a nonelastic tape. It is important that the person not wear bulky clothing during the measurement, because it could alter the measurements. During measurements, the tape should be placed snugly around the body but should not press into the skin. Record your measurements to the nearest millimeter or sixteenth of an inch. The specific procedure is detailed in Laboratory 6.1.

Laboratory Measures

Body fat measurements performed in a laboratory are considered the gold standard for assessing body composition. However, these techniques require expensive specialized equipment and are often not readily available to the general public. The methods are usually used by researchers or clinicians to determine body fat percentage in research participants or patients.

Dual Energy X-Ray Absorptiometry

Dual energy X-ray absorptiometry (DXA) involves taking a low radiation X-ray scan (involving considerably less radiation than a typical X-ray scan) of the entire body to obtain estimates of body fat percentage. In this procedure, the person lies still on a table while an X-ray arm passes over the body. The scan typically requires about 15 minutes to complete.

The advantage of using DXA is that it provides a measure of total body fat as well as a measure of regional fat distribution. It can also be used to assess bone density as it relates to osteoporosis and osteoporosis risk. However, the technique is generally not used outside research or clinical settings. The equipment is expensive, and because it uses an X ray only trained professionals can perform the scan. Therefore, most people will not have the opportunity to have this assessment.

Hydrostatic Weighing

Hydrostatic weighing, also called underwater weighing, is a technique that involves weighing the individual both on land and in a tank of water to determine body volume and body density. Lean mass has a higher density than water, whereas fat mass is less dense than water. The more muscular person will weigh more under water. Because fat tends to float, the person with more fat will weigh less under water. After the two weights are obtained, they are used to calculate percentage of body fat.

Underwater weighing is very time-consuming and requires expensive equipment. Additionally, this measure typically does not appeal to most individuals, because it involves wearing a bathing suit and being completely submerged underwater. Thus, this procedure is rarely employed to assess body composition in collegiate physical fitness courses.

Air Displacement

Air displacement is a fairly new method used to assess body composition and is similar in principle to hydrostatic weighing. Instead of being submerged in water, the individual is seated in a chamber (the Bod Pod®). Computerized sensors are used to estimate the amount of air that is displaced when the participant is in the chamber. From knowing the amount of air that is displaced, body volume and then body fat can be calculated. Estimates of body fat percentage from air displacement are similar to measures from hydrostatic weighing.

Air displacement is less time-consuming than underwater weighing; however, the equipment is expensive, so this technique is not available in fitness centers. Air displacement is more commonly used in research settings, and as a newer measure it needs more assessment in a variety of populations (e.g., athletes, older adults, ethnic minorities) to determine overall accuracy.

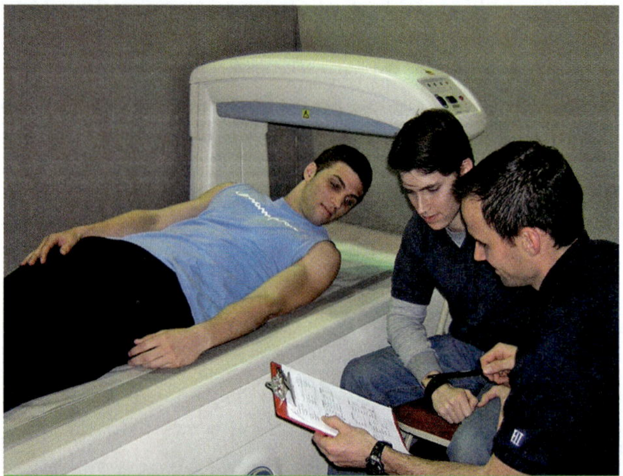

The DXA scan is considered the gold standard for measuring body composition.

Hydrostatic weighing involves being weighed while submerged in a tank of water.

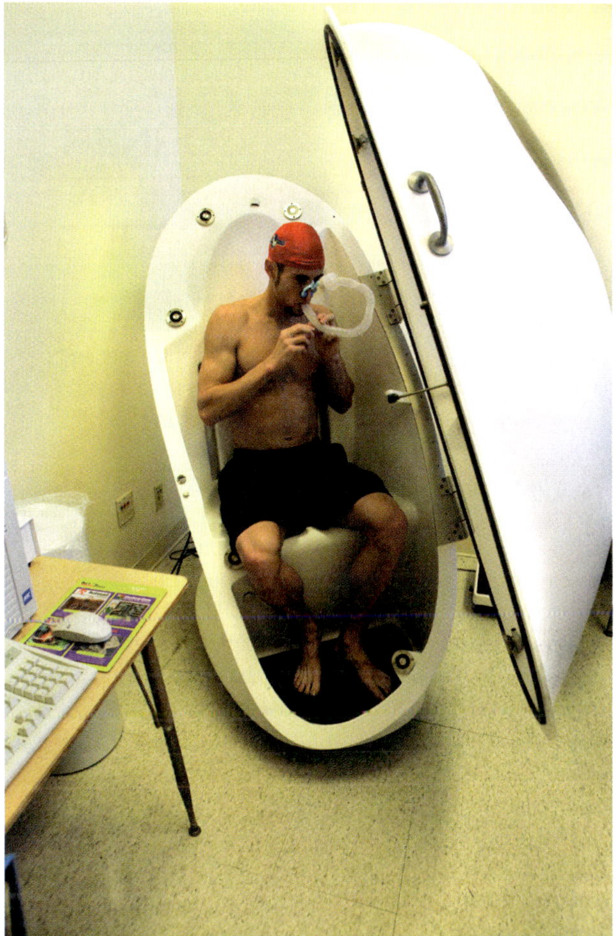

The Bod Pod® uses air displacement to measure body composition.

Bioelectrical Impedance Analysis

Bioelectrical impedance analysis (BIA) is a procedure used in fitness centers as well as in research laboratories. With commercially available BIA monitors, the person either stands on sensors of a scale-like piece of equipment or holds sensors between both hands. In the laboratory, the participant lies on a table with surface electrodes placed at the hand and foot. Then, a very low level electrical current (too low to be felt) is passed through the body between the electrodes or sensors. Because lean tissue contains more water, it is a good conductor of the current. Fat tissue, in contrast, contains less water and impedes the flow of the current. Body fat is estimated according to the resistance to the flow of the current.

BIA is typically an acceptable measure to most people. However, the commercially available monitors do not provide a total body measure, and estimates can be less accurate because a smaller area is assessed and the reading may be influenced by regional fat distribution. The total body measure used in laboratory and research settings is noninvasive and easy to administer, but its accuracy and reliability have been questioned. A significant source of error is a failure to follow instructions. If you were to have a BIA performed, the fitness professional or lab technician would give you very explicit instructions in regard to exercise, voiding, eating, and drinking prior to the assessment. The in-

dual energy X-ray absorptiometry (DXA) A technique for assessing body composition using a low radiation X ray; it is typically used in research or clinical settings and is considered a gold-standard measure.

hydrostatic weighing A method of determining body composition that involves weighing an individual on land and in a tank of water.

air displacement A technique used to assess body composition by estimating body volume based on air displaced when a person sits in a chamber.

bioelectrical impedance analysis (BIA) A method of assessing body composition by running a low-level electrical current through the body.

Consumer CORNER

USE-AT-HOME MEASUREMENT DEVICES—ARE THEY WORTH THE MONEY?

Did you know that you can buy a bathroom scale that estimates body fat? You can also purchase hand-held body fat monitors for \$40 to \$100. The question is, are such devices worth your money?

The equipment shown in the photo uses the BIA technique that was discussed on page 181. The scale assesses body fat in the lower body, and the hand-held device performs an upper body assessment. Because they do not perform total body assessments, the readings from these commercially available monitors are not as accurate as the laboratory BIA measure or other body composition techniques. Additionally, the partial body readings are influenced by the regional fat distribution. Although these devices can provide a general estimate, you are probably better served by getting a skinfold assessment performed by a trained technician.

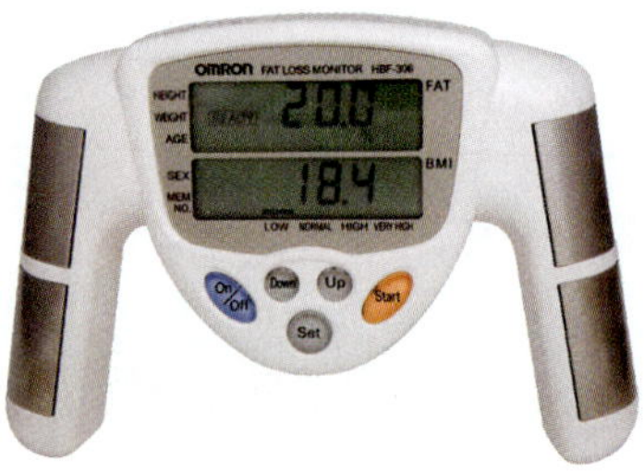

structions address factors that affect your level of hydration, which is crucial for an accurate measurement. Failure to comply with the pre-assessment instructions can significantly impair the accuracy of the reading.

Make sure you know...

- There are several laboratory and field methods used to assess body composition and weight status.
- BMI, skinfold, and waist-to-hip ratio are the most common assessments for general use in fitness courses and fitness centers.
- Laboratory assessments such as DXA, hydrostatic weighing, air displacement, and BIA provide very good estimates of body composition, but most are not practical for commercial use because of their cost.

Using Body Composition to Determine Your Ideal Body Weight

The fitness categories presented for body composition differ from those for the other components of health-related physical fitness. Whereas "superior" was the highest fitness level for cardiorespiratory, strength, and muscular endurance fitness, the classification of "optimal" is the highest standard for body composition. Any category other than "optimal" is considered unsatisfactory for health-related fitness. Therefore, your goal should be to reach and maintain an optimal body composition.

Research suggests that a range of 8%–22% body fat is an optimal health and fitness goal for men, and the optimal range for women is 20%–35% (1). These ranges provide little risk of disease associated with body fatness and permit individual differences in physical activity patterns and diet.

Once we have calculated our body fat percentage and know the optimal range of body fat, how can we determine the desired range of body weight? A typical 20-year-old man who has 30% body fat and weighs 185 pounds can calculate his optimal range of body weight in two simple steps:

Step 1. Compute fat-free weight—that is, the amount of total body weight contained in bones, organs, and muscles:

$$\text{Total body weight} - \text{fat weight} = \text{fat-free weight}$$
$$100\% - 30\% = 70\%$$

This means that 70% of total body weight is fat-free weight. Therefore, the fat-free weight for this student is

$$70\% \times 185 \text{ lb} = 129.5 \text{ lb}$$

Step 2. Calculate the optimal weight (which for men is 8–22% of total body weight): The formula to compute optimum body weight is

$$\text{Optimum weight} = \text{fat-free weight} \div (1 - \text{optimal \% fat})$$

Note that fat percentage should be expressed as a decimal. Thus, for 8% body fat,

$$\text{Optimum weight} = 129.5 \div (1 - 0.08) = 140.8 \text{ pounds}$$

For 22% body fat,

$$\text{Optimum weight} = 129.5 \div (1 - 0.22) = 166 \text{ pounds}$$

Basically, we assume that this man will maintain his lean body mass and lose fat. So, his 129.5 pounds of lean mass will be 78–92% of his new optimal body weight to achieve a healthy body composition. Hence, the optimal body weight for this individual is between 140.8 and 166.0 pounds. Laboratory 6.2 provides the opportunity to compute your optimal body weight using both body fat percentage and body mass index.

Make sure you know...

- Healthy body weight should be determined based on the optimal level of body fat for your age, height, and sex.
- Ideal weight can be easily calculated if you know your percentage of body fat.

Behavior Change: Set Goals and Get Regular Assessments

You will learn about weight management in Chapter 8, but here we want to briefly discuss the importance of getting regular body composition assessments as you attempt to lose or gain weight. When we calculated the goal weight based on the optimal level of body fat, we assumed only fat weight was lost. However, a person experiencing weight loss may also lose water weight and possibly lose lean mass. Incorporating regular aerobic and resistance exercise along with a healthy diet will maximize the amount of fat that is lost and maintain more lean mass.

As the body changes with weight loss or gain, the weights that were originally calculated might not correspond exactly with the desired body fat percentage. In the example above, the individual might lose 7 pounds and be in the optimal range if he also increased lean mass. Additionally, regular assessments will help you determine whether the weight you are losing is fat and not lean mass. Therefore, it is important to have regular body composition assessments as you are trying to reach a new goal weight. It is important to get the same type of test when you get follow-up assessments. If possible, it also is recommended that the same person perform the assessment. These factors will reduce error of the measurement. The frequency of the assessments will depend on your goal.

Make sure you know...

- You should have regular body composition assessments when trying to lose or gain weight to ensure the healthiest changes.
- Follow-up assessments should be made with the same measure as the original assessment.

Summary

1. Body composition refers to the relative amounts of fat and fat-free tissue in the body. Fat in the body can be essential fat or storage fat. A healthy body weight should be based on the recommended amount of body fat.
2. Body composition is an important component of health-related physical fitness because a high percentage of body fat is associated with an increased risk for numerous diseases. The distribution of fat also affects disease risk associated with overweight and obesity. A very low percentage of body fat is also associated with increased risk for disease.
3. Common field techniques for assessing body fat and healthy weight are skinfold measurements, BMI assessment, and examination of the waist-to-hip ratio.
4. Laboratory techniques for estimating body fat are most commonly used in research and clinical settings. DXA is considered the gold-standard measure for estimating body fat.
5. You can calculate your healthy weight range by knowing your desired percentage of body fat or BMI. You should have regular body composition assessments when trying to lose or gain weight.

Study Questions

1. How much essential fat do the average man and woman carry?
   a. 25% and 30%
   b. 3% and 12%
   c. 10% and 20%
   d. 5% and 18%
2. Which of the following is not a potential health consequence of being overweight or obese?
   a. low self-esteem
   b. gallbladder disease
   c. osteoarthritis
   d. anemia
3. Storing excess fat in the hips and thighs puts an individual at greater risk for heart disease and diabetes than storing excess fat in the abdomen.
   a. true
   b. false
4. Which technique is used to assess disease risk status associated with the regional fat distribution?
   a. waist-to-hip ratio
   b. skinfold test
   c. underwater weighing
   d. bioelectrical impedance analysis
5. For disease risk and health standards, a BMI of _______ kg/m^2 is considered obese.
   a. 27
   b. 25
   c. 30
   d. 45
6. Which of the following is a common field measure for assessing body composition?
   a. waist measurement
   b. skinfold test
   c. hydrostatic weighing
   d. DXA
7. Which is not a potential health consequence of being underweight or having an eating disorder?
   a. malnutrition
   b. menstrual abnormalities
   c. digestive disorders
   d. type 1 diabetes
8. A person classified as normal weight based on a BMI in the healthy range can be over-fat.
   a. true
   b. false
9. Discuss the different types of field measurement techniques for assessing body composition. Discuss the strengths and limitations of each.
10. Discuss potential health consequences of not maintaining a healthy body composition.
11. Define overweight and obesity. What is the public health impact of overweight and obesity in the United States?

Suggested Reading

American College of Sports Medicine. *Guidelines for Exercise Testing and Prescription*, 7th ed. Philadelphia: Lippincott Williams and Wilkins, 2006.

Heyward, V. H., and D. R. Wagner *Applied Body Composition Assessment*, 2nd ed. Champaign, IL: Human Kinetics, 2004.

Kaminsky, L. A. (ed.). *ACSM's Resource Manual for Guidelines for Exercise Testing and Prescription*. Philadelphia: Lippincott Williams and Wilkins, 2006.

Nelson, T. F., S. L. Gortmaker, S. V. Subramanian, L. Cheung, and H. Wechsler. Disparities in overweight and obesity among US college students. *American Journal of Health Behavior* 31(4):363–73, 2007.

Smith, S. C., and D. Haslem. Abdominal obesity, waist circumference and cardio-metabolic risk: Awareness among primary care physicians, the general population and patients at risk—the Shape of the Nations survey. *Current Medical Research and Opinion* 23(1):29–47, 2007.

For links to the websites below, visit The Total Fitness and Wellness Website at www.aw-bc.com/powers.

ACSM.org
Website of the American College of Sports Medicine. Provides information about all aspects of health and fitness.

Diabetes.org
Website of the American Diabetes Association.

AmericanHeart.org
Website of the American Heart Association.

References

1. Kaminsky L. A., (ed.). *ACSM'S Resource Manual for Guidelines for Exercise Testing and Prescription*. Philadelphia: Lippincott, Williams and Wilkins, 2006.
2. Bjorntorp, P., and B. Brodoff, eds. *Obesity*. Philadelphia: Lippincott, Williams and Wilkins, 1992.
3. Perri, M., A. Nezu, and B. Viegener. *Improving the Long-Term Management and Treatment of Obesity*. New York: John Wiley and Sons, 1992.
4. Stefanik, M. Exercise and weight control. In *Exercise and Sport Science Reviews*, J. Holloszy, ed. Baltimore: Williams and Wilkins, 1993.
5. Stunkard, A., and T. Wadden, eds. *Obesity: Theory and Therapy*. New York: Raven Press, 1993.
6. Atkinson, R. Treatment of obesity. *Nutritional Reviews* 50:338–345, 1992.
7. Bouchard, C., R. Shepherd, T. Stephens, J. Sutton, and B. McPherson, eds. *Exercise, Fitness, and Health: A Consensus of Current Knowledge*. Champaign, IL: Human Kinetics, 1990.
8. Cohen T., and M. Esther. Depressed mood and concern with weight and shape in normal women. *International Journal of Eating Disorders* 14:223–227, 1993.
9. Kirkcaldy, B. D., M. Eysenck, A. F. Furnham, and G. Siefen. Gender, anxiety, and self-image. *Personality and Individual Differences* 24:677–684, 1998.
10. Mokdad, A. H., M. K. Serdula, W. H. Dietz, B. A. Bowman, J. S. Marks, and J. P. Koplan, Prevalence of obesity, diabetes, and obesity-related health risk factors, 2001. *Journal of the American Medical Association* 289:76–79, 2003.
11. McGinnis, J. M., and W. H. Foege. Actual cases of death in the United States. *Journal of the American Medical Association* 270:2207–2212, 1993.
12. Kuczmarski, R. Prevalence of overweight and weight gain in the United States. *American Journal of Clinical Nutrition* 55:495s–502s, 1992.
13. Van Itallie, T. Health implications of overweight and obesity in the United States. *Annals of Internal Medicine* 103:983–988, 1985.
14. Finkelstein, E. A., I. C. Fiebelkorn, and G. Wang. National medical spending attributable to overweight and obesity: How much, and who's paying? *Health Affairs* W3:210–226, 2003.
15. Weight Control Information Network, National Institute of Diabetes and Digestive and Kidney Diseases, National Institutes of Health, http://win.niddk.nih.gov/statistics/index.htm#econ
16. Stein, C., and G. Colditz. The epidemic of obesity. *Journal of Clinical Endocrinology and Metabolism* 89:2522–2525, 2004.
17. Hedley, A., C. Ogden, C. Johnson, M. Carroll, L. Curtin, and K. Flegal. Prevalence of overweight and obesity among US children, adolescents, and adults, 1999–2002. *Journal of the American Medical Association* 16:2847–2850, 2004.
18. Bouchard, C., A. Tremblay, J. Despres, et al. The response to long-term overfeeding in identical twins. *New England Journal of Medicine* 322:1477–1482, 1990.
19. Stunkard, A., T. Sorensen, C. Hanis, et al. An adoption study of human obesity. *New England Journal of Medicine* 314:193–198, 1986.
20. Williams, M. *Lifetime Fitness and Wellness*. Dubuque, IA: William C. Brown, 1996.
21. Health implications of obesity: National Institutes of Health consensus development conference. *Annals of Internal Medicine* 103:977–1077, 1985.
22. Diabetes Prevention Research Group. Impact of intensive lifestyle and Metformin therapy on cardiovascular disease risk factors in the diabetes prevention program. *Diabetes Care* 28:888–894, 2005.
23. Wing, R. R., E. Venditti, J. M. Jakicic, B. A. Polley, and W. Lang. Lifestyle intervention in overweight individuals with a family history of diabetes. *Diabetes Care* 21:350–359, 1998.
24. Howley, E., and D. Franks. *Health Fitness Instructor's Handbook*, 4th ed. Champaign, IL: Human Kinetics, 2003.
25. DiGirolamo, M. Body composition—roundtable. *Physician and Sports Medicine* (March):144–162, 1986.
26. Van Itallie, T. Topography of body fat: Relationship to risk of cardiovascular and other diseases. In *Anthropometric Standardization Reference Manual*, T. Lohman et al., eds. Champaign, IL: Human Kinetics, 1988.
27. Stunkard, A., and T. Wadden, eds. *Obesity: Theory and Therapy*. New York: Raven Press, 1993.
28. Powers, S., and E. Howley. *Exercise Physiology: Theory and Application to Fitness and Performance*, 6th ed. St. Louis: McGraw-Hill, 2007.
29. Jackson, A., and M. Pollock. Practical assessment of body composition. *Physician and Sports Medicine* 13:76–90, 1985.
30. Racette, S. B, S. S. Deusinger, M. J Strube, G. R. Highstein, and R. H. Deusinger. Weight changes, exercise, and dietary patterns during freshman and sophomore years of college. *Journal of American College Health* 53:245–251, 2005.
31. Anderson, D. A., J. R. Shapiro, and J. D. Lundgren. The freshman year of college as a critical period for weight gain: An initial evaluation. *Eating Behaviors* 4:363–367, 2003.
32. Levitsky, D. A., C. A. Halbmaier, and G. Mrdjenovic. The freshman weight gain: A model for the study of the epidemic of obesity. *International Journal of Obesity* 28:1435–1442, 2004.
33. Haapanen N., S. Miilunpalo, M. Pasanen, P. Oja, and I. Vuori. Association between leisure time physical activity and 10-year body mass change among working-aged men and women. *International Journal of Obesity and Related Metabolic Disorders* 21:288–296, 1997.

6.1 LABORATORY

NAME ______________________________ DATE ______________

Assessing Body Composition

Equipment

Tape measure, skinfold caliper, scale

Directions

Complete the assessments described below as directed by your instructor. Then, record your body composition data and weight classifications for BMI, waist circumference, waist-to-hip ratio, skinfold, and/or other measures in the spaces below.

BMI

Weight (kg) __________

Height (m^2) __________

BMI __________

Classification (see Figure 6.2 on page 179):

__________ Underweight

__________ Normal

__________ Overweight

__________ Obese

Skinfold Test

Directions for taking skinfold measurements are on the next page.

Sum of 3 skinfolds (mm) __________
Percent body fat __________
Classification:

__________ Underweight

__________ Normal

__________ Overweight

__________ Obese

Skinfold Measurement Sites

Men

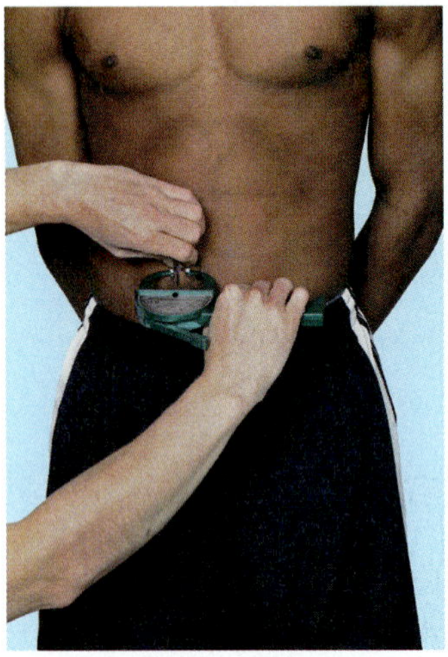

Abdomen

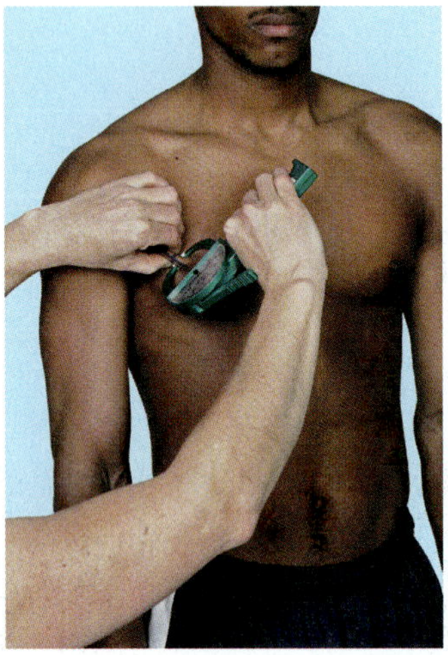

Chest

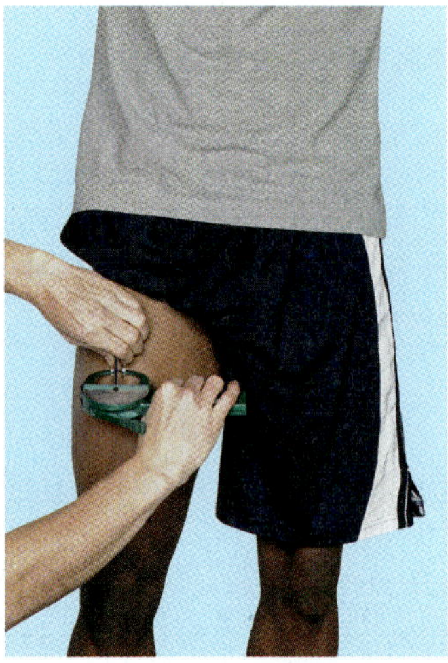

Thigh

Women

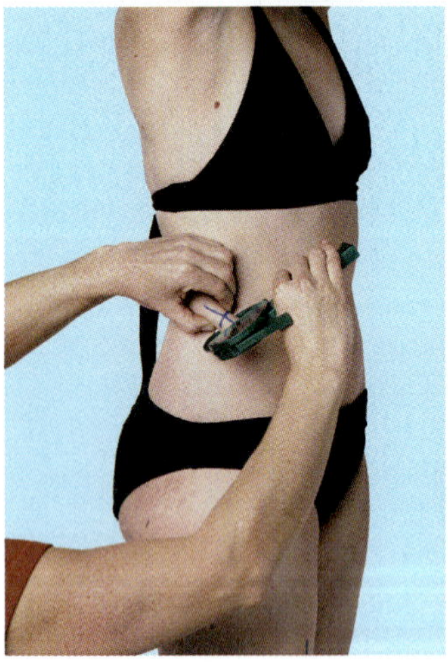

Suprailium

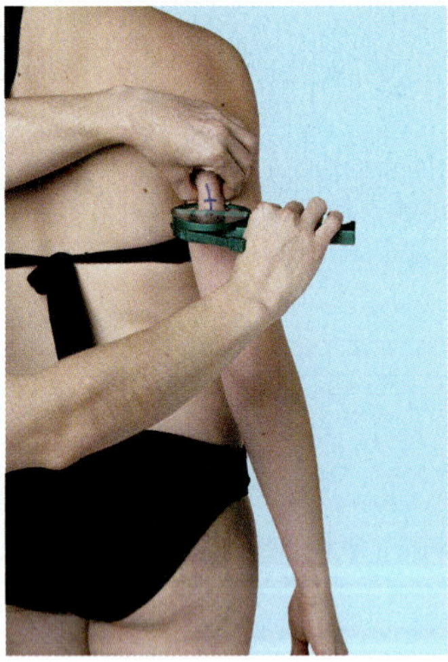

Triceps

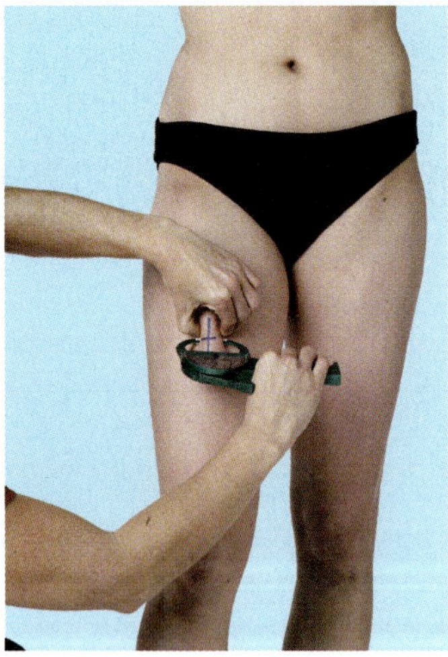

Thigh

To perform skinfold measurements:

- Hold the skinfold between your thumb and index finger.
- Slowly release the tension on the skinfold calipers to pinch the skinfold within $\frac{1}{2}$ inch of your fingers.
- Hold the skinfold, and fully release the tension on the calipers.
- Read the number (the skinfold thickness in millimeters) from the gauge.
- Release the skinfold, and allow the tissue to relax.
- Measure the skinfold thickness at each site.
- Repeat three times, and average the measurements.
- Total the measurements, and use Tables 6.2 and 6.3 on pages 189 and 190 to determine the percent body fat.
- Enter your data in the spaces on page 187.

TABLE 6.2

Percent Fat Estimate for Women

Sum of Triceps, Suprailium, and Thigh Skinfolds

Sum of Skinfolds (mm)	Age: Under 22	23–27	28–32	33–37	38–42	43–47	48–52	53–57	Over 57
23–25	9.7	9.9	10.2	10.4	10.7	10.9	11.2	11.4	11.7
26–28	11.0	11.2	11.5	11.7	12.0	12.3	12.5	12.7	13.0
29–31	12.3	12.5	12.8	13.0	13.3	13.5	13.8	14.0	14.3
32–34	13.6	13.8	14.0	14.3	14.5	14.8	15.0	15.3	15.5
35–37	14.8	15.0	15.3	15.5	15.8	16.0	16.3	16.5	16.8
38–40	16.0	16.3	16.5	16.7	17.0	17.2	17.5	17.7	18.0
41–43	17.2	17.4	17.7	17.9	18.2	18.4	18.7	18.9	19.2
44–46	18.3	18.6	18.8	19.1	19.3	19.6	19.8	20.1	20.3
47–49	19.5	19.7	20.0	20.2	20.5	20.7	21.0	21.2	21.5
50–52	20.6	20.8	21.1	21.3	21.6	21.8	22.1	22.3	22.6
53–55	21.7	21.9	22.1	22.4	22.6	22.9	23.1	23.4	23.6
56–58	22.7	23.0	23.2	23.4	23.7	23.9	24.2	24.4	24.7
59–61	23.7	24.0	24.2	24.5	24.7	25.0	25.2	25.5	25.7
62–64	24.7	25.0	25.2	25.5	25.7	26.0	26.7	26.4	26.7
65–67	25.7	25.9	26.2	26.4	26.7	26.9	27.2	27.4	27.7
68–70	26.6	26.9	27.1	27.4	27.6	27.9	28.1	28.4	28.6
71–73	27.5	27.8	28.0	28.3	28.5	28.8	29.0	29.3	29.5
74–76	28.4	28.7	28.9	29.2	29.4	29.7	29.9	30.2	30.4
77–79	29.3	29.5	29.8	30.0	30.3	30.5	30.8	31.0	31.3
80–82	30.1	30.4	30.6	30.9	31.1	31.4	31.6	31.9	32.1
83–85	30.9	31.2	31.4	31.7	31.9	32.2	32.4	32.7	32.9
86–88	31.7	32.0	32.2	32.5	32.7	32.9	33.2	33.4	33.7
89–91	32.5	32.7	33.0	33.2	33.5	33.7	33.9	34.2	34.4
92–94	33.2	33.4	33.7	33.9	34.2	34.4	34.7	34.9	35.2
95–97	33.9	34.1	34.4	34.6	34.9	35.1	35.4	35.6	35.9
98–100	34.6	34.8	35.1	35.3	35.5	35.8	36.0	36.3	36.5
101–103	35.3	35.4	35.7	35.9	36.2	36.4	36.7	36.0	37.2
104–106	35.8	36.1	36.3	36.6	36.8	37.1	37.3	37.5	37.8
107–109	36.4	36.7	36.9	37.1	37.4	37.6	37.9	38.1	38.4
110–112	37.0	37.2	37.5	37.7	38.0	38.2	38.5	38.7	38.0
113–115	37.5	37.8	38.0	38.2	38.5	38.7	39.0	39.2	39.5
116–118	38.0	38.3	38.5	38.8	39.0	39.3	39.5	39.7	40.0
119–121	38.5	38.7	39.0	39.2	39.5	39.7	40.0	40.2	40.5
122–124	39.0	39.2	39.4	39.7	39.9	40.2	40.4	40.7	40.9
125–127	39.4	39.6	39.9	40.1	40.4	40.6	40.9	41.1	41.4
128–130	39.8	40.0	40.3	40.5	40.8	41.0	41.3	41.5	41.8

Source: Jackson, A. S., and M. L. Pollock, 1985. Practical assessment of body composition. *The Physician and Sportsmedicine* 13(5):76–90, Tables 6 & 7, pp. 86, 87.

TABLE 6.3
Percent Fat Estimate for Men
Sum of Chest, Abdomen, and Thigh Skinfolds

Sum of Skinfolds (mm)	Age: Under 22	23–27	28–32	33–37	38–42	43–47	48–52	53–57	Over 57
8–10	1.3	1.8	2.3	2.9	3.4	3.9	4.5	5.0	5.5
11–13	2.2	2.8	3.3	3.9	4.4	4.9	5.5	6.0	6.5
14–16	3.2	3.8	4.3	4.8	5.4	5.9	6.4	7.0	7.5
17–19	4.2	4.7	5.3	5.8	6.3	6.9	7.4	8.0	8.5
20–22	5.1	5.7	6.2	6.8	7.3	7.9	8.4	8.9	9.5
23–25	6.1	6.6	7.2	7.7	8.3	8.8	9.4	9.9	10.5
26–28	7.0	7.6	8.1	8.7	9.2	9.8	10.3	10.9	11.4
29–31	8.0	8.5	9.1	9.6	10.2	10.7	11.3	11.8	12.4
32–34	8.9	9.4	10.0	10.5	11.1	11.6	12.2	12.8	13.3
35–37	9.8	10.4	10.9	11.5	12.0	12.6	13.1	13.7	14.3
38–40	10.7	11.3	11.8	12.4	12.9	13.5	14.1	14.6	15.2
41–43	11.6	12.2	12.7	13.3	13.8	14.4	15.0	15.5	16.1
44–46	12.5	13.1	13.6	14.2	14.7	15.3	15.9	16.4	17.0
47–49	13.4	13.9	14.5	15.1	15.6	16.2	16.8	17.3	17.9
50–52	14.3	14.8	15.4	15.9	16.5	17.1	17.6	18.2	18.8
53–55	15.1	15.7	16.2	16.8	17.4	17.9	18.5	19.1	19.7
56–58	16.0	16.5	17.1	17.7	18.2	18.8	19.4	20.0	20.5
59–61	16.9	17.4	17.9	18.5	19.1	19.7	20.2	20.8	21.4
62–64	17.6	18.2	18.8	19.4	19.9	20.5	21.1	21.7	22.2
65–67	18.5	19.0	19.6	20.2	20.8	21.3	21.9	22.5	23.1
68–70	19.3	19.9	20.4	21.0	21.6	22.2	22.7	23.3	23.9
71–73	20.1	20.7	21.2	21.8	22.4	23.0	23.6	24.1	24.7
74–76	20.9	21.5	22.0	22.6	23.2	23.8	24.4	25.0	25.5
77–79	21.7	22.2	22.8	23.4	24.0	24.6	25.2	25.8	26.3
80–82	22.4	23.0	23.6	24.2	24.8	25.4	25.9	26.5	27.1
83–85	23.2	23.8	24.4	25.0	25.5	26.1	26.7	27.3	27.9
86–88	24.0	24.5	25.1	25.7	26.3	26.9	27.5	28.1	28.7
89–91	24.7	25.3	25.9	26.5	27.1	27.6	28.2	28.8	29.4
92–94	25.4	26.0	26.6	27.2	27.8	28.4	29.0	29.6	30.2
95–97	26.1	26.7	27.3	27.9	28.5	29.1	29.7	30.3	30.9
98–100	26.9	27.4	28.0	28.6	29.2	29.8	30.4	31.0	31.6
101–103	27.5	28.1	28.7	29.3	29.9	30.5	31.1	31.7	32.3
104–106	28.2	28.8	29.4	30.0	30.6	31.2	31.8	32.4	33.0
107–109	28.9	29.5	30.1	30.7	31.3	31.9	32.5	33.1	33.7
110–112	29.6	30.2	30.8	31.4	32.0	32.6	33.2	33.8	34.4
113–115	30.2	30.8	31.4	32.0	32.6	33.2	33.8	34.5	35.1
116–118	30.9	31.5	32.1	32.7	33.3	33.9	34.5	35.1	35.7
119–121	31.5	32.1	32.7	33.3	33.9	34.5	35.1	35.7	36.4
122–124	32.1	32.7	33.3	33.9	34.5	35.1	35.8	36.4	37.0
125–127	32.7	33.3	33.9	34.5	35.1	35.8	36.4	37.0	37.6

Source: Jackson, A. S., and M. L. Pollock, 1985. Practical assessment of body composition. *The Physician and Sportsmedicine* 13(5):76–90, Tables 6 & 7, pp. 86, 87.

Waist Circumference and Waist-to-Hip Ratio

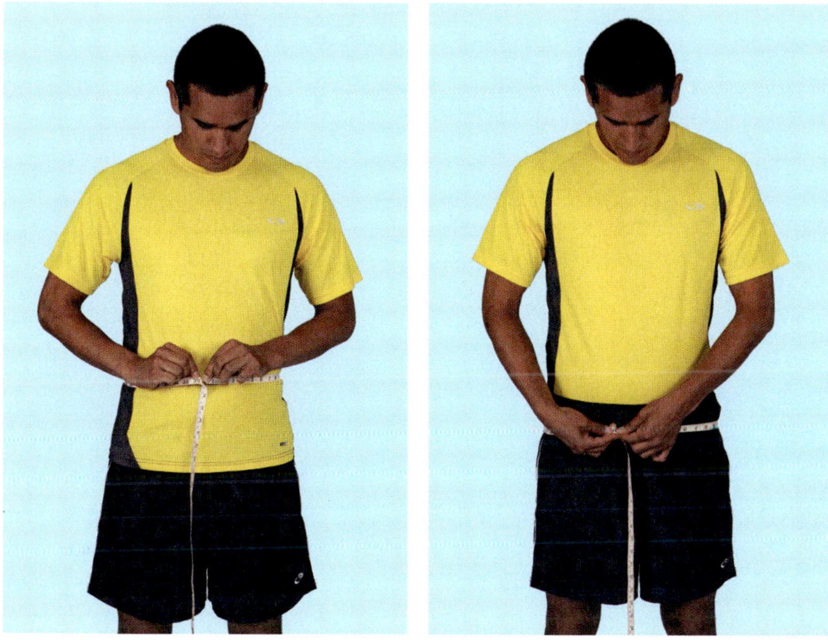

(a) (b)

To perform waist-to-hip circumference measurements.

- Perform the waist measurement first.
- Place the tape at the level of the navel (a), and make your measurement at the end of a normal breath.
- For the hip measurement, place the tape around the maxmum circumference of the buttocks (b).
- Divide the waist circumference by the hip circumference to determine the waist-to-hip ratio.
- Use Table 6.4 to determine the waist-to-hip ratio rating.
- Use Table 6.1 to determine your waist measurement rating.
- Enter your data in the spaces below.

Waist measurement __________

Hip measurement __________

Waist-to-hip ratio __________

TABLE 6.4
Waist-to-Hip Circumference Ratio Standards for Men and Women

		Risk			
	Age	Low	Moderate	High	Very High
Men	20–29	<0.83	0.83–0.88	0.89–0.94	>0.94
	30–39	<0.84	0.84–0.91	0.92–0.96	>0.96
	40–49	<0.88	0.88–0.95	0.96–1.00	>1.00
	50–59	<0.90	0.90–0.96	0.97–1.02	>1.02
	60–69	<0.91	0.91–0.98	0.99–1.03	>1.03
Women	20–29	<0.71	0.71–0.77	0.78–0.82	>0.82
	30–39	<0.72	0.72–0.78	0.79–0.84	>0.84
	40–49	<0.73	0.73–0.79	0.80–0.87	>0.87
	50–59	<0.74	0.74–0.81	0.82–0.88	>0.88
	60–69	<0.76	0.76–0.83	0.84–0.90	>0.90

Source: Reprinted with permission from Heyward, V. H., and L. M. Stolarczyk. *Applied Body Composition Assessment*. Champaign, IL: Human Kinetics, 1996, p. 82.

Classification

__________ Low risk   __________ Low risk

__________ Moderate risk   __________ Moderate risk

__________ High risk   __________ High risk

__________ Very high risk   __________ Very high risk

Other Measure ____________________

Percent body fat __________

Classification:

__________ Underweight

__________ Normal

__________ Overweight

__________ Obese

Questions

1. Are your classifications for each assessment similar? If not, why do you think there are discrepancies?

____

____

2. Which assessment did you feel was most accurate for you, and why?

____

____

6.2 LABORATORY

NAME ______________________________ DATE ______________

Determining a Healthy Body Weight

Equipment

Results from Laboratory 6.1 and a calculator

Directions

If your results from Laboratory 6.1 indicate that you need to lose or gain weight, you should calculate your goal body weight needed to achieve an optimal level of body fat or optimal BMI. Keep in mind that not everyone will need to lose or gain weight. If your weight is within the recommended levels and you are happy with your current body composition, weight maintenance should be your goal.

Part I

		Example:	
Current weight	________	*Current weight*	*176*
Current percent fat	________	*Current percent fat*	*38*
Current BMI	________	*Current BMI*	*29.3**
Goal percent fat	________	*Goal percent fat*	*25–30†*
Goal BMI	________	*Goal BMI*	*20–25 kg/m²*

Step 1: Calculate % of fat-free mass.

1 − ______ (current percent fat ‡) = ______ (% fat-free mass)

Example: 1 − (0.38) = 0.62

Step 2: Calculate fat-free weight.

______ (% fat-free mass ‡) × ______ (current body weight) = ______ (fat-free weight)

Example: 0.62 × 176 = 109.12

Step 3: Calculate optimal weight, lower and upper ends of the range.

______ (optimal weight) = ______ (fat-free weight) /(1 − ______ [optimal percent fat ‡])
Repeat for the upper end of the range.

Example: 109.12 ÷ (1 − 0.25) = 145.5
109.12 ÷ (1 − 0.30) = 155.9
Example optimal range = 146 to 156 pounds

Your optimal range: ____________ to ____________

*We used a height of 65 inches.
†We selected values within the recommended healthy range. You can use the whole range, or you can use part of the range, as we did. The important thing to remember is that your goal should be within the recommended levels for your age and activity level.
‡ Expressed as a decimal.

Step 4: Calculate BMI based on your optimal weight range.

_____________ to _____________

Example:
1 m = 39.25 in., 1 lb = 2.2 kg
65 in. ÷ 39.25 = 1.65 m
146 lb ÷ 2.2 = 66.2 kg
66.2 ÷ 1.65^2 = 24.3 kg/m^2
156 lb ÷ 2.2 = 70.7 kg
70.7 ÷ 165^2 = 25.9 kg/m^2
BMI: 24.3 to 25.9 kg/m^2

Part 2

Repeat the calculations for determining a healthy goal weight, using BMI.

$$\text{goal weight (kg)} = \text{desired BMI} \times \text{height } (m^2)$$

Repeat for the upper end of the range

_____________ to _____________

Questions

1. Do the BMI values in part 1 of the lab place you in the recommended range? If not, why not?

   ____

   ____

2. Are there any differences between the BMI values from parts 1 and 2? If so, why?

   ____

   ____

7 Nutrition, Health, and Fitness

true or false?

1. People in the U.S. don't eat enough protein.
2. Carbohydrates cause weight gain.
3. Most people need vitamin supplements.
4. All foods contain antioxidants.
5. Whole foods are more healthy than processed foods.

Answers appear on the next page.

When you sit down to lunch at your campus cafeteria, do you think to yourself, "Wow, this looks like a great plate of protein, carbohydrate, and phytochemicals"? Or are you more likely to appreciate the hamburger, french fries, and ketchup on your tray? You probably don't often consider the nutrient components of food or how they ultimately drive your body to function. However, understanding these nutrients, and the processes that break them down to make them available for use, can help you appreciate their importance to health and help you improve your food choices.

In this chapter, we'll find out how your body uses the food you eat. We'll discuss the classes of nutrients and their functions, the fundamental concepts of good nutrition, and guidelines for a healthy diet. We also explore how exercise training can modify nutritional requirements.

What Is Nutrition and Why Is it Important?

Nutrition is the study of food and the way the body uses it to produce energy and build and repair itself. It involves understanding the relationship between food and health or disease. Good nutrition means a diet that supplies all of the essential nutrients required to maintain a healthy body. Consuming too much or too little of any of the essential nutrients will eventually lead to health problems. In the past, it was dietary deficiencies of nutrients that caused health problems for many people; for example, insufficient intake of vitamin C can lead to scurvy, and insufficient iron intake can lead to a form of anemia—both of which were once prevalent in much of the world's population (and are still common in the developing world). Although these conditions still exist today, excess consumption of calories, and the overweight and obesity that result from it, are greater causes of health problems in the United States.

Diets that are too high in calories, sugar, fats, and/or sodium have been linked to diseases and conditions such as cardiovascular disease, cancer, obesity, and diabetes. These conditions are the leading killers in the United States (1). According to the U.S. Department of Health and Human Services, over half of all deaths are associated with health problems linked to poor nutrition (2). The good news is that analyzing and modifying your diet can help prevent many of these nutrition-related diseases. A basic understanding of nutrition is therefore important for everyone.

What Are Nutrients?

Nutrients are the basic substances in foods that your body uses to maintain health. They can be divided into two categories: macronutrients and micronutrients. The **macronutrients** (carbohydrates, fats, and proteins) are needed in greater amounts and primarily build and maintain body tissues and provide energy for daily activities. **Micronutrients** (vitamins and minerals) are needed in much smaller amounts by your body, but they are essential for numerous processes, including regulating cell functions. The final class of nutrient is water, which is so important for body function that you can't survive more than a few days without it.

Answers

1. **FALSE On average, most Americans consume more than the amount of protein they need for good health.**
2. **FALSE Although carbohydrates do provide calories, they don't directly cause weight gain. Too many calories, whether from carbohydrates or other nutrients, are the reason people gain weight.**
3. **FALSE Although there are some exceptions (including pregnant women and some older individuals), most people can easily obtain all the nutrients they need from a healthy diet and therefore do not need to take supplements.**
4. **FALSE Antioxidants are found in many foods, including fruits, vegetables, and some grain products, but not in all foods. Donuts, for example, do not contain antioxidants.**
5. **TRUE In general, the less processed the food, the higher it will be in nutrients, and the lower it will be in heart-unhealthy sodium and saturated fat. Fresh fruits, vegetables, and whole grains, coupled with lean meats and low-fat dairy products, are the best choices for a healthy diet.**

Macronutrients

Macronutrients provide the energy, in the form of **kilocalories** (more commonly called *calories*), that your body needs daily to function. Carbohydrates and protein provide 4 calories per gram, and fat provides 9 calories per gram. Under normal conditions, carbohydrates and fats are the primary fuels the body uses to produce energy. The primary role of protein is to build and repair tissues. However, when carbohydrate is in short supply or the body is under stress, protein can be used for energy. A well-balanced diet is composed of approximately 58% carbohydrates (including complex carbohydrates and simple sugars), 30% fat, and 12% protein (Figure 7.1).

Table 7.1 lists some major food sources of carbohydrates, proteins, and fats.

Carbohydrates

Whole grains, pasta, fruits, and vegetables are excellent sources of **carbohydrates,** the main source of fuel for your brain. Carbohydrates are especially important during many types of physical activity, because they are a key energy source for muscular contraction. However, not all carbohydrates are created equal—simple carbohydrates (or sugars) are easier for the body to break down and use for energy, and complex carbohydrates (starch and fiber) can be used for energy but also serve other purposes.

Types of Carbohydrates Simple carbohydrates consist of chains of one or two simple sugars. **Glucose** is the most noteworthy of the simple sugars because it is the only sugar molecule that can be used directly by the body. To be used for fuel, all other carbohydrates must first be converted to glucose. The body stores glucose in the form of **glycogen** in skeletal muscles and the liver. Glucose that is not immediately used for energy or stored as glycogen will be stored as fat for future energy use. The central nervous system uses glucose almost exclusively for its energy needs. If you don't consume enough carbohydrates in food, your body has to make glucose from protein. This is undesirable because it results in the breakdown of body protein for use as fuel. Dietary carbohydrates are important not only as a direct fuel source, but also for their protein-sparing effect.

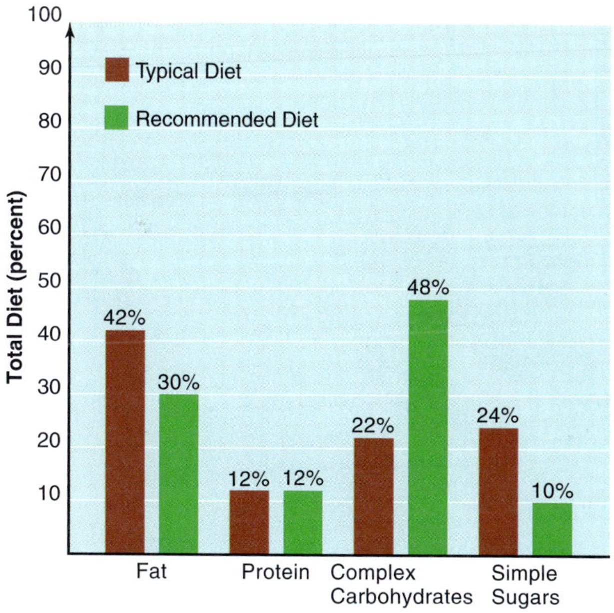

FIGURE 7.1
The recommended nutritionally balanced diet compared with the typical U.S. diet. The average American consumes too much fat and simple sugar, and too few complex carbohydrates.

Source: Block, G. Junk foods account for 30% of caloric intake. *Journal of Food Composition and Analysis* 17:439–447, 2004.

TABLE 7.1
Food Sources of the Macronutrients

Carbohydrate (4 calories/gram)	Protein (4 calories/gram)	Fat (9 calories/gram)
Grains	Meats	Butter
Fruits	Fish	Margarine
Vegetables	Poultry	Oils
Concentrated sweets	Eggs	Shortening
Bread	Milk	Cream
Beans/peas	Beans	
	Rice	

nutrition The study of food and the way the body uses it to produce energy and build or repair body tissues.

nutrients Substances in food that are necessary for good health.

macronutrients Carbohydrates, fats, and proteins, which are necessary for building and maintaining body tissues and providing energy for daily activities.

micronutrients Vitamins and minerals. Micronutrients are involved in many body processes, including regulating cell function.

kilocalorie The unit of measure used to quantify food energy or the energy expended by the body. Technically, a kilocalorie is the amount of energy necessary to raise the temperature of 1 gram of water 1°C. The terms *kilocalorie* and *calorie* are often used interchangeably.

carbohydrate A macronutrient that is a key energy source for muscular contraction.

glucose A simple carbohydrate (sugar) that can be used directly by the body. All other carbohydrates must be converted to glucose before being used for fuel.

glycogen The storage form of glucose in the liver and skeletal muscles.

Whole grains, pasta, and potatoes are excellent sources of carbohydrates.

There are several other simple sugars found in foods, including fructose, galactose, lactose, maltose, and sucrose. Fructose is found primarily in fruit, and galactose and lactose are found in milk and dairy products. Maltose is found in some grains, and sucrose, commonly known as table sugar, is the white, granular product used for household baking.

Complex carbohydrates come in the forms of starch and fiber. **Starches** are long chains of glucose units and are often used for that sudden burst of energy we need during physical activity. **Fiber** is a stringy, nondigestible carbohydrate found in plants. Because fiber is nondigestible, it is not a fuel source. However, it is important in helping prevent some chronic diseases.

The Importance of Fiber Dietary fiber provides bulk in the intestinal tract. This bulk aids in the formation and elimination of food waste products, thus reducing the time necessary for wastes to move through the digestive system and lowering the risk of colon cancer. Dietary fiber is also thought to be a factor in reducing the risk for coronary heart disease and breast cancer and in controlling blood sugar in individuals with diabetes (3). Some types of fiber bind with cholesterol in the digestive tract and prevent its absorption into the blood, thereby reducing blood cholesterol levels.

Fiber can be classified according to its viscosity (its thickness when mixed with digestive juices in the intestines). **Soluble fiber** is more viscous than **insoluble fiber** and is usually found in oats, barley, beans, peas, and citrus fruits. Insoluble fiber is typically concentrated in whole wheat and vegetables. A higher viscosity slows transit in the intestines, allowing nutrients to be absorbed more readily. This helps in regulating glucose levels, appetite, and the reabsorption of bile acids. The primary health benefit of insoluble fiber is its water-binding capacity, which quickens transit time in the large intestine. A faster transit time also helps with regularity and reduces the risk of colon cancer (4).

You should eat a minimum of 25 grams of fiber a day; however, be aware that excessive amounts of fiber in the diet can cause intestinal discomfort and decreased absorption of calcium and iron into the blood (3). Your best bet for getting plenty of fiber is to eat adequate amounts of whole grains, legumes, fruits, and vegetables (including the skins) every day. You'll also want to drink plenty of fluid to prevent constipation.

Carbohydrates in Foods Some foods, such as pasta, potatoes, and bread, are famous for containing high amounts of carbohydrates, but there are numerous other foods that can also contribute to your daily carbohydrate needs. Fruits and honey provide fructose. Dairy foods contain lactose. Sucrose is found in table sugar, including some of the packets you may use to sweeten your coffee or tea. Starch is plentiful in potatoes, corn, bread, and rice, and fiber is found in all

TABLE 7.2
Types of Carbohydrates and Their Sources

Simple Carbohydrates	Source(s)
Fructose	Fruits: apples, pears, citrus, and so on Honey
Galactose	Breast milk
Glucose	Made by the body
Lactose (galactose + glucose)	Milk products
Maltose (glucose + glucose)	Barley
Sucrose (fructose + glucose)	Table sugar
Complex Carbohydrates	**Source(s)**
Starch	Potatoes, rice, bread
Fiber	Fruits and vegetables, including apples, oranges, pears, celery, and broccoli; whole grains

TABLE 7.3
Fatty Acids, Food Sources, and Effects on Blood Cholesterol Levels

Type of Fatty Acid	Primary Sources	State at Room Temperature	Effect on Cholesterol
Monounsaturated	Canola* and olive oils; foods made from and prepared in them	Liquid	Lowers LDL; no effect on HDL
Polyunsaturated†	Soybean, safflower, corn, and cottonseed oils; foods made from and prepared in them	Liquid	Lowers both LDL and HDL
Saturated	Animal fat from red meat, whole milk, and butter; also, coconut and palm oils	Solid	Raises LDL and total cholesterol
Trans	Partially hydrogenated vegetable oils used in cooking, margarine, shortening, baked and fried foods, and snack foods	Semisolid	Raises LDL and total cholesterol

*Many nutritionists consider canola oil the most healthful vegetable oil because it's low in saturated fat, high in monounsaturated fat, and has a moderate level of omega-3 polyunsaturated fat.
†Contains the omega-3 and omega-6 essential fatty acids that the human body can't make on its own.

Source: Fats: The good, the bad, the trans. *Health News,* July 25, 1999, pp. 1–2. Massachusetts Medical Society, Published by Englander Communication, LLC, an affiliate of Behavior Publications, Inc.

plant-derived foods. See Table 7.2 for examples of food sources for different types of carbohydrates.

Fats and Lipids

Fats (technically known as triglycerides) are actually one type in a larger class of substances called **lipids.** Fats are the most common type of lipid found in foods and in your body. Once consumed, they are broken down and used to produce energy to power muscle contractions during exercise. Fat is an efficient storage form for energy, because at 9 calories per gram, it holds more than twice the energy of either carbohydrate or protein.

Excess fat in the diet is stored in fat cells located under the skin and around internal organs. In addition to fat you take in from foods, your body forms fat from excess carbohydrate and protein in the diet.

Although fat is often avoided by people who want to lose weight, you would never want to eliminate it from your diet. Dietary fat is the only source of linoleic and linolenic acids, the two fatty acids that are essential for normal growth and healthy skin. Fat also protects internal organs and assists in absorbing, transporting, and storing the fat soluble vitamins A, D, E, and K.

Types of Fats Triglycerides are made up of three **fatty acids** (essentially, chains of carbon and hydrogen atoms) attached to a glycerol backbone. Fatty acids are classified as monounsaturated, polyunsaturated, saturated, or trans, based on their structure (Table 7.3).

Unsaturated fatty acids include monounsaturated and polyunsaturated fatty acids. They are found in plants (including nuts, seeds, grains, and vegetable oils) and are liquid at room temperature. Unsaturated fats, which contain mostly unsaturated fatty acids, are thought to be the most heart healthy because of their effect on blood cholesterol levels (we'll discuss cholesterol later in the chapter).

One type of polyunsaturated fatty acid, called **omega-3 fatty acid,** is reported to lower both blood cholesterol and triglycerides. This fatty acid is found primarily in fish, especially fresh or frozen mackerel, herring, tuna, and salmon. Some researchers have argued that one or two servings per week of fish

complex carbohydrates Long chains of sugar units linked together to form starch or fiber.

starches Long chains of glucose units; commonly found in foods such as corn, grains, and potatoes.

fiber A stringy, nondigestible complex carbohydrate found in whole grains, vegetables, and fruits.

soluble fiber Viscous fiber found in oats, barley, peas, and citrus fruits.

insoluble fiber Type of fiber found in whole wheat and vegetables.

fats (triglycerides) The form of lipid that is broken down in the body and used to produce energy to power muscle contractions during exercise.

lipids A group of insoluble compounds that include fats and cholesterol.

fatty acids The basic structural unit of triglycerides; they are important nutritionally not only because of their energy content, but also because they play a role in cardiovascular disease.

unsaturated fatty acid A type of fatty acid that comes primarily from plant sources and is liquid at room temperature.

omega-3 fatty acid A type of unsaturated fatty acid that lowers both blood cholesterol and triglycerides and is found abundantly in some fish.

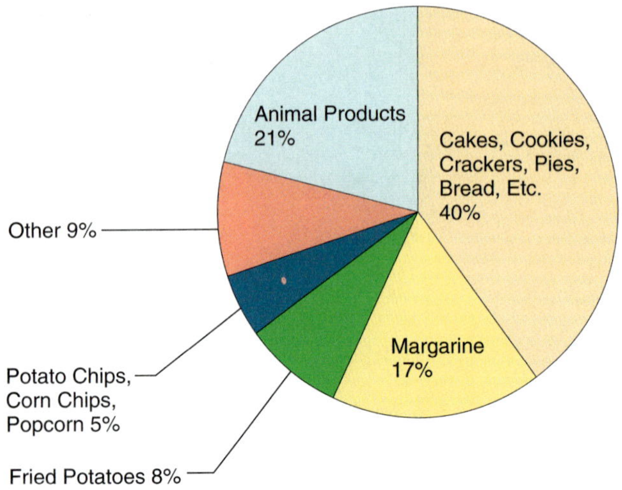

FIGURE 7.2
Major sources of trans fat in the diet.

containing omega-3 fatty acids reduces the risk of heart disease (5). However, some people, in particular pregnant women and children, may need to limit their consumption of these fish because of the possibility of methlymercury contamination (see the Appreciating Diversity box below).

Saturated fatty acids are solid at room temperature. They generally come from animal sources (meat and dairy products), but some (coconut oil, for example), come from plant sources. Saturated fatty acids increase blood levels of cholesterol. High cholesterol levels, in turn, promote the buildup of fatty plaque in the coronary arteries, which can eventually lead to heart disease (Chapter 9).

Trans fatty acids, found primarily in baked and fried foods, but also naturally in some animal foods (Figure 7.2), tend to raise total cholesterol in the blood. For this reason, they are considered to be heart-unhealthy. The U.S. Food and Drug Administration (FDA) recommends limiting the amount of trans fat in the diet—and even requires that food manufacturers list trans fat on food labels—to help consumers avoid products that contain it. Some U.S. cities, including New York and Philadelphia, have banned or greatly restricted the use of trans fats in restaurants. As more is learned about the effects of trans fats on health, food manufacturers and restaurateurs are likely to phase it out of their products.

Other Types of Lipids In addition to fat, there are two other forms of lipids: **phospholipids** and **sterols.** Phospholipids are important components of cell membranes and play a key role in emulsification. The most common sterol, **cholesterol,** is an important component of cells and is used to manufacture certain types of hormones, including some male and female sex hormones.

Lipoproteins are combinations of protein, triglycerides, and cholesterol. Although lipoproteins exist in several forms, the two primary types are low-density lipoproteins (LDL cholesterol) and high-density lipoproteins (HDL cholesterol). LDL, or "bad," cholesterol consists of a limited amount of protein and triglycerides but contains large amounts of cholesterol. It is associated with promoting fatty plaque buildup in the arteries

APPRECIATING DIVERSITY: SHOULD PREGNANT WOMEN EAT FISH?

Seafood can be an important part of a healthy diet during pregnancy. Fish is low in fat and a great source of high-quality protein and other nutrients. However, some fish may contain a form of mercury that could harm the nervous system of a developing fetus. Pregnant women need to know the types of fish that carry the highest risk of containing methylmercury and other contaminants so that they can avoid or reduce their intake of these fish during pregnancy.

Methylmercury is a toxin produced from the inorganic mercury that gets into water after the burning of wastes and fossil fuels. It enters the food chain when fish and other aquatic organisms acquire it from the water. When larger fish eat smaller fish, the methylmercury from the smaller fish will accumulate in the larger fish's body. Thus older, larger fish have higher concentrations of methylmercury in their bodies than smaller, younger fish. Some of the highest levels of methylmercury are found in large predatory fish, such as shark, swordfish, king mackerel, and tilefish, so pregnant women should avoid these species. However, eating less than 12 ounces per week of other species, such as shellfish, canned fish, small ocean fish, or farm-raised fish, can safely provide protein and other nutrients.

In addition to the wild or farmed fish found in the local grocery store, pregnant women also need to be aware of the risks for contamination of locally caught fish. The U.S. Environmental Protection Agency (EPA) provides current advice on consuming fish from your local freshwater lakes and streams. You can also contact your state or local health department for specific consumption recommendations about fish caught or sold in your area.

of the heart, which is the primary cause of heart disease. In contrast, HDL, or "good," cholesterol is primarily composed of protein, has limited amounts of cholesterol, and is associated with a low risk of heart disease. We discuss HDL and LDL cholesterol again in Chapter 9.

Fats and Lipids in Foods You can find "good" fats, including the two essential fatty acids, in fish, seeds, nuts, and vegetable oils. Unhealthy, saturated fats are in fatty meats, butter, lard, fried foods, and many baked items. These items should be avoided or eaten only in limited amounts.

Dietary cholesterol is present in many foods from animal sources, including meats, shellfish, and dairy products. Although your body needs some cholesterol for normal function, you actually don't need to consume cholesterol from foods, because your body can make all that it needs. In fact, diets high in saturated fats cause the body to produce more than normal amounts of cholesterol.

Proteins

The primary role of protein is to serve as the structural unit to build and repair body tissues, including muscle and connective tissue. Proteins are also important for the synthesis of enzymes, hormones, and antibodies. These compounds regulate body metabolism and provide protection from disease.

As mentioned earlier, proteins are not usually a major fuel source. However, if your dietary intake of carbohydrates is too low (such as during a diet or fast), proteins can be converted to glucose and used as fuel. If you consume adequate amounts of carbohydrates, excess calories from dietary protein are stored in adipose tissue as an energy reserve.

The Structure of Proteins The basic structural units of proteins are called **amino acids.** There are 20 different amino acids, and they can be linked in various combinations to create different proteins with unique functions. Some are **essential amino acids,** meaning that the body cannot make them and they must be consumed in the diet. Others are **nonessential amino acids,** meaning that the body can synthesize them in adequate amounts. There are 9 essential amino acids, and 11 nonessential amino acids.

Protein in Foods **Complete proteins** contain all of the essential amino acids and are present only in animal foods and soy products. **Incomplete proteins** are missing one or more of the essential amino acids and are present in numerous vegetable sources. Vegetarians, who avoid animal foods, must be careful to eat a variety of foods so that they consume all of the essential amino acids.

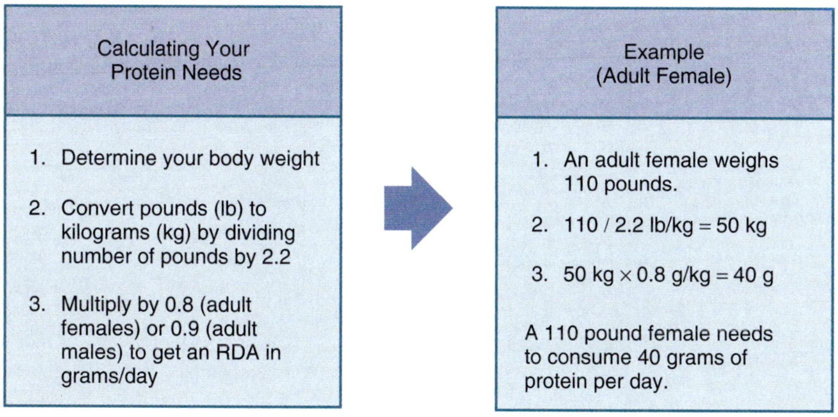

FIGURE 7.3
Estimated daily protein needs for adults. You can calculate the number of grams of protein you should consume daily.

Because of its role in building body tissue, protein is particularly important during periods of rapid growth, such as adolescence. Adolescents need to take in more than 12% of their calories from protein (the recommended amount for adults). For adolescents, the recommended dietary allowance (RDA) for proteins is 1 gram per kilogram of body weight (3). The recommendation decreases to 0.8 g/kg in women and 0.9 g/kg in men at the end of adolescence (Figure 7.3).

saturated fatty acid A type of fatty acid that comes primarily from animal sources and is solid at room temperature.

trans fatty acid A type of fatty acid that increases cholesterol in the blood and is a major contributor to heart disease.

phospholipid A type of lipid that contains phosphorus and is an important component of cell membranes.

sterol A type of lipid that does not contain fatty acids; cholesterol is the most commonly known sterol.

cholesterol A type of lipid that is necessary for cell and hormone synthesis. Found naturally in animal foods, but made in adequate amounts in the body.

lipoproteins Combinations of protein, triglycerides, and cholesterol in the blood that are important because of their role in influencing the risk of heart disease.

amino acids The building blocks of protein. There are 20 different amino acids that can be linked in various combinations to create different proteins.

essential amino acids The nine amino acids that cannot be manufactured by the body and must therefore be consumed in the diet.

nonessential amino acids Eleven amino acids that the body can make and are therefore not necessary in the diet.

complete proteins Proteins containing all the essential amino acids; found only in soy and animal foods (meats and dairy products).

incomplete proteins Proteins that are missing one or more of the essential amino acids; found in plant sources such as nuts and legumes.

TABLE 7.4
Selected Vitamins: Food Sources, Functions, and Deficiency and Toxicity Symptoms

Vitamin	Selected Food Sources	Selected Functions	Deficiency Symptoms	Toxicity Symptoms
Fat-soluble				
A	Liver, spinach, carrots, sweet potatoes; other orange and green leafy vegetables	Necessary for vision, bone growth, fertility	Night blindness, impaired immunity, infertility	Birth defects, loss of appetite, blurred vision, hair loss, liver damage
D	Fortified milk; produced in the skin with sunlight	Regulates blood calcium levels; bone health; cell differentiation	Rickets in children, bone weakness and increased fractures in adults	Hypercalcemia, calcium deposits in kidney and liver
E	Vegetable oils, whole grains, nuts, seeds	Antioxidant; improves absorption of vitamin A	Anemia, impaired nerve transmission, muscle weakness	Inhibited blood clotting
K	Green leafy vegetables; cabbage, cauliflower	Helps with blood clotting	Reduced ability to form blood clots	No known symptoms
Water-soluble				
Thiamin (B_1)	Whole grains, organ meat, lean pork	Coenzyme in carbohydrate metabolism and some amino acid metabolism	Beriberi, weight loss, confusion, muscle weakness	No known symptoms
Riboflavin (B_2)	Dairy products, enriched breads and cereals, lean meats, poultry, fish	Coenzyme; helps maintain mucous membranes	Sore throat, swelling of the tongue, anemia	No known symptoms
Niacin (B_3)	Eggs, poultry, fish, milk, whole grains, nuts, enriched breads and cereals	Coenzymes in carbohydrate and fatty acid metabolism; plays role in DNA replication and repair and cell differentiation	Pellagra, rash, vomiting, constipation or diarrhea	Flushing, liver damage, glucose intolerance, blurred vision
Vitamin B_6	Eggs, poultry, fish, whole grains, liver, kidney, pork	Coenzyme involved in amino acid and carbohydrate metabolism; synthesis of blood cells	Dermatitis, anemia, convulsions	Skin lesions
Vitamin B_{12}	Meat, fish, poultry, fortified cereals	Coenzyme that assists with blood formation and nervous system function	Pernicious anemia, pale skin, fatigue, shortness of breath, dementia	No known symptoms
Folate	Green leafy vegetables, yeast, oranges, whole grains, legumes	Coenzyme involved in DNA synthesis and amino acid metabolism	Macrocytic anemia, weakness and fatigue, headache, neural tube defects in developing fetus	Masks symptoms of vitamin B_{12} deficiency; neurological damage
Vitamin C	Citrus fruits, peppers, spinach, strawberries, tomatoes, potatoes	Antioxidant; assists with collagen synthesis; enhances immune function; enhances iron absorption	Scurvy, bleeding gums and joints, loose teeth, depression, anemia	Nausea and diarrhea, nosebleeds, abdominal cramps

Source: Thompson, J., and M. Manore. *Nutrition: An Applied Approach, MyPyramid Edition.* San Fancisco: Benjamin Cummings, 2006.

Because the average person in industrialized countries consumes more than enough protein, the nutritional problem associated with protein intake is one of excess. Protein foods from animal sources are often high in fat (and high in calories), which can lead to an increased risk of heart disease, cancer, and obesity.

Micronutrients

Micronutrients include **vitamins** and **minerals.** Though needed in smaller amounts, micronutrients are as important to body function as macronutrients and are required to sustain life. Although they do not supply energy, they are essential to the breakdown and use of the macronutrients.

Vitamins Vitamins play a key role in many bodily functions, including the regulation of growth and metabolism. Some vitamins are soluble in water; others are soluble in fat. Water-soluble vitamins include the B vitamins and vitamin C. These vitamins are generally not stored in the body and can be eliminated by the kidneys. Vitamins A, D, E, and K are fat soluble. They are stored in body fat and can therefore accumulate to toxic levels. Table 7.4 lists some functions and dietary sources of both water-soluble and fat-soluble vitamins.

In addition to their essential roles in body processes, some vitamins and minerals may also protect against tissue damage (3, 6). This has important implications for individuals engaged in an exercise program. This potential new role for micronutrients is discussed later in this chapter.

Minerals Minerals are chemical elements such as sodium and calcium that are required by the body for normal function. Like vitamins, minerals play important roles in regulating key body functions, such as the conduction of nerve impulses, muscular contraction, enzyme function, and maintenance of water balance. Minerals serve a structural function as well; calcium, phosphorus, and fluoride all are important components in bones and teeth.

Three minerals that play important roles in the body are calcium, iron, and sodium. Calcium is important in bone formation. A deficiency of calcium contributes to the development of the bone disease called **osteoporosis.** A deficiency of dietary iron may lead to iron-deficiency **anemia,** which results in chronic fatigue. High sodium intake has been associated with hypertension, a major risk factor for heart disease.

Table 7.5 summarizes several key minerals and their functions.

Vitamin and Minerals in Foods Though a few vitamins, including A, D and K, can be made in the body, most must be consumed in foods. If you're eating a balanced diet with plenty of fresh fruits, vegetables, and whole grains, and some lean meat and poultry, you're likely getting all of the vitamins and minerals that you need. (See Tables 7.4 and 7.5 for specific food sources for these and other vitamins and minerals). In general, the more brightly colored the fruit or vegetable, the higher its vitamin and mineral content. Note that some water-soluble vitamins can be destroyed during cooking or processing, so minimal cooking (such as by steaming, rather than boiling) and eating fresh rather than canned produce will provide higher amounts of micronutrients.

Water is a key ingredient in a healthy diet.

vitamins Micronutrients that play a key role in many body functions, including the regulation of growth and metabolism. They are classified according to whether they are soluble in water or fat.

minerals Chemical elements (e.g., sodium and calcium) that are required by the body in small amounts for normal functioning.

osteoporosis Bone disease in which mineral content of bone is reduced and the bone is weakened and at increased risk of fracture.

anemia Deficiency of red blood cells and/or hemoglobin that results in decreased oxygen-carrying capacity of the blood.

TABLE 7.5
Selected Minerals: Food Sources, Functions, and Deficiency and Toxicity Symptoms

Mineral	Selected Food Sources	Selected Functions	Deficiency Symptoms	Toxicity Symptoms
Major Minerals				
Calcium	Milk and milk products; sardines; dark green, leafy vegetables; fortified orange juice	Builds bones and teeth; helps maintain acid-base balance; maintains normal nerve transmission	Osteoporosis, bone fractures, convulsions and muscle spasms, heart failure	Can interfere with the absorption of iron, zinc, and magnesium; shock, fatigue, kidney failure
Phosphorus	Meat, poultry, fish, eggs, milk, soft drinks	Maintains fluid balance; plays a role in bone formation	Muscle weakness or damage, bone pain, dizziness	Muscle spasms, convulsions, low blood calcium levels
Magnesium	Grains, legumes, nuts (especially almonds and cashews), seeds, soybeans	Essential component of bone tissue; bone growth; supports muscle contraction and blood clotting	Hypomagnesemia, resulting in low blood calcium levels, muscle cramps, spasms, or seizures; chronic diseases such as heart disease, high blood pressure, and osteoporosis	Diarrhea, nausea, abdominal cramps
Potassium	Potatoes, bananas, tomato juice, orange juice	Regulates muscle contraction and transmission of nerve impulses; maintains blood pressure	Muscle weakness, paralysis, confusion	Muscle weakness, irregular heartbeat, vomiting
Sodium	Salt, soy sauce, fast foods and processed foods	Maintains acid-base balance; assists with nerve transmission and muscle contraction	Muscle cramps, dizziness, fatigue, nausea, vomiting, mental confusion	Water retention; high blood pressure; may increase loss of calcium in urine
Trace Minerals				
Iron	Meat and poultry; green, leafy vegetables; fortified grain products	Assists with oxygen transport in blood and muscle; conenzyme for energy metabolism	Anemia, fatigue, depressed immune function, impaired memory	Nausea, vomiting, diarrhea, dizziness, rapid heart beat, death
Zinc	Whole grains, meat, liver, seafood	Coenzyme for hemoglobin production; plays role in cell replication, protein synthesis	Growth retardation, diarrhea, delayed sexual maturation, hair loss	Intestinal pain, nausea, vomiting, loss of appetite, diarrhea; headache, depressed immune function
Iodine	Iodized salt, seafood, processed foods	Synthesis of thyroid hormones; temperature regulation	Goiter (enlargement of the thyroid gland), hypothyroidism; deficiency during pregnancy can cause birth defects	Goiter
Fluoride	Fluoridated water, tea, fish	Maintains health of bones and teeth	Dental caries and tooth decay; lower bone density	Teeth fluorosis (staining and pitting of the teeth); skeletal fluorisis
Selenium	Organ meats, such as liver and kidney; pork; seafood	Antioxidant; immune function; assists in production of thyroid hormone	Keshan disease, impaired immune function, infertility, muscle pain	Brittle hair, skin rashes, weakness, cirrhosis of the liver

Source: Thompson, J., and M. Manore. *Nutrition: An Applied Approach, MyPyramid Edition*. San Fancisco: Benjamin Cummings, 2006.

Water

Water makes up approximately 60–70% of your body, and it is important for everything from temperature regulation, digestion, absorption, and blood formation to waste elimination. Water is especially important for physically active people. A person engaged in heavy exercise in a hot, humid environment can lose 1 to 3 liters of water per hour through sweating (7). Losing as little as 5% of body water causes fatigue, weakness, and the inability to concentrate; losing more than 15% can be fatal. Chapter 11 provides guidelines for maintaining proper hydration during exercise training.

You should consume 8–10 cups of water per day through foods and beverages. Drinking water throughout your day will help you meet this goal, as will eating food with high water content, such as fruits and vegetables. People who experience excess sweating, diarrhea, or vomiting or who donate blood may have higher water requirements. Figure 7.4 compares the sources of water intake and output in the average person.

Daily Water Balance in the Body

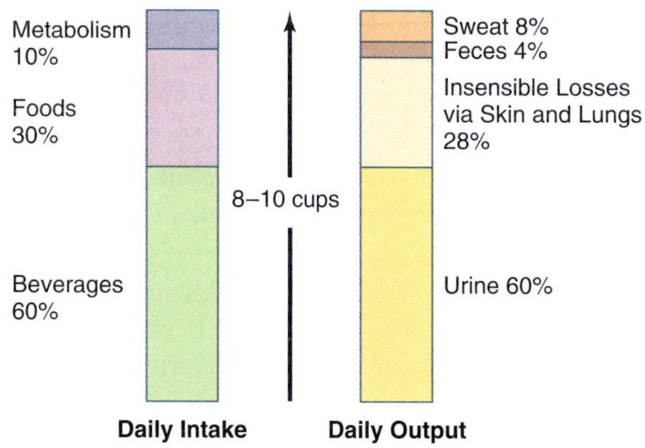

FIGURE 7.4
The amount of water you consume in food and beverages and produce during metabolism is about equal to the amount you excrete in urine, sweat, and feces and through exhalation and insensible water loss.

Make sure you know...

> Nutrition is the study of food and its relationship to health and disease.
> Carbohydrates, fat, and protein are the three calorie-containing macronutrients. A well-balanced diet is composed of approximately 58% complex carbohydrates, 30% fat, and 12% protein.
> The kilocalorie is a unit of measure for the energy in food or the energy expended by the body. The kilocalorie is more commonly referred to as the calorie.
> Carbohydrates are the primary source of fuel for the body. Glucose is the most important of the simple carbohydrates, and all other simple and complex carbohydrates must be converted to glucose before being used by the body. Starch and fiber are complex carbohydrates.
> Fats are the most common form of lipid in foods and in the body. All excess calories consumed in the diet will eventually be converted to fat for storage. Dietary cholesterol and trans fat are heart-unhealthy, and you should limit or avoid your consumption of foods containing them.
> Proteins are made up of amino acids, and are the key structural unit for building and repairing cells. All amino acids either are made by the body (nonessential amino acids) or must be consumed in the diet (essential amino acids).
> Vitamins serve many important functions in the body, including facilitating metabolism. The B vitamins and vitamin C are water soluble and are not generally stored by the body. Vitamins A, D, E and K are fat soluble and can be stored in the body.
> Minerals are chemical elements in foods that, like vitamins, play important roles in many body functions. The mineral calcium is important for bone health; iron is important for healthy blood, and too much sodium can have a negative effect on heart health.
> Approximately 60–70% of body weight is water. You should consume 8–10 cups of water from foods and beverages each day.

What Are the Guidelines for a Healthy Diet?

Nutrition may seem like a complex subject, but the basics of consuming a healthy diet are fairly simple: Balance the calories, eat a variety of foods, and consume less-healthy foods only in moderation. Additionally, everyone should strive to be physically active.

To make these points more clear, and to provide specific guidance in these areas, several national health agencies have suggested guidelines for healthy diets. For instance, the United States Department of Agriculture (USDA) released its latest version of the *Dietary Guidelines for Americans* in 2005. Among its key points of advice:

- Consume adequate nutrients within energy needs: Choose foods that limit the intake of saturated and trans fats, cholesterol, added sugars, salt, and alcohol.

- Balance energy intake with energy expended.
- Engage in regular physical activity.
- Consume sufficient amounts of fruits, vegetables, and whole grains while staying within energy needs.
- Consume less than 10% of energy intake from saturated fats and less than 300 mg per day of cholesterol; consume as little trans fat as possible.
- Choose fiber-rich fruits, vegetables, and whole grains often; choose and prepare foods and beverages with little added sugars or caloric sweeteners.
- Consume less than 1 tsp of salt per day.
- If you choose to drink alcohol, do so only in moderation.
- Take proper food safety precautions.

Let's explore some of these guidelines in more depth and discuss additional tools you can use, including MyPyramid, to plan a healthy diet.

Eat More Fruits, Vegetables, and Whole Grains

Choosing unprocessed foods that are modest in calories and low in fat and sodium is the best way to create a healthy diet. This means doing much of your grocery store shopping in the produce aisle (and perhaps stopping by the meat or seafood counter) and buying whole-grain bread and cereal products. When you eat out with friends or dine with your family, try to keep your portions of fatty meats and high-sugar desserts small, and load up on the undressed fruits and vegetables. Similarly, when you're in need of a midmorning or late afternoon snack, reach for a banana, whole-grain crackers, or air-popped popcorn rather than a bag of chips or chocolate bar.

Once you've adopted these healthy eating strategies, you're likely to see the benefits quickly. You will have more energy and feel less lethargic in the afternoon, and you may even lose weight. Over the long term, you will have a lower risk for many chronic diseases and conditions.

CONSIDER THIS!

The average American consumes more than 80 pounds of table sugar and 45 pounds of high fructose corn syrup each year.

Watch Your Intake of Calories, Sugar, Alcohol, Fat, and Sodium

With the rise in rates of overweight and obesity in the United States, it's clear that the balance of "calories in" versus "calories out" has become an issue for many individuals. Several factors are increasing calorie consumption. For example, one factor is that people consume a lot of simple sugar, often in the form of sucrose (table sugar) or high fructose corn syrup (a commercial sweetener). The problem with simple sugars is that they often contain many calories but few micronutrients (which is why they're called "empty calories"). An estimated half of the dietary carbohydrate intake of the average U.S. citizen is in the form of simple sugars (3). Sucrose and high fructose corn syrup are used to make cakes, candies, and ice cream, as well as to sweeten beverages, cereals, and other foods.

The amount of sugar in sweets adds a tremendous amount of calories to the diet. This leads to obesity, which contributes to many health problems (e.g., diabetes). Sugar in sweets also leads to tooth decay. Although brushing your teeth after eating sweets can prevent this problem, it will not solve the other problems of overconsumption of sugar. One way to trim your sucrose intake is to use sugar substitutes instead of sugar to sweeten some foods or beverages. Artificial sweeteners such as saccharin (Sweet'N Low), aspartame (Equal), or sucralose (Splenda) add sweetness with little or no calories.

Alcohol can be another breaker of a healthy diet if it's consumed in excess. Like table sugar, alcohol provides empty calories. Chronic alcohol consumption also tends to deplete the body's stores of some vitamins, possibly leading to severe deficiencies. Drinking too much alcohol can displace other, healthier foods in the diet by making you too full to eat or causing you to forget to eat. Finally, alcohol significantly increases your risk of accidents and injury. When it comes to drinking alcohol, the best plan is to avoid it or, if you do drink, to do so only in moderation.

Another factor behind the rise in overweight and obesity in the United States is the high amount of fat in many people's diets. Foods high in fat not only tend to

Guidelines for Cutting Fat from Your Diet

- Choose low-fat or nonfat foods over full-fat foods.
- For baking and sautéing, use vegetable oils, such as olive oil, that do not raise cholesterol levels.
- Choose only lean meats, fish, and poultry. Always remove the skin before eating, and bake or broil meats whenever possible. Drain off all oils from meats after cooking.
- Avoid cold cuts and processed meats (e.g., bacon, sausage, hot dogs). Beware of meat products that claim to be "95% fat-free," because they may still have a high fat content.
- Select nonfat dairy products whenever possible. Part-skim-milk cheeses such as mozzarella, farmer's, and ricotta are the best choices.
- Use broth, wine, vinegar, or low-calorie salad dressing to flavor foods during cooking rather than butter, margarine, oils, sour cream, or mayonnaise.
- Offset a high-fat breakfast with a low-fat lunch or dinner.

Ingredients	Mg sodium
Crust	
Pre-made from Pillsbury Hot Roll Mix (whole box)	1536
Sauce	
8 oz. Contadina Pizza Sauce	1350
Toppings	
Mozzarella (8–10 oz at 150 mg/oz)	1200–1500
Pork sausage (170 mg/oz) 6 oz	1020
Canadian bacon 2 oz	1450
Pepperoni 2 oz	1100
Black olives, 5 (sliced)	200
Mushrooms (raw sliced 1/2 cup)	5
Onion (1/2 cup raw)	6
Green pepper (1/2 cup raw)	10
Seasonings/herbs/spices (1 tsp)	500
	Total = 8,677 mg sodium

FIGURE 7.5
The amount of sodium in a typical medium pizza with "the works" will probably surprise you. Even if you eat only two slices, you are still likely consuming more than a 1000 mg of sodium! Note though, that cutting back on the meat toppings and loading up on the veggies will significantly lower the sodium.

be rich in cholesterol, but also contain over twice as many calories per gram than carbohydrate or protein (9 calories/gram versus 4 calories/gram). Limiting fat in the diet helps limit calories and also reduces the risk of heart disease. Both saturated and unsaturated fats are linked to heart disease, obesity, and certain cancers. The box on this page provides guidelines to help you cut your dietary fat intake.

Eating less dietary cholesterol will help lower your blood cholesterol, which will in turn lower your risk of heart disease. Research has shown that a 1% reduction in dietary cholesterol results in a 2% reduction in risk (Chapter 9). Additionally, many foods that are high in cholesterol are also high in fat (and therefore, calories).

Although salt (sodium chloride) is a necessary micronutrient, the body's daily requirement is small (less than 1/4 of a teaspoon). For very active people who perspire a great deal, this need may increase to over 1 1/2 teaspoons per day. However, most people consume much more sodium than they need, and this increased intake is putting them at increased risk for high blood pressure (hypertension). You might be surprised just how much salt is in many of your foods. For example, Figure 7.5 illustrates the "hidden" salt in an average pizza.

As mentioned, consuming too much sodium can be a complicating factor for people with high blood pressure. In countries where salt is not added to foods, either during cooking or at the table, high blood pressure is virtually unknown (8). Even if you don't already have high blood pressure, you should limit salt in your diet to only the minimal daily requirements.

CONSIDER THIS!

The average American consumes between 3 and 10 teaspoons of salt per day.

Anatomy of MyPyramid

One Size Doesn't Fit All

USDA's new MyPyramid symbolizes a personalized approach to healthy eating and physical activity. The symbol has been designed to be simple. It has been developed to remind consumers to make healthy food choices and to be active every day. The different parts of the symbol are described below.

Activity
Activity is represented by the steps and the person climbing them, as a reminder of the importance of daily physical activity.

Moderation
Moderation is represented by the narrowing of each food group from bottom to top. The wider base stands for foods with little or no solid fats or added sugars. These should be selected more often.

Personalization
Personalization is shown by the person on the steps, the slogan, and the URL. Find the kinds and amounts of food to eat each day at MyPyramid.gov.

Proportionality
Proportionality is shown by the different widths of the food group bands. The widths suggest how much food a person should choose from each group. The widths are just a general guide, not exact proportions.

Variety
Variety is symbolized by the 6 color bands representing the 5 food groups of the Pyramid and oils. Foods from all groups are needed each day for good health.

Gradual Improvement
Gradual improvement is encouraged by the slogan. It suggests that individuals can benefit from taking small steps to improve their diet and lifestyle each day.

FIGURE 7.6
The USDA's MyPyramid food guidance system reminds you to eat a varied diet with lots of nutrient dense foods and to incorporate physical activity into your daily routine.
Source: www.mypyramid.gov.

Use the Recommended Dietary Allowances, MyPyramid, and Food Labels to Plan Healthy Meals

The National Academy of Science (9) has established guidelines concerning the quantities of each micronutrient required to meet the minimum needs of most individuals. These Recommended Dietary Allowances (RDAs) are listed in Table 7.6 on pages 210–211. See also the Closer Look box on page 213 for an explanation of other important guidelines, in particular the Dietary Reference Intakes (DRIs).

Once you know the recommended daily allowances for nutrients, the key question is how to choose foods to meet these goals.

MyPyramid is the latest visual guide to eating healthy developed by the USDA. Its shape, colored bands, and other graphic elements emphasize several key aspects of planning a healthy diet. (See Figure 7.6 for a walk-through of the graphic elements of MyPyramid). For instance, you should strive to eat a wide variety of "nutrient-dense" foods—that is, foods with high nutrient content per calorie—from each of the food groups, rather than "empty-calorie" foods.

Another tool that the consumer can use when making food choices is the food label that's required on almost all packaged foods (Figure 7.7). Among the important information contained on the label is the number of calories contained per serving, a list of ingredients found in the food (listed in order of the amount contained), the amount of sodium and fat per serving, and the percent **Daily Values** of total fat, carbohydrate, and protein.

Now that we have presented the guidelines for a healthy diet, let's put these principles into practice and construct a day's healthy diet. As we discuss the steps for choosing the right foods, refer to Table 7.7 on page 214, which presents a sample of a healthful 1-day diet for a college-aged woman weighing 110 pounds and with light daily activities. Her projected daily caloric need is approximately 1690 calories. For your use of this diet plan, adjust the quantities accordingly.

Breakfast A healthy breakfast might include a grapefruit, whole-grain cereal, low-fat milk, and a banana. This meal would provide two fruits, one bread/cereal, and one dairy product to start the day. The breakfast is low in fat, cholesterol, and sodium. A large part of her daily protein need is met, as well as over 40% of her calcium and iron needs. The fruits alone provide almost all of the recommended vitamin A and C intake for the day.

Snack A morning snack adds some energy and helps to suppress the appetite before lunch. You might choose a second dairy product for the day (in this example, low-fat yogurt) that provides 130 calories of energy and lots of calcium.

Lunch For lunch, a turkey sandwich (made with low-sodium turkey) on whole-wheat bread and a handful of baby carrots will provide one serving of meat, two more servings of breads/cereals, and one vegetable. This lunch provides a low-calorie meal with lots of protein, vitamin A, and iron.

Snack A piece of cheese pizza as an afternoon snack will add a third dairy and fourth bread/cereal serving. Be careful in ordering pizza, because some toppings (meats and additional cheese) can add lots of fat, sodium, and calories to your diet. In contrast, vegetable toppings such as peppers, onions, and mushrooms can provide valuable nutrients without the fat, sodium, and calories.

Dinner You might finish the day by adding a second serving of meat and two more vegetables, to make a total of five. A peach for dessert will provide lots of vitamin A. The salmon contains protein and plenty of heart-healthy omega-3 fatty acids. The broccoli adds vitamins A and C and calcium. The lima beans add vitamin A and iron.

Watch for Special Dietary Considerations

Some people have special dietary considerations that affect their needs for certain nutrients. Strict vegetarians, for example, need to monitor their intake of protein, calcium, and some vitamins, and children and pregnant women need to be sure to consume enough iron to help with growth. Let's take a look at some of these nutrient considerations.

(*text continues on page 212*)

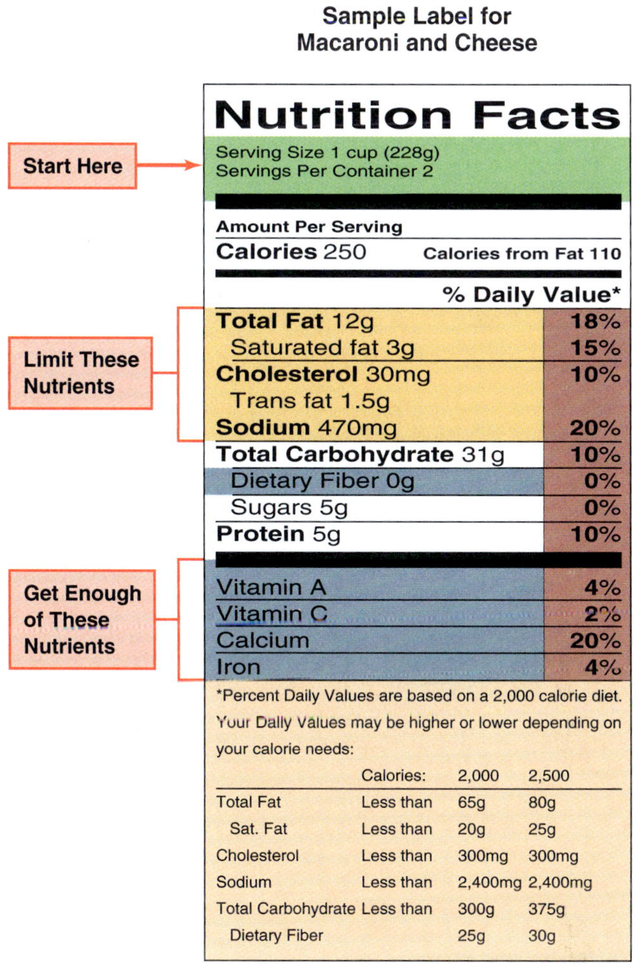

FIGURE 7.7
The Nutrition Facts Label can help you select foods that are low in fat, cholesterol, sodium, and calories and that are adequate in protein, vitamins A and C, iron, and calcium. The percent Daily Value helps you determine how good a source a food is for a given nutrient. In general, foods with less than 5% of the DV are considered low in a nutrient, whereas those with more than 20% of the DV are considered high in that nutrient.

Source: U.S. Department of Agriculture, *Dietary Guidelines for Americans 2000*. Washington, DC: U.S. Government Printing Office.

Daily Values standard values for nutrient needs, used as a reference on food labels. The Daily Values may not exactly reflect the true nutrient needs for all people.

TABLE 7.6
Recommended Dietary Allowances of Micronutrients

Minerals

Life Stage Group	Calcium (mg/d)	Phosphorus (mg/d)	Magnesium (mg/d)	Iron (mg/d)	Zinc (mg/d)	Selenium (µg/d)	Iodine (µg/d)	Copper (µg/d)	Manganese (mg/d)	Fluoride (mg/d)	Chromium (µg/d)	Molybdenum (µg/d)
Infants												
0–6 mo	210*	100*	30*	0.27*	2*	15*	110*	200*	0.003*	0.01*	0.2*	2*
7–12 mo	270*	275*	75*	11	3	20*	130*	220*	0.6*	0.5*	5.5*	3*
Children												
1–3 y	500*	460	80	7	3	20	90	340	1.2*	0.7*	11*	17
4–8 y	800*	500	130	10	5	30	90	440	1.5*	1*	15*	22
Males												
9–13 y	1300*	1250	240	8	8	40	120	700	1.9*	2*	25*	34
14–18 y	1300*	1250	410	11	11	55	150	890	2.2*	3*	35*	43
19–30 y	1000*	700	400	8	11	55	150	900	2.3*	4*	35*	45
31–50 y	1000*	700	420	8	11	55	150	900	2.3*	4*	35*	45
51–70 y	1200*	700	420	8	11	55	150	900	2.3*	4*	30*	45
>70 y	1200*	700	420	8	11	55	150	900	2.3*	4*	30*	45
Females												
9–13 y	1300*	1250	240	8	8	40	120	700	1.6*	2*	21*	34
14–18 y	1300*	1250	360	15	9	55	150	890	1.6*	3*	24*	43
19–30 y	1000*	700	310	18	8	55	150	900	1.8*	3*	25*	45
31–50 y	1000*	700	320	18	8	55	150	900	1.8*	3*	20*	45
51–70 y	1200*	700	320	8	8	55	150	900	1.8*	3*	20*	45
>70 y	1200*	700	320	8	8	55	150	900	1.8*	3*	20*	45
Pregnancy												
≤18 y	1300*	1250	400	27	12	60	220	1000	2.0*	3*	29*	50
19–30 y	1000*	700	350	27	11	60	220	1000	2.0*	3*	30*	50
31–50 y	1000*	700	360	27	11	60	220	1000	2.0*	3*	30*	50
Lactation												
≤18 y	1300*	1250	360	10	13	70	290	1300	2.6*	3*	44*	50
19–30 y	1000*	700	310	9	12	70	290	1300	2.6*	3*	45*	50
31–50 y	1000*	700	320	9	12	70	290	1300	2.6*	3*	45*	50

TABLE 7.6 (CONTINUED)

Life Stage Group	Vitamins													
	Vitamin A (μg/d)[a]	Vitamin D (μg/d)[b]	Vitamin E (mg/d)[c]	Vitamin K (μg/d)	Thiamin (mg/d)	Riboflavin (mg/d)	Niacin (mg/d)[d]	Pantothenic Acid (mg/d)	Biotin (μg/d)	Vitamin B_6 (mg/d)	Folate (μg/d)[e]	Vitamin B_{12} (μg/d)	Vitamin C (mg/d)	Choline (mg/d)
Infants														
0–6 mo	400*	5*	4*	2.0*	0.2*	0.3*	2*	1.7*	5*	0.1*	65*	0.4*	40*	125*
7–12 mo	500*	5*	5*	2.5*	0.3*	0.4*	4*	1.8*	6*	0.3*	80*	0.5*	50*	150*
Children														
1–3 y	300	5*	6	30*	0.5	0.5	6	2*	8*	0.5	150	0.9	15	200*
4–8 y	400	5*	7	55*	0.6	0.6	8	3*	12*	0.6	200	1.2	25	250*
Males														
9–13 y	600	5*	11	60*	0.9	0.9	12	4*	20*	1.0	300	1.8	45	375*
14–18 y	900	5*	15	75*	1.2	1.3	16	5*	25*	1.3	400	2.4	75	550*
19–30 y	900	5*	15	120*	1.2	1.3	16	5*	30*	1.3	400	2.4	90	550*
31–50 y	900	5*	15	120*	1.2	1.3	16	5*	30*	1.3	400	2.4	90	550*
51–70 y	900	10*	15	120*	1.2	1.3	16	5*	30*	1.7	400	2.4	90	550*
>70 y	900	15*	15	120*	1.2	1.3	16	5*	30*	1.7	400	2.4	90	550*
Females														
9–13 y	600	5*	11	60*	0.9	0.9	12	4*	20*	1.0	300	1.8	45	375*
14–18 y	700	5*	15	75*	1.0	1.0	14	5*	25*	1.2	400	2.4	65	400*
19–30 y	700	5*	15	90*	1.1	1.1	14	5*	30*	1.3	400	2.4	75	425*
31–50 y	700	5*	15	90*	1.1	1.1	14	5*	30*	1.3	400	2.4	75	425*
51–70 y	700	10*	15	90*	1.1	1.1	14	5*	30*	1.5	400	2.4	75	425*
>70 y	700	15*	15	90*	1.1	1.1	14	5*	30*	1.5	400	2.4	75	425*
Pregnancy														
≤18 y	750	5*	15	75*	1.4	1.4	18	6*	30*	1.9	600	2.6	80	450*
19–30 y	770	5*	15	90*	1.4	1.4	18	6*	30*	1.9	600	2.6	85	450*
31–50 y	770	5*	15	90*	1.4	1.4	18	6*	30*	1.9	600	2.6	85	450*
Lactation														
≤18 y	1200	5*	19	75*	1.4	1.4	17	7*	35*	2.0	500	2.8	115	550*
19–30 y	1300	5*	19	90*	1.4	1.4	17	7*	35*	2.0	500	2.8	120	550*
31–50 y	1300	5*	19	90*	1.4	1.4	17	7*	35*	2.0	500	2.8	120	550*

Source: Reprinted with permission from the National Academies Press. Copyright 1997, 1998, 2000, 2001, 2005 by the National Academy of Sciences. These reports may be accessed via www.nap.edu.

Note: This table is adapted from the DRI reports, see www.nap.edu. It lists Recommended Dietary Allowances (RDAs), with Adequate Intakes (AIs) indicated by an asterisk (*). RDAs and AIs may both be used as goals for individual intake. RDAs are set to meet the needs of almost all (97 percent to 98 percent) individuals in a group. For healthy breastfed infants, the AI is the mean intake. The AI for other life stage and gender groups is believed to cover the needs of all individuals in the group, but lack of data prevents being able to specify with confidence the percentage of individuals covered by this intake.

[a]Given as retinal activity equivalents (RAE).

[b]Also known as calciferol. The DRI values are based on the absence of adequate exposure to sunlight.

[c]Also known as α-tocopherol.

[d]Given as niacin equivalents (NIE), except for infants 0–6 months, which are expressed as preformed niacin.

[e]Given as dietary folate equivalents (DFE).

STEPS FOR BEHAVIOR CHANGE

Do you consume too much sugar?

Take the quiz below to find out whether there is too much sugar in your diet.

Y	N	
☐	☐	Do you consume a bowl of sweetened breakfast cereal more than two mornings a week?
☐	☐	Do you sweeten your tea or coffee with packets of white or brown sugar?
☐	☐	Is a morning donut or muffin or an afternoon cookie part of your regular routine?
☐	☐	Do you eat candy more than twice a week?
☐	☐	Do you consume more than one can or bottle of soda on most days of the week?

If you answered yes to to more than two of these questions, your diet could use an upgrade.

TIPS TO CUT DOWN ON SUGAR

- ☑ Know how to spot sugar. When you see terms such as *sucrose*, *glucose*, *maltose*, *dextrose*, *fructose*, or *high fructose corn syrup* on the ingredients list, beware. These are all forms of sugar. If sugar or its "pseudos" are in the first three ingredients on a label, avoid the product. It has a high sugar content by weight.
- ☑ Try a noncalorie sugar substitute, such as Sweet'N Low, NutraSweet, or Splenda in your tea or coffee, or flavor your tea with lemon instead of sugar.
- ☑ Start your morning with a piece of whole-grain toast or a fresh bowl of fruit, instead of a sugar-sweetened cereal or muffin. If you have to have cereal, opt for whole-grain granola or raisin bran, rather than sugar-sweetened puffed cereal.
- ☑ Eat graham crackers, yogurt, fresh fruits, air-popped popcorn, and other healthy substitutes for high-sugar sweets when you need a snack.

Source: Adapted from Boyle, M., and G. Zyla. *Personal Nutrition.* St. Paul, MN: West Publishers, 1991.

Vitamins: B_{12}, D, and Folate Though most people will not need vitamin supplements if they are eating a healthy diet, people who have increased nutrient needs or special circumstances may benefit from enriched or fortified foods, a multivitamin, or other vitamin supplement. For example, strict vegetarians (vegans), who eat no animal foods, need to be sure to get enough vitamin B_{12} (which is found primarily in animal products) through fortified foods, such as breakfast cereals, or by taking a supplement. Vegetarians who do not get 15 to 30 minutes of exposure to sunlight every few days may also need to take a vitamin D supplement.

Pregnant women need to be sure to consume enough folic acid, usually through a supplement, to reduce the risk of birth defects in their growing babies. And some older individuals, who may have depressed appetites or may not be able to cook or consume meals easily, may be advised to take a multivitamin to ensure that they meet their needs.

Other individuals also might benefit from vitamin supplementation:

- People with chronic illnesses that depress the appetite or the absorption of nutrients
- People on medications that affect appetite or digestion
- Athletes engaged in a rigorous training program
- Lactating women
- Individuals on prolonged low-calorie diets.

Minerals: Iron and Calcium Iron is an essential component of red blood cells, which carry oxygen

A CLOSER LOOK

DIETARY REFERENCE INTAKES

Recommended Dietary Allowances (also known as RDAs) are the daily amounts of the different food nutrients the National Academy of Sciences deems adequate for healthy individuals. However, even today, RDAs for some nutrients are not known. Thus, the Academy has issued additional indices to guide people in monitoring their diets. They refer to these indices as Dietary Reference Intakes (DRIs).

The 2005 DRIs are divided into four categories, each of which addresses a different nutritional issue:

1. *Recommended Dietary Allowance (RDA).* The RDAs are the amount of nutrient that will meet the needs of almost every healthy person in a specific age and gender group. Also, the latest RDAs are meant to reduce disease risk, not just prevent deficiency.
2. *Adequate Intake (AI).* This value is used when the RDA is not known because the scientific data aren't strong enough to produce a specific recommendation, yet there is enough evidence to give a general guideline. Thus, the AI is an "educated guess" at what the RDA would be if it were known.
3. *Estimated Average Requirement (EAR).* This is a value that is estimated to satisfy the needs of 50% of people in a given age group. It is primarily used to establish the RDA. In addition, it is used for evaluating and planning the diets of large groups of people (such as the army), not individuals.
4. *Tolerable Upper Intake Level (UL).* This is the maximal amount that a person can take without risking "adverse health effects." Anything above this amount might result in toxicity. In most cases, this number refers to the total intake of the nutrient—from food, fortified foods, and nutritional supplements.

The latest guidelines group the nutrients according to their functional properties. The following list shows the groups, the year of the latest update, and the nutrients in each.

- **Dietary Reference Intakes (DRIs) for Calcium, Phosphorus, Magnesium, Vitamin D, and Fluoride (1997).** These nutrients have key roles in developing and maintaining bone and other calcified tissues in the body.
- **DRIs for Energy, Carbohydrate, Fiber, Fat, Fatty Acids, Cholesterol, Protein, and Amino Acids (Macronutrients) (2005).** These macronutrients provide energy.
- **DRIs for Thiamin, Riboflavin, Niacin, Vitamin B_6, Folate, Vitamin B_{12}, Pantothenic Acid, Biotin, and Choline (1998).** These water-soluble vitamins are involved with energy metabolism and processes of macronutrient breakdown.
- **DRIs for Vitamin C, Vitamin E, Selenium and Carotenoids (2000).** These micronutrients have been shown to have antioxidant properties and to play important roles in combating various chronic diseases.
- **DRIs for Vitamin A, Vitamin K, Arsenic, Boron, Chromium, Copper, Iodine, Iron, Manganese, Molybdenum, Nickel, Silicon, Vanadium, and Zinc (2001):** These micronutrients have been shown to have important roles in combating various chronic diseases.
- **DRIs for Water, Potassium, Sodium, Chloride and Sulfate (2004).** These nutrients are important in maintaining fluid balance in the body.
- **DRIs: Proposed Definition of Dietary Fiber (2001).** Fiber has been shown to be important in regulating digestive tract function and preventing intestinal cancers.

Source: National Academy of Sciences. *Dietary Reference Intakes: Applications in Dietary Assessment.* Washington, DC: National Academy Press, 2005.

to all our tissues for energy production. An iron deficiency can result in decreased oxygen transport to tissues and thus an energy crisis. Getting enough iron can be a problem for women who are menstruating, pregnant, or nursing. Indeed, only half of all women of child-bearing age get the necessary 15 mg of iron per day (3). Five percent suffer from iron-deficiency anemia. Although these individuals should not take iron supplements unless their physician prescribes them (because the body excretes very little iron, there is a potential for toxicity if too much is consumed), they can modify their diets to ensure getting the RDA of iron. The following dietary modifications can help meet this requirement:

- Eat legumes, fresh fruits, whole-grain cereals, and broccoli, all of which are high in iron.
- Also eat foods high in vitamin C, which helps iron absorption.
- Eat lean red meats high in iron at least two or three times per week.
- Eat iron-rich organ meats, such as liver, once or twice per month.

TABLE 7.7
Sample Diet for a College-Aged Female Weighing 110 Pounds, Assuming Light Daily Activities

	kcal	Fat (g)	Cholesterol (mg)	Sodium (mg)	Carbohydrate (g)	Protein (g)	Vitamin A (RE)*	Vitamin C (mg)	Calcium (mg)
Breakfast									
1/2 grapefruit	38	0.1	0	0	10.7	0.8	2	41.3	14
Whole-grain cereal (1 cup)	127	0	0	244	33	3	0	0	16
Low-fat milk (1 cup)	225	2.6	10	121	42	9	20	1.4	314
1 banana	105	1	0	1	27	1	93	10	7
Snack									
Low-fat yogurt (1 cup)	130	2.6	10	121	44	9	20	1.4	314
Lunch									
Turkey sandwich: whole-wheat bread with mustard	191	3.7	9	784	25	9.4	0	0	78
Baby carrots (10)	36	1	0	35	8	1	1972	8	23
Snack									
1 slice pizza with Parmesan cheese	145	3	8	336	21	8	382	1	117
Dinner									
Broiled salmon (1/2 fillet)	180	5	83	107	0	32	169	0	21
Mushrooms (1/2 cup)	20	0	0	2	4	2	0	3	5
Whole-wheat dinner rolls (2)	150	2	0	272	27	4	0	0	60
Broccoli (3 spears)	26	0	0	25	5	3	1434	87	45
Lima beans (1/2 cup)	90	0	0	15	21	6	332	9	29
Peach (1)	37	0	0	0	10	1	465	6	4
Totals	1500	21	120	2065	247.4	88.2	4907	169.1	883
RDA	1690	<30%	<300	<3000	>58%	40	700	75	1000
% of RDA	89	14	40	68	72	220	953	225	88

*RE = retinol equivalents.

- Don't drink tea with your meals; it interferes with iron absorption.

Another mineral, calcium, is the most abundant mineral in the body and is essential for building bones and teeth, as well as for normal nerve and muscle function. Adequate calcium is especially important for pregnant or nursing women. There is some evidence that calcium may help prevent colon cancer (3).

The most recent RDAs call for a significant increase in calcium intake for both sexes beginning at age 9. Children between 9 and 18 years of age should consume a 1300 mg of calcium each day. Adequate calcium intake during those years may be a crucial factor in preventing osteoporosis in later years, which strikes one in two women and one in five men over the age of 50 (10). Adults over age 18 should consume 1000 mg of calcium per day.

A CLOSER LOOK WHAT IS THE GLYCEMIC INDEX AND WHEN IS IT HELPFUL?

Low-carbohydrate diets are based on the notion that some carbohydrate-rich foods cause a dramatic increase in blood insulin levels that results in increased storage of fat and a decrease in blood glucose that increases appetite. The diets are based on the **glycemic index** (GI) of foods, a measure of the effect a given food will have on the amount of glucose in the blood after the food is eaten. The concept is that eating foods with a low glycemic index results in less glucose fluctuation in the blood after a meal, which in turn stabilizes insulin levels and appetite. The typical reference for the GI is pure glucose, which has a GI of 100.

The GI of a food is not always easy to predict. Although some foods that contain simple sugars, such as candy, will logically have a higher GI, some foods with natural sugar, such as an apple (which is high in fructose) will have a lower GI. Additionally, the way the food is prepared and its fat and fiber content can affect its GI ranking. Instant mashed potatoes, white bread, and white rice have higher GIs than oat bran or kidney beans.

The glycemic index can be useful for some individuals, such as people with diabetes, to help them avoid fluctuations in blood glucose levels. In general, if you want to eat foods with lower, rather than higher, GIs, follow these guidelines:

- Eat breakfast cereals made of oats, barley, and bran.
- Eat dense, chewy breads made with whole seeds, not white bread.
- Eat fewer potatoes, but more al dente pasta.
- Choose basmati rather than white rice.
- Enjoy all types of vegetables.
- Eat plenty of salad vegetables with vinaigrette dressing.
- Balance a meal containing high-GI foods with extra low-GI foods.
- Add food acids (such as citrus fruits) to help slow stomach emptying and reduce the glycemic response.
- Eat fewer sugary foods, such as cookies, cakes, candy, and soft drinks.

Glycemic Index Range		
	Range	**Example Foods**
Low GI	0–55	Apples, oranges, bananas
Medium GI	56–69	White rice, ice cream
High GI	70–100	White bread, crispy rice cereal

The following recommendations can help you get the calcium you need:

- Add low-fat or nonfat dairy products to your diet.
- Choose other calcium-rich alternatives, such as canned fish (with the bones, packed in water), turnip and mustard greens, and broccoli.
- Eat foods rich in vitamin C to boost absorption of calcium.
- Use an acidic dressing, made with citrus juices or vinegar, to enhance calcium absorption from salad greens.
- Add a supplement if you can't get enough calcium in the foods you like. However, beware of supplements made with dolomite or bone meal, because they may be contaminated with lead.

Make sure you know...

> The basic guidelines for a healthy diet are to eat adequate amounts of fruits, vegetables, and whole grains and to watch your intake of calories, sugar, alcohol, fat and sodium. If you choose to drink alcohol, do so only in moderation.

> Recommended dietary allowances (RDAs), Dietary Reference Intakes (DRIs), and the USDA's MyPyramid are tools you can use to plan a healthy diet. You can use food labels to choose foods that are low in calories, fat, sodium, and sugar.

> Some people, including children, pregnant and lactating women, and strict vegetarians, may have special nutrient needs and may therefore benefit from choosing enriched or fortified foods and/or taking a vitamin or mineral supplement.

glycemic index A ranking system for carbohydrates based on a food's effect on blood glucose levels.

STEPS FOR BEHAVIOR CHANGE

Are you a fast food junkie?

Although eating at fast-food restaurants is generally not a healthy habit, there are choices you can make to improve your diet. Take the following quiz to assess your current behavior.

Y N

☐ ☐ Do you typically order the largest size on the menu?

☐ ☐ Do you always order a burger or fried fish or fried chicken sandwich?

☐ ☐ Do you always get french fries as a side?

☐ ☐ Is soda your "default" beverage for washing down your meal?

☐ ☐ Are your fast-food sandwiches and salads typically loaded up with mayonnaise, creamy dressings, or other high-fat sauces?

If you answered yes to more than two of these questions, you're probably consuming major amounts of fat and calories with every fast-food meal. Fortunately, there's a lot you can do to improve the nutritional quality of your next fast-food meal, without forgoing the drive-through altogether.

TIPS FOR THE NEXT TIME YOU'RE AT THE FAST-FOOD COUNTER

☑ Order the small-sized items. Don't "supersize" your meal. Consider these numbers: Depending on the restaurant, a double cheeseburger may contain 600–700 calories, 30–40 grams fat, 120–140 mg cholesterol, and 1000–1200 mg sodium! You'll be surprised how satisfied you'll be with just a single burger and small order of fries, and you'll save yourself a ton of calories.

☑ Forgo the sauces and creamy salad dressing. A typical tablespoon of tartar sauce contains about 20 grams of fat and 220 mg of sodium, and a tablespoon of mayonnaise will add 100 calories and 11 grams of fat to your sandwich. Ordering you sandwich without the mayo is an easy way to cut a quick 100 calories.

☑ Order grilled meat instead of fried. Breaded chicken typically contains double the amount of fat as a broiled piece.

☑ Choose healthier sides: Try ordering a small salad instead of french fries, or a fruit cup rather than an apple pie for dessert.

☑ Skip the soda or milkshake. Drink water, nonfat milk, or 100% juice with your meal. Cutting back your regular soda intake is one of the fastest ways to cut down on the calories (not to mention the sugar).

How Does Nutrition Affect Physical Fitness?

Think about the last radio, TV, or online ad you saw for a nutrition-related product. Do you remember what was said about the product, and did you question whether it was true? The reality is that much of what you see and hear in such advertisements is not based on sound research and, in some cases, is entirely made up. Often, successful athletes endorse various nutritional products and convince the public that a particular food or beverage is responsible for their success. Even though most of the claims made in commercial endorsements are not supported by research, the claims often become accepted as fact.

The truth is, there are no miracle foods to improve physical fitness or exercise performance. In the sections that follow we discuss the specific nutritional needs of individuals in a regular exercise program.

TABLE 7.8
Influence of Exercise Intensity on Fuel Use
Both intensity and duration of exercise will govern which fuel predominates during an exercise session. The following table illustrates how intensity affects fuel use during endurance-type exercises.

Exercise Intensity	Fuel Used by Muscle
Less than 30% $\dot{V}O_2max$	Mainly fat stores
40–60% $\dot{V}O_2max$	Fat and carbohydrate equally
75% $\dot{V}O_2max$	Mainly carbohydrate
Greater than 80% $\dot{V}O_2max$	Nearly 100% carbohydrate

Carbohydrates Are Used for Energy during Exercise

You need more fuel during exercise than when you're sedentary. Recall that carbohydrates and fats are the primary fuels used to provide energy for exercise. Because even very lean people have a large amount of energy stored as fat, lack of fat for fuel is not a problem during exercise. In contrast, the carbohydrate stores in the liver and muscles can reach critically low levels during intense or prolonged exercise (7) (Figure 7.8).

Because carbohydrates play a critical role in providing energy during exercise, some exercise scientists have suggested that people participating in daily exercise programs should increase the complex carbohydrates in their diet from 58–70% of the total calories consumed (fat intake is then reduced to 18% of total caloric intake) (7). If exercise is intense, carbohydrates can be depleted from the liver and muscles, resulting in fatigue. The intensity of the exercise determines whether carbohydrates or fat is the predominant source of energy production (7, 11) (Table 7.8).

In most cases, the energy you use during your workout comes from energy stored from meals eaten the previous day. Hence, products such as sports drinks and gels may not be as useful for energy during exercise as they are marketed to be. In fact, sugared sports drinks can cause a rapid rise in blood glucose, which promotes hormonal changes that reduce blood glucose to levels below normal and results in feelings of fatigue (7).

Increasing the percentage of complex carbohydrates in the diet and maintaining sufficient caloric intake can ensure that an adequate supply of energy from carbohydrates is stored in the muscles and the liver to meet the needs of a rigorous exercise training program.

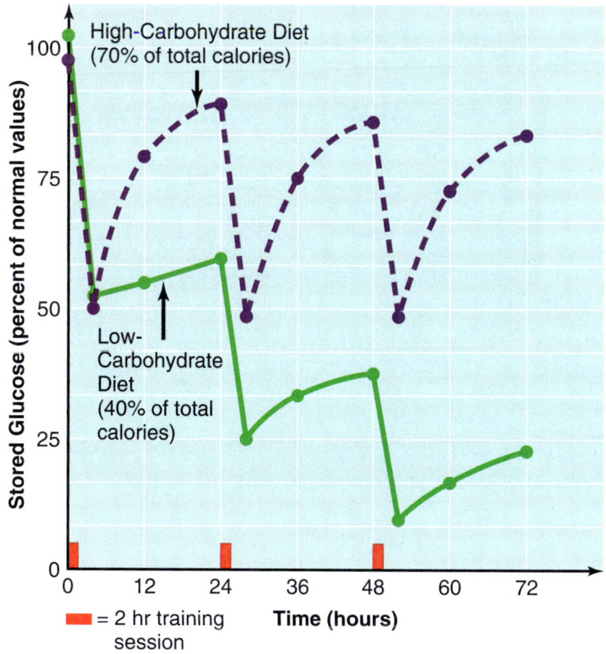

FIGURE 7.8
The importance of a high-carbohydrate diet during exercise training. With a low-carbohydrate diet (solid line), glucose stored in muscles as glycogen is depleted by daily training sessions. If a high-carbohydrate diet is consumed (dashed line), muscle glycogen levels are maintained at near normal levels.

Source: David C. Nieman, *Exercise Testing and Prescription: A Health Related Approach*. Copyright © 2003. Reprinted by permission of the McGraw-Hill Companies.

Protein Needs Can Be Met with a Healthy Diet

Many bodybuilders consume large quantities of protein in supplements, in addition to the protein they take in through their normal diet, because they think this will promote muscular growth. Unfortunately, they're drinking those shakes and eating those bars largely in vain, because research has shown that a normal, well-balanced diet meets the protein requirements of most bodybuilders (12, 13). The increased caloric needs of someone in a strength-training program should come from additional amounts of nutrient-dense foods and not simply from additional protein. This strategy supplies not only the extra macronutrients, but also the micronutrients necessary for energy production.

High Vitamin Intake Does Not Improve Performance

Some vitamin manufacturers have argued that megadoses of vitamins can improve exercise performance. This belief is based on the notion that exercise in-

Products such as sports gels and drinks are sometimes used by athletes during competition. Usually, these are unnecessary. Use caution when using them, and make sure they are appropriate for your situation.

creases the need for energy and, because vitamins are necessary for the breakdown of foods for energy, an extra load of vitamins should be helpful. There is no evidence to support this claim (14). The energy supplied for muscle contraction is not enhanced by vitamin supplements. In fact, megadoses of vitamins may interfere with the delicate balance of other micronutrients and can be toxic as well (3). For example, excess vitamin A can cause damage to the nervous system, cleft palate, and eye problems in unborn babies.

Antioxidants Help Prevent Oxidative Damage

Antioxidants are vitamins and micronutrients that protect cells by preventing a process called *oxidation*. (Oxidation is the same process that causes iron to rust over time. In fact, you can think of oxidation in the body as something like rusting from the inside.) Antioxidants work by combining with, and neutralizing, **free radicals** before they can damage cells. Excess production of free radicals has been implicated in cancer, lung disease, heart disease, and even the aging process (15). Therefore, increasing the level of antioxidants may be beneficial to health. Several micronutrients, including vitamins A, E, and C, beta-carotene, zinc, and selenium, have been identified as potent antioxidants.

Recent research suggests that the increased muscle metabolism associated with exercise may increase free radical production (16). Several studies have shown that this increase in free radicals may contribute to fatigue and perhaps even muscle damage.

Preliminary studies have indicated that antioxidants, primarily vitamin E, play a positive role in neutralizing exercise-produced free radicals. In fact, recent reports have demonstrated a reduction in muscle damage following administration of antioxidants (16). Several researchers have suggested that an additional 400 IU of vitamin E be consumed daily to protect against free radical damage. However, you should consult a nutritionist before consuming more than the RDA of fat-soluble vitamins. Remember: Fat-soluble vitamins are stored in the body, and their accumulation may lead to toxicity.

Make sure you know...

- The amount of carbohydrate and fat used as fuel during exercise will vary according to the intensity of the exercise.
- The extra energy needed for strength training should not come solely from increased protein intake.
- Excess vitamin intake does not improve exercise performance.
- Antioxidants help prevent free radicals from damaging cells. To date, vitamins A, E, and C, beta-carotene, zinc, and selenium have been identified as potent antioxidants.

Do Supplements Provide an Edge for Health and Performance?

As previously mentioned, athletes aren't the only ones who may consider taking supplements. Many less-active individuals also use (or consider using) vitamins, minerals, herbs, enzymes, amino acids, or other compounds in pill, powder, or tablet form to improve health and wellness. Over the past decade, the use of nutritional and pharmaceutical supplements has become common in the United States. The search for a speedy path to health, wellness, and fitness led Americans to spend almost $20.3 billion on nutritional supplements in 2005 (1). This has led the U.S. government to look closely at how this industry is regulated. In the following sections we examine how supplements are regulated and which ones might have the potential to be beneficial.

The Role of Supplements in a Healthy Diet

The FDA estimates that more than 25,000 products are available as dietary supplements. There is no scientific evidence to validate most of the claims that supplements improve health or exercise performance. You can view some of the more popular supplements cur-

A CLOSER LOOK

DO PHYTOCHEMICALS PROTECT AGAINST DISEASE?

Besides nutrients, plant foods—legumes, vegetables, fruits, and whole grains—contain a whole other "crop" of chemicals called phytochemicals (*phyto* means "plant"). These substances, which plants produce naturally to protect themselves against viruses, bacteria, and fungi, may help protect us from diseases as well.

Phytochemicals include hundreds of naturally occurring substances, including carotenoids, flavonoids, indoles, isoflavones, capsaicin, and protease inhibitors. And just as occurs with vitamins and minerals, different plant foods contain different kinds and amounts of phytochemicals.

Certain phytochemicals appear to protect against some cancers, heart disease, and other chronic health conditions. Until more is known, the nutrition bottom line still applies: Eat a wide variety of fruits, vegetables, legumes, and whole grains, and count on food, not diet supplements, to get the nutrients your body needs. That way, you'll reap the potential benefits of the many phytochemicals found in all kinds of plant foods.

Source: Heber, D. Vegetables, fruits and phytoestrogens in the prevention of diseases. *Journal of Postgraduate Medicine* 50(2):145–149, 2004.

rently marketed for improving health and enhancing exercise performance in Table 7.9.

Our knowledge of the relationship between diet and disease points out the importance of consuming adequate amounts of nutrients while avoiding dietary excesses. However, not much is known about newly discovered, unclassified, and naturally occurring micronutrient components of food and their effects on health and disease. For example, several studies have identified numerous plant compounds, called phytochemicals, that—when ingested by humans in small amounts—may protect against a variety of diseases. We still don't know whether the large amounts of phytochemicals typically present in supplements are safe or effective. (See the Closer Look box above). Given our current incomplete knowledge, eating a wide variety of foods and avoiding excesses from dietary supplements are the best ways to obtain adequate amounts of beneficial food components.

Regulation of Supplements

Dietary supplements are not regulated in the same way that foods and prescription and over-the-counter drugs are regulated. The difference is that foods and drugs are tested and approved by governmental agencies (such as the FDA), whereas supplements are not. Manufacturers, not the government, are responsible for the safety of supplements. Supplement manufacturers are not required to get FDA approval before they market their products, and the FDA does not test supplements. Rather, the FDA trusts the manufacturers to ensure that the products are safe and effective.

However, the claims made on supplement labels are regulated. Supplement manufacturers are allowed to claim effects on the "structure or function" of the body but are not allowed to make claims concerning the treatment, prevention, cure, or diagnosis of disease. The FDA instituted the "structure/function rule" in 2000 to distinguish disease claims, which require that evidence of safety and benefit be demonstrated to the FDA before the product is marketed, from structure/function claims, which have no such requirement. The rule prohibits both express disease claims (such as, "prevents heart disease") and implied disease claims (such as, "prevents bone fragility in postmenopausal women") without prior FDA review. However, the rule permits health-maintenance claims (such as, "maintains healthy bones"), other claims not related to disease (such as, "for muscle enhancement"), and claims for the relief of common minor symptoms associated with life stages (such as, "for common symptoms of PMS").

Since its release, the rule has been modified both to expand the number of acceptable structure/function claims and to narrow the definition of *disease* to disallow structure/function claims pertaining to aging, pregnancy, menopause, and adolescence. Supplement manufacturers are required to keep on file substantiation of any structure/function claims they make. However, the FDA neither examines nor substantiates the legitimacy of this documentation. Manufacturers must also include on their labels a disclaimer stating that their dietary supplements are not drugs and received no FDA

antioxidants Molecules that neutralize free radicals, thereby preventing them from causing damage to cells.

free radicals Oxygen molecules that can potentially damage cells.

TABLE 7.9
Comparison of Dietary Supplements

Supplement	Origin	Benefits Claimed	Evidence of Effectiveness
Androstenedione	Made by the body as part of testosterone production	Enhances the production of testosterone and causes an increase in muscle mass.	Evidence suggests that it does not increase testosterone, and it may increase female hormones in men.
Antioxidants	Produced by cells to protect against free radical production. Some vitamins, minerals, and other chemicals in foods also have antioxidant properties.	Buffer free radical damage, which could help prevent fatigue and/or muscle damage during exercise. Also, could help protect against some diseases.	No evidence to suggest enhancement of exercise performance. Some evidence to suggest a benefit in preventing damage to tissues. Growing evidence to suggest benefits in fighting many conditions such as cancer, heart and lung disease, and aging.
Caffeine	Compound found in coffee, cola, candy, stimulants, weight-loss products.	Used to increase muscle fiber activation to increase strength, or to increase fat metabolism and endurance.	Increases endurance in events lasting greater than 20 minutes. No consistent effects on strength.
Carbohydrates	Component of most food. Usually found as a dietary supplement in the form of beverages or bars.	Increase in stored glucose in muscle and liver and increase in endurance.	Improves endurance in events longer than 90–120 minutes. Also helps restore glucose after exercise.
L-carnitine	Made by the body and ingested in meat products.	Increases transport of fat in cells, reduces lactate accumulation.	Carnitine is in adequate supply in the cells, and additional amounts provide no benefit before, during, or after exercise.
Chromium picolinate	Chromium is a trace element found in several foods; picolinate is added to supplements to aid absorption.	Helps insulin action and is thought to aid glucose metabolism, blood fats, and have anabolic effects.	No good evidence for any benefits. *Side effects: Stomach upset, anemia, genetic damage, kidney damage.*
Coenzyme Q-10	Made by the body as a component of the biochemical pathway that makes adenosine triphosphate (ATP).	Enhances ATP production.	No evidence suggests a benefit during or after exercise.
Creatine	Made by the body and also found in meat products.	Decreases fatigue in short, intense exercise. Increases muscle size and strength.	Increases endurance in short, intense exercise. Causes water gain in muscle but not increases in strength.
Echinacea	Herbal supplement.	Reduces duration of colds, boosts immune system, heals wounds.	Some evidence suggests it may be beneficial for these conditions. *Side effects: Uncommon, but possible GI upset, chills, nausea.*
Ginkgo biloba	Extracts of dried leaves of *Ginkgo* plant.	Used for antioxidant properties and to improve blood flow and memory.	Does have antioxidant properties that may be beneficial in improving blood flow, improving neural function, and reducing production of stress hormones. *Side effects: nausea, headache, dizziness, skin rash, hemorrhage if used with blood thinners.*
St. John's wort	Plant extract.	Used to treat depression and external wounds, burns, and muscle aches.	Some evidence suggests that it is beneficial for treating these conditions.

CONSUMER CORNER

DETECTING SUPPLEMENT FRAUD

Most of the dietary supplements on the market today are useless. These products often do nothing more than cheat consumers out of their money or steer them away from products that have been proven useful. Some supplement products may do more harm than good.

How can you avoid being scammed by the maker of a worthless supplement? Marketers have sophisticated ways of making their products attractive to potential buyers, but you can protect yourself by learning about marketing ploys. Beware of the following techniques, claims, or catch-phrases:

- **The product "does it all."** Be suspicious of any supplement that claims to have multiple benefits. No one product is likely to be capable of so great a range of effectiveness.
- **The product is supported by personal testimonials.** Testimonials are often simply stories that have been passed from person to person, and sometimes they are completely made up. Because testimonials are difficult to prove, they may be a "tip" to the possibility of fraud.
- **The product provides a "quick fix."** Be skeptical of products that claim to produce immediate results. Among the tip-offs are ambiguous language such as, "Provides relief in days," or "You'll feel energized immediately." Unscrupulous marketers use such phrases to protect themselves against any subsequent legal action.
- **The product is "natural."** The term *natural* suggests that the product is safer than conventional treatments. However, any product—whether synthetic or natural—that is potent enough to produce a significant physiological effect is potent enough to cause side effects.
- **The product is "a new, time-tested treatment."** A product is usually one or the other, but be suspicious of any product that claims to be both a breakthrough and a decades-old treatment. If a product that claims to be an "innovation" or a "new discovery" were really so revolutionary, it would be widely reported in the media and prescribed by health professionals, not featured in obscure ads.
- **Your "satisfaction is guaranteed."** Money-back guarantees are often empty promises. The makers of this claim know most people won't go to all the trouble involved in trying to get a refund of only $9.95 or so.
- **The product's ads contain meaningless medical jargon.** The use of scientific-sounding terms such as "aerobic enzyme booster" may seem impressive and may even contain an element of truth, but these terms likely cover up a lack of scientific data concerning the product.

Always ask yourself, Does this claim seem too good to be true? If it does, then the product is probably a fraud. If you're still not sure, talk to your doctor or other health professional. The Better Business Bureau or your state attorney general's office can tell you whether other consumers have lodged complaints about a product or its marketers. If a product is promoted as being helpful for a specific condition, check with the appropriate professional group—for example, consult the American Heart Association about products that claim some effectiveness concerning heart disease.

approval before marketing. Additionally, manufacturers must notify the FDA of a product claim within 30 days of marketing it. All this means that the consumer is ultimately responsible for determining whether a given supplement is needed or safe. See the Consumer Corner box.

Make sure you know...

- Supplements should never replace foods as major sources of dietary nutrients.
- Supplements are not tested or approved by the FDA or other governmental body. However, the FDA does mandate that the only claims that can be made about supplements must relate to effects on "structure or function" of the body. Manufacturers are allowed to make no label claims about the effects of a supplement on disease.
- Because dietary supplements are poorly regulated, consumers should be cautious when choosing and using such supplements.

Washing fresh produce under running tap water will help you avoid foodborne illness.

Topics in Food Safety and Technology

The quality of your food choices and an adequate (but not too high) calorie intake are two aspects of a healthy diet. Ensuring the foods you eat are safe and free from contamination is another component of eating well. Let's discuss the specifics of food safety and technology next.

Foodborne Illness

If a food carries a disease-causing microorganism, such as a bacterium, consuming the food can potentially make you sick. According to the Institute of Food Technologists, approximately 80 million cases of foodborne bacterial disease occur each year. These illnesses produce nausea, vomiting, and diarrhea from 12 hours to 5 days after infection (17). The severity of the illness depends on the microorganism ingested and the victim's overall health. Foodborne infections can be fatal in children, people with compromised immune systems, or other people in ill health.

Two types of foodborne illness that you may have heard about are *Salmonella* contamination and botulism. The *Salmonella* bacterium is usually found in raw or undercooked chicken and eggs and in processed meats. The relatively uncommon but sometimes fatal botulism usually results from improper home-canning procedures. A particular strain of the *Escherichia coli* bacterium, O157:H7, is sometimes found in contaminated raw or undercooked ground beef and can lead to bloody diarrhea, among other symptoms.

To reduce your risk of contracting foodborne illness, follow these guidelines:

- Select foods that appear clean and fresh.
- Wash produce thoroughly with running water; use a vegetable brush on firm fruits and vegetables.
- Drink only pasteurized milk and juices.
- Don't eat raw eggs.
- When storing perishable foods for future consumption, keep them cold or frozen to prevent bacterial growth.
- Cook all meat products, such as chicken, pork, and ground beef, thoroughly. When dining out, order meats well done.
- Cook all shellfish thoroughly; steaming them open may not be sufficient.
- Avoid raw fish; it may contain parasitic roundworms. Keep fish frozen, and cook until well done.
- Use separate sets of cutting boards and utensils (e.g., knives) for meat and produce; chopping raw meat and vegetables with the same knife, without washing it thoroughly first, can lead to cross-contamination.
- Wash utensils, plates, cutting boards, knives, blenders, and other cooking equipment with soap and very hot water after each use.

See the Closer Look box on the next page for more about minimizing your risk for foodborne illness.

Food Additives

Food additives are used by manufacturers for a variety of reasons: to improve nutritional quality, as a preservative to maintain freshness and/or increase shelf life, to improve taste or color, or otherwise to make it more appealing. Among the most commonly used additives are sugar, salt, and corn syrup. Other additives, such as monosodium glutamate (MSG) and sulfites, may cause a reaction in people who are particularly sensitive to them. Nitrites, which are found in bacon, sausages, lunch meats, and other processed foods, may also form

A CLOSER LOOK KEEP HOT FOODS HOT AND COLD FOODS COLD TO AVOID FOODBORNE ILLNESS

Whether from restaurants, supermarkets, or quick-service establishments, take-out foods have become a part of our way of life. But to avoid foodborne illnesses, you must keep these foods at the appropriate temperature. The next time you order take-out or bring a hot or cold food to a party or family function, keep the following recommendations in mind.

FOR HOT FOODS

- Keep hot foods above 140°F. You can cover food with foil (to keep it moist) and keep it warm—140°F or above—in the oven (check the food's temperature with a meat thermometer). Using a slow cooker is another option for some foods. It's best to eat food within 2 hours of preparation.
- If the food won't be eaten for more than 2 hours, refrigerate it in shallow, covered containers. Before serving, reheat it in an oven to 165°F or until it's hot and steaming. If you prefer, reheat food in a microwave oven—cover and rotate—and then let it stand for 2 minutes to ensure thorough, even heating.

FOR COLD FOODS

- Keep cold foods at 40°F or below.
- If cold foods are not eaten right away, refrigerate them as soon as possible.
- Discard any foods kept at room temperature for more than 2 hours. If conditions are warmer than 90°F, toss the food after only 1 hour.
- Transport and store cold foods in chilled, insulated coolers.
- If you're going to put out a deli platter, keep it on a bowl of ice.

Source: USDA Food Safety and Inspection Service. *Cooking for Groups: A Volunteer's Guide to Food Safety*. Item #604H, Pueblo, CO 81009.

cancer-causing agents (nitrosamines) in the body. If you think you are sensitive to a particular food additive, read labels carefully and avoid foods that contain additives to which you are likely to have a reaction.

Antibiotics, Hormones, and Organically Grown Foods

As consumers become more aware of the quality of the foods they eat, they are buying increasing quantities of **organic** foods. *Organic*, in this context, refers to foods that are grown without the use of pesticides, hormones, antibiotics, or chemical fertilizers. Currently, the United States, the European Union, Japan, and many other countries require producers to obtain certification to market food as organic.

Livestock animals raised on factory farms are often treated with high doses of antibiotics to ward off potential infections. Though there is little evidence to support the view, some people are concerned that eating meat or drinking milk from these animals could lead to the development of antibiotic-resistant bacteria in humans.

Farmers also often use hormones in animals to increase production of meat and milk. Most notably, a form of growth hormone, bovine somatotropin, has been used to increase milk production in dairy cows. Some people fear that hormones in food may cause health problems, such as cancer, in humans. Many supermarkets are restricting the sale of milk produced with the aid of hormone supplements.

Should you buy organic foods? This is a decision you have to make for yourself. However, be aware that there is no research to support that organic foods are nutritionally superior to nonorganic foods, and organic foods tend to be more expensive than their nonorganic counterparts.

Irradiated and Bioengineered Foods

Irradiation is sometimes used to kill microorganisms in foods and prolong the shelf life of the food (17). In fact, irradiated food can be stored for years in sealed containers at room temperature without spoiling. In addition, irradiation can delay the sprouting of vegetables such as potatoes and onions and delay the ripening

organic Plant or animal foods that are grown without the use of pesticides, chemical fertilizers, antibiotics, or hormones.

irradiation The use of radiation (high-energy waves or particles, including radioactivity and X rays) to kill microorganisms that grow on or in food.

of fruits such as bananas, tomatoes, and avocados. This can result in significant cost savings.

Are these irradiated foods safe to eat? Currently, all research indicates that the foods are safe and nutritional content is maintained, but only limited data exist (17). Irradiated foods must carry a seal of approval to inform consumers that they have been treated.

Another practice that has become more controversial is the use of bioengineered foods. Bioengineering involves inserting the genes from one plant or animal species into another plant or animal's DNA to achieve a desired trait. Food crops such as corn and tomatoes have been bioengineered to improve yields, pest resistance, and longevity (which improves the crops' ability to be shipped long distances). Although the benefits of bioengineering can be great, the practice is considered unproven, and possibly unsafe, in some countries.

Make sure you know...

> Proper food storage and preparation are the keys to preventing foodborne illness. Select foods that appear clean and fresh; keep foods cold or frozen to prevent bacteria from growing; clean fresh fruits, vegetables, and meats thoroughly; cook all meats thoroughly; order meats well done when dining out.

> The use of the word *organic* on food labels is strictly regulated; organic foods are grown without the use of pesticides and other chemicals.

> Irradiation and bioengineering are two forms of food technology that are used to enhance food safety and increase yields and pest resistance. Despite all indications that they are safe, both techniques remain somewhat controversial.

Summary

1. Nutrition is the study of food and its relationship to health and disease. In industrialized countries, the current primary problem in nutrition is overeating.
2. A well-balanced diet is composed of approximately 58% complex carbohydrates, 30% fat, and 12% protein. The macronutrients provide the energy (kilocalories, or calories) necessary for bodily functions. The calorie is a unit of measure of the energy value of food or the energy required for physical activity.
3. Carbohydrate is a primary fuel used by the body to provide energy. Simple carbohydrates, or sugars, include glucose, fructose, sucrose, galactose, lactose, and maltose. The complex carbohydrates consist of starches and fiber. Starches are composed of chains of glucose. Fiber is a nondigestible but essential form of complex carbohydrates contained in whole grains, vegetables, and fruits. Fiber is important in regulating digestion and forming waste products.
4. Fat is an efficient storage form for energy, because each gram contains over twice the energy of carbohydrates or protein. Fat can be derived from dietary sources or formed from excess carbohydrates and protein consumed in the diet.
5. Fats are a type of lipid. Most of the fat found in foods and in your body is in the form of triglycerides. Triglycerides consist of three fatty acids attached to a glycerol backbone. Fatty acids are classified as either saturated or unsaturated, depending on their chemical structures. Cholesterol is another form of lipid. Blood cholesterol levels can affect your risk of heart disease.
6. The primary role of protein is to serve as the structural unit for building and repairing cells in all tissues of the body. Protein consists of amino acids made by the body (11 nonessential amino acids) and those available only through dietary sources (9 essential amino acids). If you consume inadequate amounts of carbohydrates or fat, protein can be broken down and used for energy.
7. Vitamins serve many important functions in the body, including regulation of growth and metabolism. The B-complex vitamins and vitamin C are water soluble and, for the most part, cannot be stored in the body. The fat-soluble vitamins A, D, E, and K can be stored in the body.
8. Minerals are inorganic chemical elements that serve many important roles in regulating body functions.
9. Approximately 60–70% of the body is water. Water is involved in all vital processes in the body and is particularly important for physically active individuals. You need to consume 8–10 cups of water in food and beverages daily.
10. A healthy diet consists of adequate amounts of fruits, vegetables, whole grains, and lean meats and dairy products, with limited amounts of sugar, fat, and sodium. You should balance the calories you consume with the calories you expend, and if you drink alcohol, do so only in moderation. You can

use the RDAs, DRIs, MyPyramid, and food labels to help you choose healthy foods.

11. The intensity of exercise dictates the relative proportions of fat and carbohydrates that are used as fuel during exercise. In general, the lower the intensity of exercise, the more fat is used as a fuel. Conversely, the greater the intensity of exercise, the more carbohydrates are used as a fuel.
12. Antioxidants are nutrients that prevent free radicals from damaging cells. Vitamins E and C, beta-carotene, zinc, and selenium have been identified as antioxidants.
13. Most people can consume adequate nutrients through a healthy diet and do not need to take supplements. However, pregnant women, strict vegetarians, older adults, and some others, may benefit from a dietary supplement.
14. The key to preventing foodborne illness is to prepare, store, and cook foods properly. Select foods that appear clean and fresh; keep foods cold or frozen to prevent bacteria from growing; thoroughly clean fresh fruits, vegetables, and meats; cook all meats thoroughly, and order well-done meats when dining out.

Study Questions

1. What is the primary role of carbohydrates in the diet?
   a. build tissue
   b. provide energy
   c. form hormones
   d. form enzymes
2. The primary role of protein in the diet is to
   a. provide energy
   b. provide hydration
   c. build tissues
   d. regulate hormones.
3. Water is important for
   a. providing energy.
   b. building bones.
   c. forming blood.
   d. building protein.
4. What approximate percentages of carbohydrates, fat, and protein in the diet are recommended daily?
   a. 60, 20, 20
   b. 58, 22, 20
   c. 40, 20, 40
   d. 58, 30, 12
5. Which of the following may protect the body's cells against damage during normal and elevated metabolism?
   a. proteins
   b. hormones
   c. antioxidants
   d. antibiotics
6. List the major food sources of dietary carbohydrates.
7. List the various subcategories of carbohydrates.
8. Define *triglyceride*, and discuss its use in the body.
9. Distinguish between saturated and unsaturated fatty acids.
10. What are omega-3 fatty acids?
11. What is the difference between essential and nonessential amino acids?
12. What are the classes of vitamins, and what role do vitamins play in body function?
13. Outline the role that minerals play in body function.
14. How many calories are contained in 1 gram of carbohydrate, fat, and protein, respectively?
15. Discuss the special need for carbohydrates in an individual who is engaging in an exercise training program.
16. Discuss the special need for protein for an individual who is engaging in an exercise training program.
17. Discuss the impact of the following on heart disease:

    high density lipoproteins (HDL cholesterol)

    low-density lipoproteins (LDL cholesterol)
18. Discuss the structure/function rule pertaining to dietary supplements.

Suggested Reading

Block, G. Junk foods account for 30% of caloric intake. *Journal of Food Composition and Analysis* 17:439–447, 2004.

Heber, D. Vegetables, fruits and phytoestrogens in the prevention of diseases. *Journal of Postgraduate Medicine* 50(2):145–149, 2004.

Kant, A. K. Dietary patterns and health outcomes. *Journal of the American Dietetic Association* 104(4):615–635, 2004.

Maughan, R. J., D. S. King, and T. Lea. Dietary supplements. *Journal of Sports Sciences* 22(1):95–113, 2004.

Position of the American Dietetic Association, Dietitians of Canada, and the American College of Sports Medicine: Nutrition and athletic performance. *Journal of the American Dietetic Association* 100(12):1543–1556, 2000.

Spriet, L. L., and M. J. Gibala. Nutritional strategies to influence adaptations to training. *Journal of Sports Sciences*. 22(1):127–141, 2004.

Srinath, R. K., and M. B. Katan. Diet, nutrition and the prevention of hypertension and cardiovascular diseases. *Public Health and Nutrition* 7(1A):167–186, 2004.

Thompson, J., and M. Manore. *Nutrition: An Applied Approach*. San Francisco: Benjamin Cummings, 2005.

Willett, W. C., and M. J. Stampfer. Rebuilding the food pyramid. In *Annual Editions: Nutrition 2004/2005*. Dubuque, IA: McGraw-Hill, 2004, pp. 11–16.

Wood, O. B., and C. M. Bruhn. Position of American Dietetic Association: Food irradiation. *Journal of the American Dietetic Association* 100(2):246–253, 2000.

For links to the websites below, visit The Total Fitness and Wellness Website at www.aw-bc.com/powers.

Center for Food Safety and Applied Nutrition
Home page for the FDA office of supplement regulation. Great information on food safety and supplements.

The Food and Nutrition Board
Part of the National Academy of Sciences, whose mission is to establish principles and guidelines of adequate dietary intake.

MEDLINE Plus Health Information: Vitamin and Mineral Supplements
A service of the National Library of Medicine, National Institutes of Health, that provides information on health topics, including vitamin and mineral supplements.

FDA Dietary Supplement Questions and Answers
Provides information about what dietary supplements are and how they are regulated, including the labeling and claims that can be made for supplements.

NUTRITION.GOV
A federal resource that provides easy access to all online federal government information on nutrition.

MEDLINEplus
Contains a wealth of up-to-date, quality nutrition information from the world's largest medical library, the National Library of Medicine at the National Institutes of Health.

Food and Drug Administration
In the summer of 2001, the FDA began publishing a quarterly newsletter titled *Dietary Supplement and Food Labeling Electronic Newsletter*. The newsletter's goal is to provide key information and updates about regulatory actions related to food labeling, nutrition, and dietary supplements, as well as educational materials and important announcements. To subscribe to the letter, visit the link.

Nutrition Café
Contains several intriguing nutritional games, including one in which you build a meal from the menu and then get nutritional information about your selections.

FoodSafety
Gateway to government food safety information. Includes news and safety alerts, consumer advice, national food safety programs, and foodborne pathogens.

Ask the Dietician
Presents sound nutritional advice on many diet-related questions. Includes an excellent "Health Body Calculator" for formulating diet and exercise programs.

USDA Center for Nutrition Policy and Promotion
Provides governmental guidelines for diets.

USDA Food Safety Publications
Contains articles about all aspects of safety in food preparation, storage, and handling.

Fast Food Finder
Enables you to search for desired fast food (by restaurant or food) and find nutritional information.

Veggies Unite! On-line guide to vegetarianism
Includes recipes, books, articles, and discussions.

American Dietetic Association
Presents nutritional resources, FAQs, links, and more.

Crunch Your Numbers
When it comes to health, everything really does add up. So here are 34 fun, easy-to-use calculators. Learn your ideal weight, determine your protein needs, assess your heart rate, determine how many calories your favorite sport will burn, and more.

References

1. Nutrition Business Journal, *NBJ's Supplement Business Report 2005,* http://Nbj.stores.yahoo.Net/Nbsupbusrep2.html.
2. Mokdad, A. H., J. S. Marks, D. F. Stroup, and J. L. Gerberding. Actual causes of death in the United States, 2000. *Journal of the American Medical Association* 291(10):1238–1245, 2004.
3. Wardlaw, G. M., J. Hampl, and R. DiSilvestro. *Perspectives in Nutrition*, 7th ed. Columbus, OH; McGraw-Hill, 2007.
4. Jenkins, D., C. Kendall, and V. Vuksan. Viscous fibers, health claims, and strategies to reduce cardiovascular disease risk. *American Journal of Clinical Nutrition* 71(2):401–402, 2000.
5. Tucker, K. L. Dietary intake and coronary heart disease: A variety of nutrients and phytochemicals are important. *Current Treatment Options in Cardiovascular Medicine* 6(4):291–302, 2004.
6. Dragsted, L. O., A. Pedersen, A. Hermetter, S. Basu, M. Hansen, G. R. Haren, M. Kall, V. Breinholt, J. J. Castenmiller, J. Stagsted, J. Jakobsen, L. Skibsted, S. E. Rasmussen, S. Loft, and B. Sandstrom. The 6-a-day study: Effects of fruit and vegetables on markers of oxidative stress and antioxidant defense in healthy nonsmokers. *American Journal of Clinical Nutrition* 79(6):1060–72, 2004.
7. Powers, S., and E. Howley. *Exercise Physiology: Theory and Application to Fitness and Performance*, 4th ed. Dubuque, IA: McGraw-Hill, 2001.
8. Karppanen, H., and E. Mervaala. Sodium intake and hypertension. *Progress in Cardiovascular Disease* 49(2): 59–75, 2006.
9. Food and Nutrition Information Center, U.S. Department of Agriculture. Dietary Reference Intakes (DRI) and Recommended Dietary Allowances (RDA), www.nal.usda.gov/fnic.
10. Keen, R. Osteoporosis: Strategies for prevention and management. *Best Practice and Research Clinical Rheumatology* 21(1):109–122, 2007.
11. Jones, N. L., and K. J. Killian. Exercise limitation in health and disease. *New England Journal of Medicine* 343(9):632–641, 2000.
12. Tipton, K. D., and R. R. Wolfe. Exercise, protein metabolism, and muscle growth. *International Journal of Sport Nutrition and Exercise Metabolism* 11(1):109–132, 2001.
13. Lemon. P. W., J. M. Berardi, and E. E. Noreen. The role of protein and amino acid supplements in the athlete's diet: Does type or timing of ingestion matter? *Current Sports Medicine Reports* 1(4):214–221, 2002.
14. Lukaski, H. C. Vitamin and mineral status: Effects on physical performance. *Nutrition* 20(7–8):632–644, 2004.
15. Young, I. S., and J. V. Woodside. Antioxidants in health and disease. *Journal of Clinical Pathology* 54(3): 176–186, 2001.
16. Powers, S. K., K. C. DeRuisseau, J. Quindry, and K. L. Hamilton. Dietary antioxidants and exercise. *Journal of Sports Sciences* 22(1):81–94, 2004.
17. Food Safety Policy, Science, and Risk Assessment: Strengthening the Connection: Workshop Proceedings (2001), Institute of Medicine, Washington, DC: National Academy Press, 2001.

NAME ______________________________ DATE ______________

Analyzing Your Diet

The purpose of this exercise is to analyze your eating habits during a 3-day period. For a 3-day period (two weekdays and one weekend day), eat the foods that typically constitute your normal diet. At the end of each day, record on the following chart the foods you ate that day and the amounts of the listed nutrients contained in each. You can use the food labels on your foods to obtain the nutrient values, or refer to the Appendix at the end of this text (you can also use a diet analysis software program, if you have access to one.)

Total the values for each nutrient at the bottom of the chart. Transfer the total to the next chart. At the end of the 3-day period, total the daily values and divide by 3 to get the average dietary intake for each of the nutrients analyzed.

Compare your average intake for each of the nutrients with those recommended at the bottom of the page for your sex and age group. (Remember that this analysis is only as representative of your normal diet as the foods you eat over the 3-day period). Then, answer the following questions:

1. How did you do on calories? Are you taking in more or fewer calories than you should be for your sex, age, and activity level?

   ____

2. Was your fat, sodium, and cholesterol intake higher than it should be?

   ____

3. What nutrients did you eat in inadequate amounts?

   ____

4. What are three substitutions you could have made that would improve the quality of your diet?

   ____

Recommended Dietary Allowances*

- Kcal total (total daily energy expenditure) equals body weight multiplied by kcal per pound per day:

  ______________ × ______________ = ______________

  body weight in lb — kcal per lb per day (from Table 8.1) — **kcal total (total daily energy expenditure)**

- Kcal from fat should be no more than 30% of total calories per day:

  ______________ × ______________ = ______________

  30% (0.3) — kcal per day — **recommended MAXIMUM kcal from fat**

- Protein intake should be 12% of total calories per day, or 0.8 to 0.9 gram per kilogram (0.36 g per pound) of body weight. (Pregnant women should add 15 g, and lactating women should add 20 g):

  ______________ × ______________ = ______________

  0.36 g — body weight in lb — **recommended protein intake**

- Carbohydrate intake should be approximately 58% of total calories per day:

  ______________ × ______________ = ______________

  58% (0.58) — kcal per day — **recommended carbohydrate intake**

Fat <30% of diet; fiber ~30% of diet; saturated fat <10% of diet; cholesterol <300 mg.; sodium <3000 mg

*See Table 7.6 on pages 210 and 211 for vitamin and mineral RDA values.

Daily Nutrient Intake

Name: ______________________________ Date: ______________

Foods	Amount	kcal (total)	kcal from fat	Protein (gm)	Carb. (gm)	Fiber (gm)	Fat (gm)	Fat % (kcal)	Sat. Fat (gm)	Chol. (mg)	Sodium (mg)	Vit. A (I.U.)	Vit. C (mg)	Calcium (mg)	Iron (mg)	Vit. B_1 (mg)	Vit. B_2 (mg)	Niacin (mg)
Totals																		

Look in your Behavior Change Log Book for an additional 3-day nutrient intake log.

Three-Day Nutrient Summary

Name: ____________________ Date: ____________

Day	kca (Total)	kcal from Fat	Protein (gm)	Carb. (gm)	Fiber (gm)	Fat (gm)	Fat % (kcal)	Sat. Fat (gm)	Chol. (mg)	Sodium (mg)	Vit. A (IU)	Vit. C (mg)	Calcium (mg)	Iron (mg)	Vit. B_1 (mg)	Vit. B_2 (mg)	Niacin (mg)
One																	
Two																	
Three																	
Totals																	
Average																	

NAME ______________________ DATE ______________

Setting Goals for a Healthy Diet

What are your three worst dietary habits?

1. ______________________
2. ______________________
3. ______________________

Check the appropriate boxes in the table below to indicate the changes that you think you need to make to improve your diet.

	Increase	Decrease	Keep the Same
Calories			
Carbohydrates			
Fat			
Protein			
Vitamins			
Minerals			

Based on your selections above, list two short-term and two long-term goals for improving your diet:

Short-term goal 1

____

Short-term goal 2

____

Long-term goal 1

____

Long-term goal 2

____

NAME ______________________________ DATE ______________________________

Planning a New Diet

The purpose of this exercise is to plan a new diet using the principles outlined in this chapter. After completing Laboratory 7.1, you should have a general idea of how your diet may need modification. Follow the example given in Table 7.7 and the discussion in the text to choose foods to build a new diet that meets the recommended dietary goals presented in this chapter. Fill in the chart on the following page with the requested information obtained from this book's appendix or from package labels. Use the totals for each column and the RDA for each nutrient in Laboratory 7.1 or Table 7.6 to determine your percentage of RDA for each nutrient.

LABORATORY 7.3 *(continued)*

	kcal (g)	Protein (g)	Sat. Fat (g)	Chol. (mg)	Sod. (mg)	Carb. (g)	Vit. A (IU)	Vit. C (mg)	Ca (mg)	Iron (mg)	GI
Breakfast											
Lunch											
Dinner											
Totals											
RDA	*	<30%†	<10%	<300	3000	>58%	1000	60	1200	12	‡
% of RDA											

*See Chapter 8 for determination of kcal requirements.

†Protein intake should be 0.8 g/kg of body weight (0.36 g/lb). Pregnant women should add 15 g, and lactating women should add 20 g.

‡For a complete list of the glycemixc index of various foods, visit www.glycemicindex.com

8

Exercise, Diet, and Weight Control

true or false?

1. The key to weight loss is to not eat snacks.
2. Low-carbohydrate diets are the only ones that really work.
3. Your genes determine whether you'll be obese.
4. A successful weight management program involves both diet and exercise.
5. Anorexia nervosa occurs only in women.

Answers appear on the next page.

Millions of people in the United States are overweight. In fact, according to the Centers for Disease Control and Prevention, the prevalence of overweight and obesity has increased sharply for both adults and children. Obesity represents a global epidemic and is now one of the leading causes of illness worldwide (1). Being overweight has been shown to be a risk factor for health problems such as diabetes, gallbladder disease, high blood pressure, high cholesterol, heart disease, and even some cancers. As a result of this connection between health and increased body weight, more people are trying to lose weight, and an estimated 43% of overweight women and 28% of overweight men attempt to lose weight each year (2).

This epidemic in overweight and obesity has given birth to a multi-billion-dollar weight-loss industry in the United States. Consumers spend about $30 billion per year on diet sodas, appetite suppressants, diet books, commercial diets, and medically supervised diets in an attempt to lose weight or prevent weight gain. In addition, the number of individuals seeking gastric bypass surgery increased from 10,000 in 1996 to more than 100,000 in 2004 (3). Many commercial weight-loss programs advertise that they are highly successful. Unfortunately, research has found that with no other treatment, only 5% of individuals maintain the weight loss for 5 years after completing the program (2). The good news is that long-term weight loss is achievable, and many people do successfully alter their diet and lifestyle habits to achieve a healthy weight. The key is to recognize that short-term diets and gimmicks work only temporarily and that the only solution for long-term weight loss is to retool one's eating and physical activity patterns.

In this chapter, we will discuss the principles of determining an ideal body weight for health and fitness; how to use a combination of diet, exercise, and behavior modification to successfully reduce body fat; and the principles involved in maintaining a desirable body weight throughout life. Finally, we will look at the symptoms and health effects of several disordered eating patterns. We begin by revisiting the concept of optimal body weight, which you read about in Chapter 6.

What Is Your Optimal Body Weight?

Before you can decide whether you should implement a weight-loss program, you need to find out whether you're currently at an optimal body weight. Recall from Chapter 6 that in general, optimal body fat for health and fitness in men ranges from 10–20%, whereas the optimal range of body fat for women ranges from 15–25% (4). These ranges allow for individual differences in physical activity and appearance and are associated with limited risk of the diseases linked to body fatness. How can you compute your desired range of body weight? The calculation can be done in two simple steps; the first step is to calculate your fat-free weight. Consider the following example of a male college student who has 25% body fat and weighs 185 pounds.

Step 1: Compute fat-free weight—that is, the amount of total body weight contained in bones, organs, and muscles:

$$\text{\% total body weight} - \text{\% fat weight} = \text{\% fat-free weight}$$
$$100\% - 25\% = 75\%$$

This means that 75% (or 0.75, expressed as a decimal) of total body weight is fat-free weight. Therefore, the fat-free weight for this student is

$$0.75 \times 185 \text{ pounds} = 138.8 \text{ pounds}$$

Answers

1. **FALSE** Snacking can help suppress the appetite between meals and can be a healthy strategy for weight management, as long as the snack foods are healthy. Fruits and raw vegetables make ideal snacks.
2. **FALSE** Low-carbohydrate diets may help you initially lose weight, but you'll likely regain the weight once you resume your normal carbohydrate intake.
3. **FALSE** Genetics do play a role in overweight and obesity; however, only 1–5% of the population have genetic conditions that are the main cause of obesity. For most obese people, the condition is a result of diet and lifestyle factors.
4. **TRUE** The combination of diet and exercise is the only effective means for losing weight and maintaining the weight loss over the long term.
5. **FALSE** Anorexia nervosa can affect both men and women.

Step 2: Calculate the optimal weight (which for men is 10–20% of total body weight). The formula to compute optimum body weight is

$$\text{Optimum weight} = \text{fat-free weight} \div (1 - \text{optimal \% fat})$$

Note that % fat should again be expressed as a decimal. Thus, for 10% body fat,

$$\text{Optimum weight} = 138.8 \div (1 - 0.10) = 154.2 \text{ pounds}$$

For 20% body fat,

$$\text{Optimum weight} = 138.8 \div (1 - 0.20) = 173.5 \text{ pounds}$$

Hence, the optimal body weight for this individual is between 154.2 and 173.5 pounds. See Laboratory 8.1 to compute your optimal body weight, using both percentage of body fat and body mass index (from Chapter 6).

Make sure you know...

- The ranges of optimal body fat for health and fitness are 10–20% for men and 15–25% for women.
- You can calculate your optimal body weight using your percent body fat and current body weight.

What Factors Can Affect Weight Management?

In most obese people, being overfat is a result of a complex interaction between internal and external (environmental) factors. Internal factors include genetics and hormonal secretions. External factors such as diet, exercise, and social settings also directly affect weight management. Let's examine these two sets of influences more closely.

Genetic Factors and Hormones

There are a few rare conditions, including Prader-Willi syndrome and Bardet-Biedl syndrome, that account for extreme obesity in about 1% of the population. These two conditions are genetic disorders and are present at birth (5). Other physiological causes of obesity may be related to the release of hormones, especially leptin and ghrelin, and much current research focuses on this area.

The hormone **leptin** appears to depress appetite by acting on areas of the brain that control hunger (6). Researchers working on the connection between hormones and obesity found that obese mice had very low levels of leptin, and when injected with leptin, the mice became lean. Leptin was believed to be the cure-all for the obesity epidemic until it was later discovered that many obese people produce abnormally high levels of leptin. Further research has focused on how leptin works with other hormones such as insulin (a hormone manufactured by the pancreas). Researchers aren't sure how leptin and insulin interact, but it provides an intriguing area of further study.

Another hormone called **ghrelin** contributes to feelings of hunger. High levels of ghrelin trigger nerve signals running from the gut to the brain, causing the hunger signal to turn on and keep ringing. Research has been conducted to determine how to suppress ghrelin production, whereas other studies have focused on the effects of exercise on ghrelin production. Although there have been no reported changes in ghrelin production following aerobic exercise, there is some evidence that moderate-intensity resistance training may suppress ghrelin production, thus reducing appetite (7). Gastric bypass surgery has also been shown to suppress ghrelin levels (8).

Hormonal influences on ghrelin have also revealed that leptin and insulin work together to lower the production levels of ghrelin. In addition, certain types of food affect the production of ghrelin. Foods rich in fat are less effective in suppressing the production of ghrelin than foods containing proteins or sugars (2). These discoveries about the hormones that affect hunger and appetite have led researchers to believe that a cure for obesity in humans may be attainable.

Environmental Factors

Environmental factors still remain the primary focus for many health care professionals in treating overweight and obese individuals. Diet and exercise are the two major factors that can be controlled and modified in fighting the obesity epidemic. What you eat, and how much you eat, as well as how much you exercise, are very much within your control.

Understanding what triggers our eating habits may be an important first step in weight management. For some people, eating has become a response to emotional stressors, both good and bad. On the one hand, think about how your family celebrates an accomplishment, such as graduation from college, or a milestone, such as a birthday or anniversary. These positive stressors bring people together to celebrate, and food is often at the center of that celebration. On the other hand, when dealing with negative feelings such as depression, loneliness, or boredom, some people turn to food for comfort. Eating habits become ingrained as part of our family practices and may be difficult to change.

leptin A hormone that appears to depress appetite.

ghrelin A hormone that contributes to feelings of hunger.

STEPS FOR BEHAVIOR CHANGE

What triggers your eating?

Take the following quiz to help assess some of the cues that cause you to eat.

Y	N	
☐	☐	I need to have a snack and a beverage nearby when I study.
☐	☐	I cannot watch television or sit through a movie without a snack in my hand.
☐	☐	I would order the small portion at a fast-food restaurant, but I get more for my money if I order the largest size possible.
☐	☐	Leaving food on my plate is wasteful.
☐	☐	I like to have a beverage in my cupholder when I'm driving.

If you answered yes to more than one of these questions, you're likely eating out of habit or because of your environment. This behavior could lead to weight gain.

TIPS TO CURB YOUR CALORIE CONSUMPTION

- ☑ Drink water while studying instead of soda, and if you get hungry, stop for a break and go get a piece of fruit for a snack.
- ☑ Visit friends or go for a walk in the evening instead of watching television. You'll eat less and work in some physical activity.
- ☑ Order only small sandwiches and fries when eating fast food, or, better yet, order no fries and a side salad instead.
- ☑ Despite what our families may have taught us, clearing your plate is probably leading to your eating long after you're full. Next time you sit down for a home-cooked meal, try grabbing smaller portions to begin with, then go back for seconds only if you're really still hungry.
- ☑ Opt for a reusable water bottle in your car, and use that to stay hydrated during road trips. The calories in sodas and sugar-and-milk-laden coffee drinks will quickly add up.

Eating habits have also changed as fast-food restaurants have proliferated throughout the country. The convenience of these food outlets has made it easy to "grab" a quick sandwich and eat it en route to work, play, or the next event. Convenience, cost, and portion size have made fast-food restaurants a likely culprit in the obesity epidemic. The restaurant industry overall has increased portion sizes to give customers more for their money. As portion sizes increase, so do the waistlines of the customers. In fact, serving sizes have increased to the point that the average person does not realize what a normal serving size should be. In the end, most people underestimate the amount of food they eat. Paying attention to how much and what we consume is an important first step in weight management.

Do you know what situations or events affect your eating habits? See the Steps for Behavior Change box above and the box on the next page to identify some of your food triggers.

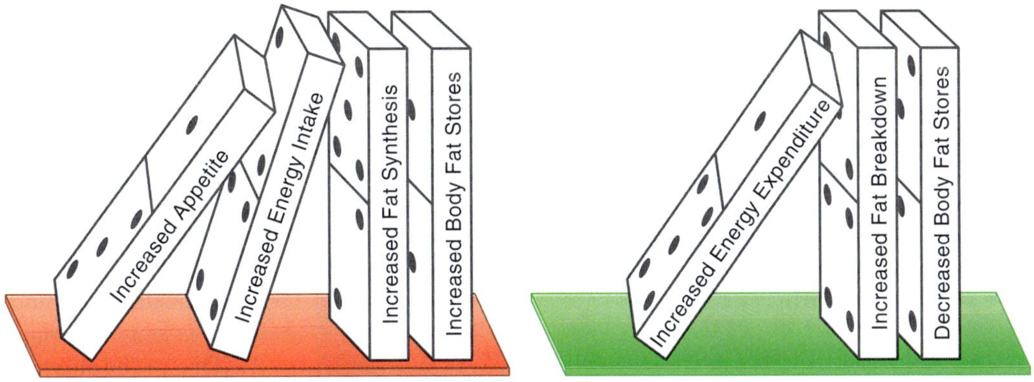

FIGURE 8.1
Numerous factors compound to lead to weight gain or weight loss.

The Concept of Energy Balance

Simply stated, body fat stores are regulated by two factors: the rate at which fat is synthesized and stored, and the rate at which energy is expended and fat is metabolized (broken down). In general, fat stores increase when energy intake ("calories in") exceeds energy expenditure ("calories out") and decrease when energy expenditure exceeds energy intake. This concept can be simplified into the phrase "calories in versus calories out." If you take in more calories than you expend, you will gain weight, and if you expend more calories than you consume, you will lose weight. You can see in Figure 8.1 that an increase in energy intake (calories) in response to increased appetite leads to increases in fat synthesis and storage. In contrast, fat stores are reduced when fat is broken down for use as a source of energy for the body.

If you want to maintain a constant body weight, your food energy intake (expressed in calories) must equal your energy expenditure; that is, you must be in **energy balance** (Figure 8.2). Healthy weight-loss

FIGURE 8.2
The concept of energy balance. To maintain body weight, the number of calories you consume must equal the number of calories you expend. An imbalance on either side of the scale will result in a change in body weight.

Social and Environmental Factors That May Contribute to Overeating

- *Activities*. You may find a correlation between specific types of activities, such as watching TV and eating snacks.
- *Emotional behavior before or during eating*. For instance, many people overeat when they are depressed or under stress.
- *Location of meals*. Do you eat your meals in front of the television? Do you associate specific rooms with snacking?
- *Time of day and level of hunger*. Do you eat at specific times of the day? Do you eat even if you are not hungry?
- *People involved*. Are specific people associated with periods of overeating?

energy balance The state of consuming a number of calories that is equal to the number expended. Over the long term, energy balance results in maintenance of a constant body weight.

Exercise is a key component to any weight-loss program.

programs include both a reduction in caloric intake and an increase in caloric expenditure achieved through exercise (4, 9, 10).

Estimating your daily energy expenditure is a key factor in planning a weight-loss program and adjusting the energy balance equation. The daily expenditure of energy involves both the resting metabolic rate and exercise metabolic rate.

Resting metabolic rate (RMR) is the amount of energy expended during all sedentary activities. That is, RMR includes the energy required to maintain necessary bodily functions (called the basal metabolic rate) plus the additional energy required to perform such activities as sitting, reading, typing, and digesting food. The RMR is an important component of the energy balance equation because it represents approximately 90% of the total daily energy expenditure in sedentary individuals (11).

Resting metabolic rate is influenced by several factors, including age, gender, and the amount of lean body mass that an individual possesses. For example, resting metabolic rate (expressed per pound of body weight) is generally higher in growing children than in adults. Moreover, resting metabolic rate declines with age, and men have a higher resting metabolic rate than women. Finally, resting metabolic rate is elevated in people with a low percentage of body fat and a high percentage of lean mass. The physiological explanation for this is that the energy required to maintain muscle tissue is greater than the energy required to maintain fat tissue (4).

Exercise metabolic rate (EMR) represents the energy expenditure during any form of exercise (walking, climbing steps, weight lifting, and so on). In sedentary individuals, EMR constitutes only 10% of the total daily energy expenditure. By comparison, EMR can account for 20–40% of the total daily energy expenditure in active individuals (11). For example, during heavy exercise, EMR may be 10–20 times greater than RMR (4). Therefore, increased daily exercise increases the EMR and is a key factor in weight control programs.

One of the simplest ways to estimate your daily caloric expenditure is to determine your activity level and use it to calculate the average number of calories you expend in a 24-hour period (Table 8.1). For example, the estimated daily caloric expenditure for a moderately active college-aged woman who weighs 120 pounds is calculated by multiplying 120 (her body weight in pounds) by 15 (the calories she expends per pound per day):

$$\text{Daily caloric expenditure} = 120 \text{ pounds} \times 15 \text{ calories/pound/day}$$
$$= 1800 \text{ calories/day}$$

If this woman takes in an average of 2000 calories per day in her meals and snacks, those extra 200 calories put her on the road to weight gain. Do this same calculation for your own daily caloric expenditure. Do you think your daily expenditure is equal to or higher than the amount of calories you take in per day? If you need to lose weight, what activities could you add to your routine to increase your daily caloric expenditure?

Now that you know the basic physiological and environmental factors that affect weight management and understand the concept of energy balance, let's discuss the strategies that can lead to safe and effective weight loss.

Make sure you know...

> Physiological (internal) factors that contribute to overweight and obesity include genetics and hormonal excretions; external factors that affect weight management include diet, exercise, and social settings.

> To maintain a constant body weight, your food energy (caloric) intake must equal your caloric expenditure; that is, you must maintain a state of energy balance. Consuming more calories than you expend results in weight gain, and consuming fewer calories than you expend results in weight loss.

TABLE 8.1
Estimating Daily Caloric Expenditure
To compute your estimated daily caloric expenditure, multiply your body weight in pounds by the calories per pound that corresponds to your activity level.

Activity Level	Description	Calories per Pound of Body Weight Expended during 24-Hour Period
1 Very sedentary	Restricted movement, such as a patient confined to a house	13
2 Sedentary	Light work or office job	14
3 Moderate activity	Some daily activity and weekend recreation	15
4 Very physically active	Vigorous activity at least 3–4 times/week	16
5 Competitive athlete	Daily activity in high energy sport	17–18

> Daily energy expenditure can be estimated by considering both your resting metabolic rate and your exercise caloric expenditure.

Designing a Successful Weight-Loss Program

The basic strategy for successful weight loss is to expend more calories than you consume and to make changes to your diet and lifestyle that you will be able to maintain over the long term. The maximum recommended rate for weight loss is 1 to 2 pounds per week. Diets resulting in a weight loss of more than 2 pounds per week are associated with a significant loss of lean body mass (i.e., muscle and body organs).

The energy deficit required to lose 1 pound per week is approximately 3500 calories. Therefore, a negative energy balance of 500 calories per day would theoretically result in a loss of 1 pound of fat per week (3500 calories per week ÷ 7 days per week = 500 calories per day).

The rate of loss during the first several days of dieting will be greater than later in the dieting period. At the onset of a diet, you lose not only fat, but also carbo hydrate and water stores, which also results in some weight loss (4). Further, you may also lose some lean tissue, such as muscle, during the beginning of any diet; therefore, you will lose more than 1 pound during the first 3500-calorie deficit. However, as the diet continues, you will lose weight at a slower rate. Don't be discouraged if weight loss levels off after the first week. The weight you lose later will come primarily from fat stores, and sticking with your weight-loss plan for several weeks will result in a significant fat loss.

To lose weight and keep it off, you need to implement four basic steps:

1. Establish a realistic goal for weight loss.
2. Assess your diet, and determine how you can modify it to reduce your caloric intake while still consuming all the nutrients you need for health.
3. Decide which physical activities you will begin doing to raise your daily caloric expenditure and increase (or maintain) muscle mass.
4. Modify your diet and lifestyle to lose the weight you want to lose and prevent future weight gain.

Let's take a closer look at what's involved in each of these steps.

Set a Realistic Goal for Weight Loss

The first step in setting a realistic weight loss goal is to decide where your percentage of body fat should fall within the optimal healthy range (10–20% for men, 15–25% for women). Many people who are beginning a comprehensive weight-loss program set a long-term weight loss goal that will place them in the middle of the optimal weight range (15% body fat for men, 20% body fat for women). After choosing your long-term goal, it is also useful to establish short-term weight-loss

resting metabolic rate (RMR) The amount of energy expended during all sedentary activities.

exercise metabolic rate (EMR) The amount of energy expended during any form of exercise.

goals—usually expressed in the number of pounds lost per week. Keep in mind that 1–2 pounds per week is a realistic weight-loss goal. Establishing a goal of losing 5 pounds in a week is not realistic and will set you up for failure.

If your goal is to lose 1 pound per week, you must establish how you will achieve that. For example, "I will lose 1 pound by walking 20 minutes each day and limiting my soda consumption to one, 8-ounce glass a day."

Remember, setting realistic goals is an important first step in weight management. Using the optimal healthy range for percent body fat as your guide is healthier and much more realistic than aiming for a tiny dress size or waist measurement. See Laboratory 8.3 for a worksheet you can use to help set your long-term and short-term goals.

CONSIDER THIS!

Approximately 90% of fat loss occurs in the body regions with the highest fat storage, generally the thighs and hips in women, and the abdominal region in men. In other words, you cannot spot-reduce fat stores.

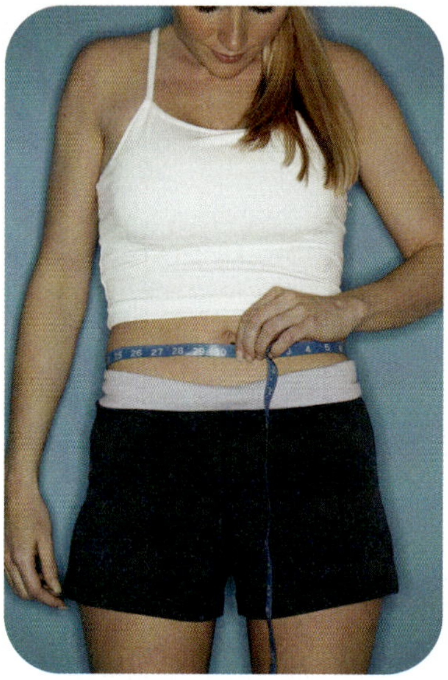

Assess and Modify Your Diet

Another key to losing weight successfully is to recognize the healthy and less healthy dietary choices you're making on a daily basis. If you're eating fast food regularly, you may be consuming too many high-fat, high-calorie foods that are impeding your ability to lose weight. Similarly, if you can't remember the last time you ate a fresh fruit or vegetable, you may be getting too few nutrients and other healthy substances. A balanced, healthy diet can naturally lead to weight loss, and once you know the areas of your diet that could be improved, you can work on making changes that are likely to help you lose weight.

Most people tend to underestimate the amount of food they consume. Keeping a food diary for as few as 2–3 days can make

TABLE 8.2
Popular Diet Plans

Diet	Description/ Examples	Recommended?	Comments
Low-carbohydrate	High in protein (meat, beans, animal products) and may also be high in fat. Examples: Atkins diet, Zone diet, and Sugar-Busters	No	Typically high in fat and cholesterol. Initial weight loss is attributed to water loss. Success in keeping weight off over time is minimal because of tendency to return to regular eating habits.
Low-calorie liquid diet	Prepackaged liquid meal replacement plans. Example: Slim-Fast	No	Although nutritionally balanced, these diets are typically monotonous and unsatisfying.
Very-low-calorie diet	Provides 300–600 calories per day.	No	Nutritionally unbalanced and unsafe for long-term use.
Balanced low-calorie diet	Typically involves reduction in calorie intake by 500–1000 calories per day. Example: diet that follows the recommendations in the MyPyramid food guidance system	Yes	Can be nutritionally balanced and safe for long-term use. Safely allows 1–2 pounds of weight loss per week.

A CLOSER LOOK FACTS AND MYTHS ABOUT LOW-FAT AND LOW-CARB DIETS

Most people are aware that eating foods high in fat can be detrimental to the waistline, so they search for foods that are labeled "low-fat" or "fat-free." This is an important first step in reducing fat intake; however, it does not always lead to weight loss. Consumers should read beyond the fat calories and be aware that many of these "reduced-fat" products may actually be higher in total calories than their alternatives. Eating less fat should not result in eating more calories, because this will be detrimental to weight loss.

Proponents of low-carbohydrate diets argue that these diets have two major advantages over conventional diet plans (24, 25). First, eating high-carbohydrate foods promotes the use of carbohydrates as fuel and reduces the rate of fat metabolism. This argument is supported experimentally, and the physiology to explain this claim is that consuming high-carbohydrate foods promotes an increase in the hormone insulin. High insulin levels are counterproductive to weight loss because insulin stimulates both fat storage and a reduction in the use of fat as a body fuel (4, 25).

The second argument in favor of low-carbohydrate diets is that high-carbohydrate foods are less satiating than foods containing high levels of proteins or fats (25). Therefore, low-carbohydrate diets may promote satiety, reduce overall caloric intake, and assist in achieving a negative caloric balance. Although evidence exists to support this argument, low-carbohydrate diets do not suppress appetite in all people.

Low-carbohydrate diets are sometimes promoted as diets on which "you never feel hungry" and "you will lose weight fast." Both claims can be misleading. As previously stated, not everyone loses appetite while on a low-carbohydrate diet. Further, the initial weight loss seen in many low-carbohydrate diets is likely temporary, because it is due to water loss rather than to fat loss. The body will regain the water after the person resumes a normal diet, thereby voiding the initial weight loss (4, 26).

Some low-carbohydrate diets have been associated with health problems, such as high blood cholesterol, hypo–glycemia, and other metabolic disorders. These observations suggest that low-carbohydrate diets can be dangerous. The evidence is somewhat contradictory: Some low-carbohydrate (and high-fat diets) have been shown to lead to high blood cholesterol, but one study reveals that a low-carbohydrate diet with relatively low fat does not elevate blood cholesterol levels or promote cardiovascular risk factors (27). Nonetheless, the safety and effectiveness of a low-carbohydrate/high-protein diet needs further long-term study before firm recommendations can be made (24, 25).

See Table 8.2 for examples of other popular weight-loss diets. Note that the only recommended solution for long-term weight loss is a balanced, low-calorie diet combined with daily physical exercise.

you aware of the food choices you are making and allow you to see where you can make changes in the future.

If you are considering a diet for the purpose of losing weight, you should be aware of the following: the diets promoted in books and on websites to promote weight loss often do not provide balanced nutrition (see the Closer Look boxes above and on page 248, and Table 8.2, for more on several specific types of weight-loss diets). When you are assessing new diets, a general rule of thumb is to avoid fad diets that promise fast and easy weight loss. If you have concerns about the safety or effectiveness of a published diet, you can either contact your local branch of the American Dietetic Association for information or approach a dietitian at a hospital or college. By learning the basic nutrition principles contained in this chapter and in Chapter 7, you should be able to critically evaluate most diet plans.

Any safe and nutritionally sound diet should adhere to the following guidelines (12–14).

- The diet should be low in calories but provide all the essential nutrients the body requires. It should be balanced with foods that provide adequate vitamins and minerals on a daily basis.
- The diet should be low in fat (less than 30% of total calories) and high in complex carbohydrates.
- The diet should promote a variety of foods to appeal to your tastes and to prevent hunger between meals, as well as to keep you from getting bored.
- The diet should be compatible with your lifestyle, and the foods should be easily obtainable.

A CLOSER LOOK FREQUENTLY ASKED QUESTIONS ABOUT WEIGHT-LOSS DIETS

WHAT IS A "FAD DIET"?

A diet is considered a "fad" if it gains fame but then fades in popularity when consumers realize that the diet does not perform as advertised. Numerous "fad" diets currently exist, and these diets come and go. Examples such as the Abs Diet, which purports to reduce stomach fat and claims that dieters will lose as much as 12 pounds in 2 weeks, and the grapefruit diet, which calls for eating only grapefruit, at the least will be ineffective and at worst may cause health problems. The fact is, there are no magical diets to lose weight. Remember, any diet plan that claims to spot-reduce or allow you to lose weight without exercising and/or reducing caloric intake will not result in the loss of body fat.

WHAT IS THE "GLYCEMIC INDEX" OF FOODS?

The "glycemic index" is a measure of how much insulin is released when a particular type of food is consumed. Foods that produce the highest release of insulin are assigned a high glycemic index. Because insulin release promotes fat storage in the body, proponents of low-carbohydrate diets argue that people should avoid foods with a high glycemic index. Most whole-grain foods, fruits, and vegetables have a low glycemic index, whereas foods such as white rice, potatoes, and pasta have a high glycemic index.

WHAT ARE HIGH-PROTEIN DIETS, AND DO THEY DIFFER FROM LOW-CARBOHYDRATE DIETS?

High-protein diets are essentially low-carbohydrate diets that emphasize consuming protein in unrestricted amounts. A health concern associated with high-protein diets is that people on them often consume large quantities of red meat, eggs, and cheese. Therefore, high-protein diets may also be high-fat diets. A high-fat diet can result in elevated blood levels of cholesterol and therefore increase the risk of cardiovascular disease. Moreover, a high fat-diet has been associated with an increased risk of certain cancers. For this reason, the World Cancer Research Fund discourages the use of any high-protein diet.

CAN CALORIC RESTRICTION SLOW AGING AND INCREASE LONGEVITY?

This practice involves consuming a balanced diet but restricting your caloric intake by approximately 20 to 40 percent below the level of energy consumed in a freely chosen diet. This practice has been shown to extend life span in a variety of animal species including rats, mice, and worms. However, whether prolonged caloric restriction increases life span or reduces the rate of aging in humans is unknown.

WHAT ROLE DO DIETARY CALCIUM AND DAIRY PRODUCTS PLAY IN WEIGHT MANAGEMENT?

New evidence suggests that dietary calcium from dairy products may play an important role in weight management. The proposed mechanism relates to the fact that calcium plays a key role in fat metabolism and fat storage. Specifically, a diet high in calcium from dairy products has been shown to promote fat metabolism, inhibit fat synthesis, and, therefore, increase the loss of body fat. These concepts have been confirmed by epidemiological data and clinical studies indicating that diets high in dairy products (more than 3 servings per day) accelerate fat loss compared with diets low in dairy products. Although these results are promising, additional studies are required to confirm that increasing calcium intake by consuming dairy products is a useful adjunct to a weight-loss program.

Sources: Heilbronn, L., and E. Ravussin. Calorie restriction and aging: Review of the literature and implications for studies in humans. *American Journal of Clinical Nutrition* 78:361–369, 2003; Zemel, M. B. Role of calcium and dairy products in energy partitioning and weight management. *American Journal of Clinical Nutrition* 79:9075–9125, 2004.

- The diet should be a lifelong diet; that is, it should be one that you can follow for the long term. This type of diet greatly increases your chances of keeping weight off once you've lost it.

In addition to these diet guidelines, here are some helpful reminders (some of which were covered in Chapter 7) for planning a healthy, balanced diet:

- Avoid high-calorie, low-nutrient foods such as those high in sugar (e.g., candy bars, cookies, soft drinks, and alcohol). Instead, select low-calorie, nutrient-dense foods such as fruits, vegetables, and whole-grain breads.
- Reduce the amount of saturated fat in your diet, and avoid trans fats (which are sometimes found in processed foods and baked goods). High-fat foods

are high in calories, and eating too much saturated fat can also increase your risk for heart disease. For example, eat less butter, and choose lean meats such as lean cuts of beef, chicken, and fish. Avoid fried foods; choose nonfat or low-fat dairy products, such as milk, yogurt, and cottage cheese.

- Select fresh fruits and vegetables whenever possible, and avoid fruits that are canned in heavy syrup.
- Limit salt intake. Use herbs and other seasonings instead of salt to flavor foods.
- Drink fewer alcoholic beverages. Alcoholic beverages are low in nutrients and high in calories.
- Eat to satisfy hunger, not boredom or other emotional situations. Remember that a negative energy balance of 500 calories per day will result in a weight loss of approximately 1 pound per week. The key to maintaining a caloric deficit of 500 calories per day is careful planning of meals and accurate calorie counting.

Plan Your Physical Activity

Physical activity and exercise play a key role in weight loss for several reasons (15, 16). Increased physical activity elevates your daily caloric expenditure and therefore helps you expend more calories, and regular cardiorespiratory exercise improves the ability of skeletal muscles to burn fat as energy. Regular resistance exercise (such as weight training) can also reduce the loss of muscle that occurs during dieting. This is important because your primary goal during weight loss is to lose fat, not muscle mass. Finally, increasing your muscle mass (as through weight training) increases resting metabolic rate, which further aids in weight loss (17).

What type of exercise is best for losing weight? You should perform both cardiorespiratory training (i.e., running, cycling, swimming, and so on) and strength training while dieting. (See the Closer Look box on page 250.) The combination of these two types of training will maintain cardiorespiratory fitness and reduce muscle loss.

How much exercise must you perform during a weight-loss program? In general, exercise sessions designed to promote weight loss should expend more than 250 calories. Further, the negative caloric balance should be shared equally by exercise and diet. For instance, an individual who wishes to achieve a 500 calorie per day deficit should increase energy expenditure (exercise) by 250 calories per day and decrease caloric intake by 250 calories.

Although intensity of exercise is an important factor in improving cardiorespiratory fitness, it is the total

Alcohol contributes calories to the diet, so people trying to lose weight should restrict the amount of alcohol they consume or avoid it altogether.

amounts of energy expended and fat burned that are important in weight loss. Some authors have argued that low-intensity prolonged exercise (such as walking 1–2 miles a day) is better than short-term high-intensity exercise (e.g., sprinting 50 yards) in burning fat calories and promoting weight loss (18). However, evidence clearly demonstrates that both high- and low-intensity exercise can promote fat loss (4). Nonetheless, for the sedentary or obese individual, low-intensity exercise is the best choice because it can be performed for longer time periods and increases the ability of skeletal muscle to metabolize fat for energy (see the Appreciating Diversity box on page 250) (11, 15).

To determine your caloric expenditure (per minute) during an activity, simply multiply your body weight in kilograms (2.2 pounds = 1 kilogram) by the calories burned per minute, per kilogram (see Table 8.3 for the calories burned per minute of some common activities) and by the exercise time. For example, suppose a 70-kilogram (kg) individual plays 20 minutes of handball. How many calories did he or she expend

A CLOSER LOOK: WHAT INTENSITY OF AEROBIC EXERCISE IS BEST FOR BURNING FAT?

Many people assume that the intensity of aerobic exercise (running, cycling, and so on) must be maintained at a low level if fat is to be burned as fuel. It is true that fat is a primary fuel source during low-intensity exercise. But as the figure in this box shows, the total amount of fat burned during exercise varies with the intensity of exercise, and for a given exercise duration, more total fat is metabolized during moderate-intensity exercise. Therefore, moderate-intensity exercise (that is, approximately 50% $\dot{V}O_2$max) is typically the optimal intensity of exercise for burning the most fat during an endurance exercise workout.

Source: Coyle, E. Fat metabolism during exercise. *Sports Science Exchange* (Gatorade Sports Science Institute) 8:6, 1995.

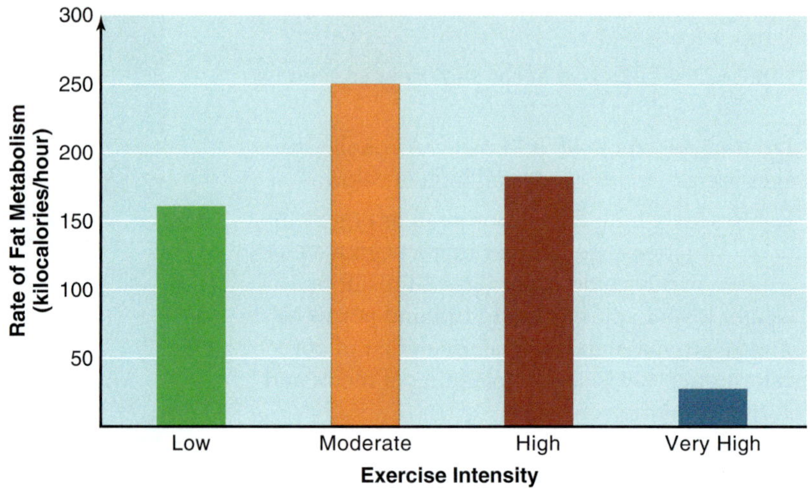

The rates of fat metabolism at low-intensity (20% $\dot{V}O_2$max), moderate-intensity (50% $\dot{V}O_2$max), high-intensity (80% $\dot{V}O_2$max), and very high intensity (100% $\dot{V}O_2$max) exercise. Although this figure is not intended to reveal any "ideal" exercise intensity for all individuals, it indicates that moderate-intensity exercise is often optimal for maximizing the amount of fat metabolized during exercise.

APPRECIATING DIVERSITY: EXERCISE PRESCRIPTIONS FOR OBESE INDIVIDUALS

Although it is well established that exercise is an important factor in promoting weight loss, exercise prescriptions for obese individuals require special attention. For example, obese individuals may be limited by the following conditions: heat intolerance, shortness of breath during heavy exercise, lack of flexibility, frequent musculoskeletal injuries, hypertension, and a lack of balance during weight-bearing activities such as walking or running.

Exercise programs for obese individuals should emphasize activities that can be sustained for long periods of time (30 minutes or more), such as walking, swimming, water exercise, or bicycling. Further, obese people should avoid exercise in a hot or humid environment. The initial goal of the exercise program should not be to improve cardiovascular fitness, but rather to increase voluntary energy expenditure and to establish a regular exercise routine. Therefore, the beginning exercise intensity should be below the typical target heart rate range for improving cardiorespiratory fitness, and the initial duration of exercise should be short (about 5–10 min/day) to reduce the risk of soreness and injury. The duration can be gradually increased in 1-minute increments to achieve an energy expenditure of approximately 300 kcal per workout. As the musculoskeletal system adapts to the exercise regimen, the intensity, too, can gradually be increased.

Sources: Fransen, M. Dietary weight loss and exercise for obese adults with knee osteoarthritis: Modest weight loss targets, mild exercise, modest effects. *Arthritis and Rheumatology* 50(5):1366–1369, 2004; Jakicic, J. M. Exercise in the treatment of obesity. *Endocrinology and Metabolic Clinics of North America* 32(4):967–980, 2003; and American College of Sports Medicine. Position stand: The recommended quantity and quality of exercise for developing and maintaining cardiorespiratory and muscular fitness, and flexibility in healthy adults. *Medicine and Science in Sports and Exercise* 30:975–991, 1998.

TABLE 8.3
Calories Expended during Selected Activities

Activity	Calories/Minute/Kilogram	Calories/Minute*	METs†
Bowling	0.0471	3.2	2.7
Golf	0.0559	3.8	3.2
Walking (17 min per mile)	0.0794	5.4	4.5
Tennis (doubles)	0.0882	6.0	5.1
Cycling (6.4 min per mile)	0.0985	6.7	5.6
Tennis (singles)	0.1029	7.0	5.8
Canoeing (15 min per mile)	0.1029	7.0	5.8
Swimming (50 yards per min)	0.1333	9.1	7.6
Running (10 min per mile)	0.1471	10.0	8.0
Cycling (5 min per mile)	0.1559	10.6	8.5
Handball (singles)	0.1603	10.9	9.1
Running (8 min per mile)	0.1856	12.6	10.0
Running (6 min per mile)	0.2350	16.0	12.8

* These values are for a 150-lb (68-kg) person.
† 1 MET equals your resting metabolic rate.

Source: From Bud Getchell, *Physical Fitness: A Way of Life,* 5th ed. Copyright © 1998. Reprinted by permission of Pearson Education, Inc.

during the time of play? The total estimated caloric expenditure is computed as follows:

$$\text{Caloric expenditure} = 70 \text{ kg} \times 0.1603 \text{ calories/kg/min} \times 20 \text{ min} = 224 \text{ calories}$$

If your exercise routine involves using fitness equipment such as stationary bicycles, treadmills, or ellipticals, the machine will probably provide a summary of caloric expenditure at the end of your exercise bout.

Focus on Behavior Modification

Research demonstrates that behavior modification plays a key role in both achieving short-term weight loss and maintaining weight loss over the long term (12, 13). Many behaviors are learned and can therefore be modified. For example, many people eat popcorn and candy when they attend a movie at the theater. Similarly, a nightly television habit is often accompanied by snacking on chips, sodas, and other high-calorie, low-nutrition items. The fact that these behaviors are learned means that they can also be unlearned. In regard to weight control, behavior modification is used primarily to reduce or (ideally) eliminate social or environmental stimuli that promote overeating.

The first step in a diet-related behavior modification program is to identify those social or environmental factors that promote overeating. This can be done by keeping a written record of daily activities for 1 or 2 weeks to identify factors associated with consumption of high-calorie meals. Refer to the box on page 243 for common social and environmental factors that may contribute to your overeating. How many of these factors occur in your food diary?

After identifying the behaviors that contribute to weight gain, you can design a program to modify those behaviors. The following weight control techniques may make weight loss easier (14).

- *Make a personal commitment to losing weight.* This is the first step toward behavior modification and weight loss. Establishing realistic short-term and long-term weight loss goals helps you maintain a lifelong commitment to weight management.
- *Develop healthy low-calorie eating patterns.* Avoid eating when you are not hungry. Learn to eat slowly and only while sitting at the table. Finally, keep food quantities to the minimum amount within your caloric guidelines.
- *Avoid social settings where you are likely to overeat.* If you go to parties where high-calorie foods are served, don't show up hungry. Eat a low-calorie meal before going.
- *Exercise daily.* Regular exercise that uses large-muscle groups can play an important role in increasing your daily caloric expenditure and can therefore assist in weight loss and weight management.

- *Reward yourself for successful weight loss with non-food rewards.* Positive feedback is an important part of behavior modification, and it doesn't have to relate to food to be effective. For example, after reaching your first short-term weight-loss goal, do something you like to do but don't get to do often, such as buying a new item of clothing or going to the movies.
- *Think positively.* Positive thinking promotes confidence and maintains the enthusiasm necessary for a lifetime of successful weight management.

Make sure you know...

> A safe rate of weight loss is 1 to 2 pounds per week; this equals approximately 3500 fewer calories consumed per week, or 500 fewer calories per day.

> There are four basic steps to designing a successful weight loss program: set realistic goals, assess and modify your diet, plan regular exercise, and modify your behavior.

Exercise and Diet Programs to Gain Weight

Thus far, this chapter has focused on how to lose body fat. However, some people may have the opposite problem—being underweight—and they may need to implement a program to gain weight. You can achieve weight gain by creating a positive energy balance, that is, by taking in more calories than you expend. When increasing body weight, however, you'll want to aim to increase muscle mass, rather than fat mass, for the sake of your health. Let's discuss how to do this.

The key to gaining muscle mass is a program of rigorous weight training combined with the increase in caloric intake needed to meet the increased energy expenditure and energy required to synthesize muscle. Exercise programs designed to improve muscular strength and size are discussed in Chapter 4 and are not addressed here. Here we focus on the dietary adjustments needed to optimize gains in muscle mass. Again, to gain muscle mass, you need to create a small positive caloric balance to provide the energy required to synthesize new muscle protein. Nonetheless, before we provide dietary guidelines, let's discuss how much energy is expended during weight training and how much energy is required to promote muscle growth.

Energy expenditure during routine weight training is surprisingly small. For instance, a 70-kg man performing a 30-minute weight workout probably burns fewer than 70 calories (14). The reason for this low caloric expenditure is that during 30 minutes in the weight room, the average person spends only 8 to 10 minutes lifting weights; much time is spent in recovery periods between sets.

Current estimates are that approximately 2500 calories are needed to synthesize one pound of muscle mass, of which about 400 calories (100 grams) must be protein (14). To compute the additional calories required to produce an increase in muscle mass, you must first estimate your rate of muscular growth. This is difficult because the rate of muscular growth during weight training varies among people. Although relatively large muscle mass gains are possible in some individuals, studies have shown that most men and women rarely gain more than 0.25 pound of muscle per week during a 20-week weight training program (3 days per week, 30 minutes per day). If we assume that the average muscle gain is 0.25 pound per week and that 2500 calories are required to synthesize one pound of muscle, a positive caloric balance of fewer than 100 calories per day is needed to promote muscle growth (0.25 pound per week $\times$ 2500 calories per pound = 625 calories per week; therefore, 625 calories per week $\div$ 7 days per week = 90 calories per day).

You can use the MyPyramid food guidance system presented in Chapter 7 to increase your caloric intake. This will ensure that your diet meets the criteria for healthful living and provides adequate protein for building muscle. Be sure to avoid high-fat foods, and limit your positive caloric balance to approximately 90 calories per day. Increasing your positive caloric balance above this level will not promote a faster rate of muscular growth but will increase body fat. Finally, if you discontinue your weight-training program, be sure to lower your caloric intake to match your daily energy expenditure.

Make sure you know...

> Gaining weight can be achieved by creating a positive caloric balance. Before deciding to gain body fat, you should consider whether your current body composition is within your desired range.

> Gaining muscle mass can be achieved by combining exercise with proper nutrition.

Lifetime Weight Management

Weight loss and weight management are not short-term events. Maintaining a healthy body weight over the long term requires adherence to several healthy diet and exercise guidelines. If you diet and exercise for a while to lose weight but then slip into unhealthy habits of overeating or being too sedentary once the weight has come off, you will likely undo your efforts. And you may even gain more weight than you initially lost. This is the reason that short-term, fad diets are typically unsuccessful.

The key factors in long-term weight management are a positive attitude, regular exercise, and a personal commitment to maintaining a desired body composition. Like many other facets of personal or professional life, weight control has its ups and downs. Be prepared for occasional setbacks. For instance, many people gain weight during holiday periods. If this happens to you, avoid self-criticism, quickly reestablish your personal commitment to a short-term weight loss goal, and develop a new diet and exercise plan to lose the undesired fat. Remember, you can lose any amount of weight you've gained by applying the principles discussed in this chapter.

Finally, we cannot overemphasize the importance of family and friends in lifetime weight management. Their encouragement and support can help you maintain healthy long-term eating habits and sustain a commitment to exercise. Losing weight is much easier if the people close to you try to help you achieve your goals rather than tempt you into unhealthy behaviors. Encourage others to join you as you exercise. Your friends and family members may need a little encouragement to get started, but you may be the role model that they need to make the change. Children are especially susceptible to live the life that you model.

Extreme Measures for Weight Loss

Most people can attain a healthy body weight through diet and exercise, but for some extremely obese individuals, these may not be enough. In such cases, surgical procedures or prescription medications may be recommended by a health care provider.

Surgery

According to the American Society for Bariatric Surgery, surgical procedures may be recommended for weight loss in severely obese individuals. The surgery is considered a last resort in weight reduction for individuals who have tried and failed at losing weight and whose obesity poses a serious health risk. Weight-loss surgery is of two types: restrictive procedures and malabsorptive procedures. Restrictive procedures, such as gastric banding, work by decreasing the amount of food consumed at one time. The reduced stomach capacity, along with behavioral changes, can result in lower caloric intake and consistent weight loss. Malabsorptive procedures alter digestion by bypassing the small intestine, thus limiting the absorption of calories. The most common bariatric surgery is a combination of restrictive and malabsorptive procedures. The combination helps patients lose weight quickly and continue to lose weight for 18–24 months after the surgery (19).

Weatherman Al Roker is one individual who underwent gastric bypass surgery and lost more than 100 pounds. Such weight-loss measures are appropriate only for people with extreme obesity.

Prescription Medications

Unlike diet pills, which are typically ineffective (Table 8.4), prescription medications such as orlistat and Meridia have been scientifically shown to help some people achieve weight loss. Orlistat (also called Xenical) works by preventing about one-third of ingested fat from being absorbed in the digestive tract. The undigested fat is eliminated in bowel movement; hence, one side effect may be an oily stool. Orlistat is the only FDA-approved weight-loss drug that acts to block fat absorption.

The prescription drug Meridia suppresses appetite by increasing serotonin levels in the brain. Meridia and Xenical are the only two weight-loss medications approved for longer term use in significantly obese people; however, their safety and effectiveness have not been established for use beyond 1 year.

TABLE 8.4
Myths and Facts about Weight Loss

Weight-Loss Myth	The Facts
Diet pills really work.	Most over-the-counter diet pills contain caffeine and other mild stimulants. Unfortunately, none of these products has been scientifically shown to assist in achieving safe and permanent weight loss. One study of individuals using commercially available diet pills reported that fewer than 3% lost weight and retained weight-loss longer than 12 months (22)
You can spot-reduce body fat.	There is no scientific evidence to show that exercising a specific area of the body promotes fat loss in that area (23). Rather, evidence suggests that when a caloric deficit exists, fat will be lost from areas where the most fat is stored (23).
Eating before bedtime causes weight gain.	Although eating a late-night meal or snack might not be a good dietary habit, this practice does not result in a greater weight gain than consuming the same meal at another time during the day. The total daily caloric intake determines fat gain, not the timing of the meal (12, 13).
Cellulite is a special form of fat.	Although many people believe that cellulite is different from other body fat, this is not true. Cellulite is just plain fat, not a special type of fat. The "dimpled" appearance comes from accumulation of fat into small clusters beneath the skin. Many products, from special creams and lotions to massage appliances, are advertised as helping reduce cellulite, but no scientific evidence exists to support these claims. The only way to lose fat is to reduce calorie intake and increase exercise. Weight training helps tighten the skin over the muscle and eliminates space between the skin and muscle for fat pockets.
Saunas, steambaths, and rubber suits can aid in weight loss.	These methods do result in body water loss due to sweating. However, the weight is regained as soon as body water is restored to normal levels. Using saunas or steambaths and exercising while wearing a rubber suit may increase body temperature well above normal, which puts additional stress on the heart and circulatory system and could increase the risk of cardiac problems for older individuals or anyone with heart problems.

What Is Disordered Eating?

Although attaining a healthy body weight is a highly desirable goal, for some people the social pressures to be thin and/or muscular can lead to a negative body image and an unhealthy relationship with food. Women may feel like they need to emulate the often unattainably thin figures of popular actresses and models, or men may wish to achieve the bulked-up look of professional athletes, in the pursuit of a more "perfect" body. When these desires lead to unhealthy behaviors, such as bouts of self-starvation, binging, and/or purging, the individual may develop a pattern of disordered eating.

Three common conditions of disordered eating that affect young adults are anorexia nervosa, bulimia nervosa, and binge eating. Let's discuss the symptoms and health consequences of these conditions.

Anorexia Nervosa

Anorexia nervosa is an eating disorder in which the individual severely limits caloric intake, resulting in an eventual state of starvation. As the condition advances, the individual becomes emaciated. The psychological cause of anorexia nervosa is unclear, but it seems to be linked to an unfounded fear of fatness that may be related to familial or societal pressures to be thin (14).

Although the condition occurs in both men and women, rates of anorexia nervosa are particularly high among adolescent girls, and as many as 1 of every 100 adolescent girls may suffer from this condition. Anorexia nervosa affects approximately 1% of the female adolescent population, with an average age of onset between 14 and 18 years (20, 21). Upper-middle-class young women who are extremely self-critical have the highest probability of developing anorexia nervosa.

People suffering from anorexia nervosa may use a variety of techniques to remain thin, including starvation, excessive exercise, and laxatives. The effects of anorexia nervosa include excessive weight loss, cessation of menstruation, and, in extreme cases, death. Because the condition is a serious mental and physical disorder, medical treatment by a team of professionals (physician, psychologist, nutritionist) is needed to correct the problem. Treatment may require years of psychological counseling and nutritional guidance.

The first step in seeking treatment for anorexia nervosa is recognizing that a problem exists. The following common symptoms may indicate that someone is exhibiting anorexia nervosa:

- An intense fear of gaining weight or becoming obese
- The feeling that one is fat even at normal or below-normal body fatness because of a highly distorted body image
- In women, the absence of three or more menstrual cycles
- The possible development of odd behaviors concerning food; for example, preparing elaborate meals for others but only a few low-calorie foods for one's own consumption

CONSIDER THIS!

The average "female" store mannequin is 6 feet tall and has a 23-inch waist, whereas the average woman is 5 feet, 4 inches tall and has a 30-inch waist.

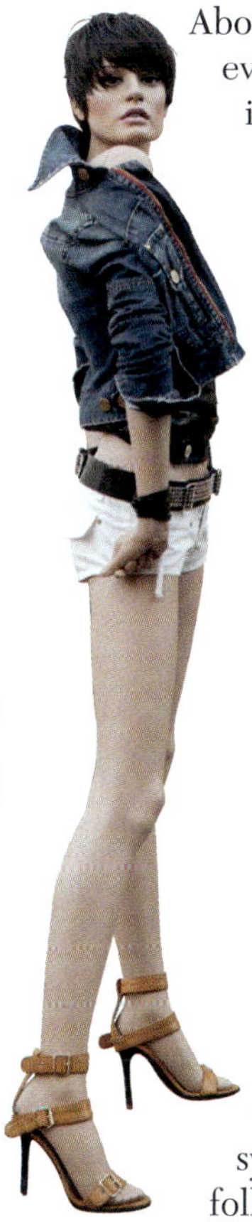

Bulimia Nervosa

About 50% of people with anorexia nervosa eventually suffer **bulimia nervosa,** which is characterized by cycles of binging and purging. People with bulimia nervosa may repeatedly ingest large quantities of food and then force themselves to vomit to prevent weight gain. The frequent vomiting associated with bulimia nervosa may result in damage to the teeth and the esophagus due to exposure to stomach acids. Like anorexia nervosa, bulimia nervosa is most common in young women, has a psychological origin, and requires professional treatment when diagnosed. Bulimia affects approximately 1–3% of adolescents in the United States. The illness usually begins in late adolescence or early adult life (21).

People with bulimia nervosa may look "normal" and be of normal weight. However, even when their bodies are slender, their stomachs may protrude because they have been stretched by frequent eating binges. Other common symptoms of bulimia nervosa include the following:

- Recurrent binge eating
- A lack of control over eating behavior
- Regular self-induced vomiting and/or use of diuretics or laxatives
- Strict fasting or use of vigorous exercise to prevent weight gain
- Averaging two or more binge eating episodes per week during a 2- to 3-month period
- Excessive concern with body shape and weight

People with anorexia nervosa restrict their caloric intake to the point of starvation.

Binge Eating Disorder

A disordered eating pattern that has recently begun to attract attention from the medical community is **binge eating disorder,** a condition in which an individual consumes mass quantities of food but, unlike people

anorexia nervosa An eating disorder in which a person severely restricts caloric intake because of an intense fear of gaining weight.

bulimia nervosa An eating disorder that involves overeating (called *binge eating*) followed by vomiting (called *purging*).

binge eating disorder The compulsive need to gorge on food without purging.

with bulimia nervosa, does not purge after binging. The person may feel embarrassed and ashamed about gorging and resolve to stop doing it, but the compulsion continues. The end result of consuming large quantities of food is that the person gains weight. The cause of binge eating is unknown, and only a very small percentage of overweight and obese individuals engage in binge eating.

Although maintaining an optimal body composition is a primary health goal, eating disorders are not appropriate means of weight loss. If you or any of your friends exhibit one or more of the symptoms cited here, please seek professional advice and treatment.

Make sure you know...

> Eating disorders such as anorexia nervosa, bulimia nervosa, and binge eating disorder involve patterns of severe calorie restriction, binging, and/or purging and can result in severe physical symptoms and possibly death.

Summary

1. Factors that can affect weight management include genetic, dietary, and lifestyle factors. Genetic disorders cause extreme obesity in about 1% of the population. For the rest, however, research supports that environmental and lifestyle factors are more likely to affect body weight than genetics.
2. Energy balance is achieved when the number of calories you take in through food and beverages equals the number of calories you expend through physical activity and normal body processes.
3. Total daily energy expenditure is the sum of resting metabolic rate and exercise metabolic rate.
4. Losing 1 to 2 pounds per week is considered a safe rate of weight loss. Body fat will be lost first in the areas of the body that store the most fat, such as the thighs and hips in women, and the abdominal region in men.
5. The four basic components of a comprehensive weight-control program are setting realistic goals for weight loss, assessing and modifying your diet, planning physical activity, and modifying your behaviors that contribute to weight gain.
6. Weight-loss goals should include both short-term and long-term goals.
7. People seeking to gain weight need to take in more calories than they expend. They should seek to gain muscle mass rather than fat by engaging in an appropriate strength-training program.
8. The eating disorders anorexia nervosa, bulimia nervosa, and binge eating disorder are serious medical conditions that require professional treatment.

Study Questions

1. The optimal percentage of body fat for men and women is
   a. 5–15% for men and 10–20% for women.
   b. 10–20% for men and 15–25% for women.
   c. 15–25% for men and 20–30% for women.
   d. 20–30% for men and 25–35% for women.
2. Hormones that play a role in appetite include which of the following?
   a. insulin
   b. ghrelin
   c. leptin
   d. estrogen
   e. both (a) and (d) are correct
   f. both (b) and (c) are correct
3. Identify the true statement regarding energy balance:
   a. Caloric intake should equal caloric expenditure.
   b. Weight gain occurs when caloric intake exceeds caloric expenditure.
   c. Weight loss occurs when caloric expenditure exceeds caloric intake.
   d. All of the above statements are true.

4. The two forms of exercise that are most beneficial in helping you lose and maintain weight are
   a. flexibility and Pilates training.
   b. yoga and anaerobic exercise.
   c. strength training and cardiorespiratory endurance training.
   d. Exercise is not helpful for weight loss.
5. Disordered eating includes all of the following except
   a. anorexia nervosa.
   b. bulimia nervosa.
   c. binge eating.
   d. using MyPyramid to plan a healthy diet.
6. What is optimal body weight, and how is optimal body weight calculated?
7. Explain the roles of resting metabolic rate and exercise metabolic rate in determining total caloric expenditure. Which is more important in total daily caloric expenditure in a sedentary individual?
8. Outline a simple method for computing your daily caloric expenditure. Give an example.
9. List the four major components of a weight-loss program.
10. Discuss the role of behavior modification in weight loss.
11. Compare and contrast the symptoms of anorexia nervosa, bulimia nervosa, and binge eating disorder.
12. Define the following terms:
    energy balance
    resting metabolic rate
    fad diet
13. Compare exercise metabolic rate with resting metabolic rate.

Suggested Reading

Acheson, K. Carbohydrate and weight control: Where do we stand? *Current Opinion in Clinical Nutrition and Metabolic Care* 7:485–492, 2004.

Buchholz, A., and D. Schoeller. Is a calorie a calorie? *American Journal of Nutrition* 79:899–906S, 2004.

Heilbronn, L., and E. Ravussin. Calorie restriction and aging: Review of the literature and implications for studies in humans. *American Journal of Clinical Nutrition* 78:361–369, 2003.

Jakicic, J., et al. Appropriate intervention strategies for weight loss and prevention of weight regain for adults. (ACSM Position Stand). *Medicine and Science in Sports and Exercise* 33:2145–2156, 2001.

Stein, C., and G. Colditz. The epidemic of obesity. *Journal of Clinical Endocrinology and Metabolism* 89:2522–2525, 2004.

For links to the websites below, visit The Total Fitness and Wellness Website at www.aw-bc.com/powers.

American Dietetic Association
Contains articles about nutrition and fad diets.

MyPyramid.gov
Walks you through the advice illustrated in the MyPyramid food guidance system.

References

1. Kopelman, P. G. Obesity as a medical problem. *Nature* 404:635–643, 2000.
2. Sordula, M. K., A. H. Mokdad, D. F. Williamson, D. A. Galuska, J. M. Mendlein, and G. W. Heath. Prevalence of attempting weight loss and strategies for controlling weight. *Journal of the American Medical Association* 282:1353–1358, 1999.
3. National Center for Health Statistics. *Health, United States, 2006, With Chartbook on Trends in the Health of Americans*. Hyattsville, Md; 2006, pp. 58–59.
4. Powers, S., and E. Howley. *Exercise Physiology: Theory and Application to Fitness and Performance*, 4th ed. St. Louis: McGraw-Hill, 2004.
5. Raloff, J. Still hungry? Fattening revelations—and new mysteries—about the hunger hormone. *Science News Online* 167: April 2, 2005.
6. Frubeck, G., J. Gomez-Amrosi, F. Muruzabal, and M. Burrell. The adipocyte: A model for integration of endocrine and metabolic signaling in energy metabolism regulation. *American Journal of Physiology* 280: E827–E847, 2001.
7. Kraemer, R. R., and V. D. Castracane. Exercise and humoral mediators of peripheral energy balance: Ghrelin and adiponectin. *Experimental Biology and Medicine* 232:184–194, 2007.

8. Cummings, D. E., D. S. Weigle, R. S. Frayo, P. A. Breen, M. K., Ma, E. P. Dellinger, and J. Q. Purnell. Plasma ghrelin levels after diet-induced weight loss or gastric bypass surgery. *New England Journal of Medicine* 346:1623–1630, 2002.
9. Bailey, J., R. Barker, and R. Beauchene. Age-related changes in rat adipose tissue cellularity are altered by dietary restriction and exercise. *Journal of Nutrition* 123:52–58, 1993.
10. Blair, S. Evidence for success of exercise in weight loss control. *Annals of Internal Medicine* 119:702–706, 1993.
11. Poehlman, E. A review: Exercise and its influence on resting energy metabolism in man. *Medicine and Science in Sports and Exercise* 21:515–525, 1989.
12. Bjorntorp, P., and B. Brodoff, eds. *Obesity*. Philadelphia: Lippincott, 1992.
13. Perri, M., A. Nezu, and B. Viegener. *Improving the Long-term Management and Treatment of Obesity*. New York: John Wiley and Sons, 1992.
14. Williams, M. *Lifetime Fitness and Wellness*. Dubuque, IA: Wm. C. Brown, 1996.
15. Ross, R., J. Freeman, and I. Janssen. Exercise alone is an effective strategy for reducing obesity and related co-morbidities. *Exercise and Sport Sciences Reviews* 28(4):165–170, 2000.
16. Jakicic, J. et al. Appropriate intervention strategies for weight loss and prevention of weight regain for adults. (ACSM Position Stand). *Medicine and Science in Sports and Exercise* 33:2145–2156, 2001.
17. Broeder, C., K. Burrhus, L. Svanevik, and J. Wilmore. The effects of either high intensity resistance or endurance training on resting metabolic rate. *American Journal of Clinical Nutrition* 55:802–810, 1992.
18. Romijn, J., E. Coyle, L. Sidossis, et al. Regulation of endogenous fat and carbohydrate metabolism in relation to exercise and duration. *American Journal of Physiology* 265:E380–E391, 1993.
19. Weight-control Information Network. Gastrointestinal surgery for severe obesity. NIH Publication no. 04-4006. December 2004. http://win.niddk.nih.gov/publications/gastric.htm.
20. American Psychiatric Association. APA Expert Opinion: Pauline S. Powers, MD. http:/healthyminds.org/expertopinion9.cfm. Accessed July 2007.
21. Office on Women's Health, U.S. Department of Health and Human Services. Eating disorders. February 2000. www.4woman.gov.owh/pub/factsheets/eatingdisorders.pdf.

NAME ______________________________ DATE ____________

Determining Ideal Body Weight Using Percent Body Fat and the Body Mass Index

There are several different ways to compute an ideal body weight. In Chapter 6 we discussed body fat percentage (estimated from skinfold measurements). Method A of this laboratory enables you to compute and record your ideal body weight using that method. Method B enables you to calculate and record your ideal body weight using the body mass index (BMI) procedure (Chapter 6). Choose one of these techniques, and complete the appropriate section.

Method A: Computing Ideal Body Weight Using Percent Body Fat

Step 1: Calculate fat-free weight

100% − your percent body fat estimated from skinfold measurement = _____ % fat free weight.

Therefore,

_____ % fat-free weight expressed as a decimal × _____ your body weight in pounds
= _____ pounds of fat-free weight.

Step 2: Calculate optimal weight

Remember: Optimal body fat ranges are 10–20% for men and 15–25% for women.

Optimal weight = fat-free weight ÷ (1.00 − optimal %fat), with optimal %fat expressed as a decimal. Therefore, the low and high optimal weight ranges for your gender are as follows:

For low %fat: Optimal weight _____ pounds
For high %fat: Optimal weight _____ pounds

Method B: Computing Ideal Body Weight Using Body Mass Index (BMI)

The BMI uses the metric system. Therefore, you must express your weight in kilograms (1 kilogram = 2.2 pounds) and your height in meters (1 inch = 0.0254 meter).

Step 1: Compute your BMI

BMI = body weight (kg) ÷ (height in meters)^2
Your BMI =

Step 2: Calculate your ideal body weight based on BMI*

The ideal BMI is 21.9 to 22.4 for men and 21.3 to 22.1 for women. The formula for computing ideal body weight using BMI is

$$\text{Ideal body weight (kilograms)} = \text{Desired BMI} \times (\text{height in meters})^2$$

Consider the following example as an illustration of the computation of ideal body weight. A man who weighs 60 kilograms and is 1.5 meters tall computes his BMI to be 26.7. His ideal BMI is between 21.9 and 22.4; therefore, his ideal body weight range is as follows:

Low end range: 21.9 × 2.25 = 49.3 kilograms
High end of range: 22.4 × 2.2550.4 kilograms

Now complete this calculation using your values for BMI.

My ideal body weight range using the BMI method is _____ to _____ kilograms.

*Note: BMI may not be a good method to determine ideal body weight for a highly muscled individual.

NAME ______________________________ DATE ______________

Estimating Daily Caloric Expenditure and the Caloric Deficit Required to Lose 1 Pound of Fat per Week

Part A: Estimating Your Daily Caloric Expenditure

Using Table 8.1, compute your estimated daily caloric expenditure.

Estimated daily caloric expenditure = ____________ calories/day.

Note: For you to maintain current body weight, your caloric intake should equal your daily caloric expenditure.

Part B: Calculating Caloric Intake Required to Promote 1 Pound Per Week of Weight Loss

Recall that 1 pound of fat contains approximately 3500 calories. Therefore, a negative caloric balance of 500 calories per day will result in a weight loss of 1 pound per week. Use the following formula to compute your daily caloric intake to result in a daily caloric deficit of 500 calories.

Estimated daily caloric expenditure − 500 calories (deficit) = Daily caloric intake needed to produce a 500-calorie deficit

In the space provided, compute your daily caloric intake needed to produce 1 pound per week of weight loss.

________ (estimated caloric expenditure)
− 500 (caloric deficit)
= ________ (target daily caloric intake)

Note: To increase body weight by 1–2 pounds per week, increase daily caloric intake by 90–180 calories per day.

NAME ______________________ DATE ______________

Weight-Loss Goals and Progress Report

In the spaces provided, record your short-term and long-term weight-loss goals. Then keep a record of your progress on the chart.

Ideal body weight (range): __________

Short-term weight loss goal: ___1–2___ (pounds/week)

Long-term weight loss goal: __________ pounds

Week No.	Body Weight	Date	Weight Loss
1			
2			
3			
4			
5			
6			
7			
8			
9			
10			
11			
12			
13			
14			
15			

Appendix A Answers to Study Questions

Chapter 1

1. c. Physical activity is any type of occupational, leisure, or lifestyle related physical movement. Exercise is one example of leisure physical activity.

2. a. Although exercise is not a component of wellness, it can help you achieve physical health, which is one of the components of total wellness.

3. c. Agility may be important for sport performance, but it is not linked to improved overall health and therefore is not considered a major component of health-related physical fitness.

4. d. Reduced risk for osteoporosis and heart disease, as well as improved mental health are all benefits of regular physical activity.

5. a. Current goals of Healthy People 2010 seek to improve the quantity and quality of life for all Americans. Eliminating health disparities is also a key objective to meet these goals.

6. b. An individual in the action stage of change has been participating in a new health behavior for 6 months or less, but once this individual has moved beyond 6 months, he or she will be in the maintenance stage of change.

7. d. Developing a plan, getting the support of friends and family, and seeking outside help from others are all important actions to take in initiating a health behavior change.

8. d. Assessing your current behavior—including number and effort of behaviors you want to change, your motive for behavior change and current behaviors patterns—is an important step to take when planning a change.

Chapter 2

1. d. Supercompensation is not one of the five key principles of exercise training.

2. c. Current guidelines indicate that a minimum of 30 minutes of moderate exercise each day can produce numerous health benefits.

3. a. A few minutes of low intensity exercise (a warm-up) at the beginning of an exercise training session benefits the body by increasing both muscle temperature and blood flow to active muscles.

Chapter 3

1. c. Aerobic exercises include activities that promote cardiorespiratory fitness, such as jogging, swimming, and cycling.

2. a. Activities that promote muscle strength and endurance, such as wrestling, utilize the anaerobic energy pathway to create ATP and provide energy to muscles.

3. b. As an individual's cardiorespiratory fitness level increases, resting heart rate will decrease because the heart becomes more efficient at pumping blood throughout the body. This allows the heart to beat fewer times per minute to pump the same amount of blood.

4. c. You should exercise at a level of at least 50% of your heart rate reserve in order to improve health-related physical fitness and cardiorespiratory endurance.

5. d. Increases in heart rate, cardiac output, and breathing are normal physical changes you will experience during cardiorespiratory exercise.

6. a. Arteries are the blood vessels that move oxygen-rich blood away from your heart. Veins return oxygen-depleted blood back to the heart.

Chapter 4

No multiple choice questions in chapter 4.

Chapter 5

1. d. The shape of the bones, and tight skin and tendons can all affect one's flexibility at a joint. Bone length is typically not a factor.

2. c. The two types of proprioceptors are Golgi organs and muscle spindles, and they are found in tendons and muscles, respectively. Motor units are not a type of proprioceptor.

3. b. False. Most people, including athletes and non athletes, would benefit from the improved flexibility that results from regular static stretching.

4. b. A few minutes of light exercise before stretching will minimize your risk of injury. Where and when you stretch is not likely to affect your risk. Stretching to the point of pain is more likely to result in injury than stretching to the point of mild discomfort.

5. d. An imbalance in muscle strength caused by weak hamstrings or abdominal muscles (or a combination of both) can result in a forward curve (or hyperextension) of the lower back, resulting in back pain. Stretching and strengthening these muscles are important for avoiding LBP.

Chapter 6

1. b. Essential fat, necessary fat the body requires to maintain certain functions, should be at least 3 percent of total body weight in men and 12 percent in women.

2. d. Anemia is not a health consequence of overweight or obesity.

3. b. False. Excess fat in the abdomen or waist can put one at greater risk for heart disease and diabetes than an individual who stores body fat in their hips and thighs and lower part of the body.

4. a. While skinfold testing, underwater weighing, and bioelectrical impendence analysis are reliable methods for assessing body composition, the waist-to-hip ratio is the technique used to determine disease risk associated with body fat distribution.

5. c. A BMI of 30 kg/m^2 or greater is considered obese. A healthy BMI is less than 25 for men and less than 27 for women.

6. b. A Skinfold test is an easy measure to obtain and can provide good estimates when done properly.

7. d. Type 1 diabetes is not a health consequence of being underweight or having an eating disorder. Being underweight is associated with health problems such as malnutrition and osteoporosis.

8. a. True. Your BMI is a good estimate of your weight status, however, BMI does not give you a direct measure of percent fat. The method can over- or underestimate body fatness

Chapter 7

1. b. Carbohydrates provide the main source of fuel for your brain, and are the main source of energy during exercise.

2. c. Protein is used by the body to build muscle, skin, connective tissues, and other structural body tissues.

3. c. While water doesn't provide energy or build bone or protein, it is involved in numerous metabolic and other body processes, including blood formation.

4. d. A well-balanced diet consists of 58 percent carbohydrates, 30 percent fats, and 12 percent protein.

5. c. Antioxidants neutralize free radicals in the body, which prevent them from causing damage to cells.

Chapter 8

1. b. Optimal body fat percentages for health and fitness in men range from 10–20%, and from 15%–25% in women. The ranges allow for individual differences in physical activity and appearance.

2. f. Leptin and ghrelin are hormones that play a role in appetite. Leptin depresses appetite, while ghrelin contributes to appetite.

3. d. Energy balance occurs when the amount of calories you consume is equal to the amount of calories you consume, and therefore your weight will not change. If you consume more calories then you burn, you will gain weight. If you consume fewer calories than you burn, you will lose weight.

4. c. Physical activity that uses large muscle groups, such as cardiovascular and strength training is best to achieve weight loss. While flexibility training, yoga and Pilates can be part of a physical fitness program, cardiovascular training improves muscles' ability to burn fat as energy, resulting in weight loss.

5. d. Using the MyPyramid plan is a healthy way to eat for nutrition and overall health. Drastic measures for weight loss such as anorexia, bulimia, or using diet pills can be harmful to your health and constitute disordered eating.

Chapter 9

1. d. Smoking, hypertension, and high blood cholesterol are major risk factors for cardiovascular disease. Resting pulse rate is not a risk factor.

2. d. Normal blood pressure is 120/80 mm/Hg, so a blood pressure reading of 140/90 would be considered high blood pressure, or hypertension.

3. b. HDL is "good" cholesterol and LDL is "bad" cholesterol. When your LDL is high you are at increased risk for CHD, but if your HDL is high, your risk for developing CHD decreases.

4. c. Cardiovascular disease is leading cause of death in the United States for all ages.

5. b. Obesity, hypertension, and diabetes can all be modified by healthy lifestyle changes, however heredity, or the genes you are born with, cannot be changed.

Chapter 10

1. d. There are a variety of physical symptoms associated with stress, including headaches, anxiety, and muscle tension.

2. c. Eustress is positive stress that motivates and energizes us. Distress is the type of stress that can have a negative impact on our mental and physical health.

3. a. Epinephrine, cortisol, and norepinephrine are hormones released into the bloodstream during the stress response. Dopamine does not play a role in the body's response to stress.

4. d. Every day life situations can contribute our stress levels. These situations can include financial responsibilities, interpersonal relationship problems, and academic pressures.

5. b. Alcohol is not an effective way to cope with stress. Using alcohol to cope may eventually increase your stress level by affecting your ability to sleep, be productive, and may even lead to alcohol abuse.

Chapter 11

1. c. Evaporation is the body's major mechanism of heat loss during exercise. It is the only method that can dissipate enough heat during exercise to maintain a core temperature close to normal.

2. b. High humidity inhibits sweat evaporation. So, along with high heat, high humidity can cause a rapid rise in body temperature.

3. d. Layering clothing is the best method to insulate your body. Air is an excellent insulator, and layering clothing traps air between layers to insulate the body.

4. b. In cold weather the body's core temperature can decrease to dangerous levels, causing hypothermia.

5. b. At high alitudes, there is less oxygen available in the air, and thus, there is a reduced level of oxygen in the blood. In order to compensate, breathing increases to maximize the available oxygen.

Chapter 12

1. d. Any abnormal stress in the form of improper shoes, training techniques, or alignment abnormalities can impact muscles, tendons, joints, etc., and cause injury to a runner.

2. a. Because back pain is often associated with muscle weakness, exercise plays a role in prevention. In particular, core strength training, including your abdominal muscles, can readily prevent such damage.

3. b. Acute muscle soreness immediately after exercise is usually due to overuse or injury.

4. d. Because shin splints are typically caused by stress on the soft tissues, each of the listed precautions can reduce the stress on the tissues and reduce the risk of injury.

5. d. Ligaments cannot withstand much movement without injury. Thus, refraining from exercises that place a strain on joints is the best way to prevent damage.

Chapter 13

1. b. Lung cancer is the leading cause of cancer deaths for women in United States. While more women are diagnosed with breast cancer per year than lung cancer, breast cancer is typically detected earlier and is more treatable than lung cancer.

2. d. When a malignant tumor (one that is cancerous) metastisizes this means that the cancer cells have spread to other parts of the body. A benign tumor is not cancer.

3. c. Performing regular breast self exams is one thing you can do to prevent your cancer risk. However, behaviors such as poor diet, physical inactivity, and excessive alcohol consumption can increase your risk.

4. a. Skin cancer is the most common type of cancer, but is highly treatable if detected early. For people under the age of 30 melanoma is the most common type of skin cancer.

5. d. A nagging cough or hoarseness, a sore that does not heal, and unusual bleeding or discharge are three of the seven warning signs of cancer. If you have any one of these, make an appointment to see your doctor right away.

Chapter 14

1. d. Hepatitis B promotes an inflammatory response in the liver that results in a decrease in normal liver function. For this reason, Hepatitis B, which can be transmitted via bodily fluids, is a serious disease.

2. a. There are over 30 strains of human papillomavirus (HPV), and while many infected individuals do not experience noticeable symptoms, some strains of HPV are responsible for genital warts.

3. d. Syphilis is a bacterial infection. If it is treated early, it can be cured with antibiotics.

4. a. Stage 1, primary syphilis, generally includes a dime-sized, painless sore, called a chancre, located at the initial site of infection.

5. b. These infections are all caused by parasites

Chapter 15

1. d. A key factor in preventing an addiction is to abstain from the addictive behavior in the first place.

2. e. Each trait is associated with an addiction. Addictive behaviors begin as a single use of the drug, but over time cravings become stronger and an individual can lose control. This results in an escalation of drug use. When confronted, most addicts will deny that they have a drug problem.

3. a. Some drugs are more addictive than others. Each drug affects the brain in different ways.

4. b. Babies born to mothers who drink alcohol while pregnant may be born with fetal alcohol syndrome. One effect of FAS is low birth weight; however, a newborn can have low birth weight without having FAS.

5. e. Secondhand smoke is derived from a smoker's exhaled smoke (mainstream smoke) and the smoke given off from burning tobacco products (sidestream smoke).

Chapter 16

1. b. Pregnant women should avoid exercises that require them to lie on their backs for five minutes or more. For this reason, pregnant women should avoid floor-based abdominal toning exercises.

2. d. As you age, your maximal heart rate, cardiorespiratory fitness, and muscle mass all decrease.

3. a. Taking a daily vitamin or herbal supplement is not proven to ensure successful aging; however, regular exercise, regular medical screenings, and not smoking are all ways to age successfully.

4. a. Spending time in a sauna or steam bath to lose weight is a common fitness misconception. You may lose weight temporarily due to water loss, but as soon as you eat or drink, you will replace the lost fluids and your weight will return.

5. c. A fee for service plan provides the most freedom, but this type of health plan can be more costly than PPOs or HMOs.

APPENDIX B Nutritive Value of Selected Foods and Fast Foods

This section presents nutritional information about a wide array of foods, including many fast foods. Values are given for calories, protein, carbohydrates, fiber, fat, saturated fat, and cholesterol for common foods and serving sizes. Use this information to assess your diet and make improvements. This is only a sampling of the most common foods. See the MyDietAnalysis database for a more extensive list of foods.

MDA Code	Food Name	Amt	Wt (g)	Ener (kcal)	Prot (g)	Carb (g)	Fiber (g)	Fat (g)	Sat (g)	Chol (g)
Beverages										
Alcoholic Beverages										
22831	Beer	12 fl. oz	360	157	1	13		0	0	
34053	Beer, light	12 fl. oz	353	105	1	5	0	0	0	
22606	Beer, non alcoholic	12 fl. oz	353	73	1	14	0	0	0	
22884	Wine, red	1 fl. oz	29	24	0	1		0	0	
22861	Wine, white	1 fl. oz	29.3	24	0	1		0	0	
22514	Gin, 80 proof	1 fl. oz	27.8	64	0	0	0	0	0	
22593	Rum, 80 proof	1 fl. oz	27.8	64	0	0	0	0	0	
22515	Tequila, 80 proof	1 fl. oz	27.8	64	0	0	0	0	0	
22594	Vodka, 80 proof	1 fl. oz	27.8	64	0	0	0	0	0	
22670	Whiskey, 80 proof	1 fl. oz	27.8	64	0	0	0	0	0	
Coffee, Tea and Dairy Drink Mixes										
20012	Coffee, brewed	1 cup	237	2	0	0	0	0	0	0
20686	Coffee, decaffeinated, brewed	1 cup	237	0	0	0	0	0	0	0
20439	Coffee, espresso	1 cup	237	5	0	0	0	0	0.2	0
20402	Coffee, from mix, French vanilla, sugar & fat free	1 ea	7	25	0	5	0	0	0.1	0
85	Chocolate milk, prepared w/syrup	1 cup	282	254	9	36	1	8	4.7	25
46	Hot cocoa, w/aspartame, sodium, vitamin A, prepared w/water	1 cup	256	74	3	14	1	1	0	0
48	Hot cocoa, prep from dry mix with water	1 cup	275	151	2	32	1	2	0.9	3
166	Hot cocoa, w/marshmallows, from dry packet	1 ea	28	112	1	24	1	1	0.4	2
39	Chocolate flavor, dry mix, prepared w/milk	1 cup	266	226	9	32	1	9	4.9	24
41	Strawberry flavor, dry mix, prepared w/milk	1 cup	266	234	8	33	0	8	5.1	32
20014	Tea, brewed	1 cup	237	2	0	1	0	0	0	0
20036	Tea, herbal (not chamomile) brewed	1 cup	237	2	0	0	0	0	0	0
Fruit and Vegetable Beverages and Juices										
71080	Apple juice, canned or bottled, unsweetened	1 ea	262	123	0	31	0	0	0	0
20277	Capri Sun All Natural Juice Drink, Fruit Punch	1 ea	210	99	0	26	0	0	0	0
5226	Carrot juice, canned	1 cup	236	94	2	22	2	0	0.1	0
3042	Cranberry juice cocktail	1 cup	253	137	0	34	0	0	0	0
20024	Fruit punch, canned	1 cup	248	117	0	30	0	0	0	0
20035	Fruit punch, from frozen concentrate	1 cup	247	114	0	29	0	0	0	0
20101	Grape drink, canned	1 cup	250	153	0	39	0	0	0	0
3053	Grapefruit juice, from frozen concentrate, unsweetened	1 cup	247	101	1	24	0	0	0	0
20045	Lemonade flavor drink, from dry mix	1 cup	266	112	0	29	0	0	0	0
20047	Lemonade w/aspartame, low kcal, from dry mix	1 cup	237	5	0	1	0	0	0	0

Ener = energy (kilocalories); **Prot** = protein; **Carb** = carbohydrate; **Fiber** = dietary fiber; **Fat** = total fat; **Sat** = saturated fat; **Chol** = cholesterol.

*This food composition table has been prepared for Pearson Education, Inc. and is copyrighted by ESHA Research in Salem, Oregon, the developer of the MyDietAnalysis software program.

Appendix B
Nutritive Value of Selected Foods and Fast Foods

MDA Code	Food Name	Amt	Wt (g)	Ener (kcal)	Prot (g)	Carb (g)	Fiber (g)	Fat (g)	Sat (g)	Chol (g)
20070	Orange drink, canned	1 cup	248	122	0	31	0	0	0	0
20004	Orange flavor drink, from dry mix	1 cup	248	122	0	31	0	0	0	0
71108	Orange juice, canned, unsweetened	1 ea	263	110	2	26	1	0	0	0
3090	Orange juice, fresh	1 cup	248	112	2	26	0	0	0.1	0
3091	Orange juice, from frozen concentrate, unsweetened	1 cup	249	112	2	27	0	0	0	0
5397	Tomato juice, canned w/o salt	1 cup	243	41	2	10	1	0	0	0
20849	Vegetable and fruit, mixed juice drink	4 oz	113	33	0	8	0	0	0	0
20080	Vegetable juice cocktail, canned	1 cup	242	46	2	11	2	0	0	0
Soft Drinks										
20006	Club soda	1 cup	237	0	0	0	0	0	0	0
20685	Low-calorie cola, with aspartame, caffeine free	12 fl. oz	355	4	0	1	0	0	0	0
20843	Cola, with higher caffeine	12 fl. oz	370	152	0	39	0	0	0	0
20008	Ginger ale	1 cup	244	83	0	21	0	0	0	0
20032	Lemon-lime soft drink	1 cup	246	98	0	25	0	0	0	0
20027	Pepper-type soft drink	1 cup	246	101	0	26	0	0	0.2	0
20009	Root beer	1 cup	246	101	0	26	0	0	0	0
Other										
20033	Soy milk	1 cup	245	127	11	12	3	5	0.6	0
20041	Water, tap	1 cup	237	0	0	0	0	0	0	0
Breakfast Cereals										
40095	All-Bran/Kellogg	0.5 cup	30	78	4	22	9	1	0.2	0
40032	Cap'n Crunch/Quaker	0.75 cup	27	108	1	23	1	2	0.4	0
40297	Cheerios/Gen Mills	1 cup	30	111	4	22	4	2	0.4	0
40126	Cinnamon Toast Crunch/Gen Mills	0.75 cup	30	127	2	24	1	3	0.5	0
40195	Corn Flakes/Kellogg	1 cup	28	101	2	24	1	0	0.1	0
40089	Corn Grits, instant, plain, prepared/Quaker	1 pkg	137	93	2	21	1	0	0	0
40206	Corn Pops/Kellogg	1 cup	31	117	1	28	0	0	0.1	0
40179	Cream of Rice, prepared w/salt	1 cup	244	127	2	28	0	0	0	0
40182	Cream of Wheat, instant, prepared w/salt	1 cup	241	149	4	32	1	1	0.1	0
40104	Crispix/Kellogg	1 cup	29	109	2	25	0	0	0.1	0
40218	Froot Loops/Kellogg	1 cup	30	118	2	26	1	1	0.5	0
40217	Frosted Flakes/Kellogg	0.75 cup	31	114	1	28	1	0	0	0
11916	Frosted Mini-Wheats, bite size/Kellogg	1 cup	55	189	6	45	6	1	0.2	0
40209	Raisin Bran/Kellogg	1 cup	61	195	5	47	7	2	0.3	0
40210	Rice Krispies/Kellogg	1.25 cup	33	128	2	28	0	0	0.1	0
60887	Shredded wheat, large biscuit	2 ea	37.8	127	4	30	5	1	0.2	0
40211	Special K/Kellogg	1 cup	31	117	7	22	1	0	0.1	0
Dairy and Cheese										
500	Cream, half & half	2 Tbs	30	39	1	1	0	3	2.1	11
11	Milk, condensed, sweetend, canned	2 Tbs	38.2	123	3	21	0	3	2.1	13
19	Milk, lowfat, 1% fat, chocolate	1 cup	250	158	8	26	1	2	1.5	8
218	Milk, 2%, w/added vitamins A & D	1 cup	245	130	8	13	0	5	3	
6	Milk, nonfat/skim, w/added vitamin A	1 cup	245	83	8	12	0	0	0.1	5
1	Milk, whole, 3.25%	1 cup	244	146	8	11	0	8	4.6	24
20	Milk, whole, chocolate	1 cup	250	208	8	26	2	8	5.3	30
72088	Yogurt, fruit variety, nonfat	1 cup	245	230	11	47	0	0	0.3	5
1287	American Cheese, nonfat slices	1 pce	21.3	32	5	2	0	0	0.1	3
13349	Cheez Whiz cheese sauce/Kraft	2 Tbs	33	91	4	3	0	7	4.3	25

MDA Code	Food Name	Amt	Wt (g)	Ener (kcal)	Prot (g)	Carb (g)	Fiber (g)	Fat (g)	Sat (g)	Chol (g)
1014	Cottage cheese, 2% fat	0.5 cup	113	102	16	4	0	2	1.4	9
1015	Cream cheese	2 Tbs	29	101	2	1	0	10	6.4	32
1452	Cream cheese, fat free	2 Tbs	29	28	4	2	0	0	0.3	2
1016	Feta, crumbled	0.25 cup	37.5	99	5	2	0	8	5.6	33
47887	Mozzarella, whole milk, slice	1 ea	34	102	8	1	0	8	4.5	27
1075	Parmesan, grated	1 Tbs	5	22	2	0	0	1	0.9	4
1024	Ricotta, part skim	0.25 cup	62	86	7	3	0	5	3.1	19
1064	Ricotta, whole milk	0.25 cup	62	108	7	2	0	8	5.1	32
Eggs and Egg Substitutes										
19525	Egg substitute, liquid	0.25 cup	62.8	53	8	0	0	2	0.4	1
19506	Egg, white, raw	1 ea	33.4	17	4	0	0	0	0	0
19509	Egg, whole, fried	1 ea	46	92	6	0	0	7	2	210
19515	Egg, whole, hard boiled	1 ea	37	57	5	0	0	4	1.2	157
19521	Egg, whole, poached	1 ea	37	54	5	0	0	4	1.1	156
19516	Egg, whole, scrambled	1 ea	61	101	7	1	0	7	2.2	215
19508	Egg, yolk, raw, fresh	1 ea	16.6	53	3	1	0	4	1.6	205
Fruit										
72101	Apricots, canned, heavy syrup, drained	1 cup	182	151	1	39	5	0	0	0
3164	Fruit cocktail canned in juice	1 cup	237	109	1	28	2	0	0	0
71079	Apple w/skin, raw	1 cup	125	65	0	17	3	0	0	0
3331	Applesauce, canned, sweetened w/added Vit C	0.5 cup	128	97	0	25	2	0	0	0
3657	Apricot, raw	1 cup	165	79	2	18	3	1	0	0
3210	Avocado, California, peeled, raw	1 ea	173	289	3	15	12	27	3.7	0
71082	Banana, peeled, raw	1 ea	81	72	1	19	2	0	0.1	0
71976	Grapefruit, fresh	0.5 ea	154	60	1	16	6	0	0	
3055	Grapes, Thompson seedless, fresh	0.5 cup	80	55	1	14	1	0	0	4
3642	Melon, fresh, wedge	1 pce	69	23	1	6	1	0	0	5
3168	Mixed fruit (prune, apricot & pear) dried	1 oz	28.4	69	1	18	2	0	0	0
3216	Nectarine, raw	1 cup	138	61	1	15	2	0	0	0
3726	Peach, peeled, raw	1 ea	79	31	1	8	1	0	0	0
3106	Pear, raw	1 ea	209	121	1	32	6	0	0	0
3766	Raisins, seedless	50 ea	26	78	1	21	1	0	0	0
72113	Pineapple, fresh, slice	1 pce	84	38	0	10		0		5
3085	Orange, fresh	1 ea	184	86	2	22	4	0	0	
3135	Strawberries, halves/slices, raw	1 cup	100	53	1	13	3	0	0	0
Grain Products										
Breads, Rolls, and Bread Crumbs										
71170	Bagel, cinnamon raisin	1 ea	20	71	3	14	1	0	0.1	0
71167	Bagel, egg	1 ea	26	72	3	14	1	1	0.1	6
71152	Bagel, plain/onion/poppy/sesame, enriched	1 ea	26	67	3	13	1	0	0.1	0
42433	Biscuit, w/butter	1 ea	82	280	5	27	0	17	4	0
71192	Biscuit, Plain or Buttermilk, refrig dough, baked, reduced fat	1 ea	21	63	2	12	0	1	0.3	0
42004	Bread crumbs, dry, plain, grated	1 Tbs	6.8	27	1	5	0	0	0.1	0
49144	Bread, crusty Italian w/garlic	1 pce	50	186	4	21	10	2.4	6	
70964	Bread, garlic, frozen/Campione	1 pce	28	101	2	12	1	5	0.8	
42069	Bread, oat bran	1 pce	30	71	3	12	1	1	0.2	0

Appendix B (continued)
Nutritive Value of Selected Foods and Fast Foods

MDA Code	Food Name	Amt	Wt (g)	Ener (kcal)	Prot (g)	Carb (g)	Fiber (g)	Fat (g)	Sat (g)	Chol (g)
42095	Bread, wheat, reduced kcal	1 pce	23	46	2	10	3	1	0.1	0
71247	Bread, white, commercially prepared, crumbs/cubes/slices	1 pce	9	24	1	5	0	0	0.1	0
42084	Bread, white, reduced kcal	1 pce	23	48	2	10	2	1	0.1	0
26561	Buns, hamburger, Wonder	1 ea	43	117	3	22	1	2	0.4	
42021	Hamburger/hot dog bun, plain	1 ea	43	120	4	21	1	2	0.5	0
42115	Cornbread, prepared from dry mix	1 pce	60	188	4	29	1	6	1.6	37
71227	Pita bread, white, enriched	1 ea	28	77	3	16	1	0	0	0
71228	Pita bread, whole wheat	1 ea	28	74	3	15	2	1	0.1	0
71368	Roll, dinner, plain, homemade w/reduced fat (2%) milk	1 ea	43	136	4	23	1	3	0.8	15
42161	Roll, French	1 ea	38	105	3	19	1	2	0.4	0
71056	Roll, hard/kaiser	1 ea	57	167	6	30	1	2	0.3	0
42297	Tortilla, corn, w/o salt, ready to cook	1 ea	26	58	1	12	1	1	0.1	0
90645	Taco shell, baked	1 ea	5	23	0	3	0	1	0.2	0
Crackers										
71451	Cheez-its/Goldfish crackers, low sodium	55 pce	33	166	3	19	1	8	3.2	4
43507	Oyster/soda/soup crackers	1 cup	45	193	4	32	1	5	0.7	0
70963	Ritz crackers/Nabisco	5 ea	16	79	1	10	0	4	0.6	0
43587	Saltine crackers, original premium/Nabisco	5 ea	14	59	2	10	0	1	0.3	0
43545	Sandwich crackers, cheese filled	4 ea	28	134	3	17	1	6	1.7	1
43546	Sandwich crackers, peanut butter filled	4 ea	28	138	3	16	1	7	1.4	0
44677	Snackwell Wheat Cracker/Nabisco	1 ea	15	62	1	12	1	2		
43581	Wheat Thins, baked/Nabisco	16 ea	29	136	2	20	1	6	0.9	0
43508	Whole wheat cracker	4 ea	32	142	3	22	3	6	1.1	0
Muffins and Baked Goods										
42723	English muffin, plain	1 ea	57	132	5	26		1	0.2	
62916	Muffin, blueberry, commercially prepared	1 ea	11	30	1	5	0	1	0.2	3
44521	Muffin, corn, commercially prepared	1 ea	57	174	3	29	2	5	0.8	15
44514	Muffin, oat bran	1 ea	57	154	4	28	3	4	0.6	0
44518	Toaster muffin, blueberry	1 ea	33	103	2	18	1	3	0.5	2
Noodles and Pasta										
38048	Chow mein noodles, dry	1 cup	45	237	4	26	2	14	2	0
38047	Egg noodles, enriched, cooked	0.5 cup	80	110	4	20	1	2	0.3	23
38060	Spaghetti, whole wheat, cooked	1 cup	140	174	7	37	6	1	0.1	0
38251	Egg noodles, enriched, cooked w/salt	0.5 cup	80	110	4	20	1	2	0.3	
38102	Macaroni noodles, enriched, cooked	1 cup	140	221	8	43	3	1	0.2	
38118	Spaghetti noodles, enriched, cooked	0.5 cup	70	111	4	22	1	1	0.1	4
Grains										
38076	Couscous, cooked	0.5 cup	78.5	88	3	18	1	0	0	0
38080	Oats	0.25 cup	39	152	7	26	4	3	0.5	0
38010	Rice, brown, long grain, cooked	1 cup	195	216	5	45	4	2	0.4	0
38256	Rice, white, long grain, enriched, cooked w/salt	1 cup	158	205	4	45	1	0	0.1	0
38019	Rice, white, long grain, instant, enriched, cooked	1 cup	165	193	4	41	1	1	0	0
Pancakes, French Toast, and Waffles										
42156	French Toast, homemade w/reduced fat (2%) milk	1 pce	65	149	5	16	1	7	1.8	75
45192	Pancake/waffle, buttermilk/Eggo/Kellogg	1 ea	42.5	99	3	16	0	3	0.6	5

MDA Code	Food Name	Amt	Wt (g)	Ener (kcal)	Prot (g)	Carb (g)	Fiber (g)	Fat (g)	Sat (g)	Chol (g)
45117	Pancakes, plain, homemade	1 ea	77	175	5	22	1	7	1.6	45
45193	Waffle, lowfat, homestyle, frozen	1 ea	35	83	2	15	0	1	0.3	9
Meat and Meat Substitutes										
Beef										
10093	Beef, average of all cuts, lean & fat (1/4″ trim) cooked	3 oz	85.1	260	22	0	0	18	7.3	75
10705	Beef, average of all cuts, lean (1/4″ trim) cooked	3 oz	85.1	184	25	0	0	8	3.2	73
10133	Beef, whole rib, roasted, 1/4″ trim	3 oz	85.1	305	19	0	0	25	10	71
58129	Ground beef (hamburger), 25% fat, cooked, pan-browned	3 oz	85.1	236	22	0	0	15	6	76
58119	Ground beef (hamburger), 15% fat, cooked, pan-browned	3 oz	85.1	218	24	0	0	13	5	77
58109	Ground beef (hamburger), 5% fat, cooked, pan-browned	3 oz	85.1	164	25	0	0	6	2.9	76
10791	Porterhouse steak, lean & fat (1/4″ trim) broiled	3 oz	85.1	280	19	0	0	22	8.7	61
58257	Rib eye steak, small end (ribs 10-12), 0″ trim, broiled	3 oz	85.1	210	23	0	0	13	4.9	94
58094	Skirt steak, trimmed to 0″ fat, broiled	3 oz	85.1	187	22	0	0	10	4	51
58328	Strip steak, top loin, 1/8″ trim, broiled	3 oz	85.1	171	25	0	0	7	2.7	67
10805	T-Bone steak, lean & fat (1/4″ trim) broiled	3 oz	85.1	260	20	0	0	19	7.6	55
11531	Veal, average of all cuts, cooked	3 oz	85.1	197	26	0	0	10	3.6	97
Chicken										
15057	Chicken breast, w/o skin, fried	3 oz	85.1	159	28	0	0	4	1.1	77
15080	Chicken, dark meat, w/skin, roasted	3 oz	85.1	215	22	0	0	13	3.7	77
15026	Chicken, dark meat, w/o skin, fried	3 oz	85.1	203	25	2	0	10	2.7	82
15042	Chicken drumstick, w/o skin, fried	3 oz	85.1	166	24	0	0	7	1.8	80
15048	Chicken, wing, w/o skin, fried	3 oz	85.1	180	26	0	0	8	2.1	71
15059	Chicken, wing, w/o skin, roasted	3 oz	85.1	173	26	0	0	7	1.9	72
Turkey										
51151	Turkey bacon, cooked	1 oz	28.4	108	8	1	0	8	2.4	28
51098	Turkey patty, breaded, fried	1 ea	42	119	6	7	0	8	2	26
16110	Turkey breast w/skin, roasted	3 oz	85.1	130	25	0	0	3	0.7	77
16038	Turkey breast, no skin, roasted	3 oz	85.1	115	20	0	0	1	0.2	71
16101	Turkey, dark meat w/skin, roasted	3 oz	85.1	155	24	0	0	6	1.8	100
16003	Turkey, ground, cooked	1 ea	82	193	22	0	0	11	2.8	84
Lamb										
13604	Lamb, average of all cuts (1/4″ trim) cooked	3 oz	85.1	250	21	0	0	18	7.5	83
13616	Lamb, average of all cuts, lean (1/4″ trim) cooked	3 oz	85.1	175	24	0	0	8	2.9	78
Pork										
12000	Bacon, broiled, pan-fried, or roasted	3 pcs	19	103	7	0	0	8	2.6	21
28143	Canadian bacon	1 ea	56	68	9	1	3	1	27	
12211	Ham, cured, boneless, regular fat (11% fat) roasted	1 cup	140	249	32	0	0	13	4.4	83
12309	Pork, average of retail cuts, cooked	3 oz	85.1	232	23	0	0	15	5.3	77
12097	Pork, ribs, backribs, roasted	3 oz	85.1	315	21	0	0	25	9.4	100
12099	Pork, ground, cooked	3 oz	85.1	253	22	0	0	18	6.6	80

Appendix B (continued)
Nutritive Value of Selected Foods and Fast Foods

MDA Code	Food Name	Amt	Wt (g)	Ener (kcal)	Prot (g)	Carb (g)	Fiber (g)	Fat (g)	Sat (g)	Chol (g)
Lunchmeats										
13000	Beef, thin slices	1 oz	28.4	42	5	0	0	2	0.8	20
58275	Bologna, beef and pork, low fat	1 ea	14	32	2	0	0	3	1	5
13157	Chicken breast, oven roasted deluxe	1 oz	28.4	29	5	1	0	1	0.2	14
13306	Corned beef, cooked, chopped, pressed	1 ea	71	101	14	1	0	5	2	46
13264	Ham, slices, regular (11% fat)	1 cup	135	220	22	5	2	12	4	77
13101	Pastrami, beef, cured	1 oz	28.4	41	6	0	0	2	0.8	19
13215	Salami, beef, cotto	1 oz	28.4	59	4	1	0	4	1.9	24
16160	Turkey breast slice	1 pce	21	22	4	1	0	0	0.1	9
58279	Turkey ham, sliced, extra lean, prepackaged or deli-sliced	1 cup	138	163	27	2	0	5	1.8	92
Sausage										
13070	Chorizo, pork & beef	1 ea	60	273	14	1	0	23	8.6	53
57877	Frankfurter, beef	1 ea	45	148	5	2	0	13	5.3	24
13012	Frankfurter, turkey	1 ea	45	102	6	1	0	8	2.7	48
57890	Italian sausage, pork, cooked	1 ea	83	286	16	4	0	23	7.9	47
13021	Pepperoni sausage	1 pce	5.5	26	1	0	0	2	0.9	6
13185	Pork sausage links, cooked	2 ea	48	165	8	0	0	15	5.1	37
58227	Sausage, pork, pre-cooked	3 oz	85	321	12	0	0	30	9.9	63
58007	Turkey sausage, breakfast links, mild	2 ea	56	132	9	1	0	10	4.4	34
Meat Substitutes										
7509	Bacon substitute, vegetarian, strips	3 ea	15	46	2	1	0	4	0.7	0
7722	Garden patties, frozen/Worthington, Morningstar	1 ea	67	119	11	10	4	4	0.5	1
7674	Harvest burger, original flavor, vegetable protein patty	1 ea	90	138	18	7	6	4	1	0
90626	Sausage, vegetarian, meatless	1 ea	28	72	5	3	1	5	0.8	0
7726	Spicy Black Bean Burger/Worthington, Morningstar	1 ea	78	115	12	15	5	1	0.2	1
Nuts										
4519	Cashews, dry roasted w/salt	0.25 cup	34.2	196	5	11	1	16	3.1	0
4728	Macadamia nuts, dry roasted, unsalted	1 cup	134	962	10	18	11	102	16	0
4592	Mixed nuts, w/peanuts, dry roasted, salted	0.25 cup	34.2	203	6	9	3	18	2.4	0
4626	Peanut butter, chunky w/salt	2 Tbs	32	188	8	7	3	16	2.6	0
4756	Peanuts, dry roasted w/o salt	30 ea	30	176	7	6	2	15	2.1	0
4696	Peanuts, raw	0.25 cup	36.5	207	9	6	3	18	2.5	0
4540	Pistachio nuts, dry roasted, salted	0.25 cup	32	182	7	9	3	15	1.8	0
Seafood										
17029	Bass, freshwater, cooked w/dry heat	3 oz	85.1	124	21	0	0	4	0.9	74
17037	Cod, Atlantic, baked/broiled (dry heat)	3 oz	85.1	89	19	0	0	1	0.1	47
19036	Crab, Alaskan King, boiled/steamed	3 oz	85.1	83	16	0	0	1	0.1	45
17090	Haddock, baked or broiled (dry heat)	3 oz	85.1	95	21	0	0	1	0.1	63
17291	Halibut, Atlantic & Pacific, baked or broiled (dry heat)	3 oz	85.1	119	23	0	0	3	0.4	35
17181	Salmon, Atlantic, farmed, cooked w/dry heat	3 oz	85.1	175	19	0	0	11	2.1	54
17099	Salmon, Sockeye, baked or broiled (dry heat)	3 oz	85.1	184	23	0	0	9	1.6	74
71707	Squid, fried	3 oz	85.1	149	15	7	0	6	1.6	221
17066	Swordfish, baked or broiled (dry heat)	3 oz	85.1	132	22	0	0	4	1.2	43
56007	Tuna salad, lunchmeat spread	2 Tbs	25.6	48	4	2	0	2	0.4	3
17151	White tuna, canned in H_2O, drained	3 oz	85.1	109	20	0	0	3	0.7	36
17083	White tuna, canned in oil, drained	3 oz	85.1	158	23	0	0	7	1.1	26

MDA Code	Food Name	Amt	Wt (g)	Ener (kcal)	Prot (g)	Carb (g)	Fiber (g)	Fat (g)	Sat (g)	Chol (g)
Vegetables and Legumes										
Beans										
7038	Baked beans, plain or vegetarian, canned	1 cup	254	239	12	54	10	1	0.2	0
5197	Bean sprouts, mung, canned, drained	1 cup	125	15	2	3	1	0	0	0
7012	Black beans, boiled w/o salt	1 cup	172	227	15	41	15	1	0.2	0
5862	Beets, boiled w/salt, drained	0.5 cup	85	37	1	8	2	0	0	0
90018	Cowpeas, cooked w/salt	1 cup	171	198	13	35	11	1	0.2	0
7081	Hummus, garbanzo or chickpea spread, homemade	1 Tbs	15.4	27	1	3	1	1	0.2	0
7087	Kidney beans, canned	1 cup	256	210	13	37	11	2	0.2	0
7006	Lentils, boiled w/o salt	1 cup	198	230	18	40	16	1	0.1	0
7051	Pinto beans, canned	1 cup	240	206	12	37	11	2	0.4	0
6748	Snap green beans, raw	10 ea	55	17	1	4	2	0	0	0
5320	Snap yellow beans, raw	0.5 cup	55	17	1	4	2	0	0	0
90026	Split peas, boiled w/salt	0.5 cup	98	116	8	21	8	0	0.1	0
7054	White beans, canned	1 cup	262	307	19	57	13	1	0.2	0
Fresh Vegetables										
9577	Artichokes (globe or French) boiled w/salt, drained	1 ea	20	10	1	2	1	0	0	0
6033	Arugula/roquette, raw	1 cup	20	5	1	1	0	0	0	0
90406	Asparagus, raw	10 ea	35	7	1	1	1	0	0	0
5558	Broccoli stalks, raw	1 ea	114	32	3	6	4	0	0.1	0
5036	Cabbage, raw	1 cup	70	17	1	4	2	0	0	0
90605	Carrots, baby, raw	1 ea	15	5	0	1	0	0	0	0
5049	Cauliflower, raw	0.5 cup	50	12	1	3	1	0	0	0
90436	Celery, raw	1 ea	17	2	0	1	0	0	0	0
7202	Corn, white, sweet, ears, raw	1 ea	73	63	2	14	2	1	0.1	0
5900	Corn, yellow, sweet, boiled w/salt, drained	0.5 cup	82	89	3	21	2	1	0.2	0
5908	Eggplant (brinjal) boiled w/salt, drained	1 cup	99	35	1	9	2	0	0	0
5087	Lettuce, looseleaf, raw	2 pcs	20	3	0	1	0	0	0	0
51069	Mushrooms, brown, Italian, or crimini, raw	2 ea	28	6	1	1	0	0	0	0
90472	Onions, chopped, raw	1 ea	70	29	1	7	1	0	0	0
5116	Peas, green, raw	1 cup	145	117	8	21	7	1	0.1	0
7932	Peppers, jalapeno, raw	1 cup	90	27	1	5	2	1	0.1	0
90493	Peppers, sweet green, chopped/sliced, raw	10 pcs	27	5	0	1	0	0	0	0
6990	Pepper, sweet red, raw	1 ea	10	3	0	1	0	0	0	0
9251	Potatoes, red, flesh and skin, baked	1 ea	138	123	3	27	2	0	0	0
9245	Potatoes, russet, flesh and skin, baked	1 ea	138	134	4	30	3	0	0	0
5146	Spinach, raw	1 cup	30	7	1	1	1	0	0	0
90525	Squash, zucchini w/skin, slices, raw	1 ea	118	19	1	4	1	0	0	0
6924	Sweet potato, baked in skin w/salt	0.5 cup	100	90	2	21	3	0	0.1	0
5180	Tomato sauce, canned	0.5 cup	123	39	2	9	2	0	0	0
90532	Tomato, red, ripe, whole, raw	1 ea	15	3	0	1	0	0	0	0
5306	Yam, peeled, raw	0.5 cup	75	88	1	21	3	0	0	0
Soy and Soy Products										
7564	Tempeh	0.5 cup	83	160	15	8	9	1.8	0	
7015	Soybeans, cooked	1 cup	172	298	29	17	10	15	2.2	0
7542	Tofu, firm, silken, 1″ slice	3 oz	85.1	53	6	2	0	2	0.3	0
Meals and Dishes										
92216	Tortellini with cheese filling	1 cup	108	332	15	51	2	8	3.9	45
57658	Chili con carne w/beans, canned entree	1 cup	222	269	16	25	9	12	3.9	29

Appendix B (continued)

Nutritive Value of Selected Foods and Fast Foods

MDA Code	Food Name	Amt	Wt (g)	Ener (kcal)	Prot (g)	Carb (g)	Fiber (g)	Fat (g)	Sat (g)	Chol (g)
57703	Chili, vegetarian chili w/beans, canned entree/Hormel	1 cup	247	205	12	38	10	1	0.1	0
57068	Macaroni and cheese, unprepared/Kraft	1 ea	70	259	11	48	1	3	1.3	10
70958	Stir fry, rice & vegetables, w/soy sauce/Hanover	1 cup	137	130	5	27	2	0		
70943	Beef & bean burrito/Las Campanas	1 ea	114	296	9	38	1	12	4.2	13
16195	Chicken & vegetables/Lean Cuisine	1 ea	297	252	19	32	5	6	1	24
70917	Hot Pockets, beef & cheddar, frozen	1 ea	142	403	16	39		20	8.8	53
70918	Hot Pockets, croissant pocket w/chicken, broccoli, & cheddar, frozen	1 ea	128	301	11	39	1	11	3.4	37
56757	Lasagna w/meat sauce/Stouffer's	1 ea	215	277	19	26	3	11	4.7	41
11029	Macaroni & beef in tomato sauce/ Lean Cuisine	1 ea	283	249	14	37	3	5	1.6	23
5587	Mashed potatoes, from granules w/milk, prep w/water & margarine	0.5 cup	105	122	2	17	1	5	1.3	2
70898	Pizza, pepperoni, frozen	1 ea	146	432	16	42	3	22	7.1	22
56703	Spaghetti w/meat sauce/Lean Cuisine	1 ea	326	313	14	51	6	6	1.4	13
Snack Foods										
10051	Beef jerky	1 pce	19.8	81	7	2	0	5	2.1	10
63331	Breakfast bars, oats, sugar, raisins, coconut	1 ea	43	200	4	29	1	8	5.5	0
61251	Cheese puffs and twists, corn based, low fat	1 oz	28.4	123	2	21	3	3	0.6	0
44032	Chex snack mix	1 cup	42.5	181	5	28	2	7	2.4	0
23059	Granola bar, hard, plain	1 ea	24.5	115	2	16	1	5	0.6	0
23104	Granola bar, soft, plain	1 ea	28.4	126	2	19	1	5	2.1	0
44012	Popcorn, air-popped	1 cup	8	31	1	6	1	0	0.1	0
44076	Potato chips, plain, no salt	1 oz	28.4	152	2	15	1	10	3.1	0
5437	Potato chips, sour cream & onion	1 oz	28.4	151	2	15	1	10	2.5	2
44015	Pretzels, hard	5 pcs	30	114	3	24	1	1	0.1	0
44021	Rice cake, brown rice, plain, salted	1 ea	9	35	1	7	0	0	0.1	0
44058	Trail mix, regular	0.25 cup	37.5	173	5	17	2	11	2.1	0
Soups										
50398	Beef barley, canned/Progresso Healthy Classics	1 cup	241	142	11	20	3	2	0.7	19
50081	Chicken noodle, chunky, canned	1 cup	240	175	13	17	4	6	1.4	19
50085	Chicken rice, chunky, ready to eat, canned	1 cup	240	127	12	13	1	3	1	12
50088	Chicken vegetable, chunky, canned	1 cup	240	166	12	19	0	5	1.4	17
90238	Chicken, chunky, canned	1 cup	240	170	12	17	1	6	1.9	29
50697	Cup of Noodles, ramen, chicken flavor, dry/ Nissin	1 ea	64	296	6	37	14	6.3		
50009	Minestrone, canned, made w/water	1 cup	241	82	4	11	1	3	0.6	2
92163	Ramen noodle, any flavor, dehydrated, dry	0.5 cup	38	172	4	25	1	6	2.9	0
50043	Tomato vegetable, from dry mix, made w/water	1 cup	253	56	2	10	1	1	0.4	0
50028	Tomato, canned, made w/water	1 cup	244	85	2	17	0	2	0.4	0
50014	Vegetable beef, canned, made w/water	1 cup	244	78	6	10	0	2	0.9	5
50013	Vegetarian vegetable, canned, made w/water	1 cup	241	72	2	12	0	2	0.3	0
Desserts										
62904	Brownie, commercially prepared, square, lrg, 2-3/4″ × 7/8″	1 ea	56	227	3	36	1	9	2.4	10
46062	Cake, chocolate, homemade, w/o icing	1 pce	95	340	5	51	2	14	5.2	55
46091	Cake, yellow, homemade, w/o icing	1 pce	68	245	4	36	0	10	2.7	37

MDA Code	Food Name	Amt	Wt (g)	Ener (kcal)	Prot (g)	Carb (g)	Fiber (g)	Fat (g)	Sat (g)	Chol (g)
71337	Doughnut, cake, w/chocolate icing, lrg, 3 1/2″	1 ea	57	270	3	27	1	18	4.6	35
45525	Doughnut, cake, glazed/sugared, med, 3″	1 ea	45	192	2	23	1	10	2.7	14
47026	Animal crackers/Arrowroot/Tea Biscuits	10 ea	12.5	56	1	9	0	2	0.4	0
90636	Chocolate chip cookie, commercially prepared 3.5″ to 4″	1 ea	40	196	2	26	1	10	3.1	0
47006	Chocolate sandwich cookie, creme filled	3 ea	30	140	2	21	1	6	1.1	0
62905	Fig bar, 2 oz	1 ea	56.7	197	2	40	3	4	0.6	0
90640	Oatmeal cookie, commercially prepared, 3-1/2″ to 4″	1 ea	25	112	2	17	1	5	1.1	0
47010	Peanut butter cookie, homemade, 3″	1 ea	20	95	2	12	0	5	0.9	6
62907	Sugar cookie, refrigerated dough, baked	1 ea	23	111	1	15	0	5	1.4	7
57894	Pudding, chocolate, ready to eat	1 ea	113	158	3	26	1	5	0.8	3
2612	Pudding, vanilla, ready-to-eat	1 ea	113	147	3	25	0	4	1.7	8
2651	Rice pudding, ready-to-eat	1 ea	142	231	3	31	0	11	1.7	1
57902	Tapioca pudding, ready-to-eat	1 ea	113	135	2	22	0	4	1.1	1
71819	Frozen yogurt, chocolate, nonfat	1 cup	186	199	8	37	2	1	0.9	7
72124	Frozen yogurt, flavors other than chocolate	1 cup	174	221	5	38	0	6	4	23
2010	Ice cream, light, vanilla, soft serve	0.5 cup	88	111	4	19	0	2	1.4	11
90723	Ice popsicle	1 ea	59	47	0	11	0	0	0	0
42264	Cinnamon rolls w/icing, refrigerated dough/ Pillsbury	1 ea	44	150	2	24	5	1.2		
71299	Croissant, butter	1 ea	67	272	5	31	2	14	7.8	45
45572	Danish, cheese	1 ea	71	266	6	26	1	16	4.8	11
45593	Toaster pastry, Pop Tart, apple-cinnamon/ Kellogg	1 ea	52	205	2	37	1	5	0.9	0
23014	Chocolate syrup, fudge-type	2 Tbs	38	133	2	24	1	3	1.5	1
510	Whipped cream topping, pressurized	2 Tbs	7.5	19	0	1	0	2	1	6
54387	Whipped topping, frozen, low fat	2 Tbs	9.4	21	0	2	0	1	1.1	0
Fats, Oils, and Condiments										
90210	Butter, unsalted	1 Tbs	14	100	0	0	0	11	7.2	30
8084	Oil, vegetable, canola	1 Tbs	14	124	0	0	0	14	1	0
8008	Oil, olive, salad or cooking	1 Tbs	13.5	119	0	0	0	14	1.9	0
8111	Oil, safflower, salad or cooking, greater than 70% oleic	1 Tbs	13.6	120	0	0	0	14	0.8	0
44483	Shortening, household	1 Tbs	12.8	113	0	0	0	13	2.6	0
1708	Barbecue sauce, original	2 Tbs	36	63	0	15	0			
27001	Catsup	1 ea	6	6	0	2	0	0	0	0
50523	Cheese sauce, ready-to-eat	0.25 cup	63	110	4	4	0	8	3.8	18
54388	Cream substitute, powdered, light	1 Tbs	5.9	25	0	4	0	1	0.2	0
50939	Gravy, brown, homestyle, canned	0.25 cup	60	25	1	3	1	0.3	2	
23003	Jelly	1 Tbs	19	51	0	13	0	0	0	0
25002	Maple syrup	1 Tbs	20	52	0	13	0	0	0	0
44476	Margarine, regular, 80% fat, with salt	1 Tbs	14.2	102	0	0	0	11	1.8	0
8116	Mayonnaise, safflower/soybean oil	1 Tbs	13.8	99	0	0	0	11	1.2	8
8502	Miracle Whip, light/Kraft	1 Tbs	16	37	0	2	0	3	0.5	4
435	Mustard, yellow	1 tsp	5	3	0	0	0	0	0	0
23042	Pancake syrup	1 Tbs	20	47	0	12	0	0	0	0
23172	Pancake syrup, reduced kcal	1 Tbs	15	25	0	7	0	0	0	0
53524	Pasta sauce, spaghetti/marinara	0.5 cup	125	92	2	14	1	3	0.4	0
53646	Salsa picante, mild	2 Tbs	30.5	8	0	1	0	0		0
504	Sour cream, cultured	2 Tbs	28.8	62	1	1	0	6	3.8	13
53063	Soy sauce	1 Tbs	18	11	2	1	0	0	0	0

Appendix B (continued)
Nutritive Value of Selected Foods and Fast Foods

MDA Code	Food Name	Amt	Wt (g)	Ener (kcal)	Prot (g)	Carb (g)	Fiber (g)	Fat (g)	Sat (g)	Chol (g)
53652	Taco sauce, red, mild	1 Tbs	15.7	7	0	1	0	0		0
53004	Teriyaki sauce	1 Tbs	18	15	1	3	0	0	0	0
8024	1000 Island, regular	1 Tbs	15.6	58	0	2	0	5	0.8	4
8013	Blue/Roquefort cheese, regular	2 Tbs	30.6	154	1	2	0	16	3	5
90232	French, regular	1 Tbs	12.3	56	0	2	0	6	0.7	0
44498	Italian, fat-free	1 Tbs	14	7	0	1	0	0	0	0
44696	Ranch, reduced fat	1 Tbs	15	33	0	2	0	3	0.2	3
8035	Vinegar & oil, homemade	2 Tbs	31.2	140	0	1	0	16	2.8	0
Fast Food										
6177	Baked potato, topped w/cheese sauce	1 ea	296	474	15	47		29	10.6	18
56629	Burrito w/beans & cheese	1 ea	93	189	8	27		6	3.4	14
66023	Burrito w/beans, cheese & beef	1 ea	102	165	7	20	2	7	3.6	62
66024	Burrito w/beef	1 ea	110	262	13	29	1	10	5.2	32
56600	Biscuit w/egg sandwich	1 ea	136	373	12	32	1	22	4.7	245
66029	Biscuit w/egg, cheese & bacon sandwich	1 ea	144	477	16	33	0	31	11.4	261
66013	Cheeseburger, double, condiments & vegetables	1 ea	166	417	21	35		21	8.7	60
56649	Cheeseburger, large, one meat patty w/condiments & vegetables	1 ea	219	563	28	38		33	15	88
15063	Chicken, breaded, fried, dark meat (drumstick or thigh)	3 oz	85.1	248	17	9	1	15	4.1	95
15064	Chicken, breaded, fried, light meat (breast or wing)	3 oz	85.1	258	19	10	1	15	4.1	77
56000	Chicken filet, plain	1 ea	182	515	24	39		29	8.5	60
56635	Chimichanga w/beef & cheese	1 ea	183	443	20	39		23	11.2	51
5461	Cole slaw	0.75 cup	99	147	1	13		11	1.6	5
56606	Croissant w/egg & cheese sandwich	1 ea	127	368	13	24		25	14.1	216
56607	Croissant w/egg, cheese & bacon sandwich	1 ea	129	413	16	24		28	15.4	215
66021	Enchilada w/cheese	1 ea	163	319	10	29		19	10.6	44
66020	Enchirito w/cheese, beef & beans	1 ea	193	344	18	34		16	7.9	50
66031	English muffin w/cheese & sausage sandwich	1 ea	115	393	15	29	1	24	9.9	59
66010	Fish sandwich w/tartar sauce	1 ea	158	431	17	41	0	23	5.2	55
90736	French fries fried in vegetable oil, medium	1 ea	134	427	5	50	5	23	5.3	0
56638	Frijoles (beans) w/cheese	0.5 cup	83.5	113	6	14		4	2	18
56664	Ham & cheese sandwich	1 ea	146	352	21	33		15	6.4	58
56662	Hamburger, large, double, w/condiments & vegetables	1 ea	226	540	34	40		27	10.5	122
56659	Hamburger, one patty w/condiments & vegetables	1 ea	110	279	13	27		13	4.1	26
66007	Hamburger, plain	1 ea	90	274	12	31		12	4.1	35
5463	Hash browns	0.5 cup	72	151	2	16		9	4.3	9
66004	Hot dog, plain	1 ea	98	242	10	18		15	5.1	44
2032	Ice cream sundae, hot fudge	1 ea	158	284	6	48	0	9	5	21
6185	Mashed potatoes	0.5 cup	121	100	3	20		1	0.6	2
56639	Nachos w/cheese	7 pcs	113	346	9	36		19	7.8	18
6176	Onion rings, breaded, fried	8 pcs	78.1	259	3	29		15	6.5	13
6173	Potato salad	0.333 cup	95	108	1	13		6	1	57
56619	Pizza w/pepperoni 12" or 1/8	1 pce	108	275	15	30		11	3.4	22
66003	Roast beef sandwich, plain	1 ea	139	346	22	33		14	3.6	51
56671	Submarine sandwich, cold cuts	1 ea	228	456	22	51	2	19	6.8	36
57531	Taco	1 ea	171	369	21	27		21	11.4	56
71129	Shake, chocolate 12 fl. oz	1 ea	250	317	8	51	5	9	5.8	32
71132	Shake, vanilla, 12 fl. oz	1 ea	250	369	8	49	2	16	9.9	57

Photo Credits

All photos by Creative Digital Visions, Pearson Benjamin Cummings, except the following:

p. 1: Carl Schneider/Taxi/Getty Images; p. 3: Giantstep/Photonica/Getty Images; p. 4: DAJ/Getty Images; p. 8: MIXA/Getty Images; p. 9: David Stoecklein/Corbis; p. 10: Tim de Waele/Corbis; p. 11: Mark Dadswell/Getty Images; p. 15: Stone/Getty Images; p. 32: Daniel Hurst/Daniel Hurst Photography/images.com; p. 33 (top) JGI/Getty Images; p. 33 (second from top) David Madison/Getty Images; p. 33 (third from top) Tom Kola/Jupiter Images; p. 33 (bottom) John Kelly/Getty Images; p. 34: Richard Price/Taxi/Getty Images; p. 35: Comstock/Jupiter Images; p. 38 (left) Arthur Tilley/Stone/Getty Images; p. 38 (right) Anthony Neste; p. 49: Bubbles Photolibrary/Alamy; p. 51: altrendo images/Getty Images; p. 53: David Sacks/Image Bank/Getty Images; p. 58: Comstock/Jupiter Images; p. 60: Anthony Neste; p. 61: Paul Hill/iStockphoto; p. 83 (a–d): Anthony Neste; p. 95: Alan Jacubek/Corbis; p. 111: Elena Dorfman, Pearson Benjamin Cummings; p. 132 (bottom a&b): Elena Dorfman, Pearson Benjamin Cummings; p. 137: Elena Dorfman, Pearson Benjamin Cummings; p. 139: Anthony Redpath/Corbis; p. 144: Spike Mafford/Getty Images; p. 148: Spencer Grant/PhotoEdit; p. 155 (bottom) Elena Dorfman, Pearson Benjamin Cummings; p. 169: Patrik Giardino/Corbis; p. 171: Gregg Adams/Getty Images; p. 172 (left): Mike Brinson/Image Bank/Getty Images; p. 172 (right): Jeff Green-Martin/PhotoEdit; p. 173: Guryanov Oleg/Shutterstock, Tom McNemar/iStockphoto; p. 176 (top): David Freund/iStockphoto; p. 176 (bottom): Janet Duran/Black Star; p. 180: Fitness Institute of Texas/University of Texas; p. 181 (left & right): David Young-Wolff/PhotoEdit; p. 182: Kristin Piljay, Pearson Benjamin Cummings; p. 188 (all): Elena Dorfman, Pearson Benjamin Cummings; p. 195: Brooke Fasani/Corbis; p. 198: Brian Hagiwara/Foodpix/Jupiter Images; p. 203: Philip Harvey/Corbis; p. 206: Alice Edward/Getty Images; p. 207:Lew Robertson/Getty Images; p. 218: Kristin Piljay, Pearson Benjamin Cummings; p. 222: Pascal Broze/age footstock; p. 239: Corbis; p. 244: Larry Dale Gordon/Getty Images; p. 246: Comstock/Corbis; p. 249: Elizabeth Etienne/Alamy; p. 253: Nancy Kaszerman/ZUMA/Corbis; p. 255 (top): Rootstein; p. 255 (bottom): Nina Berman/Sipa Press; p. 269: John Henley/Corbis; p. 272: NiKreationS/Alamy; p. 274: David Bishop/Phototake; p. 277: Getty Photodisc; p. 279: Jeff Boyle/Asia Images/Jupiter Images; p. 293: Jonathan Andrew/Corbis; p. 294: Jeffrey Coolidge/Corbis; p. 298: Ryan McVay/Getty Images; p. 299: Andersen Ross/Getty Images; p. 306: Anthony Neste; p. 307: Scott K. Powers; p. 325: John Kelly/Image Bank/Getty Images; p. 329: Owen Franken/Corbis; p. 332: Dorling Kindersley Media Library; p. 333: Mike Powell/Corbis; p. 335: S. P. Gillette/Corbis; p. 343: Corbis; p. 349: Princess Margaret Rose Orthopedic Hospital/SPL/Photo Researchers; p. 355: David Crausby/Alamy; p. 357: Dorling Kindersley Media Library; p. 369: Syracuse Newspapers/The Image Works; p. 370: vario images GmbH & Co.KG/Alamy; p. 376: Kristin Piljay, Pearson Benjamin Cummings; p. 377 (top left): ISM/Phototake; p. 377 (top right/bottom right): CNRI/Photo Researchers; p. 377 (bottom left): P. Marazzi/Photo Researchers; p. 379: Tony Freeman/PhotoEdit; p. 391: Tony Freeman/PhotoEdit; p. 395: sgame/Shutterstock; p. 402: Photo Researchers; p. 403: Eye of Science/Photo Researchers; p. 405: Ronnie Kaufman/Corbis; p. 413: Stockbyte/Getty Images; p. 415: Wang Leng/Asia Images/Jupiter Images; p. 418: Tom Croke/Acclaim Images; p. 419: Comstock/Jupiter Images; p. 420: Leonid Smirnov/Shutterstock; p. 423: Don Farrall/Getty Images; p. 423 (top): David Young-Wolff/PhotoEdit; p. 424: David H. Wells/Corbis; p. 426: Bananastock/Jupiter Images; p. 439: Larry Williams/Corbis; p. 443: Jeffrey Aaronson/Network Aspen; p. 444: Leland Bobbe/Stone/Getty Images; p. 445: Steven Peters/Stone/Getty Images; p. 446: Photodisc/Getty Images; p. 450: Anthony Neste

Index

NOTE: A *t* following a page number indicates tabular material, an *f* following a page number indicates an illustration, and a *b* following a page number indicates a boxed feature.

Abdominal curl, 115
Abdominal muscles
  flexibility exercises for, 158
  isotonic exercises for, 115
  spinal alignment/low back pain and, 142*f*, 143
Abdominal thrusts (Heimlich maneuver), for choking victim, 356, 357*f*
Abs Diet, 248*b*
Abstinence, STI risk reduction and, 404–405
Acamprosate, for alcohol dependence, 422
Accident(s), 354, 355*b*
  reducing risk/prevention of, 354–355, 356*b*, 358*b*
Acclimatization, heat, 329, 329*b*
Achilles' tendon, stretching exercises for, 150
Acquired immunodeficiency syndrome (AIDS), 393, 393*b*, 394–395, 395*f*. *See also* HIV infection/AIDS
Action stage, of behavior change, 12
Active stretching, 146, 146*f*, 147*f*
Acute mountain sickness, 335
Acute muscle soreness, 346, 347*b*
Addiction, 414–417, 415*b*
  behavioral, 415
  causes of, 416–417, 416*t*
  commonly abused substances and, 416*t*, 417–429. *See also specific substance and* Substance use/abuse
  definition of, 414, 415*b*
  physical/psychological, 415–416, 416*t*
Adductor muscles of thigh, flexibility exercises for, 153
Adenosine triphosphate (ATP), 55, 55*b*
  production of, 55–56, 55*b*, 56*f*
Adequate Intake (AI), 213*b*
Adherence goals, 37
Adipose tissue, 171, 171*b*
Adrenaline. *See* Epinephrine
Adult-onset diabetes, 176. *See also* Diabetes
  obesity and, 175–176
Aerobic capacity, maximal ($\dot{V}O_2$max), 52, 53*b*, 58
  aging affecting, 444, 444*f*, 445*f*
  altitude affecting, 334–335, 334*f*
  estimation of, 59–60, 60*f*
  exercise affecting, 58, 58*f*
  target heart rate and, 61–62, 61*b*, 62*f*
  training threshold and, 61, 61*b*
Aerobic exercise, 53*b*. *See also* Cardiorespiratory endurance; Exercise
  ability to perform, 52–53
  adaptations to, 57–58, 57*b*
  cool-down activities for, 45, 64
  designing program for, 60–64
  energy continuum and, 56, 57*f*
  injuries and, 344
  questions about, 63*b*
  responses to, 56–57, 57*b*
  warm-up activities for, 45
  weight control/weight loss and, 249–251, 250*b*, 251*t*
Aerobic fitness. *See* Aerobic exercise; Cardiorespiratory endurance
Aerobic system/aerobic energy production, 55, 55–56, 55*b*, 56*f*. *See also* Cardiorespiratory endurance
  energy continuum and, 56, 57*f*
Age/aging
  coronary heart disease risk and, 277, 278*t*
  diet and, 248*b*
  exercise affecting, 7*f*, 8, 8*f*, 9
  exercise guidelines and, 447–448
  heart rate affected by, 61, 62*f*
  lifetime fitness/wellness and, 441*f*, 444–448, 444*f*, 445*f*, 447*b*, 467–468
  physical and mental changes of, 445–446, 445*f*
  strength training and, 118*b*
  successful, 446–448, 447*b*
  wellness issues and, 5*b*
AI. *See* Adequate Intake
AIDS, 393, 393*b*, 394–395, 395*f*. *See also* HIV infection/AIDS
Air displacement, in body fat measurement, 180, 181*b*, 181*f*
Air pollution, exercise/environmental health and, 4, 335–336, 336*f*, 337*b*
Alarm stage, of general adaptation syndrome, 300
Alcohol abuse, 422. *See also* Alcohol use/abuse
Alcohol dependence (alcoholism), 422–423, 423*b*. *See also* Alcohol use/abuse
Alcoholism, 422–423, 423*b*. *See also* Alcohol use/abuse
Alcohol poisoning, binge drinking and, 423
Alcohol use/abuse, 420–425
  abuse versus addiction, 422–423
  accidents/unintentional injury and, 355
  assessment (inventory) of, 433
  behavioral/physical effects and, 421–422, 422*t*
  behavior change and, 424*b*
  binge drinking and, 423, 423*b*, 423*f*
  blood concentration and, 420–421, 421*b*, 422*t*
    alcohol poisoning and, 423
  cancer risk and, 378, 381, 381*b*
  coronary heart disease risk and, 278, 278*t*
  dependence potential and, 416, 416*t*
  health effects of, 423–425
  healthy diet and, 206
  malnutrition and, 424, 425*b*
  during pregnancy (fetal alcohol syndrome), 424–425, 425*b*
  prevalence of, 423
  STI risk and, 406
  stress and, 307
Alignment
  lower extremity, exercise-related injuries and, 344
  spinal, low back pain and, 142*f*
Allostasis, 301, 301*b*
Allostatic load, 301, 301*b*
Altitude, exercise and, 334–335, 334*f*, 335*f*, 341–342
Alveoli, 53, 53*b*
Amino acids, 201, 201*b*
  DRI for, 213*b*
Amphetamines, dependence potential of, 416*t*
AMS. *See* Acute mountain sickness
Anabolic steroids, 102*b*, 421*t*, 427–428, 427*b*
  dependence potential of, 416*t*
Anaerobic–aerobic energy continuum, 56, 57*f*
Anaerobic system/anaerobic energy production, 55, 55*b*
  energy continuum and, 56, 57*f*
Android pattern, 172, 172*f*, 173*b*
Androstenedione, supplementary, 220*t*
Anemia, iron-deficiency, 203, 203*b*, 213
Anesthesiologist, 452*b*
Angina pectoris, 271
Animals/pets, HIV transmission and, 396
Anorexia nervosa, 177, 254–255, 255*b*, 255*f*
Antabuse. *See* Disulfiram
Antagonist muscle, 145, 145*b*
  in CRAC stretching, 145–146, 146*f*
Antibiotics, food from animals treated with, 223
Antidotes, 357
Antioxidants, 218, 219*b*
  cancer prevention and, 379
  supplementary, 220*t*
Appetite
  aging affecting, 446
  leptin affecting, 241
Arm ergometry, cardiorespiratory fitness in individuals with disability and, 87, 88*t*
Arm muscles
  flexibility exercises for, 155
  isotonic exercises for, 111–112
Arrhythmias, 274, 275*b*
  smoking and, 274
Arsenic, DRI for, 213*b*
Arteries, 53, 53*b*
  exercise affecting, 56
Arteriosclerosis, 270, 271*b*, 271*f*. *See also* Atherosclerosis
Arthritis, obesity and, 176
Arthroscopic surgery, 349*b*
Artificial sweeteners, 206, 212*b*

Aspirin, in heart disease prevention, 280*b*
Atherosclerosis, 270, 271*b*, 271*f*
aging and, 445
coronary heart disease and, 271, 271*f*, 272*f*, 280*b*
smoking and, 274
Atherosclerotic plaque, 270, 271*b*, 271*f*
in coronary arteries, 271, 271*f*, 272*f*
ATP (adenosine triphosphate), 55, 55*b*
production of, 55–56, 55*b*, 56*f*
Atypical mycobacterial infection, in HIV infection/AIDS, 396*t*
Autonomic nervous system, 295, 295*b*
in stress response, 295–296

BAC. *See* Blood alcohol concentration
Back extension exercise, 115, 167
Back muscles
flexibility/stretching exercises for, 45, 152, 154, 157, 158, 167
isotonic exercises for, 112–113, 115, 117
Back pain, 345–346
assessing risk of, 365–366
causes/risk factors for, 143*b*
prevention of, 143
flexibility/stretching exercises in, 143, 167
spinal alignment and, 142*f*
Back to wall test, 365
Bacteria, 401*b*. *See also specific organism*
sexually transmitted infection caused by, 400, 401*b*
Balance, decisional, in behavior modification, 12
Balanced diet. *See* Diet, healthy/balanced
Balanced low-calorie diet, 246*t*
aging/longevity affected by, 248*b*
Ballistic stretching, 144, 145*b*
Barbiturates, dependence potential of, 416*t*
Bardet-Biedl syndrome, 241
Bariatric surgery, 253
Barriers, behavior change, identifying, 13
Basal metabolic rate, 244. *See also* Resting metabolic rate
Behavior(s), addictive, 414, 415. *See also* Addiction
Behavior change, 11–16, 13*b*, 14*b*, 25
alcohol use/abuse and, 424*b*
assessing habits and, 12–13
behavior modification strategies and, 12, 15–16
cardiorespiratory endurance and, 70, 70*b*
cardiovascular disease risk and, 281*b*
goals for, 14
realistic, 12, 37
health care consumer improvement and, 453*b*
identifying barriers to, 13
injury prevention and, 356*b*
physical activity in daily routine and, 41*b*
skin protection and, 383*b*
sleep habits and, 302*b*, 303
smoking cessation and, 15
Stages of Change Model and, 11–12, 11*b*
steps in, 13*b*
STI prevention and, 407*b*
strength/endurance/weight training and, 106*b*
time management and, 301*b*, 303
unhealthy behaviors and, 14
in weight control/nutrition, 15–16, 242*b*, 251–252
body composition assessments and, 183
eating triggers and, 241, 242*b*, 267–268
fast food and, 216*b*
sugar consumption and, 212*b*
Behavior change contracts, 12, 13*b*
Behavior modification, 12, 15–16. *See also* Behavior change
for smoking cessation, 15
for weight loss, 15–16, 251–252
Bench press, 116
Benign tumor, 368, 369*b*
BIA. *See* Bioelectrical impedance analysis
Biceps curl, 111
Biceps femoris, isotonic exercises for, 114
Biceps muscle
flexibility exercises for, 156
isotonic exercises for, 111
Bicycle, stationary
for cycle ergometer fitness test, 60, 60*f*, 61*b*, 79, 79–81*t*
for spinning, 69*b*
Bicycle accidents, reducing risk of, 358*b*
Binge drinking, 423, 423*b*, 423*f*
Binge eating
in bulimia, 255
stress and, 307
Binge eating disorder, 255–256, 255*b*
Bioelectrical impedance analysis (BIA), in body fat measurement, 181–182, 181*b*
"at home" devices based on, 182*b*
Biopsy, in cancer diagnosis, 368, 369*b*
Biotin
DRI for, 213*b*
RDA for, 211*t*
Bleeding, treatment of, 357–358
Blood alcohol concentration, 420–421, 421*b*, 422*t*
alcohol poisoning and, 423
Blood pressure, 272
exercise affecting, 59, 59*b*
in hypertension, 272. *See also* Hypertension
lowering, coronary heart disease risk and, 279, 286
measurement of, 272
normal, 272
Blood transfusion, HIV transmission and, 395
Blood vessels, 53
BMI. *See* Body mass index
BodPod, in body fat measurement, 180, 181*f*
Body composition, 10–11, 11*b*, 169–194, 171*b*. *See also* Body fat
assessment of, 178–182, 182*b*, 187–192, 189*t*, 190*t*, 192*t*, 259
behavior change and, 183
field methods for, 178–180, 179*t*
laboratory measurements and, 180–182, 180*f*, 181*f*
behavior change and, 183
definition of, 170, 171*b*
exercise affecting, 58
goals for, 183
ideal (healthy/optimal) body weight and, 170, 171, 172*f*, 182–183, 193–194, 240–241, 259
overweight/obesity and, 170, 171, 172*f*, 173
relationship to health, 171–178, 171*f*
underweight and, 176–177
Body fat, 170
losing. *See* Weight control
need for, 171–173, 171*f*, 172*f*
percentage of, 170, 171. *See also* Body composition
assessment of, 178–182, 182*b*, 187–192, 189*t*, 190*t*, 192*t*, 259
behavior change and, 183
exercise affecting, 58
health and, 171, 172, 172*f*
ideal (healthy/optimal) body weight and, 170, 171, 172*f*, 182–183, 193–194, 240–241, 259
overweight/obesity and, 170, 171, 172*f*, 173
underweight and, 176–177
regional storage/distribution of, 171–173, 171*f*, 172*f*
coronary heart disease risk and, 173, 277
Body image
assessing, 265–266
healthy weight and, 173
Body mass index (BMI), 178–179, 179*b*, 179*t*, 187, 194, 259–260
Body temperature regulation, 326, 327*f*
Body weight. *See also* Obese/obesity
ideal (healthy/optimal), 182–183, 193–194, 240–241, 259–260
benefits of, 173
body composition/percent of body fat and, 170, 171, 172, 172*f*, 182–183, 193–194, 240–241, 259
body mass index and, 178–179, 179*t*, 194, 259–260
energy balance and, 243–245, 243*f*, 244*f*, 245*t*
losing. *See* Weight control
Bone(s)
aging affecting, 445–446, 445*f*
movement limitations and, 141
Bone mass
age-related changes in, 7, 445–446, 445*f*
exercise affecting, 7–8, 7*f*, 8*f*, 59
loss of (osteoporosis), 7, 7*b*, 445–446
Borg Rating of Perceived Exertion, 62, 62*f*, 63*b*, 93–94
Boron, DRI for, 213*b*
Botulism, 222
Bovine somatotropin, milk from animals treated with, 223
Brachialis muscle, isotonic exercises for, 111

Brachioradialis muscle, isotonic exercises for, 111
Brain
age-related changes in, 446
"exercising" mind and, 446
arteries supplying, atherosclerotic blockage of, 271–272, 272*f*
Breast cancer, 371*f*, 372–375, 372*f*, 373*b*
metastasis of, 369*f*
self-examination in detection of, 373, 374*b*
Breastfeeding (lactation), RDAs during, 210–211*t*
Breast self-examination, 373, 374*b*
Breathing
exercise affecting, 57, 58
stopped, CPR for, 358–359
Breathing exercises, 305
Bulimia nervosa, 177, 255, 255*b*
Burnout, 304*b*, 305*b*
Buttocks
flexibility exercises for, 153, 157, 158, 159
isotonic exercises for, 114

Caffeine, 426–427, 427*b*, 428*b*
in supplements, 220*t*, 428*b*
Calcium, 203, 204*t*, 214–215
DRI for, 213*b*
food sources of, 204*t*, 215
in healthy/balanced diet, 214*t*
RDA for, 210*t*, 214
supplementary, 215
weight control and, 248*b*
Calf muscles
flexibility exercises for, 150, 152
isotonic exercises for, 117
Calf stretch, 45
Calipers, for skinfold measurements, 179
Caloric expenditure. *See* Energy balance; Energy expenditure
Caloric restriction
aging/longevity affected by, 248*b*
weight control and, 243–245, 243*f*, 244*f*, 245*t*
Calorie(s), 197, 197*b*
energy balance and, 243–245, 243*f*, 245*t*. *See also* Energy balance
in healthy/balanced diet, 206, 214*t*
RDA for, diet analysis and, 229
reducing intake of, 242*b*
strength/endurance/weight training and, 108*b*
Campral. *See* Acamprosate
Cancer, 367–389. *See also specific type or structure affected*
definition of, 368–369, 369*b*
early detection of, 389
incidence/death rates of, 368, 371*f*, 372*f*
normal cell transformation and, 369, 370*f*
obesity and, 176
phytochemicals in prevention of, 219*b*
risk factors for, 378–384. *See also specific factor*
determining, 387
self-examination in detection of
breast cancer and, 373, 374*b*
skin cancer, 376, 377*b*
testicular cancer and, 375, 376*b*
types of, 370–378, 371*f*
warning signs of, 369, 370*b*
Candidiasis, (*Candida albicans*/yeast infection), 404
Canon, Walter, 296
Capillaries, 53, 53*b*
Carbohydrate(s), 197–199, 197*b*, 220*t*
diets low in, 215*b*, 246*t*, 247*b*, 248*b*
DRI for, 213*b*
diet analysis and, 229
as energy source, 55, 56, 56*f*, 197, 217, 217*f*, 217*t*, 218*f*
food sources of, 197, 197*t*, 198–199, 198*f*, 198*t*
in healthy/balanced diet, 197, 197*f*, 206, 214*t*
physical fitness and, 217, 217*f*
supplementary, 220*t*
types of, 197–198
Carbon monoxide, 336, 336*f*, 337*b*
Carcinogens, 369, 369*b*, 370*f*
occupational, 383–384
Cardiac output, 53, 53*b*
age affecting, 445, 445*f*
exercise affecting, 56, 57–58
Cardiac rate. *See* Heart rate
Cardiologist, 452*b*
Cardiopulmonary resuscitation (CPR), 358–359
Cardiorespiratory endurance, 9–10, 9*b*, 10*f*, 51–94, 53*b*, 53*f*. *See also* Aerobic exercise
adaptations to exercise and, 57–58, 57*b*
aerobic system in development of, 55, 55–56
cross training in, 66–67, 67*b*
in daily living, 52, 59, 59*b*
designing program for, 60–64
cool-down activities for, 45, 64
personalization of, 64–66, 66*b*, 67*b*, 68*b*, 91
warm-up activities and, 45, 61
workout activities and, 61–64, 62*f*, 63*b*, 64*b*, 64*f*
evaluation of, 59–60, 60*f*, 75–88
goals for, 60
health benefits of, 52, 59, 59*b*
importance of, 52
injuries and, 344
interval training in, 67–68, 67*b*
maintenance of, 65
motivation for, 68–70
responses to exercise and, 56–57, 57*b*
training techniques for, 66–68
weight control/weight loss program and, 249–251, 250*b*, 251*t*
Cardiorespiratory fitness. *See* Cardiorespiratory endurance
Cardiorespiratory system, 52–53. *See also* Cardiovascular disease
exercise and training affecting, 56–58, 57*b*, 58*f*
Cardiovascular disease, 7, 7*b*, 269–291, 271*b*
arteriosclerosis, 270, 271*b*, 271*f*
coronary heart disease, 271, 271*b*, 272*f*, 273*b*. *See also* Coronary heart disease
hypertension, 272–273, 273*b*, 273*f*
incidence/prevalence/costs of, 270, 271*f*
risk of developing, 274*b*. *See also* Coronary heart disease, risk factors for
body fat storage and, 173
exercise affecting, 7, 7*f*, 59, 59*b*
hereditary factors in, 277, 278*t*
risk assessment and, 291
obesity and, 175
reducing, 281*b*
understanding, 289–290
stroke, 271–272, 271*b*, 272*f*
types of, 270–273, 271*f*, 272*f*, 273*b*, 273*f*
Cardiovascular system, 53, 54*f*, 55*f*. *See also* Cardiovascular disease
adaptation to exercise by, 57–58
response to exercise by, 56–57
L-Carnitine, supplementary, 220*t*
Carotenoids. *See also* Vitamin A
DRI for, 213*b*
Carotid artery, heart rate measured at, 55*f*
Cartilage, 141*b*, 141*f*
movement limitations and, 141
torn, 349–350
Cat stretch, 167
Cell transformation, in cancer, 369, 370*f*
Cellulite, 254*t*
Central nervous system, age-related changes in, 446
Cervical cancer, 378
HPV infection and, 378, 379*b*, 383
Chancre, syphilitic, 402, 402*f*, 403*b*
CHD. *See* Coronary heart disease
Checkups (medical), 454, 454*t*
successful aging and, 447
Chemical dependence, 416, 417*b*
Chest muscles
flexibility exercises for, 156
isotonic exercises for, 112, 116, 117
Chest pain, in coronary heart disease/heart attack, 271, 273*b*
Chest press, for muscular strength evaluation, 123–125, 123*f*, 125*t*
Chest stretch, 156
Children, RDAs for, 210–211*t*
Chlamydia infection, 400–401, 400*f*, 401*b*
incidence of, 393*f*, 400, 400*f*
Chloride, DRI for, 213*b*
Choking, treatment of, 355–356
Cholesterol, 200, 275–276, 276*b*
coronary heart disease risk and, 200, 275–276, 275*f*, 276*b*, 278*t*, 285–286
lowering, 279, 280*b*, 280*t*
dietary, 201
in healthy/balanced diet, 207, 214*t*
reducing intake of, 207, 279, 280*t*
DRI for, 213*b*
fatty acids affecting, 199, 199*t*, 200
obesity and, 175
omega-3 fatty acid affecting, 199
smoking and, 274
Choline
DRI for, 213*b*
RDA for, 211*t*

Chromium
- DRI for, 213b
- RDA for, 210t

Chromium picolinate, supplementary, 220t
Cigarette smoking. *See* Smoking
"Clap." *See* Gonorrhea
"Club drugs," 418–419
Cocaine (coke), 418, 419b, 420t
- dependence potential and, 416, 416t, 418
- long term complications of use of, 419, 420t

Codeine, dependence potential of, 416, 416t
Coenzyme Q-10, supplementary, 220t
Coke. *See* Cocaine
Cold/cold weather, exercise in, 331–333, 332b, 333f, 334b, 341–342
Cold medications, abuse of, 419
Cold sore (herpes), 400
Colonoscopy, in colorectal cancer screening, 372
Colon and rectal cancer (colorectal cancer), 371–372, 371f, 372f, 373b
Complete proteins, 201, 201b
Complex carbohydrates, 198, 199b. *See also* Carbohydrate(s)
- in balanced diet, 197, 197f
- physical fitness and, 217

Compulsive gambling, 415
Compulsive shoppers/spenders, 415
Concentric muscle action (positive work), 100, 100f, 101b
Conditioning. *See* Exercise training; Workout
Conditioning period, primary (workout). *See* Workout
Condoms, STI risk reduction and, 405
Connective tissue, movement limitations and, 141
Consumer issues, fitness products and, 448–449
- evaluating, 461

Contemplation stage, of behavior change, 11
Contract-relax (CR) stretching, 145
Contract-relax/antagonist contract (CRAC) stretching, 145–146, 146f
Contracts, in behavior modification, 12, 13b
- weight loss and, 15

Convection, heat loss by, 327, 327b
Cool-down, 39, 39b, 45
- for cardiorespiratory exercise program, 45, 64

Copper
- DRI for, 213b
- RDA for, 210t

Core strength, measuring, 137–138
Corn syrup, high fructose, reducing intake of, 206, 212b
Coronary arteries, atherosclerotic blockage of, 271, 271f, 272f
Coronary heart disease, 271, 271b, 272f, 273b. *See also* Heart attack
- risk factors for, 273–278, 274b, 275f, 278t
  - aging, 277, 278t
  - alcohol consumption, 278, 278t
  - assessment of, 285–286
  - cholesterol, 200, 275–276, 275f, 276b, 278t, 285–286
    - lowering, 279, 280b, 280t
  - contributory/secondary, 273, 277–278, 278t
  - diabetes, 277, 278t
  - exercise affecting, 7, 7f, 276–277, 277f, 279, 280b
  - gender, 277, 278t
  - hereditary, 277, 278t
    - risk assessment and, 291
  - hypertension, 274–275, 275f, 278t, 286
    - lowering, 279
  - major/primary, 273, 274–277, 275f, 275t, 276b, 278t
  - modification of, 278–281, 278t, 279f, 281b
  - obesity and overweight, 175, 277, 278t
  - omega-3 fatty acids affecting, 199–200
  - personality type, 297–298, 297t
  - physical inactivity, 276–277, 278t
    - exercise affecting, 7, 7f, 276–277, 277f, 279, 280b
  - reducing risk and, 278–281, 279f, 280b, 280t, 281b
  - smoking, 274, 274f, 278t, 286, 421t, 426
    - cessation and, 278–279
  - stress, 278, 278t
    - reduction of, 279–281
  - understanding, 289–290

Cortisol, 295, 295b
- in stress response, 295, 296
  - illness and, 301

Cough suppressants, abuse of, 419
Counter conditioning, in behavior modification, 12
- weight loss and, 16

CPR (cardiopulmonary resuscitation), 358–359
Crabs (pubic lice), 404, 405b
"Crack babies," 419
CRAC stretching. *See* Contract-relax/antagonist contract (CRAC) stretching
Cramp (muscle), 149b
- heat injury and, 329

Creatine, supplementary, 220t
Creeping obesity, 174, 175b, 175f
Cross training, 66–67, 67b
CR stretching. *See* Contract-relax (CR) stretching
Cryokinetics, 353, 353b, 353f
Curl up, 158
Curl-up test, 103, 103b, 132, 135t
CVD. *See* Cardiovascular disease
Cycle ergometer fitness test, 60, 60f, 61b, 79, 79–81t
Cytomegalovirus infection, in HIV infection/AIDS, 396t

Daily Values, on food labels, 209, 209b, 209f
Dairy products, weight control and, 248b
DASH (Dietary Approach to Stop Hypertension) eating plan, 275
Decisional balance, in behavior modification, 12
Deep knee bends, injury and, 157
Dehydration, 330b, 331b
- effects of, 331b
- exercise in hot environment and, 330b, 331b
- mountain sickness and, 335

Dehydroepiandrosterone (DHEA), muscle increase and, 102b
Delayed-onset muscle soreness (DOMS), 346–347, 347b
Deltoid muscles
- flexibility exercises for, 156
- isotonic exercises for, 112, 116, 117

Denial, 415b
- addiction and, 414

Depade. *See* Naltrexone
Dependence, 415, 415b
- alcohol, 422–423. *See also* Alcohol use/abuse
- chemical, 416, 417b

Dermatologist, 452b
Dextromethorphan (DXM), 419, 421t
Dextrose, reducing intake of, 212b
DHEA. *See* Dehydroepiandrosterone
Diabetes, 7, 7b, 175b
- coronary heart disease risk and, 277, 278t
- exercise affecting risk of, 7, 7f, 59, 59b
- obesity and, 175–176
- reducing risk of, 177b

Diaphragm (breathing muscle), exercise affecting, 58
Diastolic blood pressure, 272. *See also* Blood pressure
Diet, 195–238. *See also* Nutrition
- analysis of, 229–231, 237–238
- cancer risk and, 379–381, 381b
  - colorectal cancer, 372, 379–381
- exercise and, 249–251, 250b, 251t, 261
- fast food and, 216b
- food safety/technology and, 222–224, 222f, 223b
- healthy/balanced, 197, 197f, 206–207, 207t
  - behavior change and, 212b, 216b
  - cancer prevention and, 372, 379–381, 381b
  - coronary heart disease risk lowered by, 279, 280b
  - guidelines for, 205–218, 212b, 213b, 216b
  - low-calorie, 246t
    - aging/longevity affected by, 248b
  - planning, 235–236, 246–249, 246t, 247b, 248b
    - RDAs/MyPyramid/food labels in, 208–209, 208f, 209f, 210–211t, 214t, 235–236
  - sample diet, 209, 214t
  - setting goals for, 233
  - successful aging and, 446
  - supplements and, 218–219
- muscle mass gain and, 252
- special considerations and, 209–215
- strength/endurance/weight training and, 108b, 217

supplements and, 218–221, 220*t*, 221*b*. *See also* Dietary supplements
for weight control/weight loss, 246–249, 246*t*, 247*b*, 248*b*. *See also* Weight control
for weight gain, 252
Dietary Approach to Stop Hypertension (DASH) eating plan, 275
Dietary Guidelines for Americans, 205–206
Dietary Reference Intakes (DRIS), 208, 213*b*
Dietary supplements, 218–221, 220*t*, 221*b*
ergogenic aids, 448, 449*b*
fraud detection and, 221*b*
in healthful diet, 218–219
regulation of, 219–221, 221*b*
stress reduction and, 307*b*
Diet pills, 254*t*
Digital rectal exam, in prostate cancer screening, 375
Dip exercise, 117
Disability
assessing cardiorespiratory fitness and, 87, 88*t*
cardiorespiratory exercise for person with, 69*b*
Disordered eating patterns. *See also* Eating disorders
stress and, 307
Distress (negative stress), 295, 295*b*, 295*f*, 304*b*
Disulfiram, for alcohol dependence, 422
DNA, damage to, cell transformation in cancer and, 369, 370*f*
viruses causing, 383
Doctor. *See* Health care provider
DOMS. *See* Delayed-onset muscle soreness
Donkey kick, injury and, 159
Drinking water, contaminated, environmental health and, 4
DRIS. *See* Dietary Reference Intakes
Driving stress, road rage and, 299, 300*b*
Drowning, reducing risk of, 358*b*
Drug(s), illicit, 416*t*, 417–429, 417*b*
Drug addiction. *See* Addiction; Substance use/abuse
Dual energy X-ray absorptiometry (DXA), for body fat measurement, 180, 180*f*, 181*b*
Dumbbell fly, 112
Duration of exercise, 39, 39*b*, 39*t*
in cardiorespiratory workout, 62–63, 64*f*
energy continuum and, 56, 57*f*
in flexibility/stretching routine, 146–148, 147*t*
DXA. *See* Dual energy X-ray absorptiometry
DXM (dextromothorphan), 419, 421*t*
Dynamic (isotonic) exercise, 99, 99*b*
weight-training program/exercises and, 106, 111–117
Dynamic stretching, 144, 145*b*

EAR. *See* Estimated Average Requirement
Eating disorders, 177, 254–256. *See also* Diet; Nutrition
stress and, 307
Eating habits. *See also* Diet; Nutrition
assessment of, 229–231, 237–238
weight loss and, 15, 242
changes in, burnout and, 304*b*
triggers and, 241, 242*b*, 267–268
Eccentric muscle action (negative work), 100, 100*f*, 101*b*
Echinacea, 220*t*
Ecstasy (MDMA/methylenedioxymethamphetamine), 418, 421*t*
dependence potential of, 416*t*
Effective temperature
heat index, 328, 328*f*
wind-chill index, 333, 333*f*
Elbow flexor muscles, isotonic exercises for, 111
Elderly. *See* Age/aging
Emergency room specialist, 451, 452*b*
Emotional (mental) health, 3, 3*f*
assessment of, 22, 459
exercise affecting, 7*f*, 8, 59, 59*b*
Empty calories, avoiding, 206
EMR. *See* Exercise metabolic rate
Endocrine system, 295, 295*b*
in stress response, 295, 296
Endometrial cancer, 377
Endorphins, 295, 295*b*
in stress reduction, exercise and, 303
in stress response, 295
Endurance
cardiorespiratory. *See* Cardiorespiratory endurance
muscular. *See* Muscular endurance
Energy, 55
for arm ergometry, 88*t*
DRI for, 213*b*
diet analysis and, 229
expenditure of. *See* Energy balance; Energy expenditure
production of, 55–56, 56*f*, 57*f*
requirements for, 108*b*
Energy balance. *See also* Energy expenditure; Energy intake
weight control and, 243–245, 243*f*, 244*f*, 245*t*
exercise/physical activity and, 249–251, 250*b*, 251*t*, 261
Energy continuum, 56, 57*f*
Energy expenditure. *See also* Calorie(s); Energy balance
diet analysis and, 229
estimating, 229, 244, 249–251, 251*t*, 261
resting (resting metabolic rate), 97*b*, 244, 245*b*
strength training affecting, 96–97, 249
weight control and, 243–244, 243*f*, 244*f*
exercise/physical activity and, 249–251, 250*b*, 251*t*, 261
Energy intake. *See also* Calorie(s); Energy balance
weight control and, 243
Environment
accidents/unintentional injury and, 355
exercise and, 325–342. *See also* Environmental health
overweight/obesity and, 241–242, 242*b*
Environmental health, 3*f*, 4, 325–342
air pollution and, 4, 335–336, 336*f*, 337*b*, 341–342
altitude and, 334–335, 334*f*, 335*f*, 341–342
assessment of, 22, 460
cold/cold weather and, 331–333, 332*b*, 333*f*, 334*b*, 341–342
heat/hot weather and, 326–331, 328*f*, 329*f*, 330*b*, 331*b*, 341–342
water contamination and, 4
Epinephrine, 295, 295*b*
in stress response, 295
Erector spinae muscles
flexibility exercises for, 152, 154
isotonic exercises for, 115
Ergogenic aids, 448, 449*b*
Ergometer
arm, 87, 88*t*
cycle, 60, 60*f*, 61*b*, 79, 79–81*t*
Escherichia coli O157:H7, foodborne infection caused by, 222
Essential amino acids, 201, 201*b*
Essential fat, 171, 171*b*
Estimated 1 RM test, 103, 127–128, 128*t*
Estimated Average Requirement (EAR), 213*b*
Ethnicity, wellness issues and, 5*b*
Ethyl alcohol. *See* Alcohol
Eustress, 295, 295*b*, 295*f*
Evaporation, heat loss by, 327, 327*b*
Exercise, 5–11. *See also* Exercise prescription; Exercise training
adherence to program for/lifetime fitness and wellness and, 440–441, 441*b*, 442*t*, 443*b*. *See also* Lifetime fitness/wellness
successful aging and, 446, 447–448
cancer risk/prevention and, 381*b*, 382, 382*f*
colorectal cancer, 372
cardiorespiratory adaptations to, 57–58, 57*b*
cardiorespiratory responses to, 56–57, 57*b*
definition of, 6, 7*b*
designing program for, 36–40. *See also* Exercise prescription
diet and, 249–251, 250*b*, 251*t*, 261
duration of, 39, 39*b*, 39*t*. *See also* Duration of exercise
energy sources for, 55–56, 56*f*, 57*f*
environment and, 325–342. *See also* Environmental health
air pollution and, 4, 335–336, 336*f*, 337*b*, 341–342
altitude and, 334–335, 334*f*, 335*f*, 341–342
temperature and, 326, 327*f*, 341–342
cold/cold weather and, 331–333, 332*b*, 333*f*, 334*b*, 341–342
heat/hot weather and, 326–331, 328*f*, 329*f*, 330*b*, 331*b*, 341–342
equipment for, 64*b*, 448–449
fitness evaluation and, 459–460. *See also* Fitness evaluation
health assessment and, 27, 29

frequency of, 39, 39*b*, 39*t*, 40*f*. *See also* Frequency of exercise
goal setting and, 36–38, 37*f*. *See also* Fitness goals
health benefits of, 6–9, 7*f*, 8*f*, 9*f*, 59, 59*b*
threshold for, 40–42, 41*b*, 41*f*
health-related fitness and, 9–11
principles of, 31–50
heart disease risk affected by, 7, 7*f*, 276–277, 277*f*, 279, 280*b*
injuries and. *See* Exercise-related injuries
intensity of, 39, 39*b*, 39*t*. *See also* Intensity of exercise
mode of, 38, 39*b*, 40*f*
for cardiorespiratory workout, 63–64, 63*b*, 64*f*
obesity prevention/treatment and, 249–251, 250*b*, 251*t*, 261. *See also* Energy balance; Weight control
in older adulthood, 444–448, 444*f*, 445*f*, 447*b*, 467–468
selecting activities for, 38, 40*f*, 47. *See also* Exercise prescription
specificity of, as training principle, 33–34, 33*b*, 34*b*, 105*b*
strength/endurance/weight training and, 104, 105*b*
in stress management, 303–304, 303*f*
sudden cardiac death and, 280*b*
for weight control/weight loss, 249–251, 250*b*, 251*t*, 261. *See also* Energy balance; Weight control
for weight gain, 252
Exercise clothing
for cold environment, 332–333, 332*b*, 333*f*, 334*b*
for hot environment, 329
Exercise cycle
for cardiorespiratory endurance evaluation (cycle ergometer fitness test), 60, 60*f*, 61*b*, 79, 79–81*t*
for spinning, 69*b*
Exercise equipment, 64*b*, 448–449
Exercise metabolic rate (EMR), 244, 245*b*
Exercise prescription, 36–40, 37*b*. *See also specific component and specific type of training*
for cardiorespiratory endurance, 60–64
cool-down, 39, 39*b*, 45
goal setting and, 36–38, 37*f*. *See also* Fitness goals
mode of exercise and, 38, 39*b*, 40*f*
for older adults, 447–448
personalization of, 39–40, 47
pregnancy and, 441–444, 444*f*, 463
for strength/weight training program, 107–108, 107*f*, 109–110, 109*t*, 110*t*
sample exercises and, 111–117
warm-up and, 38–39, 39*b*, 45
workout and, 39, 39*t*
Exercise-related injuries, 344–354. *See also specific type*
acute muscle soreness, 346, 347*b*
back pain, 345–346
assessing risk of, 365–366
causes of, 344–345
delayed-onset muscle soreness, 346–347, 347*b*
ligament sprains, 348–349, 348*f*, 349*b*
lower extremity involvement and, 350–352
management of, 352–354
arthroscopic surgery in, 349*b*
initial treatment and, 352–353
rehabilitation and, 353, 353*f*
muscle strain, 347–348, 347*b*, 347*f*
patellofemoral pain syndrome, 350–351, 350*f*, 351*b*
prevention of, 363
risk of, 344–345, 345*b*
reducing, 354*b*
shin splints, 351, 351*b*, 351*f*
stress fractures, 351–352, 351*b*, 352*f*
tendonitis, 348, 349*b*
torn cartilage, 349–350
Exercise shoes, selecting, 34*b*
Exercise training. *See also specific type of training*
overload principle and, 32, 33*b*, 33*f*. *See also* Progressive resistance exercise
overtraining and, 35, 35*b*, 36*b*
principles of, 32–36
progression principle and, 32–33, 33*b*, 33*f*
recuperation principle and, 34–35, 35*b*, 35*f*
reversibility and, 35, 35*b*, 35*f*
specificity of exercise and, 33–34, 33*b*, 34*b*, 105*b*
strength/endurance/weight training and, 104, 105*b*
Exertion, perceived, rate of, 62, 62*f*, 63*b*, 93–94
Exhaustion
feelings of, burnout and, 304*b*
heat, 330
Exhaustion stage, of general adaptation syndrome, 300
Experience(s), stress affected by, 298
Extensor digitorum longus muscle, flexibility exercises for, 151
Extensor hallucis longus muscle, flexibility exercises for, 151
Extreme environment, exercise in. *See* Environmental health
Eyes
age-related changes in, 446
poisons in, treatment of, 357
protection of from sun damage, successful aging and, 447

"Fad diets," 248*b*
Falls, reducing risk of, 358*b*
Family practitioner, 451
FAS. *See* Fetal alcohol syndrome
Fascia, 97, 97*b*, 97*f*
Fast food, 216*b*, 242
Fast-twitch fibers, 100, 101*b*, 101*t*
exercise intensity and, 101, 102*f*
individual variations/genetics and, 101
Fat (body), 170
losing. *See* Weight control
need for, 171–173, 171*f*, 172*f*
percentage of, 170, 171. *See also* Body composition
assessment of, 178–182, 182*b*, 187–192, 189*t*, 190*t*, 192*t*, 259
behavior change and, 183
exercise affecting, 58
health and, 171, 172, 172*f*
ideal (healthy/optimal) body weight and, 170, 171, 172*f*, 182–183, 193–194, 240–241, 259
overweight/obesity and, 170, 171, 172*f*, 173
underweight and, 176–177
regional storage/distribution of, 171–173, 171*f*, 172*f*
coronary heart disease risk and, 173, 277
Fat(s), 199–201, 199*b*, 199*t*, 200*f*
cancer risk and, 372, 379
DRI for, 213*b*
diet analysis and, 229
as energy source, 55, 56, 56*f*, 199, 217*t*
food sources of, 197*t*, 199, 199*t*, 200, 200*b*, 200*f*, 201
in healthy/balanced diet, 197, 197*f*, 206–207, 214*t*
diet analysis and, 229
reducing intake of, 206–207, 207*b*
coronary heart disease risk and, 279, 280*b*, 280*t*
types of, 199–200, 199*t*
Fat-soluble vitamins, 202*t*
Fatty acids, 199–200, 199*b*, 199*t*, 200*f*
DRI for, 213*b*
Fecal immunochemical test, for colorectal cancer screening, 372
Fecal stool blood test, for colorectal cancer screening, 372
Fee-for-service insurance plan, 451
Female condoms, STI risk reduction and, 405
Females. *See* Women
Fetal alcohol syndrome (FAS), 424–425, 425*b*
Fetus
HIV infection of, 395
maternal alcohol use and (fetal alcohol syndrome), 424–425, 425*b*
maternal drug use and, 419
maternal tobacco use and, 426
Fever blister (herpes), 400
Fiber (dietary), 198, 199*b*
in cancer prevention, 372, 379
DRI for, 213*b*
Fiber(s) (muscle), 97, 97*f*
in muscle action, 98, 99*f*
recruitment of, 101, 101*b*, 102*f*
muscular strength and, 102, 103*f*
types of, 100, 101*t*
individual variations/genetics and, 100–101
"Fight or flight" response, 296, 297*b*, 300
Financial responsibilities, stress and, 298–299
reducing, 303
Fire, reducing risk of, 358*b*

Fish
consumption of during pregnancy, 200*b*
contamination of, 200*b*
omega-3 fatty acids in, 199–200
FIT/FITT principle, 39, 39*t*
in cardiorespiratory workout, 61–64, 62*f*, 63*b*, 64*f*
in stretching routine, 146–148, 147*t*
Fitness. *See also* Physical health/fitness; Wellness
basic principles of
exercise and, 31–50
understanding, 1–29
books/magazines related to, 449
evaluation of, 459–460. *See also* Fitness evaluation
exercise/activity for, 9–11
lifetime, 439–468. *See also* Lifetime fitness/wellness
during older adulthood, 444–448, 444*f*, 445*f*, 447*b*, 467–468
during pregnancy, 441–444, 444*f*, 463
Fitness evaluation, 459–460
for body composition, 178–182, 182*b*, 187–192, 189*t*, 190*t*, 192*t*, 259
for cardiorespiratory endurance, 59–60, 60*f*, 75–88
for flexibility, 143–144, 163–164, 164*t*
health status evaluation and, 27, 29
for muscular endurance, 103, 131–135
for muscular strength, 103, 123–129
Fitness expert, 450*b*
Fitness facility/health club, selecting, 443*b*, 450*b*
Fitness goals, 36–38, 37*f*
lifetime fitness/wellness and, 37
for muscular strength/endurance, 108–109
obstacles to achieving, recognition of, 38
realistic, 12, 37
Fitness products, 448–449
evaluation of, 461
Flexibility, 10, 11*b*, 139–167, 141*b*. *See also* Stretches
back pain risk/prevention and, 143, 167, 365–366
benefits of, 142–143
cool-down after cardiorespiratory workout and, 64
in daily living, 140
evaluation of, 143–144, 163–164, 164*t*
intensity of stretching and, 39
joint health and, 142
mechanics of, 140–142, 141*f*, 141*t*, 142*f*
motivation for maintenance of, 149
training program for. *See also* Stretches
designing, 144–149, 145*b*
injury prevention/hazardous exercises and, 147, 149*b*
contraindicated and substitute exercises and, 157–159
progression log for, 165–166
sample exercises in, 150–159
weight training and, 104
Flexibility progression log, 165–166
Fluid intake, exercise in hot environment and, 330*b*
Fluoride, 204*t*
DRI for, 213*b*
RDA for, 210*t*
Folate/folic acid, 202*t*
DRI for, 213*b*
RDA for, 211*t*
supplementary, 212
Food. *See also* Diet; Nutrient(s); Nutrition
animal treatment with antibiotics and hormones and, 223
energy from, 55
organic, 223, 223*b*
proper handling/storage of, 222, 223*b*
Food additives, 222–223
Foodborne illness, 222, 223*b*
Food cravings, stress and, 304*b*, 307
Food diary
3-day diet record, 229–231
weight control and, 246–247
Food intake. *See* Energy intake
Food labels, planning healthy diet and, 208–209, 209*f*
Food safety/technology, 222–224, 222*f*, 223*b*
additives and, 222–223
foodborne illness and, 222, 223*b*
irradiation and, 223–224
Footwear, running/exercise
injuries and, 344
selecting, 34*b*
Free radicals, 218, 219*b*
cancer risk and, 379
Frequency of exercise, 39, 39*b*, 39*t*, 40*f*
in cardiorespiratory workout, 61, 64*f*
in flexibility/stretching routine, 146–148, 147*t*
in strength/weight training program, 107, 107*f*
Fructose (fruit sugar), 198
in high fructose corn syrup, reducing intake of, 206, 212*b*
reducing intake of, 212*b*
Fruit, in healthy diet, 206
Fruit sugar. *See* Fructose
Functional capacity, age-related changes in, 445

Galactose, 198
Gallbladder disease, obesity and, 176
Gambling, compulsive, 415
Gaming, as addiction, 415
Gamma-hydroxybutyrate (GHB), 418
Gastric banding, 253
Gastric bypass surgery, 253
Gastrocnemius muscle
flexibility/stretching exercises for, 45, 150, 152
isotonic exercises for, 117
Gastroenterologist, 452*b*
Gender
coronary heart disease risk and, 277, 278*t*
strength/endurance/weight training differences and, 105
stress levels and, 298
General adaptation syndrome, 300, 301*b*
Genetics
cancer risk and, 378–379
breast cancer, 374
colorectal cancer, 372
coronary heart disease risk and, 277, 278*t*
assessment of, 291
muscle fiber types and, 101
obesity and, 173*b*, 241
Genital herpes, 399–400
incidence of, 393*f*, 400
Genital warts, 399, 399*b*. *See also* Human papillomavirus (HPV) infection
incidence of, 393*f*, 399
GHB (gamma-hydroxybutyrate), 418
Ghrelin, 241, 241*b*
GI. *See* Glycemic index
Ginkgo biloba, 220*t*
Glucose, 197, 197*b*
as energy source, 55, 197
reducing intake of, 212*b*
Gluteals, flexibility exercises for, 153, 154
Gluteus maximus
flexibility exercises for, 152, 155
isotonic exercises for, 113
Glycemic index, 215*b*, 248
Glycogen, 197, 197*b*
as energy source, 55, 197
Glycolysis, 55, 55*b*
Goals
behavior change, 12, 14
fitness. *See* Fitness goals
national wellness, 5, 6*b*
realistic, 12, 37
Golgi tendon organ(s), 142, 143*b*
Gonorrhea, 401–402, 401*b*, 401*f*
incidence of, 393*f*, 401, 401*f*
Grains (whole), in healthy diet, 206
Grapefruit diet, 248*b*
Group health insurance, 451
Growth hormones, food from animals treated with, 223
Gynecologist, 452*b*
Gynoid pattern, 172*f*, 173, 173*b*

Hair, age-related changes in, 446
Hamstring curl, 114
Hamstring muscles
flexibility/stretching exercises for, 45, 152, 158
isotonic exercises for, 113, 114
in spinal alignment/low back disease, 142*f*, 143
Hamstring stretch, sitting, 158
Hand weights, 448
Harsh environment, exercise in. *See* Environmental health
HBV. *See* Hepatitis B
HDL. *See* High-density lipoproteins
Head rotation, muscles used in (neck muscles), flexibility exercises for, 156, 159
Health, 2. *See also* Wellness
body composition and, 171–178, 171*f*
emotional (mental), 3, 3*f*
assessment of, 22, 459
exercise affecting, 7*f*, 8, 59, 59*b*

environmental, 3*f*, 4
assessment of, 22, 460
healthy weight and, 173
intellectual, 3, 3*f*
assessment of, 22, 459
overweight/obesity and, 173, 175–176
physical, 2–3, 3*f*
assessment of, 21–22, 459
social, 3*f*, 4
assessment of, 22, 459
spiritual, 3–4, 3*f*, 4*f*
assessment of, 23, 460
development of in stress management, 306
stress and, 299–302, 300*f*
assessing risk for illness and, 321–323
burnout and, 304*b*
underweight and, 176–177, 176*f*
Health benefits of exercise, 6–9, 7*f*, 8*f*, 9*f*, 59, 59*b*
threshold for, 40–42, 41*b*, 41*f*
Health care choices, lifetime fitness/wellness and, 449–455, 453*b*
assessing need for health care provider visit and, 453–454
communication with health care provider and, 454–455
insurance and, 450–451, 451*b*, 465–466
regular checkups and, 454, 454*t*
selecting health care provider and, 451–453, 452*b*
Health care provider
communicating with, 454–455
need for visit to, 453–454
selecting, 451–453, 452*b*
Health club, selecting, 443*b*, 450*b*
Health information, sources of, 14*b*
Health insurance, 450–451, 451*b*, 465–466
Health Maintenance Organization (HMO), 451
Health-related fitness. *See* Fitness
Health risk status, assessment of, 12–13
Healthy diet. *See* Diet, healthy/balanced
Healthy People 2010, 5, 6*b*
Heart, 53, 54*f*
exercise affecting, 57
Heart attack (myocardial infarction), 271, 271*b*, 272*f*, 273*b*. *See also* Coronary heart disease
aspirin in prevention of, 280*b*
assessing risk for, 285–286
exercise protecting against injury during, 7, 7*f*
smoking and, 274
Heartbeat, stopped, CPR for, 358–359
Heart disease, 271, 271*b*, 272*f*, 273*b*. *See also* Coronary heart disease
Heart rate, 53, 55*f*
age affecting, 61, 62*f*, 445, 445*f*
exercise affecting, 56
altitude and, 334*f*, 335
in heat/hot weather, 328, 329*f*
exercise intensity estimated by, 39, 61–62, 62*f*
maximal, 61, 62*f*
target, 61–62, 61*b*, 62*f*, 89–90
Heart rate reserve (HRR), 61, 61*b*, 62*f*
Heat/hot weather, exercise in, 326–331, 328*f*, 329*f*, 330*b*, 331*b*, 341–342
acclimatization and, 329, 329*b*
fluid intake/dehydration and, 330*b*, 331*b*
heat loss and, 327–329
Heat index, 328, 328*f*
Heat injury/illness (heat cramps/exhaustion/stroke), 326, 328, 328*f*, 329–330, 329*b*
Heat loss, 327–328, 328*f*, 329*f*
Heimlich maneuver, for choking victim, 356, 357*f*
Hematologist, 452*b*
Hepatitis B, 398–399, 399*b*
incidence of, 393*f*
Hereditary factors
cancer risk and, 378–379
breast cancer, 374
colorectal cancer, 372
coronary heart disease risk and, 277, 278*t*
risk assessment and, 291
muscle fiber types and, 101
obesity and, 173*b*, 241
Heroin, 420*t*
dependence potential of, 416, 416*t*
Herpes infection, 399–400, 399*b*
genital, 399–400
incidence of, 393*f*, 400
High-density lipoproteins/high-density cholesterol (HDL/HDL cholesterol), 200, 201, 275–276, 275*b*, 276*b*, 286
High-fiber diet, 198
in cancer prevention, 372, 379
High fructose corn syrup, reducing intake of, 206, 212*b*
High-impact activities, 38
High protein diet, 247*b*, 248*b*
Hip and gluteal stretch, 153
Hip muscles
flexibility/stretching exercises for, 45, 152, 153, 155
isotonic exercise for, 113
in spinal alignment/low back disease, 142*f*, 143
HIV (human immunodeficiency virus), 393, 393*b*. *See also* HIV infection/AIDS
HIV infection/AIDS, 393–398
incidence of, 393–394, 393*f*, 394*f*
worldwide distribution of, 397*b*
opportunistic infections and, 395, 396*t*
stages of, 394–395, 395*f*
testing for, 406*b*
transmission of, 395, 396*f*
myths about, 395–398
treatment/cure research and, 395, 398*b*
HMO (Health Maintenance Organization), 451
Homeostasis, stress affecting, 254
Homeotherms, 326, 327*b*
Hopelessness, feelings of, burnout and, 304*b*
Hormones
food from animals treated with, 223
overweight/obesity and, 241
in stress response, 295, 296
Hot environment. *See* Heat
Hot tubs, 449
HIV transmission and, 396
HPV infection. *See* Human papillomavirus (HPV) infection
HPV vaccine, 399
HR_{max}. *See* Maximal heart rate
HRR. *See* Heart rate reserve
Human immunodeficiency virus (HIV), 393, 393*b*. *See also* HIV infection/AIDS
Human papillomavirus (HPV) infection, 379*b*, 399
cervical cancer and, 378, 379*b*, 383, 399
incidence of, 393*f*, 399
vaccine for, 399
Humidity, 327, 327*b*
heat loss affected by, 327–328, 328*f*, 329*f*
Hunger, ghrelin affecting, 241
Hurdler's stretch, modified, 152
Hydrostatic weighing, in body fat measurement, 180, 181*b*, 181*f*
Hyperplasia, 104, 105*b*
Hypertension, 272–273, 273*b*, 273*f*
aging and, 445
coronary heart disease risk and, 274–275, 275*f*, 278*t*, 286
lowering, 279
obesity and, 175, 277
sodium intake and, 207
Hypertrophy, 104, 105*b*
Hypokinetic disease, 143, 143*b*
low back pain as, 143
Hypothalamus, in stress response, 295
Hypothermia, 331–332, 331*b*, 332*b*

Illicit drugs, 416*t*, 417–429, 417*b*
Imagery (visualization), 306, 307*b*
Immunity, overtraining affecting, 36*b*
Improvement phase, in cardiovascular endurance program, 65
Inactivity (physical)
coronary heart disease risk and, 276–277, 278*t*
exercise affecting, 276–277, 277*f*, 279, 280*b*
obesity and, 10
Incomplete proteins, 201, 201*b*
Individual health insurance, 451
Infant(s), RDAs for, 210–211*t*
Infection
opportunistic, HIV infection/AIDS and, 395, 396*t*
overtraining affecting risk of, 36*b*
Ingested poisons, treatment of, 357
Inhalants, use/abuse of, 421*t*
Inhaled poisons, treatment of, 357
Initial conditioning phase, in cardiovascular endurance program, 64–65
Injection drug use, HIV transmission and, 395, 395*f*
Injuries
exercise-related, 344–354. *See also* Exercise-related injuries
unintentional, 354–359, 354*t*, 355*b*
leading causes of death and, 354*t*
prevention of, 354–355, 356*b*, 358*b*

risk of, 354–355
reducing, 355, 356*b*, 358*b*
Insect bites, HIV transmission and, 398
Inside leg stretch, 153
Insoluble fiber, 198, 199*b*
Insulin, leptin interaction and, 241
Insulin sensitivity, decreased, 176. *See also* Diabetes
Insurance (health), 450–451, 451*b*, 465–466
Intellectual health, 3, 3*f*
assessment of, 22, 459
Intensity of exercise, 39, 39*b*, 39*t*
in cardiorespiratory workout, 61–62, 62*f*, 64*f*
fitness maintenance and, 65
energy sources and, 55, 56, 57*f*
estimation of, 39, 61–62, 62*f*
in flexibility/stretching routine, 146–148, 147*t*
fuel use and, 217, 217*f*
muscle fiber recruitment and, 101, 102*f*
repetition maximum (RM) and sets and, 107, 107*f*
for strength/weight training program, 107, 107*f*
stress reduction and, 303, 303*f*
weight loss and, 249, 250*b*
Intermediate fibers, 100, 101*b*, 101*t*
exercise intensity and, 101, 102*f*
individual variations/genetics and, 101
Internal rotator muscles of thigh, flexibility exercises for, 153
Internist, 451, 452*b*
Interpersonal relationships
emotional health and, 3
social health and, 4
stress and, 298
Interval training, 67–68, 67*b*
Iodine, 204*t*
DRI for, 213*b*
RDA for, 210*t*
Iron, 203, 204*t*
DRI for, 213*b*
food sources of, 204*t*, 213
RDA for, 210*t*
supplementary, 212–214
Iron-deficiency anemia, 203, 203*b*, 213
Irradiation, in food preservation/safety, 223–224, 223*b*
Isokinetic exercise, 99–100, 99*b*
weight-training program/exercises and, 107
Isometric (static) exercise, 99, 99*b*
weight-training program/exercises and, 106–107
Isotonic (dynamic) exercise, 99, 99*b*
weight-training program/exercises and, 106, 111–117

Joint(s)
aging affecting, 445–446, 445*f*
injuries of
arthroscopic surgery for, 349*b*
ligament sprains, 348–349, 348*f*, 349*b*
mobility/health of. *See also* Flexibility
evaluation of, 143–144
flexibility/stretching exercises and, 142
limitations to, 141, 141*t*
Joint capsule, 141*f*
movement limitations and, 141, 141*t*

Kaposi's sarcoma, in HIV infection/AIDS, 396*t*
kcal(s) (kilocalories), 197, 197*b*. *See also* Calorie(s)
RDA for, diet analysis and, 229
Ketamine, 418
Kilocalorie(s), 197, 197*b*. *See also* Calorie(s)
Kilopond meters per minute (KPMs), 79
Knee bends, injury and, 157
Knee to chest test, 365–366
Knee injury, patellofemoral pain syndrome (PFPS) and, 350–351, 350*f*, 351*b*
Knee muscles, isotonic exercises for, 113
Knee pull, injury and, 157
Knee-to-nose touch, 159
KPMs. *See* Kilopond meters per minute

Lactation, RDAs during, 210–211*t*
Lactic acid/lactic acid system, 55, 55*b*
Lactose (milk sugar), 198
Latex condoms, STI risk reduction and, 405
Latissimus dorsi muscle
flexibility exercises for, 155
isotonic exercises for, 116
Laughing gas, 421*t*
Layering, for cold weather exercise, 332–333, 333*f*
LBP. *See* Low back pain
LDL. *See* Low-density lipoproteins
Leg extension exercise, 114
Leg hug exercise, 45
Leg muscles
flexibility exercises for, 157
isotonic exercises for, 114
Leg press, for muscular strength evaluation, 123–125, 124*f*, 126*t*
Leg pull, 157
Leg stretch, 152
inside leg, 153
Leptin, 241, 241*b*
Leukemia, 371*f*, 372*f*, 378
Lice (pubic/crabs), 404, 405*b*
Lifestyle
assessment of, 12–13, 21–23
healthy/active, 440–441, 441*b*, 442*t*, 443*b*. *See also* Behavior change; Lifetime fitness/wellness; Physical health/fitness
behavior change in achieving, 11–16, 13*b*, 14*b*
cancer risk/prevention and, 381*b*, 382, 382*f*
colorectal cancer, 372
heart disease prevention and, 276–277
older adults and, 444–448, 444*f*, 445*f*, 447*b*, 467–468
pregnancy and, 441–444, 444*f*, 463
successful aging and, 446
wellness and, 2–4, 3*f*, 4*f*
sedentary
coronary heart disease risk and, 276–277
exercise affecting, 276–277, 277*f*, 279, 280*b*
obesity and, 10
Lifetime fitness/wellness, 439–468
assessment of, 459–460
diet/fitness products (consumer issues) and, 448–449
exercise adherence/active lifestyle and, 440–441, 441*b*, 442*t*, 443*b*
goal setting and, 37
successful aging and, 446, 447–448
health care choices and, 449–455
keys to success in, 446–448, 447*b*
for older adult, 444–448, 444*f*, 445*f*, 447*b*, 467–468
pregnancy and, 441–444, 444*f*, 463
Ligament(s), 141*b*, 141*f*
movement limitations and, 141
Ligament sprains, 348–349, 348*f*, 349*b*
Linoleic acid, 199
Linolenic acid, 199
Lipid(s), 199–201, 199*b*, 199*t*, 200*f*. *See also* Fat(s)
Lipoprotein(s), 200–201, 201*b*, 275–276, 276*b*
Liquid diet, low-calorie, 246*t*
Longevity
diet affecting, 248*b*
exercise affecting, 7*f*, 8, 9*f*, 59
Lordosis, 143
Low back pain, 345–346
assessing risk of, 365–366
causes/risk factors for, 143*b*, 346
prevention of, 143, 346
flexibility/stretching exercises in, 143, 167
spinal alignment and, 142*f*
Low-calorie balanced diet, 246*t*
aging/longevity affected by, 248*b*
Low-calorie liquid diet, 246*t*
Low-carbohydrate diet, 215*b*, 246*t*, 247*b*, 248*b*
Low-cholesterol diet, 207
coronary heart disease risk affected by, 279, 280*b*, 280*t*
Low-density lipoprotein (LDL) treatment plan, 286–287
Low-density lipoproteins/low density cholesterol (LDL/LDL cholesterol), 200, 200–201, 275–276, 275*b*, 276*b*
Lower back stretch, 154
Lower extremity, exercise-related injuries of, 350–352
Lower leg stretch, 150
Low-fat diet, 206–207, 207*b*, 247*b*
in cancer prevention, 372, 379–381
coronary heart disease risk and, 279, 280*b*, 280*t*
in weight control, 247*b*
Low-impact activities, 38
LSD (lysergic acid diethylamide), 418, 421*t*
dependence potential of, 416*t*
Lung cancer, 370–371, 371*f*, 372*f*, 373*b*, 381

Lunges, 113, 157
Lymphoma, 371*f*
  of brain, in HIV infection/AIDS, 396*t*
Lysergic acid diethylamide (LSD), 418, 421*t*
  dependence potential of, 416*t*

Macronutrient(s), 196, 197–203, 197*b*. *See also specific type*
  in balanced diet, 197, 197*f*
  DRI for, 213*b*
  food sources of, 197*t*
Magnesium, 204*t*
  DRI for, 213*b*
  RDA for, 210*t*
Mainstream smoke, 426. *See also* Secondhand smoke
Maintenance phase/program, 33, 33*b*, 33*f*, 109*b*
  for cardiorespiratory endurance, 65
    motivation for, 68–70
  for flexibility/stretching routine, 147, 147*t*
    motivation for, 149
  for strength/endurance/weight training, 109, 109*b*, 109*t*
    motivation for, 110
Maintenance stage, of behavior change, 12
Males. *See* Men
Malignant melanoma, 371*f*, 375–376, 375*b*
Malignant tumor, 368, 369*b*. *See also* Cancer
Malnutrition, 425*b*
  alcohol use/abuse and, 424, 425*b*
  underweight and, 176
Maltose (malt sugar), 198
  reducing intake of, 212*b*
Mammograms, 373, 373*b*
Manganese
  DRI for, 213*b*
  RDA for, 210*t*
Mantra, 306
Marijuana, 418, 419*b*, 420*t*
  dependence potential and, 416, 416*t*
  long term complications of use of, 419, 420*t*
Maximal aerobic capacity ($\dot{V}O_2max$)), 52, 53*b*, 58
  aging affecting, 444, 444*f*, 445*f*
  altitude affecting, 334–335, 334*f*
  estimation of, 59–60, 60*f*
  exercise affecting, 58, 58*f*
  target heart rate and, 61–62, 61*b*, 62*f*
  training threshold and, 61, 61*b*
Maximal heart rate, 61, 62*f*
MDMA (methylenedioxymethamphetamine/ecstasy), 418, 421*t*
  dependence potential of, 416*t*
Medical examination. *See also* Health care choices
  assessing need for, 453–454
  regular checkups and, 454, 454*t*
    successful aging and, 447
  successful communication with health care provider and, 454–455
Medical history, assessment of, 27
Medical specialists, 451, 452*b*
Meditation, 303*f*, 306, 306*f*, 307*b*
Melanoma, 371*f*, 375–376, 375*b*
Men
  body fat storage in, 171, 172*f*
  body mass index (optimal) in, 178
  chest press results for, 125*t*
  curl-up test results for, 135*t*
  cycle ergometer fitness test results for, 79–81*t*
  leg press results for, 126*t*
  muscle mass in, 102, 102*b*, 105
  1-mile walk test results for, 78*t*
  1.5-mile run test results for, 76*t*
  one-repetition maximum (1 RM) test results for, 125*t*, 126*t*
  percent fat estimates for, 190*t*
  push-up/modified push up test results for, 134*t*
  RDAs for, 210–211*t*
  shoulder flexibility test results for, 164*t*
  sit and reach test results for, 164*t*
  sit-up test results for, 134*t*
  skinfold measurement sites for, 179, 188
  skinfold test results for, 190*t*
  step test fitness results for, 85*t*
  strength/weight training responses and, 105
  trunk flexibility test results for, 164*t*
  waist-to-hip ratio results for, 179*t*, 192*t*
Mental (emotional) health, 3, 3*f*
  assessment of, 22, 459
  exercise affecting, 7*f*, 8, 59, 59*b*
  healthy weight and, 173
Mercury, seafood contamination by, 200*b*
Meridia, 253
Mescaline, dependence potential of, 416*t*
Metabolic rate
  exercise, 244, 245*b*
  resting (resting energy expenditure), 97*b*, 244, 245*b*
    strength training affecting, 96–97, 249
Metastasis, 369, 369*b*, 369*f*
Metatarsal stress fractures, 351–352, 351*b*, 352*f*
Methadone, dependence potential of, 416*t*
Methamphetamine, 418–419, 420*t*
  dependence potential of, 416*t*
  long term complications of use of, 419, 420*t*
Methylenedioxymethamphetamine (MDMA/ecstasy), 418, 421*t*
  dependence potential of, 416*t*
Methylmercury, seafood contamination by, 200*b*
Micronutrient(s), 196, 197*b*, 202*t*, 203, 204*t*
  RDAs for, 210–211*t*
Milk sugar (lactose), 198
Mind, "exercising," 446
Mineral(s), 203, 203*b*, 204*t*. *See also specific type*
  food sources of, 203, 204*t*
  RDAs for, 210*t*
  supplementary, 212–215
Mode of exercise, 38, 39*b*, 40*f*
  for cardiorespiratory workout, 63–64, 63*b*, 64*f*
Modified hurdler's stretch, 152
Modified push-up test, 134*t*
Moles (skin), examination of in skin cancer detection, 376, 377*b*
Molybdenum
  DRI for, 213*b*
  RDA for, 210*t*
Monogamy, STI risk reduction and, 405, 405*f*
Monounsaturated fatty acids, 199, 199*t*
Morphine, dependence potential of, 416, 416*t*
Mother
  alcohol use/abuse during pregnancy (fetal alcohol syndrome) and, 424-425, 425*b*
  HIV transmission to fetus by, 395
  substance use during pregnancy and, 419
Motorcycle accidents, reducing risk of, 358*b*
Motor neuron, 98, 99*f*
Motor unit, 98, 99*b*, 99*f*
Motor vehicle accidents, reducing risk of, 358*b*
Mountain sickness, acute, 335
Movement. *See also* Range of motion
  structural limitations to, 141, 141*f*, 141*t*
Muscle(s). *See also under Muscular*
  aging affecting, 445*f*, 446
  function of, 98–99, 99*f*
  hyperplasia of, 104, 105*b*
  hypertrophy of, 104, 105*b*
  movement limitations and, 141, 141*t*
  size of
    strength and, 102
      anabolic steroid use and, 102*b*, 427
    strength/endurance/weight training affecting, 104
  structure of, 97–98, 97*f*, 98*f*
Muscle action, 97, 97*b*, 98–99
  classification of, 100
  energy sources for, 55–56, 56*f*, 57*f*
Muscle cramp, 149*b*
Muscle exercise, 99–100
Muscle fibers, 97, 97*f*
  in muscle action, 98, 99*f*
  recruitment of, 101, 101*b*, 102*f*
    muscular strength and, 102, 103*f*
  types of, 100, 101*t*
    individual variations/genetics and, 100–101
Muscle mass
  aging affecting, 446
  diet/exercise in gaining, 252
  strength training affecting. *See also* Strength/endurance training
    resting metabolic rate and, 97, 249
  testosterone affecting, 102, 102*b*, 105
Muscle soreness
  acute, 346, 347*b*
  delayed-onset, 346–347, 347*b*
Muscle spindles, 141–142, 141*b*
Muscle strain, 347–348, 347*b*, 347*f*
Muscle tension, in stress, progressive relaxation and, 304–305, 305*b*
Muscular endurance, 10, 11*b*, 11*f*, 95–138
  in daily living, 96–97
  definition of, 96
  evaluation of, 103
  goals for, 108–109

maintenance of, 109, 109*b*, 109*t*
motivation for, 110
training program for. *See* Strength/endurance training
Muscular strength, 10, 95–138
aging affecting, 445*f*, 446
in daily living, 96–97
definition of, 96
evaluation of, 103
factors affecting, 102
goals for, 108–109
maintenance of, 109, 109*b*, 109*t*
motivation for, 110
muscle size and, 102
anabolic steroid use and, 102*b*, 427
recruitment and, 102, 103*f*
training program for. *See* Strength/endurance training
Mycobacterial infections, in HIV infection/AIDS, 396*t*
Myocardial infarction (heart attack), 271, 271*b*, 272*f*, 273*b*. *See also* Coronary heart disease
aspirin in prevention of, 280*b*
assessing risk for, 285–286
exercise protecting against injury during, 7, 7*f*
smoking and, 274
MyPyramid food guidance system, 208, 208*f*

Naltrexone, for alcohol dependence, 422
Neck circles, injury and, 159
Neck muscles, flexibility exercises for, 156, 159
Neck stretches, 156, 159
Needle sharing, HIV transmitted by, 395, 395*f*
Negative stress (distress), 295, 295*b*, 295*f*, 304*b*
Negative work (eccentric muscle action), 100, 100*f*, 101*b*
Neisseria gonorrhoeae, gonorrhea caused by, 401*b*, 402
Nerve impulse, in muscle action, 98–99
Nervous system, in stress response, 295
Neurologist, 452*b*
Neuromuscular facilitation, proprioceptive (PNF), 144, 145–146, 145*b*, 146*f*, 147*f*
Neurons, aging affecting, 446
Neurosurgeon, 452*b*
Neurotransmitters, aging affecting, 446
Niacin (vitamin B_3), 202*t*
DRI for, 213*b*
RDA for, 211*t*
Nickel, DRI for, 213*b*
Nicotine, 420*t*, 425, 425–426, 425*b*. *See also* Smoking
addiction to, 425–426
dependence potential of, 416, 416*t*
heart rate/blood pressure affected by, 274
stress and, 307
tobacco usage inventory and, 435–437
Nonessential amino acids, 201, 201*b*
Non-insulin-dependent diabetes, 176. *See also* Diabetes
obesity and, 175–176
Nonmelanoma, 375, 375*b*, 376
Nonoxynal 9, STI risk and, 406–407
Norepinephrine, 295, 295*b*
in stress response, 295
Nutrient(s), 196–205, 197*b*, 197*f*, 197*t*. *See also specific type*
intake of
dietary analysis and, 229–231
planning new diet and, 235–236
RDAs for, 208, 210–211*t*, 213*b*
Nutrition, 195–238, 197*b*. *See also specific nutrient and under Diet*
alcohol use/abuse and, 424, 425*b*
cancer risk and, 379–381
definition of, 196, 197*b*
dietary supplements and, 218–221, 220*t*, 221*b*. *See also* Dietary supplements
eating disorders and, 177
food safety/technology and, 222–224, 222*f*, 223*b*
goals for healthy diet and, 233
guidelines for healthy diet and, 205–218. *See also* Diet, healthy/balanced
importance of, 196
physical fitness and, 216
strength/endurance/weight training and, 108*b*, 217
successful aging and, 446
Nutritional supplements, 218–221, 220*t*, 221*b*. *See also* Dietary supplements
stress reduction and, 307*b*
Nutrition Facts (food labels), 208–209, 209*f*

Obese/obesity, 10, 170, 171*b*, 173–176. *See also* Weight control
android pattern of, 172, 172*f*, 173*b*
body composition and, 170, 171, 172*f*, 173
body mass index and, 178, 179*t*
cancer risk and, 175
chronic conditions associated with, 175–176
creeping, 174, 175*b*, 175*f*
diabetes and, 175–176
disease risk and, 173, 175–176
environmental factors and, 241–242, 242*b*, 243*f*
exercise prescription for individuals with, 250*b*
genetics and, 173*b*, 241
gynoid pattern of, 172*f*, 173, 173*b*
heart disease and, 175, 277, 278*t*
hypertension and, 175, 277
inactivity and, 10
mental/physical health and, 173
rates of, 173–174, 174*f*
weight loss and. *See* Weight control
Oblique muscles
flexibility exercises for, 155
isotonic exercises for, 115
Obstetrician, 452*b*
Occult blood in stool, in colorectal cancer screening, 372
Occupational carcinogens, 383–384
Older adulthood. *See also* Age/aging
fitness during, 444–448, 444*f*, 445*f*, 447*b*, 467–468
Omega-3 fatty acid, 199–200, 199*b*
Oncologist, 452*b*
1-mile walk test, 60, 77, 78*t*
1.5-mile run test, 59–60, 59*b*, 75, 76*t*
1.5-mile run/walk test, 60
One-repetition maximum (1 RM) test, 103, 103*b*, 123–126, 125*t*, 126*t*
estimated, 103, 127–128, 128*t*
Opium, 420*t*
Opportunistic infection, HIV infection/AIDS and, 395, 396*t*
Oral cancer(s), 371*f*, 378
smoking/tobacco use and, 381
Organic foods, 223, 223*b*
Orlistat, 253
Osteoarthritis. *See* Arthritis
Osteoporosis, 7, 7*b*, 203, 203*b*
aging and, 7, 445–446
calcium and, 214
exercise affecting bone mass and, 7–8, 7*f*, 8*f*
Otorhinolaryngolist, 452*b*
Ovarian cancer, 371*f*, 372*f*, 377–378
Overeating, stress and, 307
Over-fat, body composition/health and, 171
Overload principle, 32, 33*b*, 33*f*. *See also* Progressive resistance exercise
Overnutrition, 425*b*
alcohol use/abuse and, 425*b*
Overtraining/overtraining syndrome, 35, 35*b*, 36*b*, 344, 345*b*
illness risk affected by, 36*b*
Overweight, 170, 171*b*, 173–176. *See also* Obese/obesity; Weight control
body composition/health and, 170, 171, 172*f*, 173
body mass index and, 178, 179*t*
chronic conditions associated with, 175–176
fitness and, 178*b*
heart disease risk and, 277
mental/physical health and, 173
OxyContin, 419
Oxygen consumption/oxygen uptake
altitude affecting, 334–335, 334*f*
exercise affecting, 56
maximal. See $\dot{V}O_2$max
Ozone, 336, 336*f*, 337*b*

Pancreas, cancer of, 371*f*, 372*f*, 378
Pandemic, 395*b*
HIV infection/AIDS as, 394
Pantothenic acid
DRI for, 213*b*
RDA for, 211*t*
Parasympathetic branch of autonomic nervous system, 295, 295*b*
Par-Q and You, 29
Passive stretching, 146, 146*f*, 147*f*
Patellofemoral pain syndrome (PFPS), 350–351, 350*f*, 351*b*
Pectoralis major
flexibility exercises for, 156
isotonic exercises for, 112, 116, 117
Pediatrician, 452*b*

Pedometer, measuring physical activity and, 49–50
Pelvic inflammatory disease (PID), 401, 401*b*, 406*b*
Pelvic tilt, 167
Perceived exertion, rate of, 62, 62*f*, 63*b*, 93–94
Performance goals, 37, 37*f*. *See also* Fitness goals
Personality type
  assessment of, 319–320
  stress levels/heart disease risk and, 297–298, 297*t*
Pets, HIV transmission and, 396
Peyote, dependence potential of, 416*t*
PFPS. *See* Patellofemoral pain syndrome
Phospholipids, 200, 201*b*
Phosphorus, 204*t*
  DRI for, 213*b*
  RDA for, 210*t*
Physiatrist, 452*b*
Physical (medical examination). *See also* Health care choices
  assessing need for, 453–454
  regular checkups and, 454, 454*t*
    successful aging and, 447
  successful communication with health care provider and, 454–455
Physical activity. *See also* Exercise
  definition of, 6, 7*b*
  energy sources for, 55–56, 56*f*, 57*f*
  health benefits of, 6–9, 7*f*, 8*f*, 9*f*, 59, 59*b*
    threshold for, 40–42, 41*b*, 41*f*
  levels of, 41–42, 41*f*
    pedometer for measurement of, 49–50
  in weight control program, 249–251, 250*b*, 251*t*, 261
Physical health/fitness, 2–3, 3*f*
  books/magazines related to, 449
  evaluation of, 21–22, 459. *See also* Fitness evaluation
  exercise and, 9–11
    health benefits of, 6–9, 7*f*, 8*f*, 9*f*, 59, 59*b*
      threshold for health benefits and, 40–42, 41*b*, 41*f*
    principles of, 31–50
  health-related, 9–11
  healthy weight and, 173
  lifetime, 439–468. *See also* Lifetime fitness/wellness
  motivation/goal setting and. *See* Fitness goals
  nutrition and, 216, 217–218
  obesity and, 173, 175–176
Physical inactivity
  cancer risk/prevention and, 381*b*, 382, 382*f*
    colorectal cancer, 372
  coronary heart disease risk and, 276–277, 278*t*
    exercise and, 276–277, 277*f*, 279, 280*b*
  obesity and, 10
Physician. *See* Health care provider
Phytochemicals, 219*b*
PID. *See* Pelvic inflammatory disease
Pilates, 148*b*
Ping-pong effect, in trichomoniasis infection, 404
Plaque, atherosclerotic, 270, 271*b*, 271*f*
  in coronary arteries, 271, 271*f*, 272*f*
Plasticity, of brain, mental activity/successful aging and, 446
Pneumocystis pneumonia, in HIV infection/AIDS, 396*t*
Pneumonia, in HIV infection/AIDS, 396*t*
PNF. *See* Proprioceptive neuromuscular facilitation
Poisoning
  reducing risk of, 358*b*
  treatment of, 357
Polyps, colorectal cancer and, 372, 373*b*
Polyunsaturated fatty acids, 199, 199*t*
Positive stress (eustress), 295, 295*b*, 295*f*
Positive work (concentric muscle action), 100, 100*f*, 101*b*
Potassium, 204*t*
  DRI for, 213*b*
PPO (Preferred Provider Organization), 451
Prader-Willi syndrome, 241
Precontemplation stage, of behavior change, 11
Pre-diabetes, 176. *See also* Diabetes
Preferred Provider Organization (PPO), 451
Pregnancy
  alcohol use during (fetal alcohol syndrome), 424–425, 425*b*
  caffeine use during, 428*b*
  drug use during, 419
  fish/seafood in diet and, 200*b*
  fitness/exercise during, 441–444, 444*f*, 463
  folic acid supplements during, 212
  RDAs during, 210–211*t*
  smoking during, 426
Preparation stage, of behavior change, 11–12
Presbyopia, 446, 447*b*
Prescription medications, for weight loss, 253
Press up position, for testing core strength and stability, 137–138
Primary care physician, 451
Primary conditioning period (workout), 39, 39*t*, 40*f*
  for cardiorespiratory exercise program, 61–64, 62*f*, 63*b*, 64*b*, 64*f*
  personalization of, 39–40, 47
    for cardiorespiratory exercise program, 64–66, 66*b*, 67*b*, 68*b*, 91
Principles of exercise training, 32–36. *See also specific principle and specific type of training*
  overload, 32, 33*b*, 33*f*. *See also* Progressive resistance exercise
  progression, 32–33, 33*b*, 33*f*
  recuperation, 34–35, 35*b*, 35*f*
  reversibility, 35, 35*b*, 35*f*
  specificity of exercise, 33–34, 33*b*, 34*b*, 105*b*
Progression, principle of, 32–33, 33*b*, 33*f*
Progressive relaxation, 304–305, 305*b*
Progressive resistance exercise (PRE), 104, 105*b*
Proprioceptive neuromuscular facilitation (PNF), 144, 145–146, 145*b*, 146*f*, 147*f*
Proprioceptor(s), 143*b*
  muscle spindles as, 142
  structure of, 201
Prostate cancer, 371*f*, 372*f*, 373*b*, 375
Prostate-specific antigen blood test, in cancer screening, 375
Protein, 201–203, 201*b*, 201*f*
  DRI for, 213*b*
    diet analysis and, 229
  as energy source, 55–56
  food sources of, 197*t*, 201
  in healthy/balanced diet, 197, 197*f*, 214*t*, 217
  requirements for, 108*b*, 201, 201*f*, 217
  strength/endurance/weight training and, 108*b*, 217
  supplementary, 217
Psychiatrist, 452*b*
Psychoactive drugs, use/abuse of, 418–419, 418*f*, 419*b*, 420–421*t*
  health effects and, 419, 420*t*
Psychological well-being. *See* Emotional (mental) health
Pubic lice (crabs), 404, 405*b*
"Pulled muscle." *See* Muscle strain
Pullover exercise, 116
Pulmonary circuit, 53, 53*b*, 54*f*
Pulmonary system. *See* Respiratory system
Pulse/pulse rate, 53, 55*f*. *See also* Heart rate
Purging, in bulimia, 255
Push-up test, 103, 103*b*, 131, 134*t*
  modified, 134*t*

Quadratus lumborum muscle, isotonic exercises for, 115
Quadriceps muscles
  flexibility/stretching exercises for, 45, 151
  isotonic exercises for, 113, 114

Race, cancer risk and, 379, 380*b*
  breast cancer, 374–375
Radial artery, heart rate measured at, 55*f*
Radiation, cancer risk and, 383
Radiologist, 452*b*
Rain/wind, hypothermia and, 332*b*
Range of motion, 100, 101*b*. *See also* Flexibility
  flexibility and, 140–142, 141*f*, 141*t*, 142*f*
  isokinetic exercises and, 100
  structural limitations to, 141, 141*f*, 141*t*
Rating of Perceived Exertion, 62, 62*f*, 63*b*, 93–94
RDA. *See* Recommended Dietary Allowance
Recommended Dietary Allowance (RDA), 208, 210–211*t*, 213*b*
  diet analysis and, 229
  planning new diet and, 235–236
Recruitment, 101, 101*b*, 102*f*
  muscular strength and, 102, 103*f*
Rectal cancer/colorectal cancer, 371–372, 371*f*, 372*f*, 373*b*

Rectus abdominus muscle, isotonic exercises for, 115
Rectus femoris muscle, isotonic exercises for, 114
Recuperation, principle of, 34–35, 35*b*, 35*f*
Rehabilitation, after exercise-related injury, 353, 353*f*
Relapse prevention, in behavior modification, 12
  weight loss and, 16
Relationships. *See* Interpersonal relationships
Relaxation techniques, 303*f*, 304–306, 306*f*
  progressive relaxation and, 304–305, 305*b*
  stress-related coronary heart disease and, 279–281
Repetition(s) (reps), strength gains and, 107–108, 107*f*
Repetition maximum (RM), 107
  muscular strength evaluation and, 103, 103*b*, 107, 123–128
Resistance exercise. *See also* Strength/endurance training; Weight training
  in weight control, 249
Resistance stage, of general adaptation syndrome, 300
Respiratory system, response to exercise by, 56–57
Rest/ice/compression/elevation (RICE), 352–353, 353*b*
Resting metabolic rate (resting energy expenditure), 97*b*, 244, 245*b*
  strength training affecting, 96–97, 249
Rest/sleep, stress management and, 302*b*, 303, 303*f*
Reversibility, principle of, 35, 35*b*, 35*f*
ReVia. *See* Naltrexone
Rhomboid muscles, isotonic exercises for, 112
Riboflavin (vitamin B2), 202*t*
  DRI for, 213*b*
  RDA for, 211*t*
RICE (rest/ice/compression/elevation), 352–353, 353*b*
Risk-taking behavior(s)
  alcohol use/abuse and, 420
  unintentional injury and, 354–355
RM. *See* Repetition maximum
RMR. *See* Resting metabolic rate
Road rage, 299, 300*b*
Rohypnol, 418
RPE. *See* Rating of Perceived Exertion
"Runner's knee" (patellofemoral pain syndrome), 350–351, 350*f*, 351*b*
Running shoes, selecting, 34*b*

Safety issues, for strength/endurance/weight training program, 105
Saliva, HIV transmission and, 396
Salmonella food poisoning, 222
Salt. *See* Sodium
Sarcopenia, 446, 447*b*
Saturated fatty acids, 199*t*, 200, 201*b*
  cholesterol and, 199*t*, 200, 201
Saunas, 449
Scabies, 404, 405*b*
Seafood, consumption of during pregnancy, 200*b*
Secondhand smoke, 426, 427*b*
  cancer risk and, 381
  coronary heart disease risk and, 274
Sedentary lifestyle
  coronary heart disease risk and, 276–277
    exercise affecting, 276–277, 277*f*, 279, 280*b*
  obesity and, 10
Selenium, 204*t*
  DRI for, 213*b*
  RDA for, 210*t*
Self-esteem, healthy body weight and, 173
Self-examination
  breast, 373, 374*b*
  skin, 376, 377*b*
  testicular, 375, 376*b*
Self-monitoring, in behavior change, 12
Self-reinforcement, in behavior modification, 12
  achieving fitness goal and, 38
  weight loss and, 16
Selye, Hans, 296, 299–300
Semimembranosus muscle, isotonic exercises for, 114
Semitendinosus muscle, isotonic exercises for, 114
Set(s), 107, 107*b*
  strength gains and, 107–108, 107*f*
Sex (gender)
  coronary heart disease risk and, 277, 278*t*
  strength/endurance/weight training differences and, 105
  stress levels and, 298
Sexually transmitted infection(s), 391–412, 393*b*. *See also specific disease*
  definition of, 392–393, 393*b*
  incidence of, 392, 393*f*, 406*b*
    worldwide distribution of, 397*b*
  inventory of attitudes/behaviors about, 411–412
  questions about, 406*b*
  reducing risk of, 404–407, 405*f*, 407*b*
Sexual partners, STI risk reduction and
  discussing high-risk behavior and, 405–406
  limiting number and, 405, 405*f*
Shaping, as behavior change strategy, 14, 15*b*
Shin muscles, flexibility exercises for, 151
Shin splints, 351, 351*b*, 351*f*
Shin stretch, 151
Shoes, running/exercise
  injuries and, 344
  selecting, 34*b*
Shoppers, compulsive, 415
Shoulder
  flexibility exercises for, 156
  isotonic exercises for, 112, 116, 117
Shoulder flexibility test, 144, 145*b*, 163–164, 164*t*
Sidestream smoke, 426. *See also* Secondhand smoke
Side stretch, 45, 155
Sigmoidoscopy, in colorectal cancer screening, 372
Silicon, DRI for, 213*b*
Simple carbohydrates (simple sugars), 197–198. *See also* Carbohydrate(s)
  in balanced/healthy diet, 197, 197*f*, 206
  reducing intake of, 206, 212*b*
Sit-and-reach test, 144, 145*b*, 163–164, 164*t*
Sitting hamstring stretch, 158
Sitting toe touch, 45
Sit-up (hand behind head), injury and, 158
Sit-up test, 103, 103*b*, 132, 134*t*
Skeletal muscle, 97–98, 97*f*, 98*f*. *See also under Muscle*
Skin
  aging affecting, 446
  movement limitations and, 141, 141*t*
  poisons on, treatment of, 357
  protection of
    cancer prevention and, 376, 382–383, 383*b*
    successful aging and, 447
Skin cancer, 371*f*, 375–376, 377*b*
  self-examination/early detection of, 376, 377*b*
  ultraviolet radiation exposure and, 376, 382–383, 383*b*
Skinfold test, 179, 179*b*, 187–188, 189*t*, 190*t*
Sleep apnea, obesity and, 176
Sleep deprivation, exercise affecting, 59, 59*b*
Sleep/rest
  changes in, burnout and, 304*b*
  stress management and, 302*b*, 303, 303*f*
Slow progression phase, 109*b*
  for flexibility/stretching routine, 146–147, 147*t*
  for strength/endurance/weight training program, 109, 109*b*, 109*t*
Slow-twitch fibers, 100, 101*b*, 101*t*
  exercise intensity and, 101, 102*f*
  individual variations/genetics and, 101
Smell sensation, aging affecting, 446
Smoking, 15, 425–426, 426*f*
  addiction to nicotine and, 15, 416, 416*t*, 420*t*, 425–426
  assessment (inventory) of, 435–437
  cancer risk and, 371, 381–382, 426
  cessation of, 15
    behavior modification strategies for, 15
    cancer risk affected by, 371, 381–382
    coronary heart disease risk and, 278–279
  coronary heart disease risk and, 274, 274*f*, 278*t*, 286, 426
  health effects of, 426
  stress and, 307
Social health, 3, 4*f*
  assessment of, 22, 459
Social support, stress management and, 306
Socioeconomic status, wellness issues and, 5*b*
Sodium, 203, 204*t*, 275*t*
  DRI for, 213*b*
  in healthy/balanced diet, 207, 207*f*, 214*t*
  hypertension and, 274–275, 275*t*
  reducing intake of, 207, 207*f*, 275, 275*t*
Soft tissues, flexibility/movement limitations and, 141, 141*t*

Soleus muscle
flexibility/stretching exercises for, 45, 150, 152
isotonic exercises for, 117
Soluble fiber, 198, 199*b*
Somatotropin, bovine, milk from animals treated with, 223
Specificity of exercise, 33–34, 33*b*, 34*b*, 105*b*
strength/endurance/weight training and, 104, 105*b*
Spenders, compulsive, 415
Spermicides, with nonoxynal 9, STI risk and, 406–407
SPF (sun protection factor), 376, 377*b*
Spinning, 69*b*
Spiritual health/wellness, 3–4, 3*f*, 4*f*
assessment of, 23, 460
development of in stress management, 306
Sports activities
HIV transmission and, 396
injuries and. *See* Exercise-related injuries
Sports drinks/gels, 217, 218*f*
Spot reduction, 254*t*
Sprains, 348–349, 348*f*, 349*b*
Stability, measuring, 137–138
Stages of Change Model, 11–12, 11*b*
Standing toe touch, injury and, 158
Starch(es), 198, 199*b*
Starter phase, 109*b*
for flexibility/stretching routine, 146, 147*t*
for strength/endurance/weight training program, 109, 109*b*, 109*t*
Static (isometric) exercise, 99, 99*b*
weight-training program/exercises and, 106–107
Static stretching, 144, 145*b*
Statin drugs (statins), for cholesterol lowering, 280
Stationary bikes
for cycle ergometer fitness test, 60, 60*f*, 61*b*, 79, 79–81*t*
for spinning, 69*b*
Steambaths, 449
Step stretch, 45
Step test, 60, 83–84, 83*f*, 84*f*, 85*t*
Sternocleidomastoid muscle, flexibility exercises for, 156
Steroids, anabolic, 102*b*, 421*t*, 427–428, 427*b*
dependence potential of, 416*t*
Sterol(s), 200, 201*b*
STI(s). *See* Sexually transmitted infection(s)
Stiff muscle, movement limitations and, 141
St. John's Wort, 220*t*
Storage fat, 171–173, 171*b*, 171*f*, 172*f*
heart disease risk and, 173, 277
Straight leg lift, 365
Strain (muscle), 347–348, 347*b*, 347*f*
Strength, muscular, 10, 95–138. *See also* Muscular strength; Strength/endurance training
Strength/endurance training. *See also* Weight training
adaptation to, 104–105
benefits of, 96, 104
designing program for, 105–107, 106*b*, 109*t*
principles for, 102–104
dietary/protein requirements and, 108*b*, 217
exercise prescription for, 107–108, 107*f*, 109–110, 109*t*, 110*t*
individualization of, 109, 109*t*
gender differences and, 105
goals for, 108–109
guidelines/precautions for, 109*b*
maintenance phase for, 109, 109*b*, 109*t*
motivation and, 110
muscle mass gain and, 252
for older adults, 118*b*
physiological changes caused by, 104
progressive resistance exercise (PRE) and, 104, 105*b*
protein needs and, 108*b*, 217
rate of improvement and, 104–105
safety concerns and, 105
sample exercises and, 111–117
slow progression phase for, 109, 109*b*, 109*t*
specificity of training and, 104, 104*f*, 105*b*
starter phase for, 109, 109*b*, 109*t*
starting and maintaining, 108–110, 109*b*, 109*t*, 110*t*
training log for, 129
types of programs for, 105–107
Stress, 294–302, 295*b*, 295*f*
accidents/unintentional injury and, 355
allostasis/allostatic load and, 301, 301*b*
assessment of, 311–313
burnout and, 304*b*, 305*b*
chronic, 296
health affected by, 299–302, 300*f*
assessing risk for illness and, 321–323
college students and, 298–299, 299*f*
common causes of, 298–299
coronary heart disease risk and, 278, 278*t*
stress management/relaxation techniques and, 279–281
definition of, 294–295, 295*b*, 295*f*
excessive, 304*b*
factors affecting levels of, 297–299, 297*t*
gender and, 298
health and, 299–302, 300*f*
assessing risk for illness and, 321–323
management of. *See* Stress management
negative (distress), 295, 295*b*, 295*f*, 304*b*
nutritional supplements and, 307*b*
past experiences and, 298
personality type and, 297–298, 297*t*, 319–320
positive (eustress), 295, 295*b*, 295*f*
response to, 294, 295–296, 295*b*, 296*f*
emotional health and, 3
Stress diary, 313
Stress fractures, 351–352, 351*b*, 352*f*
Stress index questionnaire, 311–312
Stress management, 301*b*, 302–307, 302*b*, 303*f*
breathing exercises and, 305
coronary heart disease risk and, 279–281
counterproductive behaviors in, avoidance of, 306–307
exercise and, 303–304, 303*f*
meditation and, 303*f*, 306, 306*f*, 307*b*
nutritional supplements and, 307*b*
reducing stressors and, 303
relaxation techniques and, 303*f*, 304–306, 306*f*
rest and sleep and, 302*b*, 303, 303*f*
spiritual wellness and, 306
successful aging and, 447
support network and, 306
time management and, 301*b*, 303, 315–317
visualization (imagery) and, 306, 307*b*
Stressor(s), 294, 295*b*
reducing, in stress management, 303
Stress response, 294, 295–296, 295*b*, 296*f*
Stretches. *See also* Flexibility
back pain prevention and, 143, 167
ballistic, 144, 145*b*
for cool-down after cardiorespiratory workout, 64
designing program of, 144–149
dynamic, 144, 145*b*
injury prevention/hazardous exercises and, 147, 149*b*
contraindicated and substitute exercises and, 157–159
intensity of, 39
joint health and, 142
passive and active, 146, 146*f*, 147*f*
progression log for, 165–166
proprioceptive neuromuscular facilitation and, 144, 145–146, 145*b*, 146*f*, 147*f*
sample, 150–159
static, 144, 145*b*
for warm-up, 39, 45
Stretch reflex, 141–142, 141*b*
Stroke, 271–272, 271*b*, 272*f*
heat, 330
Stroke volume, 53, 53*b*
exercise affecting, 56, 57
"Structure/function rule," 219
Subcutaneous fat, 171, 171*b*, 171*f*
Submaximal cycle test (cycle ergometer fitness test), 60, 60*f*, 61*b*, 79, 79–81*t*
Substance abuse, 417, 417*b*. *See also* Substance use/abuse
Substance use/abuse, 413–437
accidents/unintentional injury and, 355
addiction and, 414–417, 415*b*
avoiding, 429
STI risk reduction and, 406
successful aging and, 446–447
causes/risk of addiction and, 416–417, 416*t*
chemical dependence and, 416, 417*b*
drugs commonly used, 416*t*, 417–429
stress and, 307
use versus abuse and, 417
withdrawal and, 416, 417*b*
Sucrose (table sugar), 198
reducing intake of, 206, 212*b*
Sudden cardiac death, exercise and, 280*b*
Sugar (sucrose), 198
reducing intake of, 206, 212*b*
Sugar substitutes, 206, 212*b*
Sulfate, DRI for, 213*b*
Sun exposure, protecting skin from

cancer prevention and, 376, 382–383, 383*b*
successful aging and, 447
Sun protection factor (SPF), 376, 377*b*
Sunscreen, in skin cancer prevention, 376, 382, 383*b*
Supplements (dietary), 218–221, 220*t*, 221*b*
ergogenic aids, 448, 449*b*
fraud detection and, 221*b*
in healthful diet, 218–219
regulation of, 219–221, 221*b*
stress reduction and, 307*b*
Support network, stress management and, 306
Surgeon, 452*b*
Swallowed poisons, treatment of, 357
Sweating, heat loss by, 327
Swimming pools, HIV transmission and, 396
Sympathetic branch of autonomic nervous system, 295–296, 295*b*
Syphilis, 402, 402*f*, 403*b*
incidence of, 393*f*
Systemic circuit, 53, 53*b*, 54*f*
Systolic blood pressure, 272. *See also* Blood pressure

Table sugar (sucrose), 198
reducing intake of, 206, 212*b*
Tanning beds, skin cancer and, 376, 382
Target heart rate, 61–62, 61*b*, 62*f*, 89–90
Taste sensation, aging affecting, 446
Temperature
body, regulation of, 326, 327*f*, 328*f*
environmental
effective
heat index, 328, 328*f*
wind-chill index, 333, 333*f*
exercise and, 326, 327*f*
cold/cold weather and, 331–333, 332*b*, 333*f*, 334*b*, 341–342
heat/hot weather and, 326–331, 328*f*, 329*f*, 330*b*, 331*b*, 341–342
Tendonitis, 348, 349*b*
Tendons, 97, 97*b*, 97*f*, 141*f*
exercise-related injury of (tendonitis), 348, 349*b*
movement limitations and, 141, 141*t*
Ten percent rule, 33, 33*b*
Ten-repetition maximum (10 RM) test, estimating 1 RM from, 127–128, 128*t*
Tensor fasciae latae, flexibility exercises for, 153
Teres major muscle, isotonic exercises for, 116
Testicular cancer, 373*b*, 375
self-examination in detection of, 375, 376*b*
Testosterone, muscle mass and, 102, 105
anabolic steroid abuse and, 102*b*, 427
Tetrahydrocannabinol (THC), 418
Thiamin (vitamin B_1), 202*t*
DRI for, 213*b*
RDA for, 211*t*
Thigh muscles, flexibility exercises for, 151, 152, 153
Thigh stretch, 151
THR. *See* Target heart rate
3-day diet record, for diet analysis, 229–231
Threshold for health benefits, 40–42, 41*b*, 41*f*
Tibialis anterior muscle, flexibility exercises for, 151
Time (duration) of exercise, 39, 39*b*, 39*t*
in cardiorespiratory workout, 62–63, 64*f*
in stretching routine, 146–148, 147*t*
Time management, 301*b*, 303, 315–317
Tobacco use, 425–426, 426*f*. *See also* Smoking
addiction to nicotine and, 15, 416, 416*t*, 420*t*, 425–426
assessment (inventory) of, 435–437
cancer risk and, 371, 378, 381–382, 426
health effects of, 426
stress and, 307
Toe raise exercise, 117
Toe touch
sitting, 45
standing, injury and, 158
Tolerable Upper Intake Level (UL), 213*b*
Tolerance, 416, 417*b*
Torso, stretching exercises for, 45
Total body resistance training program, 110*t*
Trace minerals, 204*t*. *See also specific type*
Traffic, road rage and, 299, 300*b*
Training log
for flexibility/stretching exercises, 165–166
for strength/endurance/weight training, 129
Training threshold, 61, 61*b*
Trans fatty acids, 199*t*, 201*b*
sources of in diet, 200, 200*f*
Trapezius muscles, isotonic exercises for, 112
Treponema pallidum, syphilis caused by, 402, 403*b*
Triceps extension exercise, 111
Triceps muscle
flexibility exercises for, 155
isotonic exercises for, 111, 116, 117
Trich. *See* Trichomoniasis
Trichomoniasis (*Trichomonas vaginalis* infection/trich), 403–404, 403*b*, 403*f*
incidence of, 393*f*, 403
Triglycerides, 199, 199*b*. *See also* Fat(s)
Trunk flexibility, evaluation of, 144, 163–164, 164*t*
Trunk muscles
isotonic exercises for, 116
stretching exercises for, 155
Trunk twister, 155
Tuberculosis, in HIV infection/AIDS, 396*t*
Tumor, 368, 369*b*. *See also* Cancer
Type A/B/C/D personalities
assessment of, 319–320
stress levels/heart disease risk and, 297–298, 297*t*

UL. *See* Tolerable Upper Intake Level
Ultraviolet light, exposure to, protecting skin from
cancer prevention and, 376, 382–383, 383*b*
successful aging and, 447
Undereating, stress and, 307
Undernutrition, 425*b*
alcohol use/abuse and, 425*b*
Underwater (hydrostatic) weighing, in body fat measurement, 180, 181*b*, 181*f*
Underweight
exercise and diet for weight gain and, 252
health effects of, 176–177, 176*f*
Unintentional injuries, 354–359, 354*t*, 355*b*
leading causes of death and, 354*t*
prevention of, 354–355, 356*b*, 358*b*
risk of, 354–355
reducing, 355, 356*b*, 358*b*
treatment of, 355–359
United States Department of Agriculture (USDA), *Dietary Guidelines for Americans* of, 205–206, 208*f*
Unsaturated fatty acids, 199–200, 199*b*, 199*t*
Upper arm, back of, isotonic exercises for, 111, 116
Upright row, 112
Urologist, 452*b*
USDA (United States Department of Agriculture), *Dietary Guidelines for Americans* of, 205–206, 208*f*
Uterine cancer, 371*f*, 372*f*, 377

Vaginal spermicides, with nonoxynal 9, STI risk and, 406–407
Vaginitis, candidal, 404
Valsalva maneuver, 106–107, 107*b*
Vanadium, DRI for, 213*b*
Vascular system (blood vessels), 53
Vastus lateralis/intermedius/medialis muscles, isotonic exercises for, 114
Vegetables, in healthy diet, 206
Vegetarian diet
obtaining essential amino acids in, 201
vitamin supplementation and, 212
Veins, 53, 53*b*
Venereal disease. *See* Sexually transmitted infection(s)
Very-low-calorie diet, 246*t*
Virus(es), 393*b*
cancer caused by, 383
Visceral fat, 171, 171*b*, 171*f*
Vision, age-related changes in, 446
Visualization, 306, 307*b*
Vitamin(s), 202*t*, 203, 203*b*. *See also specific type*
food sources of, 202*t*, 203
RDAs for, 211*t*
supplementary, 212, 217–218
physical fitness and, 217–218
Vitamin A, 202*t*. *See also* Antioxidants
in cancer prevention, 370
DRI for, 213*b*
in healthy/balanced diet, 214*t*
RDA for, 211*t*
Vitamin B_1 (thiamin), 202*t*
DRI for, 213*b*
RDA for, 211*t*
Vitamin B_2 (riboflavin), 202*t*
DRI for, 213*b*
RDA for, 211*t*
Vitamin B_3 (niacin), 202*t*
DRI for, 213*b*
RDA for, 211*t*

Vitamin B_6, 202*t*
DRI for, 213*b*
RDA for, 211*t*
Vitamin B_{12}, 202*t*
DRI for, 213*b*
RDA for, 211*t*
supplementary, 212
Vitamin C, 202*t*. *See also* Antioxidants
in cancer prevention, 379
DRI for, 213*b*
in healthy/balanced diet, 214*t*
RDA for, 211*t*
Vitamin D, 202*t*
DRI for, 213*b*
RDA for, 211*t*
supplementary, 212
Vitamin E, 202*t*. *See also* Antioxidants
as antioxidant, 218, 379
in cancer prevention, 379
DRI for, 213*b*
RDA for, 211*t*
Vitamin K, 202*t*
DRI for, 213*b*
RDA for, 211*t*
$\dot{V}O_2$max (maximal aerobic capacity), 52, 53*b*, 58
aging affecting, 444, 444*f*, 445*f*
altitude affecting, 334–335, 334*f*
estimation of, 59–60, 60*f*
exercise affecting, 58, 58*f*
target heart rate and, 61–62, 61*b*, 62*f*
training threshold and, 61, 61*b*

Waist measurement/waist-to-hip ratio, 179–180, 179*b*, 179*t*, 191–192, 192*t*
coronary heart disease risk and, 277
Walk-in medical clinics, 451
Warm-up, 38–39, 39*b*, 45
for cardiorespiratory exercise program, 45, 61
Warts, genital, 399, 399*b*. *See also* Human papillomavirus (HPV) infection
incidence of, 393*f*, 399
Water, 196, 205
contamination of, environmental health and, 4
DRI for, 213*b*
importance of in diet, 196, 203*f*, 205, 205*f*. *See also* Dehydration
as nutrient, 196, 203*f*, 205, 205*f*
Water-soluble vitamins, 202*t*
Weight (body). *See also* Obese/obesity
ideal (healthy/optimal), 182–183, 193–194, 240–241
benefits of, 173
body composition/percent of body fat and, 170, 171, 172, 172*f*, 182–183, 193–194, 240–241, 259
body mass index and, 178–179, 179*t*, 194, 259–260
energy balance and, 243–245, 243*f*, 244*f*, 245*t*
losing. *See* Weight control
Weight control/weight loss, 239–268
behavior change and, 15–16, 242*b*, 251–252
behavior modification strategies and, 15–16
contract and, 15
diet modifications/plans and, 246–249, 246*t*, 247*b*, 248*b*
energy balance and, 243–245, 243*f*, 244*f*, 245*t*
environmental factors and, 241–242, 242*b*, 243*b*
exercise/physical activity and, 249–251, 250*b*, 251*t*, 261
lifetime fitness/wellness and, 252–253
factors affecting, 241–245, 242*b*, 243*f*
genetic factors and, 241
goals for, 15, 245–246, 263
hormones and, 241
lifetime, 252–253
low-carbohydrate diets and, 215*b*, 246*t*, 247*b*, 248*b*
low-fat diets and, 206–207, 207*b*, 247*b*
medications (prescription) for, 253
metabolic rate and, 244
strength training affecting, 96–97, 249
myths about, 254*t*
optimal body weight and, 240–241, 259–260. *See also* Body weight, ideal
program for
designing, 245–252
establishing, 15–16
evaluation of, 16
progress report and, 263
questions about, 248*b*
spot reduction and, 254*t*
surgery for, 253, 253*f*
Weight gain, exercise and diet programs for, 252
Weights, hand, 448
Weight training. *See also* Strength/endurance training
benefits of, 104
designing program for, 105–107, 106*b*, 109–110, 109*t*, 110*t*
principles of, 102–104
exercise prescription for, 107–108, 107*f*, 109–110, 109*t*, 110*t*
individualization of, 109, 109*t*
gender differences and, 105
goals for, 108–109
guidelines/precautions for, 109*b*
maintenance phase for, 109, 109*b*, 109*t*
motivation and, 110
muscle mass gain and, 252
muscular strength and, 10
older adults and, 118*b*
physiological changes caused by, 104
progressive resistance exercise (PRE) and, 104, 105*b*
protein needs and, 108*b*, 217
rate of improvement and, 104–105
safety concerns and, 105
sample exercises and, 111–117
slow progression phase for, 109, 109*b*, 109*t*
starter phase for, 109, 109*b*, 109*t*
starting and maintaining, 108–110, 109*b*, 109*t*, 110*t*
training log for, 129
types of programs for, 105–107
weight control and, 249
Wellness. *See also* Fitness
basic principles of
exercise and, 31–50
understanding, 1–29
components of, 2–4, 3*f*, 4*f*
interactions of, 4–5
concept/definition of, 2, 3*b*
evaluation of, 459–460. *See also* Fitness evaluation
lifetime, 439–468. *See also* Lifetime fitness/wellness
national goals for, 5, 6*b*. *See also* Fitness goals
population/socioeconomic issues and, 5*b*
Wellness profile, 459–460
Whippets (inhalants), 421*t*
Whirlpool baths, HIV transmission and, 396
Whole grains, in healthy diet, 206
"Wind-chill" index, 333, 333*f*
Withdrawal symptoms, 416, 417*b*
Women
body fat storage in, 171, 172*f*
body mass index results for, 178
chest press results for, 125*t*
curl-up test results for, 135*t*
cycle ergometer fitness test results for, 79–81*t*
leg press results for, 126*t*
muscle mass in, 102, 105
1-mile walk test results for, 78*t*
1.5-mile run test results for, 76, 76*t*
one-repetition maximum (1 RM) test results for, 125*t*, 126*t*
percent fat estimates for, 189*t*
push-up/modified push-up test results for, 134*t*
RDAs for, 210–211*t*
shoulder flexibility test results for, 164*t*
sit and reach test results for, 164*t*
sit-up test results for, 134*t*
skinfold measurement sites for, 179, 188
skinfold test results in, 189*t*
step test fitness results for, 85*t*
strength/weight training responses and, 105
trunk flexibility test results for, 164*t*
waist-to-hip ratio results for, 179*t*, 192*t*
Workout (primary conditioning period), 39, 39*t*, 40*f*
for cardiorespiratory exercise program, 61–64, 62*f*, 63*b*, 64*b*, 64*f*
personalization of, 39–40, 47
for cardiorespiratory exercise program, 64–66, 66*b*, 67*b*, 68*b*, 91
Workout hangover, 35, 35*b*, 36*b*. *See also* Overtraining

Xenical (orlistat), 253

Yeast infection (candidiasis), 404

Zinc, 204*t*
DRI for, 213*b*
RDA for, 210*t*